The need to control violent and non-violent harm has been central to human existence since societies first emerged. This book analyses the problem of harm in world politics which stems from the fact that societies require the power to harm in order to defend themselves from internal and external threats, but must also control the capacity to harm so that people cannot kill, injure, humiliate or exploit others as they please. Andrew Linklater analyses writings in moral and legal philosophy that define and classify forms of harm, and discusses the ways in which different theories of international relations suggest the power to harm can be controlled so that societies can co-exist with the minimum of violent and non-violent harm. Linklater argues for new connections between the English School study of international society and Norbert Elias's analysis of civilizing process in order to advance the study of harm in world politics.

ANDREW LINKLATER is Woodrow Wilson Professor of International Politics at Aberystwyth University as well as a Fellow of the British Academy, a member of the Academy of Social Sciences, and a Founding Fellow of the Learned Society of Wales. He has published several major works on the theory of international relations including *Critical Theory and World Politics* (2007), *The English School of International Relations* (Cambridge, 2006, with Hidemi Suganami), *The Transformation of Political Community* (1998), *Beyond Realism and Marxism* (1990) and *Men and Citizens in the Theory of International Relations* (1982/1990).

THE PROBLEM OF HARM IN WORLD POLITICS

Theoretical investigations

ANDREW LINKLATER

Aberystwyth University

CAMBRIDGE
UNIVERSITY PRESS

CAMBRIDGE UNIVERSITY PRESS
Cambridge, New York, Melbourne, Madrid, Cape Town,
Singapore, São Paulo, Delhi, Tokyo, Mexico City

Cambridge University Press
The Edinburgh Building, Cambridge CB2 8RU, UK

Published in the United States of America by Cambridge University Press, New York

www.cambridge.org
Information on this title: www.cambridge.org/9780521179843

© Andrew Linklater 2011

First published 2011

Printed in the United Kingdom at the University Press, Cambridge

A catalogue record for this publication is available from the British Library

Library of Congress Cataloguing in Publication data
Linklater, Andrew, 1949–
The Problem of Harm in World Politics : Theoretical Investigations / Andrew Linklater.
p.   cm
Includes bibliographical references and index.
ISBN 978-0-521-17984-3 (pbk.)
1. International relations–Moral and ethical aspects.   2. Harm
reduction–Political aspects.   I. Title.
JZ1306.L56 2011
172′.4–dc22
2010045744

ISBN 978-1-107-00443-6 Hardback
ISBN 978-0-521-17984-3 Paperback

For Jane

CONTENTS

Preface   *Page* ix

Introduction   1

1   The concept of harm   29

Harm conventions   29
International and cosmopolitan forms   35
Conceptualizing harm   41
Classifying harms   49
Applications to international politics   61
Conclusion   73

2   The harm principle and global ethics   76

Defending the harm principle   77
Criticisms of the harm principle   88
Pain, suffering and vulnerability   90
A hierarchy of harms?   105
Conclusion   111

3   Harm and international relations theory   112

War and injury   116
The forces of necessity   122
The attractions of society   127
The perils of collective identities   133
The vagaries of class   139
The potentialities for care   145
Conclusion   151

4   The sociology of civilizing processes   154

Civilizing processes   157
The European civilizing process   163
Decivilizing processes   172
A global civilizing process?   175

Process sociology and critical theory   185
Conclusion   191

5   Historical sociology and world politics: structures, norms and emotions   194

Historical sociology and international relations   199
Historical social psychology   207
Emotionology and emotional identification   217
Cosmopolitan emotions   222
Conclusion   230

6   Civilizing processes and international systems   232

The idea of a states-system   237
The sociology of states-systems   240
Towards a sociology of civilizing processes in states-systems   244
Collective learning in world history   250
Modernity, collective learning and global civilization   253

Conclusion   258

Bibliography   267
Index   299

PREFACE

There is probably nothing more fundamental in social life than how people deal with the problem of harm in their relations with each other – how they protect themselves from the various forms of suffering to which they are susceptible by virtue of their mental and physical vulnerability, and how they deal with those who are prepared to kill, injure, exploit and in other ways harm them. There is no lack of literature that considers different aspects of harm in society and world politics. Invaluable resources can be found in many disciplines: criminology, psychology, jurisprudence, anthropology, sociology, political theory and International Relations. But there has been precious little work that draws their findings together with the aim of constructing a conceptual framework that unifies largely unrelated modes of analysis – and there is no body of literature that starts with the assumption that the study of harm can usefully promote higher-level synthesis in the social sciences.

As its subtitle indicates, this book is about theorizing harm, and not about providing a theory of harm. It is a ground-clearing exercise that aims to establish the foundations on which future work on the problem of harm in world politics can build. The longer-term ambition is to produce two other works that consider, first, the relationship between violence and civilization in the Western states-systems and, second, the problem of harm from the vantage-point of world history. No doubt, those volumes will require many revisions to the main arguments of this book. Adjustments will be made in due course. The prior task is to plot a preliminary course by drawing together themes from several literatures, including International Relations, in order to explain what is involved in studying harm in world politics.

The overall project is designed to extend Martin Wight's pioneering essays on the sociology of states-systems. A personal reminiscence is necessary here. Around 1974, when I was a graduate student at the LSE, I spent a week in the library tracking down references for what is now the widely-celebrated collection of Wight's essays, *Systems of States*. Then based in Canberra, Hedley Bull (who was behind this serendipitous employment) sent me only those pages where references were at the time missing or incomplete, but I saw enough to have some sense of the unique quality of those essays and the immense scholarship that underpinned them. The influence of Wight's sociology of states-systems runs through much of the argument that follows. Few have sought to build upon them (the major exception is Adam Watson's *The Evolution of International Society*); curiously, they have not been at the heart of the recent revival of the English School perspective on international society; those who have been involved in building connections between International Relations and historical sociology have rarely mentioned them; they are virtually invisible in the sociological literature or in studies of world history. The great achievement of those essays was to put the comparative analysis of societies of states at the heart of the study of International Relations, and to outline the questions that the sociology of those distinctive forms of world political organization should investigate. This volume and the one that will follow it build on those papers through an inquiry into the study of the problem of harm.

To extend Wight's analysis, it is necessary to confront one of its main shortcomings which was the lack of any serious engagement with the classical sociological tradition, which is usually thought to include Comte, Marx, Durkheim and Weber and all those who have followed their lead by analysing long-term processes of change that have forged modern societies. The problem was that Wight's analysis of societies of states paid insufficient attention to broader patterns of social and political change that influenced developments within and between societies. Scholars who have explored connections between historical sociology and International Relations invariably draw attention to the significance of one or more of the authors mentioned in order to explain the links between changes in inter-state politics and the larger transformation of human society. But few have devoted any attention to the writings of the one last major representatives of that tradition, namely Norbert Elias's whose analysis of 'the civilizing process' rehabilitated the study of long-term social patterns. The omission is all the more significant because, from the late 1930s onwards, Elias devoted more attention than most sociologists at the time, and subsequently, to the impact of war and geopolitical competition on social development. Indeed, at the core of his thinking was the claim that 'internal' social developments cannot be understood without analysing relations between the societies involved. That standpoint now commands general assent as a result of the intellectual developments that have occurred in the attempt to comprehend the most recent phase of globalization. But such is the gravitational pull of disciplinary loyalties that sociologists rarely attempt to incorporate the arguments of major works in International Relations into frameworks of analysis that are designed to cast light on global processes. Nor, for that matter, do specialists in International Relations regularly venture beyond disciplinary boundaries to consider how the most sophisticated forms of sociology can contribute to their endeavours.

The logic of Elias's inquiry – nowhere does he state this explicitly – is that International Relations has no greater claim than Sociology to exist as a freestanding discipline. Readers of his work will find little indication that he read the principal writings in that field (although he knew E. H. Carr and very probably read his work). Elias's study of the civilizing process therefore has some of the same problems as Wight's sociology of systems of states. It left open large questions about how the most sophisticated forms of analysis in the two disciplines could be combined in a higher synthesis. As far as I know, there is no evidence that Elias read any of Wight's publications – and there is no evidence that they ever met. Had they done so, they might have discovered that they shared an interest in civilizing processes. Elias's preoccupation was with how Europeans came to regard themselves as more civilized than their ancestors and more advanced than peoples in other regions. The analysis of that development noted in passing what International Relations scholars call 'the standard of civilization' – the formalization of the conditions that would have to be met before non-European societies could be considered for membership of the European society of states. Elias's comments on the Europeans' orientation towards other peoples therefore noted how the process of civilization had influenced their thinking about relations between societies. But in the main, he did not examine civilizing processes in different systems of states, and was inclined to think that there was little in the way of processes of civilization in international relations. The very idea of international society, which is at the centre of English School inquiry, embodies rather different conclusions, without assuming that civilized norms do much more than mitigate the effects of the competition for security and power – some of its more harmful consequences, it might be added. There lies the most obvious point of convergence between English School analysis and Eliasian or process sociology which defined the civilizing process as one in which different peoples are organized so that they can go about satisfying basic needs and promoting vital interests without harming each other over and over again. The details will follow, but perhaps enough has been said to indicate that the study of harm in world politics can integrate those schools of thought – seemingly very different standpoints but, at a fundamental level, united in attempting to understand how people control their capacity to cause violent and non-violent harm, and how their efforts both within their respective societies and in international systems have shaped the long-term development of human society.

I have been working on this book – and on the two volumes to come – for almost ten years. The project grows out of a book on political community which was completed while I was a member of the Department of International Relations at Keele University. I thank my former colleagues at Keele who offered advice and encouragement when I first began to think about this project, and I thank my current colleagues at Aberystwyth for their interest in, and support for, a project that has gone some way beyond the one-volume work that was envisaged back in 1999. Thanks to the University's generous support for the Department – evident in its magnificent sabbatical scheme – I enjoyed two years of research leave on completing a two-year period as Director of Research in the International Relations Department. During that sabbatical, I revised an earlier manuscript of this book, drafted the eleven chapters that currently make up volume two, and laid the theoretical foundations for the last book in the trilogy. I have benefitted from discussions, both inside and outside the seminar room, with three excellent cohorts of Masters' students enrolled in my module, Harm in World Politics. Many in the exceptional PhD community at Aberystwyth have also contributed to the development of the project. Elaine Lowe has been exceptional in providing administrative support (not only during the period when I was preparing the 2008 RAE submission) but throughout the ten years I have been at Aberystwyth. I thank her for easing my burden with unfailing cheerfulness and efficiency.

Different parts of the argument have been tested before several audiences in Schools and Departments in the UK (the Universities of Aberdeen, Bath, Belfast, Birmingham, Cambridge, Keele, Kent, Leicester, the LSE, Newcastle, Oxford, St Andrews, Sussex and Warwick); in Australia (the Australian National University, Deakin University and the University of Queensland); in the United States (Columbia and the University of Southern California); and more recently at Ristumeikan University and the International Christian University in Japan, and at University College Dublin. I am grateful to more people than I can begin to mention here for suggesting directions, advising on reading material, and for engaging with the argument in highly supportive ways. Special thanks are owed to John Hobson at Sheffield University and Stephen Mennell at University College Dublin for incisive comments and advice on the penultimate draft. I am particularly grateful to Stephen for his friendship, generosity and support ever since he first received an unsolicited paper on Elias with a plea for advice on whether my interpretation of the latter's explanation of the civilizing process was broadly accurate. Stephen has not only deepened my understanding of Elias's writings; he has promoted discussions with the larger community of process sociologists (the 'figurational family') who have offered invaluable advice and encouragement over the last few years. My closest colleagues are aware of how my views about history, society and politics have been transformed by reading Elias's work, and they know that I believe that many specialist areas of International Relations could profit from engaging with his writings. I hope this book will encourage others in International Relations to consult Elias's various books and essays (now in the process of being published in eighteen volumes by University College Dublin Press), and that it will lead more process sociologists to turn to the literature in that field with a view to developing Elias's insights into society and politics.

Some parts of this book have been published – albeit in different form – in various journals and edited collections over the last few years. I thank the publishers for permission to draw on material that has appeared in the *European Journal of International Relations*, 16 (2) 2010, 155–78 ; *Global Society*, 20 (3) 2006, 329–43; *Global Change, Peace and Security*, 21 (1) 2009, 3–17; *International Affairs*, 78 (2) 2002, 319–38; *International Political Science Review*, 22 (3) 2001, 261–77; *International Politics*, 41 (1) 2004, 3–35 and 44 (1) 2007, 3–35; *International*

Relations, 21 (3) 2007, 355–59, 21 (1) 2007, 119–30 and 23 (3) 2009, 481–97; *Review of International Studies*, 31 (1) 2005, 141–54 and 33 (1) 2007, 135–50; and *Theory, Culture and Society*, 24 (4) 2007, 31–7.

I dedicate this book to my wife, Jane, in gratitude for her love and support during the years spent on this book, and in the hope that her tolerance and understanding will cover the period that will be devoted to the next two volumes.

~

Introduction

Zealous devotees of the Buddhist doctrine of *ahimsa* (or non-harming) are reported to wear masks and strain drinking water lest they kill insects unintentionally (Amore 1996: 244). Jain monks are alleged to carry small brushes to clear the path ahead of them so they avoid killing unseen insects; they are said to refrain from lighting fires or lamps in case insects are drawn towards them and destroyed (Bowker 1975: 281–2). Even though they may seem excessively burdensome to those brought up in Western ways of life, and may also attract ridicule, such precautions merit respect as codes of conduct that display powerful commitments to avoiding unnecessary harm in daily life. Laudable though the devotion to avoiding unnecessary suffering may be as a personal ideal, the realist will stress that adherents enjoy the moral luxury that comes with freedom from the responsibilities that are linked with the public duty to ensure the security and survival of the state. In the international political domain, circumstances frequently arise where compromising far less exacting moral codes than that enshrined in the notion of *ahimsa* is inescapable. Those who believe that 'brute force has hitherto governed the world' (Wollstonecraft 1992 [1792]: 40), and will forever do so, may add that the ideal of avoiding harm is not just politically irresponsible but destined to permanent ruination at the hands of the unforgiving logic of international anarchy. From that standpoint, the duty to violate the harm principle when vital national interests are at stake will remain a critical tenet of foreign policy – as will the responsibility to outmanoeuvre and overwhelm adversaries by accumulating instruments of violence that can inflict levels of suffering that were unimaginable only a few decades ago.

The last point raises large questions about the course of human development. It is clear that the species has an unusual capacity for harmful action which is especially evident in the history of international relations, and particularly in successive military revolutions that have made the destruction of all human, and virtually all non-human, life possible. That power is no less evident in one outcome of the long journey to the human monopolization of the most destructive technologies, namely the extermination or domination of many threatening animal species. The ability to develop new technologies of harm is one reason why humans have triumphed in this way, converting themselves in the process from the hunted to the hunters, but increasing the dangers they pose to each other as they reduced the threats emanating from nature (Elias 2007a [1987]: 25; Goudsblom 1992: 20–3). Not only human development but also natural history and the fate of the environment have been shaped by the species' unrivalled inventiveness in designing effective instruments of harm. Creativity in that realm is as old as the species itself. Early hunting and gathering societies could not have survived without using force to defend possessions from human and non-human predators. Threats from other species declined with the introduction of technologies of harm including mastery of the monopolization of fire, an innovation that altered the nature of warfare and all subsequent human development (Goudsblom 1992). Decisive technological breakthroughs occurred as a result of warring relations between the first cities and states and then, particularly over the last five and a half millennia, in struggles between ever-larger territorial monopolies of power that increased the capacity to cause distant harm. That development has been one of the main overall trends in world history. But it does not end there. As a result of environmental degradation, societies have the ability to harm generations that have yet to be born. Whether or not the more pessimistic interpretations of the future prove to be correct, few doubt that the destruction of the biosphere on which all complex life depends is conceivable. That possibility is testimony to the species' unique power to cause harm, and evidence of how inventiveness in that domain has come to endanger its potential to direct its future development and, quite possibly, to ensure its own survival.

Advances in that sphere – most clearly in the ability to wage warfare in the heartland of enemy societies and to do so over larger territorial areas – have been amongst the most powerful features of social and political evolution. Humans have developed the ability to harm one another in remarkably diverse ways throughout their history – hence Karamazov's lament that 'no animal could ever be so cruel as a man, so artfully, so artistically cruel'. The ingenuity of humans has been to extend capabilities that formed part of their animal inheritance. The upshot has been that killing or maiming, deceiving, humiliating, or exploiting others, behaving recklessly or negligently, and responding with cold indifference to their plight have existed in all times and places, albeit in different quantities and degrees. Conservative modes of Western political theory have been assiduous in drawing attention to such features of human existence – rather more so than utopian theories of politics and, of course, those apocalyptic perspectives that hold that force or terror can have the long-term effect of purging violence from social and political affairs. That is not to argue that utopian visions should be placed to one side; it is only to suggest that no such exercise of the political imagination can ignore Freud's safe prediction that societies may never reach the point where they no longer need to guard against those who will seize any opportunity to exploit the vulnerable and to inflict harm in other ways (Freud 1939: 85).

Considerable effort has been devoted to establishing whether or not human aggression is anchored in genetic foundations, but on one level, whether there are such underpinnings is immaterial (Pinker 2003). Humans have, if not a genetic disposition to behave aggressively, then a biological capacity to initiate harmful action which has evolved as part of the armoury of survival (but they also have the ability to learn how to curb the power to harm). How those powers are exercised depends on social conditions and circumstances most of all. Unlike predatory animals, humans can undergo cultural development that enables them to organize their interaction with a view to checking aggressive impulses and controlling the capacity to harm. Other species, including primates, do not lack such mechanisms, but they are either fixed genetically or evolve far more slowly than human cultural development. The question is how far cultural forces that have replaced biological properties as the main pacemaker of human evolution can bring the genetically-based capacity to injure under greater control (Elias 2007a [1987]: 31ff.; Elias 2007b [1992]: 125). The historical evidence appears to confirm Freud's contention that the future does not belong to societies that will eradicate the disposition to harm, even though such a condition is desirable, and may be attainable in some distant era (Freud 1939: 85ff.). The injunction to 'do no harm', or to refrain from causing unnecessary harm, will remain a central ethical dictate as long as the problem of preventing humans from injuring each other unnecessarily – whether members of the same social group or, more ambitiously, those who belong to other communities – persists. No doubt, there are more uplifting social ideals than aiming for a condition in which human beings do not harm one another without justification – though much depends on whether the harm principle is understood to generate only negative duties of refraining from injury, or entails, as some have argued, positive duties of assistance that provide the basis for more far-reaching advances in transnational solidarity. The point is that those more limited ambitions must have a central place in any vision of how humans should live together. More radical political visions cannot escape the issue of what they propose in response to breakthroughs in harming others in ingenious ways (Elshtain 1999).

None of those comments is designed to lend support to the Hobbesian perspective that 'the will to hurt' has always had a greater impact on social evolution than have acts of charity and kindness, commitments to justice, or notions of respect for other persons (Hobbes 1949 [1651]: 25). Nor are they offered as a blanket endorsement of Adorno's contention that human history is no different from the world of nature where the dominant tendency is to devour and be devoured (Breuer 1993: 274). The disposition to cause harm exists alongside powerful efforts to check violent and non-violent action and to encourage sympathy and benevolence. It is relevant that evil acts that involve delight in causing and/or witnessing suffering constitute only a small percentage of criminal behaviour in modern societies (Baumeister 1997). But their social effects can outweigh the benefits of beneficence, if not objectively because of the actual incidence of violence, then subjectively by generating high levels of fear and insecurity that lead many to support extraordinary or 'emergency' measures. All human groups therefore have to protect themselves from sources of harm, but it is crucial not to deflect attention from acts of kindness and commitments to justice, or to devalue political projects that aim to extend solidarity between members of the same society and, more adventurously, between those who belong to different communities.

Some of the seemingly more prosaic, but remarkable, features of social life are worth noting at this point. Not even the most violent societies can function without child-rearing practices that place constraints on the carers' ability to harm, while encouraging positive values of love and affection. But such necessities require limited applications of the higher virtues. The latter have rarely governed the conduct of relations with outsiders that include subordinate groups in the same society and, crucially as far as the present work is concerned, the members of other groups. But they have not been wholly absent either. Patterns of harmful behaviour must be understood alongside measures to prevent, alleviate or eradicate suffering that have existed in all societies, and which have influenced, though usually to a lesser extent, their relations with the wider world. The fact that most humans share basic mental and physical vulnerabilities, and depend on others to care for them at various points in the life-cycle, has great significance for how they might organize relations between societies. Such common vulnerabilities provide the foundation for trans-cultural support for the ideal of eradicating unnecessary harm from world politics – or the grounding for shared beliefs that have proved elusive when the preferred starting-point has been the quest for a potentially universalizable notion of the good life. The process that societies need to undergo is therefore clear. Separately, societies face basic moral questions that are not easy to answer, and which arouse heated controversies about how to distinguish between harms such as methods of punishment that are essential for the preservation of society, and harms such as cruelty, exploitation and so forth that exceed what is strictly necessary for their survival. Similar difficulties arise in the context of rising levels of global interconnectedness where the parallel task is deciding the forms of harm that are essential for world society to function and the forms that are inhumane, superfluous and eradicable. The political challenges are eased by focusing on obvious points of solidarity between strangers.

Since the Enlightenment, many social and political theorists have argued that the highest political goal is to end needless suffering in line with what has been called the 'affirmation of ordinary life' (Taylor 1989: 13–16, 209–302). Marx's thought is especially significant because his emancipatory project included support for universal cooperation to liberate all people from unnecessary harm, insecurity and suffering as part of a larger political quest to create the conditions that facilitate the expansion of individual and collective freedom. That remains one of the great visions of politics, notwithstanding the catastrophic failures of

Marxism in practice. Certainly, the achievements that the medical sciences have made in conquering or easing pain that would have ended or crippled life in earlier epochs have demonstrated that, in some respects, the more prosaic elements of the Marxian ideal are more achievable than ever before (Marx made the same point with respect to famine and economic misery). It may be that the vision of a world in which harm is greatly reduced is taken more seriously now than in most previous epochs, not least because of the influence that liberalism and socialism, the two principal heirs of the Enlightenment, have had on the 'civilizing process' in modern societies. What is not in dispute is that the condition in which all people closely monitor their behaviour in order to avoid unnecessary harm would be 'a very advanced form of human civilisation' indeed (Elias 2007a [1987]: 141) – as would a global political order in which most people are linked by a common desire to progress together in that general direction, however uncertain they may be about how to realize that ethical ideal, or unsure about the precise implications of their joint commitment. No civilization has succeeded in raising itself to such levels of eradicating force, and it is possible that no future civilization will succeed where others have failed (Toynbee 1978). But for the reasons given earlier, the remoteness of a state of affairs in which all people are linked by the ambition to prevent or reduce unnecessary harm does not justify abandoning this, the most realistic and realizable of cosmopolitan ethical ideals.

The purpose of this work is to reflect on core theoretical issues that surround any effort to understand the problem of harm in world politics. As its title indicates, the commitment is to theorizing harm and not to developing a theory of harm. The objective is to lay the foundations and prepare the way for future work. A second volume will connect the following exercise in theorizing harm with reflections on different states-systems in the West. A third will broaden the perspective to consider the problem of harm in world history. A central aim of the overall project is to understand whether, or how far, the modern world has made progress in making harm a key moral and political question for humanity as a whole – and, more radically, whether Enlightenment ideals have made sufficient inroads into the 'barbarism' of world politics to justify the claim that the modern states-system has succeeded in forbidding actions that were permitted in earlier times. The main features of perspectives that warn against the dangers of inflated claims about the special character of modernity are well-known. Especially important is the contention that one of the great illusions of the epoch is the belief that humanitarian sentiments have come to enjoy unusual influence on human affairs. Belief in growing humanitarianism has been interpreted as an exercise in constructing flattering self-images that critical social theory must expose (Foucault 1979). The aim has been to undermine modernist conceits anchored in arbitrary and self-satisfying dichotomies between the progressive nature of contemporary social life and the grotesque violence and cruelty of earlier epochs. That critique has raised intriguing debates about the 'progressive' nature of modern societies, but the disputants have rarely tried to settle their disagreements by engaging in the comparative analysis of different historical epochs. The resulting challenge is especially acute in International Relations where there has been little historically-informed discussion of whether, and how far, the modern states-system remains trapped in the age-old quest for power and security, as neo-realists contend, or has undergone progressive development in morally significant respects as, for instance, many contemporary liberals believe.

Reference has been made to the problem of harm in human affairs, and some further comments about that expression are needed before proceeding further. The term is designed to stress that the need to control the power to harm is a universal feature of social existence. All societies have had to deal with the harm that members can do to each other, not only through direct physical violence but also through damage to institutions and the natural world (not to mention the separate category of harm to the self). Some caution is necessary here because this tripartite division is a modern invention, possibly first suggested by Freud (1939: 28). The taxonomy may be perfectly intelligible to all societies, but most groups over the millennia almost certainly did not classify harm in that way but emphasized, for example, the greater danger of offending, or in other ways harming, supernatural or spiritual forces that were assumed to govern, or stand in judgment of, human affairs. It is clear that many societies have believed that harm to supernatural beings is the most serious injury of all, and that harm to other people or to the self has to be viewed as part of a larger struggle to resist evil or defeat satanic forces. No sociology of harm conventions can ignore the extraordinarily diverse ways in which societies have understood harm and the various justifications that have been advanced for inflicting harm, just as no sociology can neglect the ingenuity of the species in creating new ways of making others suffer. Yet the stress on cultural diversity can be pressed too far, as occurred in much post-Second World War anthropology where the well-intended ambition of escaping ethnocentrism led to an emphasis on social differences that deflected attention from properties and problems that all societies have in common (Brown 1991). Harm conventions have precisely that quality since they address challenges that are part of the universal grammar of social life.

The universality of harm conventions exists on several levels. Every functioning society must possess some concept of harm in an inventory of moral concepts that addresses the problem of how to regulate human behaviour; all societies must distinguish between serious and trivial harms, and between permissible and prohibited harm. Systems of punishment often provide insights into how core distinctions are drawn: they express the dominant beliefs about what is harmful to people and society, and about what is justifiable as opposed to cruel punitive action. The place of such beliefs in the moral grammar of societies cannot be understood in isolation from the power hierarchies that explain unequal vulnerabilities to harm and the uneven distribution of security, and which invariably lead to perceptions of injustice, and can cause civil unrest or violent conflict in the most extreme cases. The problem of harm is compounded by the politics of decision-making structures – and specifically by often socially divisive questions about where the ultimate authority for creating harm conventions lies (and about the protocols and procedures that should restrain the governing social strata). All of those features of social structures are mirrored in everyday life. Through routine socialization processes, every society must make infants aware of their capacity to cause harm (and therefore inculcate socially relevant concepts of agency, responsibility, shame, and so forth), and they must gradually lead them to the realization that other people are independent centres of experience with the ability to feel pain and to suffer (Aronfreed 1968: 68ff.; Hoffman 2000). The routines that promote the internalization of the social standards that govern the dominant conceptions of responsibility to others will reflect broader patterns of inclusion and exclusion in society, not least by reflecting and reproducing more general beliefs about the groups that have the greatest entitlement to be protected from significant harm and the strata whose interests count for less, or are simply ignored.

Enough may have been said to support earlier claims about the universality of the problem of harm. All that is assumed is that every society has to find ways of protecting vulnerable humans from harms that may shorten or disfigure their lives. For that reason, the dominant harm conventions can be the subject of comparative inquiry. It is possible to analyse the development of any society to ascertain how far, if at all, harm conventions changed over time. It is feasible to compare different societies at a precise moment in their life-cycle, or over long-term intervals, in order to cast light on the enormous range of harm conventions and to identify similarities. The same holds for relations between societies. It is possible to ask how far different conceptions of the problem of harm, different strategies for curtailing harm, and different levels of success existed in different stages in the evolution of any states-system (or how far continuities existed across all periods). The same questions can be asked of all known international systems. It is possible to compare specific phases in their life-cycle, and to compare long-term patterns of development, with the aim of understanding the dominant views about permissible and forbidden behaviour, and in order to identify any common trends. Whether there were similar trajectories, whether moral concerns about unnecessary pain and suffering shaped their evolution, and whether the constituent parts cooperated to reduce or eliminate forms of harm that were widely held to be unjustifiable or reprehensible – those are central questions for this mode of sociological investigation.

The last few comments about a comparative analysis of harm conventions may give the impression that domestic and international politics can be regarded as autonomous spheres of action. But that is not the intention. Separating those spheres has been an obstacle to understanding one of the central processes in human history – how all societies have become more closely interconnected over the millennia, but never more so than in the last few centuries, and at an ever-accelerating rate in recent decades. One might hope through studying the problem of harm in world politics to shed some light on the social and political evolution of humanity as a whole, and to place current global developments in an appropriately broad historical context. It might be surmised that certain patterns recur. In general, lengthening webs of human interconnectedness have almost always been superimposed on parochial moral codes that privileged the interests of insiders, or the needs of the most powerful or high-status groups. Sectional interests have shaped the patterns of global interconnectedness or they have tried to bend them to their cause in ways that have often generated resistance. The perennial question has been whether the dominant strata had the desire (or were forced or persuaded by vulnerable groups and those who claimed to represent them) to establish cosmopolitan harm conventions that had the purpose of protecting all people from unnecessary harm, irrespective of their nationality, ethnicity, citizenship, class, race, gender, sexual orientation and so forth.

That has usually been a normative ideal rather than a determining influence on political practice. More often than not, societies have struggled to develop broader frameworks of thought and action that keep pace with extended webs of interdependence that make it easier for some groups to cause harm over greater distances (Sherratt 1995). Responses to such dangers that build solidarities based on the widespread aversion to pain and suffering have not been the historical norm. Certainly, the world religions often took the initiative in promoting more inclusive solidarities, but invariably limited their scope by creating distinctions between believers and non-believers – between the faithful and heretics or apostates. That recurrent problem exemplifies the more general failure to create principles of co-existence that seem just from the perspectives of all those who have been forced to live together. The history of empires reveals that colonizers rarely strained to ascertain whether their social standards were appropriate for organizing relations with cultures that they might stumble across. As a general rule, they arrived in distant places with an uncontested faith in the superiority of their values and way of life, and treated vulnerable outsiders accordingly. In the same way, following first contact with each other, egocentric civilizations relied on their parochial worldviews to decide how to conduct a new web of relations. The interesting question has been whether they could devise, or felt obliged to work towards, more detached worldviews that could enable them to co-exist as equals (Bull and Watson 1984). Rising levels of global interconnectedness have always raised the issue of whether societies can find common moral and political ground when forced to live together in such haphazard or coercive ways. The earlier query about whether the modern states-system is distinctive leads to the question of how far its constituent political units have made advances in establishing 'transcultural principles' that eluded earlier world orders (Watson 1987: 152).

That question can be rephrased to ask how far cosmopolitan harm conventions have influenced the evolution of international systems, and whether such

conventions helped bridge the gulf between parochial moral codes and lengthening social connections. International societies have been the highest 'steering mechanisms' that have developed thus far for organizing relations between
largely autonomous communities; they have been the arenas in which possibilities for agreeing on global harm conventions can be explored. But as with
relations within societies, so it has been with relations between them. All such
orders have faced the problem of violent harm. They have had to distinguish,
insofar as they could, between harmful actions that are widely thought to be
acceptable (the use of force in self-defence, for example) and reprehensible
harmful behaviour that should be removed from external relations, wherever
possible. They have done so in a hostile or uncertain environment where prepa-
rations for injuring, weakening and disadvantaging other societies have been
widely regarded as the inevitable consequence of the seemingly endless competition for security and survival.

The scale of the problem of harm in world politics has been documented
at length by mainstream analyses of international politics. Those approaches
have stressed that societies often disagree fundamentally about what counts
as permissible or prohibited harm. Disputes have reflected moral and cultural
differences and asymmetries of wealth and power. Unequal levels of security,
and different levels of vulnerability, have compounded the problem of achieving consensus. Such factors shape the scope of any agreement about conventions that are designed to maintain order between independent communities.
The difficulties are still greater when the issue is whether those associations can
introduce cosmopolitan conventions that protect certain rights or entitlements
that many now regard as the 'natural' possession of all persons.

To use that discourse immediately drives a wedge between the individual
and the state, the implication being that the international community, or who-
ever claims to represent it, can stand in judgment of national governments
and assert the right to be the true custodian of their citizens' interests. In
the modern world, progress in that sphere has been difficult because of an
unwillingness to relinquish sovereign prerogatives, but also because of disagreements about fundamental human entitlements, and understandable fears
that cosmopolitan discourses will provide the pretext for occasional great
power intervention in the internal affairs of smaller states, and possibly for the
re-imposition of imperial authority. However, the problem of harm in contemporary world politics has acquired a quite distinctive configuration. The question of whether 'pluralist' agreements that are geared towards the maintenance
of order can accommodate 'solidarist' principles that express commitments to
a universal community of humankind has arisen in this states-system, and
probably in no other to anything like the same extent (Linklater and Suganami
2006: part two).

Connections can be made with the 'comparative sociology of states-systems'
which considers, amongst other things, ways of organizing the diplomatic

dialogue and the means of controlling force (Wight 1977: ch. 1). Comparisons of levels of institutionalization in different states-systems indicate that contemporary international society has developed an unusual battery of practices for managing increasing levels of interdependence – diplomacy and diplomatic immunity, the contrived balance of power, the doctrine that the great powers have special responsibilities for preserving international order, as well as global institutions and public international law (Little 2000: 410; Wight 1977: ch. 1). As earlier comments about the human rights culture and humanitarian intervention reveal, the inquiry can be broadened to ask whether the sovereign members of the modern society of states have surpassed their predecessors in cooperating not only to prevent unnecessary harm to each other but also to offer protection to individuals in their own right.

The distinction between international and cosmopolitan harm conventions can clarify the point. The purpose of international conventions includes upholding rights to territorial integrity and controlling violence. In various periods, such conventions were created by autocrats for autocrats who were not influenced by the universalistic and egalitarian conviction that each person's interests merit equal consideration. Individual people may have profited from general compliance with such harm conventions, but that was not the reason for creating them. The rise of the human rights culture is instructive in this regard. Throughout its history, the modern society of states has usually combined indifference to human rights with firm opposition to humanitarian intervention. The democratization of Western societies led to pressures for the parallel transformation of global harm conventions, although, as recent debates about intervention have shown, complex practical questions remain about the relationship between national sovereignty, individual rights and 'humanitarian war'. The fact those debates exist at all is evidence of the distinctive nature of modern international society. They indicate that unprecedented levels of global interconnectedness have encouraged discussions about how far the society of states can go in institutionalizing cosmopolitan principles that uphold the equal rights of people everywhere.

The comparative sociology of states-systems has the task of understanding the relationship between international and cosmopolitan harm conventions in different historical eras. A central question is how different systems coped with the discrepancies between the then current level of global integration, the prevailing harm conventions within the constituent political communities, and the understandings that existed between them. Those conventions usually revolved around insider–outsider distinctions that made it impossible to organize human interconnectedness around the principle that the interests of all people deserve equal moral consideration. They usually failed to overcome the ambiguities of global interconnectedness – the condition in which the ability to cause harm in remote places forged ahead of any willingness to develop cosmopolitan commitments to assist distant strangers. Such ambiguities arise in particularly dramatic ways in the modern international system which has been the location for rapid advances in global interconnectedness, but it is possible to trace their evolution across the entire history of international relations. It is then essential to ask what different societies of states contributed to the emergence and implementation of universal moral and political principles that embodied a collective interest in controlling the capacity to cause more destructive forms of harm over greater distances.

It will be apparent that certain normative interests underpin this approach to the sociology of states-systems. Of course it is entirely legitimate to compare harm conventions in international systems without adopting any ethical stance towards them – that is, without assuming that any system is more advanced than the others in taking practical measures to remove needless suffering. The arguments against grading states-systems according to their remoteness from, or proximity to, any ethical ideal are formidable. Many argue that there is no obvious universal ethical yardstick that can support such an endeavour, adding that all such assessments inevitably betray the prejudices of particular stand-points. There is a need to guard against the danger that any moral commitments that underpin the comparative analysis of international systems are so biased towards the modern era that claims about its progressive character triumph by default. The risk is that comparative investigation will reinforce uplifting but spurious self-images, that the limitations of the modern states-system will be conveniently ignored, and that the achievements of earlier forms of world polit-ical organization will be overlooked.

Debates about the adequacy of any principles of trans-historical compari-son are not about to be settled one way or the other, but the aim of this study is to bring certain ethical criteria to bear to the discussion of how different international systems responded to the moral and political challenges that stemmed from rising levels of interconnectedness. No assumption is made here that earlier systems faced a choice between their values and ours, and failed through some inherent defect to reach the correct decision (see pp. 159–60). Societies were not required to choose in that way. Their values have to be understood in conjunction with the distinctive problems they faced rather than judged by the standards of later times where the awareness of alternative ethical and political possibilities may be greater – not because of any higher intelligence but because of different circumstances. For example, the relatively pacified societies of the modern era have opportunities that did not exist in Ancient Greece or in Renaissance Italy for significant periods when prolonged civil strife was the cause and effect of external interference that ensured high levels of domestic and international instability. That is one reason why distin-guishing between more and less advanced international societies is a troubled endeavour.

Whether societies of states must be judged on their own terms is not straight-forward, however. It is important to ask how far the dominant harm conventions in earlier systems reflected the interests of the most powerful social strata, and whether they took account of the needs of the vulnerable. Future generations may ask similar questions about the modern era in the course of assessing its achievements and imperfections. The critic may argue that such preoccupations reflect modern concerns about suffering that earlier societies did not have, but such judgments are vulnerable to the contention that they go beyond what it is reasonable to suppose on the basis of the existing historical knowledge, and that they need to consider what may be impossible to recover – namely evidence that subordinate groups resented or resisted the dominant harm conventions, and that their public protests or private complaints imagined alternative possibilities that went unheard at the time and did not find their way into surviving narratives.

It is clear that some social systems acted on pernicious representations of outsiders that were based, for example, on cosmological worldviews that have been undermined by the natural sciences. It is necessary to add that those societies followed the apparent rationality of those beliefs and cannot be faulted for doing so. Whether, compared with liberal societies today, they were extraordinarily violent and excessively cruel is beside the point. But such an approach leaves the door open to the analysis of forms of collective social learning in which the issue is the extent to which societies of states developed principles and practices that enabled them to live together amicably, in a condition that all parties could regard as just because international arrangements were sympathetic to their desire to be free from unnecessary suffering. A related issue is whether global orders improved the prospects for amicable co-existence through a search for 'generalizable interests' that relied on open dialogue between equal interlocutors (Habermas 1975, 1990). Those are interests that each person has the right to promote in a condition of equal liberty with all others. The language of generalizability raises large philosophical questions, but here that issue is not considered in the 'abstract' but analysed in conjunction with the enduring practical problem of how societies can co-exist with the minimum of violent and non-violent harm. The attraction of the language of generalizable interests lies then in its utility, in its practical use in facilitating movement to a condition in which no individual, social stratum or community achieves security and happiness by imposing insecurity and misery on others.

The issue remains of how serious harm is understood in this discussion, and whether any definition can avoid the difficulties that have been mentioned. As already noted, an obvious criticism is that there is no trans-historical agreement about what constitutes serious harm – no far-reaching global consensus about forms of harm that are plainly incompatible with a humane way of life. One response to such criticisms is that it is possible – and indeed necessary – to settle for less than total universality in this sphere. All that need be assumed is that the majority of people in most times and places have recognized that certain acts are harmful to them, and to be avoided wherever possible. Shared biological characteristics are crucial factors in this discussion. It is clear that, from the start of the life-cycle, human beings respond in similar, but not in identical, ways to the same painful stimuli. At a certain stage of their development, they may decline to be governed by such imperatives, choosing instead to embrace suffering for the sake of religious martyrdom, or welcoming pain in order to undergo rites of passage in which warriors test and establish their mental and physical endurance. But such decisions to override physiological aversion to pain do not alter the reality that human beings generally prefer to avoid conditions that may greatly shorten their lives or burden them with unrelieved suffering. So much is nearly, if not entirely, universal. It is the reason why the most basic points of solidarity between strangers are to be found in the widely shared aversion to pain and suffering – a recognition that has been central to many world religions, as noted earlier (Bowker 1975). That is why most humans can agree on certain generalizable interests, and that is why there are more direct routes to cosmopolitanism than the Habermasian claim that the first 'speech act' already contained the promise of a universal association. On the argument thus far, it is essential to ask if the first displays of sympathy for suffering strangers in human history testified to the existence of a unique 'species power' to extend the boundaries of community so that all people can live without the fear of unnecessary harm. A significant convergence of moral codes in recent times – as demonstrated by the universal human rights culture – is the main example of the capacity to organize global relations around that most elementary of cosmopolitan ideals.

As for the extent to which affinities based on actual or potential suffering have influenced international relations, the evidence is that transnational solidarities based on mutually intelligible fears of pain and suffering have had only limited impact in most phases of human history. Most states-systems have not made what O'Neill (1996: 165–6) calls opposition to a 'principle of injury' central to their mode of organization. Observations about the most accessible points of solidarity between strangers may seem trivial if a principle of resistance to injury has had such little effect on long-term developments. Insider–outsider dualisms, that were often fostered or consolidated by fear and insecurity, have invariably had the upper hand. Their impact on the course of history has blocked the development of transnational solidarities based on the common aversions mentioned earlier. For that reason, the idea of moral learning is a valuable concept for the comparative analysis of states-systems precisely because it highlights the ways in which societies can transcend such dualisms by making shared aversions to pain and suffering the basis for collective resistance to those who employ a 'principle of injury' in relations with others (O'Neill 1996: 166). It is then possible to ask how far different international systems developed the relevant cosmopolitan understandings. As noted above, the key question is what international states-systems contributed to identifying generalizable interests and universal principles that allow societies to co-exist harmonious!

that standpoint, later eras that have progressed beyond earlier epochs must be placed in their historical context, and due recognition must be paid to earlier breakthroughs without which later innovations would not have occurred (Elias 2007b [1992]: 110, 143).

It is peculiar that no single strand of social and political inquiry has been devoted to understanding the problem of harm in domestic and international politics. No body of literature has concentrated in a systematic way on some of the most fundamental challenges that all societies have to face; no body of work has considered how the analysis of harm can integrate the contributions of different disciplines in a higher synthesis. There is, of course, no shortage of discussion of the history of force within, and in relations between, states; moreover, various approaches to international politics have debated the extent to which force can be tamed, if not eradicated, from relations between separate communities. Harm and violence are not co-extensive categories however. The former is the broader concept, encompassing actions that may be non-violent in nature. Questions immediately arise about the variety of forms of harm in world politics. Given the importance of harm in the history of international relations, it is perhaps strange that there is no plain answer to that question in the principal writings on the field.

The varieties of harm have been considered elsewhere, in the areas of jurisprudence and criminology. From Feinberg (1984) to Hillyard *et al.* (2004), scholars in those fields have debated the meaning of the concept of harm, whether in an attempt to carry forward the liberal attempt to determine 'the limits of the criminal law' or to criticize such endeavours. The key departure point for such inquiries is Mill's harm principle which held that the state should only use its coercive power when a person or group has harmed others – and not to promote the individual's own good or moral improvement. That thesis has spawned numerous debates about what counts as serious harm and about what properly falls within the jurisdiction of the criminal law. The issues have been explored in a large and complex literature on ethics and jurisprudence which has reconsidered Mill's objections to legal paternalism in the light of recent contentions, including the claim that pornography should be illegal because it harms women or the belief that abortion should be prohibited because it is no different from homicide. Various works on jurisprudence and criminology have debated whether the harm principle provides precise guidelines on how societies should respond to such developments.

Ensuing disputes reveal that a consensus on what counts as serious harm eludes liberal societies whose members have so much in common. How much more difficult must be any attempt to promote a global consensus about the meaning and implications of the harm principle for world politics – where ideological and cultural differences are much more pronounced. The central issues have been debated at length in connection with human rights, and in especially interesting ways with respect to the rights of women where the moral status of such cultural practices as 'female genital mutilation' has led to well-documented controversies about what counts as cruelty and unnecessary suffering, about what warrants external criticism and condemnation, and what counts as 'paternalistic' interference. But by analysing the concept of harm, leading works in criminology and jurisprudence provide an indispensable starting-point for any examination of the problem of harm in world politics. They provide insights into the difficulties involved in classifying harms, and they contain an invaluable discussion of the case for and against an ethic that is anchored in the harm principle. Very few of those writings address related issues in world politics – or indeed devote much time to international issues of any kind – but they are the first port of call for any exercise in theorizing harm at that level.

The point was made that different approaches to international relations have analysed the extent to which something like the harm principle can alter the course of world politics by alleviating suffering caused by the state and war. The discussion of harm is usually implicit or confined to questions about the threat and use of violence. Those perspectives are important for speculating about what a comparative study of harm conventions in different systems of states might reveal – whether, for example, such an inquiry is likely to discover that the same patterns appear again and again because of the unvarying effects of international anarchy on foreign policy conduct or because, as Thucydides alleged, human nature is the same everywhere. Many conjectures have been advanced about the extent to which modern international society seems likely to suffer the fate of previous world political orders, or has unusual possibilities for progressive development. On the one hand, there is an influential literature that portrays international relations as a 'realm of recurrence and repetition' in which there is little scope for promoting the good life (Wight 1966a: 26). On the other hand, there is the optimistic spectrum of opinion which focuses on the unique liberal zone of peace or on how the 'global business civilization' releases unusual, if not unprecedented, opportunities for pacifying relations between the industrial or post-industrial powers. Critical approaches have stressed the dangers of such discourses of progress and specifically, as suggested earlier, the risk that proponents may assume that dominant forms of power are being dismantled when, in reality, they are only being reconstituted in less violent ways that 'progressivist' analysis may fail to detect. At the same time, they have declined to lend support to the 'recurrence theorem' – to the idea that the same struggles for power and security are bound to be repeated in future eras.

Since the Enlightenment, social and political theorists have debated whether modern social and political arrangements represent a major advance beyond earlier forms of society. The main lines of debate, as we have seen, have also influenced the study of international relations. Few positions present matters as 'either/or'. As Foucault (1984) maintained, the question is not whether to be for or against the Enlightenment – which was not a monolithic movement in any case, but a tapestry of perspectives that unfolded through many arguments and counter-arguments. Those approaches often highlighted the achievements of modern ways of life while emphasizing their precariousness and unrivalled destructiveness. Accurate judgments about the nature of modern arrangements require an analysis of long-term trends in human society that considers changing relationships between the evolution of the ability to cause destruction over larger areas and political achievements in making unnecessary harm a moral problem for humanity as a whole.

That approach to history has an ancient pedigree which can be traced back at least to Thucydides' account of the rise of a unique Hellenic civilization and the patterns of self-destruction that occurred during the Peloponnesian War. In the modern era, Kant (1965 [1797]: 126) formulated the central issue regarding the ambiguities of interconnectedness with great acuteness when he observed that societies enjoy the benefits of global commerce, and are sufficiently enlightened to protest against violations of human rights in any part of the world. However, those very ties also make it easier for states to cause evil in the most distant places, which they could not do before. Kant's claim that people have a moral duty to enter into a civil constitution with those they are in a position to injure is perhaps the first statement of a key ethical theme in the study of harm in world politics, namely that cosmopolitan harm conventions are essential to remove the ambiguities of human interconnectedness, or to bridge the gulf between advancing transnational social and economic processes and parochial moral codes (Kant 1970a [1784]: 206). To use the language that Marx employed in the course of analysing the relationship between the forces and relations of production, it is as if those moralities had become 'fetters' on new social bonds – the source of contradictions between traditional ways of life and social arrangements that are waiting to be born.

A related approach to the ambiguities of interconnectedness is evident in the comment that the members of the most secure and pacified social systems enjoy unusually high levels of personal security in everyday life, while facing the danger of complete annihilation should the most sophisticated instruments of warfare be used against them (Elias 2007b [1992]: 129). Elias regarded that paradox as the outcome of long-term civilizing processes, although his use of that term has led to the mistaken view that he reproduced pernicious distinctions between 'higher' and 'lower' ways of life by assuming that modern societies are more civilized than their predecessors. But Elias did not use the idea of 'the civilizing process' to celebrate modern social arrangements. He may have thought that there have been progressions in contemporary societies, but nothing so grand as to justify speaking of overall progress (Elias 2007a [1987]: 156). The 'civilizing process' was employed in a neutral or non-celebratory way to analyse the rise of Europeans' supreme confidence in the superiority of their civilization, the development of modes of thought that marked them off from their 'barbarian' ancestors, and the appearance of contrasts between their mode of existence and 'primitive' or 'savage' ways that it was their self-appointed mandate to civilize. That perspective on modern societies, and the approach to human history with which it was linked, contain invaluable resources for a comparative study of harm conventions in different international systems – for a comparative investigation of global civilizing processes. But since that was not Elias's main preoccupation, it is important now to provide a short overview of some of his central ideas which will be applied in later parts of the discussion.

A useful starting-point is Elias's thesis that from around the fifteenth century the inhabitants of Western European societies began to acquire a strong distaste for public and private acts of violence, as exemplified by changing modes of punishment and a heightened sensitivity to cruelty to women, children and animals. For Elias, those changes were key features of the European civilizing process which derived its immediate impetus from the rise of monopolies of state power. His technical use of the term is evident in the observation that all societies have civilizing processes since all must educate the young to follow the relevant social standards governing elementary body functions, and all must control their efforts to satisfy basic physical needs; they must teach them to observe principles of social interaction that include rules of etiquette and bodily comportment; they must train them to tame aggressive impulses and angry or violent dispositions as part of the duty to protect their members from serious harm (Elias 1996: 31).

The sociology of civilizing processes has explored the different standards that regulate those aspects of human behaviour; it has provided a detailed examination of the evolution and character of the European civilizing process, including the rise in the nineteenth century of the conviction that Europeans had reached a much higher level of civilization than their medieval forebears and outlying societies. Elias insisted that, in some respects, modern societies have established levels of personal security that are unusual in human history, but that achievement was not unambiguous because those societies simultaneously created dangers for themselves that earlier ways of life did not have to confront. In an argument that is, at first glance, similar to Bauman's thesis that central features of 'modernity' found expression in the Holocaust – this is a matter to come back to in the second volume – Elias stressed the need to understand what in the structure of modern, industrial societies made the Nazi genocide possible. His thesis was that success in dampening the 'pleasure in killing', and in imposing restraints on violent conduct, exposed 'civilized' societies to the new danger of impersonal, industrialized killing. The point also applies to long-distance mass killing in warfare that may owe more to the sophistication of weapons' operators than to military valour, the hatred of enemies, or joy in killing. Influenced by Freud, and witness to the rise of National Socialism, Elias thought that the civilizing process was as much a trial or test as a long-term pattern of development.[1] Freud argued that civilization compelled people to suppress impulses that then found an outlet in all manner of neuroses. In a parallel with that conception of the ambiguities of civilized life, Elias stressed that civilizing processes always develop hand-in-hand with decivilizing processes. Efforts to create civilized practices and habits have usually generated their own dangers and the possibility that the overall process could be thrown into reverse. For those reasons, civilization was precarious and 'unfinished'.

Elias stressed that two main features of the civilizing process – territorial pacification and the widening of the scope of emotional identification to include all or most members of society – had made little impression on international relations. Although the realism of that standpoint did not go unqualified, the presumption was that a global civilizing process was improbable in the absence of a worldwide monopoly of power. Societies that have regarded their pacified condition as evidence of their state of civilization have seen no contradiction in regarding international politics as a sphere in which violent force is necessary and legitimate. High levels of 'self-restraint' in stable territorial monopolies of power are therefore largely missing, Elias argued, from relations between communities. Forms of violence that are, for the most part, taboo within such societies are not only acceptable but are often actively encouraged and highly valued in that domain. Elias regarded that double standard as evidence of a 'contradiction' at the heart of the civilizing process, and added that limited civilizing restraints on the conduct of foreign relations often break down when fears for security or survival run high. In short, warfare produces a coarsening of the sensibilities that can result in acts of violence that transgress civilized standards in modern states, but with justification from the standpoint of those involved. The analysis of the civilizing process led directly to the question of whether the species can make progress in overcoming divisions between the relatively restrained, peaceful character of life within secure, stable states and the more violent, or violence-prone, conditions that typify international politics. The related issue was whether sovereign communities will ever voluntarily accept the levels of self-restraint that are critical for building world peace, or must await the appearance of a global monopoly of power that can enforce constraints that societies are unwilling to impose on themselves, with all the dangers that transformation will involve.

There are problems with Elias's characterization of international politics, and they are best summarized by recalling the English School claim that elements of society exist even in the absence of a higher sovereign power. Indeed, some proponents of that perspective refer to 'civility' and to a global 'civilizing process'

---

[1] The sense of trial is integral to the German term, *Prozess*. It is not clear whether Elias chose to call his first major book *The Civilizing Process* in order to convey that subtlety, but the sentiment runs through that book and many subsequent writings. I am grateful to Stephen Mennell for advice on this matter.

to describe relations within the 'anarchical society' (Linklater and Suganami 2006: ch. 4). In fact, Elias did not always portray the international system in quintessentially realist terms – and rightly so, because it would be curious if the European civilizing process had not influenced that realm to some degree. He contrasted the excessive violence of Graeco-Roman war and medieval warfare (exemplified, in turn, by frequent genocidal killing and by a high incidence of rape and pillage) with more civilized, or less bloodthirsty, modern warfare. Elias referred to contemporary moral concerns about civilian suffering and the cruel treatment of prisoners of war, implying that they reflected the lower tolerance of violence that is a central feature of the modern civilizing process. Whether he was right to draw those contrasts is a matter for future investigation. It is clear that they were not based on an extensive discussion of international relations in the ancient and medieval worlds. Elias insisted that civilizing and decivilizing processes invariably developed in tandem; however little attention was paid to the interplay between them in, for example, Ancient Greece where, if Thucydides is a reliable guide, a long-term civilizing process was thrown into reverse by the Peloponnesian War, producing, on some accounts, atrocities that many, including Thucydides himself, regarded as abhorrent by the higher standards of the time. In addition, little attention was paid to the inter-relations between medieval civilizing offensives to tame the warrior and the decivilizing processes that resulted from the fusion of violence and piety in, for example, Christian notions of crusading warfare.

Such observations are in line with Elias's statement that his position was preliminary; they point to lacunae in his approach; but they do not question the essential validity of his account of the civilizing process or diminish its importance for the sociology of global harm conventions. Although Elias's comments often incline towards realism, his approach invites the union of two traditions of international thought: the realist perspective that stresses recurrent decivilizing processes and potentials, and English School analysis of the precarious 'civilized' properties of societies of states, to which one might add those cautiously optimistic approaches that focus on security communities and the inter-liberal peace. The point is that it is necessary to avoid the extremes (and most observers do this in practice) of supposing that nothing of substance has changed in world politics for millennia, or proclaiming that the modern society of states represents an entirely new and progressive stage in the history of international relations. From that perspective, a sociology of global civilizing processes must highlight efforts to control violent harm and also emphasize the sinister forces that often stalk them, qualifying, and at times reversing, important advances.

Nowhere does Elias claim that there is evidence of progress in international history and, at times, there is no obvious difference between his position and the neo-realist thesis that the same patterns of conflict and competition have been repeated endlessly over the millennia (see, however, Linklater 2009). But nowhere does he maintain that setbacks and regressions prove that the species is incapable of pacifying relations between independent communities. His remarks about the recent phase of the globalization of society provide a more nuanced approach to world politics that reflects his broader perspective on the interplay between civilizing and decivilizing processes. It was stressed that longer chains of interconnectedness have made more people more aware than ever before of distant suffering. Globalization has introduced the possibility that the scope of emotional identification might yet extend beyond co-nationals, and that compassion for all people may come to have a major influence on the next phase of 'global integration'. But globalization issues no firm guarantees. Decivilizing trends can be released by collective resentment at the loss of power, prestige and autonomy, or by fears and anxieties about the social and political effects of encroaching external influences. Whether the modern states-system can succeed in pacifying world politics was, for Elias, an open question. His comments on whether globalization can alter the course of world events invite a larger comparative study of global civilizing processes that focuses on the prevalent attitudes to violent and non-violent harm in different phases in international history, and assesses arguments that the modern system may yet break the historical mould.

Such an inquiry can build on and extend Elias's discussion of civilizing processes. The envisaged approach resonates with the interest, which was pronounced in his later writings, in understanding processes that now affect the species as a whole. Focusing on the human capacity for symbolization and time-measurement, those later works sought to understand how cultural evolution displaced biological evolution as the principal determinant of social development. Central to the perspective was the capacity to form larger social units and to participate in the longer webs of interconnectedness that have profoundly transformed the planet. Increases in violent capabilities were an integral part of the globalization of social and political relations, as were advances in modes of social regulation and related internalized restraints. Process or figurational sociologists who have built on Elias's work have stressed that states have been the principal architects of globalization throughout history (Mennell 1990a). An additional point is suggested by Elias's comment that balance of power systems are the highest 'steering mechanisms' that have evolved thus far in response to the challenge of controlling global interconnections. It is a short step from there to the claim that systems of states have been intermediaries between separate political communities and global civilizing processes – they have been the instruments that have enabled states to build elements of civility into their relations, even in the unpromising condition of international anarchy. That observation underlines the importance of integrating Wight's sociology of states-systems with Elias's discussion of long-term civilizing processes.

The analysis of the European civilizing process focused on structural changes such as territorial pacification and the emergence of long-range commercial ties. But one of the distinctive features of Elias's approach was its investigation of the relationships between social-structural and psychological developments or, to use his expression, between sociogenetic and psychogenetic forces. The discussion emphasized changes in emotional responses to violence, in the scope of identification with other people, and in the dominant forms of conscience and self-restraint. It is entirely characteristic of Elias's approach that his reflections on the most recent phase of globalization raised the question of whether it might lead to new 'personality structures', or a new social 'habitus', and specifically to a willingness to assume global responsibilities for alleviating the misery of strangers because of the moral conviction that relievable suffering had become intolerable.

The approach has great significance for the sociology of states-systems. Structuralist perspectives have dominated the study of international relations although English School, constructivist and related standpoints have drawn attention to the place of norms and values in the formation of collective identities and interests, and in the evolution of global constitutional frameworks. An important comment in the 1920s by the *Annales* historian, Lucien Febvre, is worth noting at this point. There was, he argued, no history of pity or cruelty. His ambition was to defend what has been called historical psychology – the analysis of collective emotions in social life (Burke 1973: 18ff.). Elias's analysis of the civilizing process was exemplary because its account of the reasons for changing attitudes to violence and suffering was specifically concerned with emotional codes: with the scope of identification, levels of tolerance of violent harm, and the governance of universal moral emotions such as disgust, guilt and shame, all to be understood in conjunction with power structures, social inequalities, levels of interconnectedness and so forth.

One of the greatest works on politics and international relations (and possibly the first to analyse tensions between civilizing and decivilizing processes) considered the interplay between long-term structural developments and changes in personality traits (Thucydides 1928). The greater tolerance of brutality as security fears intensified and traditional constraints on force declined was a central theme in his account of the Peloponnesian War. In contemporary writings, the case for analysing 'the passions in world politics' has been made in criticism of materialist perspectives that insist that raw interests dominate politics (Bleiker and Hutchison 2008; Crawford 2001). Valuable studies of changing emotional responses to violence and suffering in world politics have appeared in recent years (Crawford 2002b; Rae 2002; Thomas 2001). Such works are instructive for a sociology of states-systems that grapples with emotional responses to the fundamental realities of violent and non-violent harm. To illustrate the point, it is useful to consider what the conventions that governed Greek hoplite warfare, or medieval notions of chivalry, or the modern international legal principles that developed in response to the slave trade and slavery, apartheid, unnecessary suffering in war, genocide and other serious human rights violations reveal about global civilizing processes. The degree to which normative structures are embodied in personality systems at either the mass or elite levels is central to that inquiry. But for the reasons that were provided earlier, the relationship between cruelty and compassion as societies have become more closely interconnected has special importance. So is the issue that was raised in Elias's writings of whether the modern states-system is witnessing the growth of cosmopolitan emotional responses to unnecessary harm that is inflicted on any member of the species.

The case for a sociology of states-systems is constructed in the light of the moral belief, which moved to the forefront of social inquiry during the Enlightenment, that human beings can reorganize the social world to end cruelty and misery. The emergence and development of International Relations as an academic discipline, and the many variations on debates between realism and liberalism, testify that the question of whether the species can progress in that direction has been at the centre of social and political analysis ever since – almost certainly to an unprecedented degree. Given the importance of Elias's ideas for the current project, it is essential to note his preference for avoiding partisan inquiry. However, many asides in his writings display a humanistic commitment to a world in which all people live together more harmoniously, free from violence, oppression, exploitation, humiliation, stigmatization or disrespect. A particular conception of world order is implicated in such hopes. Overviews of the history of humanity revealed, according to Elias, that from the earliest times the use of force has been ubiquitous in relations between groups. Violent responses to immediate fears and insecurities have repeatedly compounded the problem of how independent communities can free themselves from cycles of competition and distrust. But in an immensely important comment, Elias (2007b [1992]: 128) added that it is easy to forget that we live in what might be called 'humankind's prehistory'. The point was that the species – and here it is worth adding that current assessments are that anatomically modern humans appeared between 100,000 and 150,000 years ago – may have hundreds of millions of years in which to learn how to tame violence. The time interval was based on calculations about how long humanity will survive before the expanding sun destroys all life on earth, assuming, and this was no small qualification, that the species does not destroy itself first. But it should not be beyond the ingenuity of humans to solve the problem of violent harm in the time that is left (Elias 1991: 146–7).

Elias's support for non-partisan inquiry was based on the need for high levels of detachment from immediate political considerations and aspirations in order to acquire 'reality congruent' knowledge that could improve the species' prospects of mastering uncontrolled processes. The argument was that analyses of society had yet to free themselves from false hopes and from collective myths and fantasies (Elias 1978: ch. 2). Exposing deluded belief-systems was a central task for social-scientific inquiry that might one day equip people with a deeper understanding of the constraints that are essential for preserving any orderly society and the restraints that have no other purpose than ensuring the continuing dominance of sectional interests (Elias 1978: 153–4; 1998: 145). By shattering delusions and exposing mystification, sociology could assist people in under-going a global civilizing process in which, and here Elias (2007a [1987]: 13) makes his moral commitments perfectly clear, it 'should be recognised as a basic human right that human beings can live out their natural lives to their natural limits if that is their own wish, and that people who use or advocate and threaten the use of force as a means of shortening other people's lives have therefore to be regarded as criminals or as insane'.

Advocacy of non-partisan inquiry will not blind the reader to parallels between Elias's conception of social inquiry and Frankfurt School critical the-ory. First-generation Frankfurt School theorists defended normative commit-ments that often lurk in the background of Elias's inquiry. There is an affinity between Elias's humanism and Horkheimer's thesis that universal solidarity can be based on the fact that humans are 'finite beings whose community consists of fear of death and suffering', and on their related capacity to sympathize with each other's desire 'to improve and lengthen life' (see Linklater 2007a). Elias was concerned about the dangers of allying social inquiry to any political project such as lending 'a voice to suffering' (Adorno 1973: 17). But it is far from obvi-ous that such explicit normative commitments must compromise the quest for 'reality congruent' knowledge (Kilminster 2007). Consequently, the following discussion forges connections between process sociology and critical theory, incorporating the moral dimensions of Horkheimer and Adorno's writings that found only muted support in Elias's analysis of global civilizing processes.

Undoubtedly, that decision complicates the task ahead, but the argument will be that the capacity to sympathize with other peoples' endeavours to extend and improve their lives provides the key, as Horkheimer maintained, to 'correct solidarity'. It is recognized that any claims about the path to true solidarity will arouse suspicion and attract criticism, and it is acknowledged that groups that are locked in violent conflict often do not believe they have the luxury of com-plying with the restraints that Horkheimer's position supports. All that will be maintained here is that an overlapping global moral consensus on the virtues of a harm principle is possible, and indeed that one has already been built into the constitution of the modern society of states to a significant extent in the shape of international law (see Rawls 1993 on the idea of an overlapping consensus). The additional point is that most societies can recognize the contribution that a cosmopolitan harm principle can make to learning how to co-exist amicably in the context of increasing human interconnectedness. On that argument, that principle can play a central role in any future collective endeavour to promote a global civilizing process that is designed to benefit all persons.

The principal sociological objective is to understand the extent to which dif-ferent international systems made progress in institutionalizing a harm principle that can be said to be immanent in all societies because they all have mechanisms for protecting (at least high status) members from unnecessary harm. The fact that they have often declined to observe that principle in their external relations has largely been the result of insider–outsider dualisms that thwarted any efforts to extend the boundaries of moral and political community. It is important to ask whether the constituent political units in societies of states have transcended those limits by insisting that the legal and moral rights and duties that tie citizens together have to be consistent with cosmopolitan obligations to avoid inflicting unnecessary harm on other people – or alternatively, whether they believe that the tensions between citizenship and humanity can be overcome by exploring the image of solidarity noted earlier (Linklater 1982/1990). As part of that discussion, one must ask whether the modern society of states represents a new phase in the development of global harm conventions.

A second volume will analyse the claim that there have been progressions in the modern states-system which reflect the influence of the Enlightenment notion of the 'affirmation of ordinary life'. It will be framed by an apparent ambiguity in Elias's writings, namely a tension between the argument that nothing seems to change in international history – other than the methods of killing and the number of people involved – and the observation that the contemporary era differs from classical antiquity, for example, by virtue of its greater antipathy to mass slaughter in war. The focus on Western international relations requires explanation given sensibilities about the Eurocentric nature of dominant approaches to the field, and serious doubts that those progressions have improved the position of non-European peoples in a Western-dominated global system.

Numerous historical studies have discussed the impact of non-European civilizations on Western development. But it was the European world that created the international political framework that now embraces the entire world, which is why the adequacy of Western principles of international relations in an increasingly post-European era has been at issue (Bull and Watson 1984). There may come a time when those principles are forgotten, or when they only interest scholars who are researching the history of civilizations and international relations. But it is the adequacy of the Western political framework that matters most in the current phase of global integration. How far progress in creating cosmopolitan harm conventions will take place depends above all on the diplomatic dialogue that takes place within the society of states that first developed in Europe and, increasingly, on the relationship between discourse at that level and the claims that are advanced by global civil society actors (Clark 2007). The significance of Western ideas about the emancipatory project must be considered here, where emancipation refers not to some dreamy utopia in which people are entirely at one with each other, and violent conflict has been eradicated, but to the more prosaic vision that is mindful of the plight and priorities of the world's most vulnerable people. Reflecting those realities, the emphasis is on emancipation from unnecessary and relievable harm which may be violent, as in the case of serious abuse of human rights, or non-violent, as in the silent operation of world markets or in the calm deliberations within global regimes that have profound effects on the lives of the poorest people. What is at stake is the extent to which Western principles of international relations can inspire efforts to reduce or eradicate violent and non-violent harm – it is whether the legacy of European modernity to future generations and their collective efforts to organize humanity will be little more than unprecedented levels of economic and technological interconnectedness – little more than the tightening grip of global structures and processes without parallel moral developments.

Those issues can be linked with familiar debates about the achievements of Western societies and about the relevance of notions of progress for representations of modern political life. Reference has been made to tensions between liberal and realist or neo-realist approaches to the question of whether the perpetuation of cycles of violent harm is inevitable, or whether the modern states-system may be undergoing a fundamental transformation that shares some broad similarities with the civilizing process as described by Elias. Those debates revolve around the question of whether there have been marked progressions in the history of the modern states-system and whether they have secured improvements for the whole species as a result of the revolutionary expansion of international society during the last few decades. Those questions lead to divided opinion. On the one hand, there is Toynbee's arresting claim that there has been no significant progress in history beyond the technological sphere (Toynbee 1978: 590). On the other hand, there are claims about the 'expanding circle' of moral concern from the first small-scale societies with populations of a few dozen to modern states with populations in the tens or hundreds of millions, and indeed to transnational movements that promote identification with humankind as a whole (Singer 1981). From that second standpoint, there have been progressions in enlarging the constituency of those whose interests merit equal consideration. The overall process can be characterized as one in which the idea of humanity has come to enjoy increased moral significance relative to the claims asserted in support of particularistic communities (Mazlish 2006).

Such differences can be linked with the argument that approaches to world history often seem to be inconclusive about whether Western brutality, greed and exploitation outweigh its 'beneficent and humane' qualities (Duchesne 2005: 166). At first glance, the positions struck by Toynbee and Singer seem incompatible. But on one level they are not irreconcilable. The advances that Singer identifies cannot be explained without considering the processes that have led to larger political communities and which have compelled people to become more attuned to each other over greater distances. Current levels of global interconnectedness have extended this process in ways that have led many liberals to think that the global business civilization will have a long-term pacifying effect. Learning processes over many thousands of years that have led to the 'expanding circle' are therefore not easily disentangled from the technological and political advances that have resulted in greater territorial monopolies of power that can cause devastating harm over larger areas (de Swaan 1995; Liston and Mennell 2009; Mennell 1994). As noted earlier, the idea of the ambiguities of interconnectedness is designed to integrate elements from those different interpretations of long-term processes that now affect the species as a whole.

It is in principle possible to construct a history of social and political development from the earliest times to the present day around a study of those ambiguities. Such an approach would explain the rise of the ambiguities of interconnectedness, beginning with the formation of the first cities and states, tracing their evolution through the history of empires, and finally turning to the impact of modern states and global political and economic associations on the ways in which all peoples are now bound together. That perspective on the past would stress the 'lag effect' in which rising levels of global interconnectedness have generally outpaced the widening of moral horizons; it would raise questions about the extent to which societies that were caught up in those processes adapted to them by creating new normative frameworks that demonstrated their capacity to become more responsive to each others' interests and beliefs, or reacted with hostility to what they saw as unwelcome threats to their status, power and autonomy (Elias 2007a [1987]: 67). It would then ask whether, faced with the problems of modern weaponry and global environmental degradation, the modern states-system has better prospects than past systems of using cosmopolitan principles to reduce the ambiguities of interconnectedness.

A third volume will consider the modern states-system in the light of recent approaches to world history. Whereas a second work will offer some preliminary observations about how modern international society differs from earlier states-systems in the West (the Hellenic and Hellenistic, the medieval, and the Renaissance systems), the following volume will analyse the impact of Western and non-Western states-systems on the overall trend towards higher levels of human interconnectedness. It may suffice at this stage to note that studies of world history have only recently devoted more attention to the importance of 'encounters with strangers' for the long-term trend towards the social and political integration of humanity (McNeill 1990). In so doing, they have echoed initiatives in International Relations that place relations between political communities at the heart of the study of world history (Buzan and Little 2000; Mansbach and Ferguson 1996; van der Pijl 2007). The realist or neo-realist will argue that what International Relations can contribute is a detailed understanding of the impact of war and geopolitics on the evolution of human society. But it is no less important to recognize that relations between groups have been one source of growing 'reflexivity' in the form of 'the detachment of consciousness from its immediacy in … traditions and customs' that has been a 'critical step in the progression of humanity' (Duchesne 2005: 160). The English School analysis of the expansion of international society lends support to that theme by showing how contacts between independent political communities have created pressures and incentives to become detached from traditional egocentric worldviews in order to reach agreements about the constitutive principles of international order. It is necessary to extend that investigation by noting how an appreciation of how humans can harm one another, often indirectly or unintentionally, as a result of the global structures and processes that lock them together, invites all peoples to achieve similar forms of detachment from their immediate circumstances and to reflect on the cosmopolitan principles that can bind them to one another as equal members of a world society. Universal history stands in a special relationship with that cosmopolitan idea. Kant (1970a [1784]: 191) believed that world history could combine a modicum of detachment from the current era with an orientation to the future that asked how 'posterity will be able to cope with the burden of history as ... transmitted to them after a few centuries'. The defence of world history in recent times has maintained that it can encourage detachment from the central issues of the era, or place immediate concerns in long-term perspective, and in other ways 'diminish the lethality of group encounters by cultivating a sense of individual identification with the trials and tribulations of humanity as a whole' (McNeill 1986: 16). That is one reason why the study of Western international relations in the second volume will be followed by reflections on harm from the standpoint of world history – and why a discussion that builds on Wight's vision of a sociology of states-systems will be followed by an exploration of the place of different international orders in the overall trend towards higher levels of human interconnectedness: and specifically with their role in promoting longer webs of interdependence and in identifying, and trying to solve, the problem of harm.

Given the breakthroughs that have resulted from greater academic specialization in recent years, projects of this kind are bound to raise concerns about partiality and selectivity, and to prompt efforts to identify errors and omissions. Many years ago, Schwarzenberger (1941: 27) warned that 'the shortcomings of the specialist, who is at least master in his own field, are nothing compared with the harm which can be done by the dilettante'. Exercises in intellectual synthesis, it might be added, largely depend on existing specialist works, and they are bound to contain errors and oversights. But specialization or 'pseudo-specialization' has its own costs that include the fragmentation of knowledge which then forms a barrier to studying long-term processes that stretch over centuries or millennia (Elias 1978: 59ff.; 2007a [1987]: 176–7). The fact that analysis runs ahead of synthesis is not merely an academic problem. When making that comment, Elias (1998: 144) maintained that investigations of long-term patterns have an important role to play in producing knowledge that may eventually be used to give societies greater control over their development. As has been claimed for world history, the prize would be sufficient detachment from contemporary problems – particularly those that are national in scope – so that due attention can be paid to the challenges that have resulted from long-term changes in social and political structures that will take decades, if not centuries, to alter. Despite numerous problems, the great theories of history, and especially those advanced by Kant and Marx, combined a focus on the evolution of society with normative reflections on how future trajectories could liberate all peoples, and not just Europeans, from avoidable suffering. More than ever, it is imperative to keep faith with that mode of inquiry.

As for the organization of the present volume, Chapter 1 analyses the concept of harm and develops a classification of forms of harm in domestic society and international politics. Chapter 2 turns to the significance of the harm principle for a global ethic. Chapter 3 discusses approaches to world politics that contain important conjectures about long-term developments that the sociology of cosmopolitan harm conventions must examine. Chapter 4 considers Elias's account of the civilizing process, noting how it can combine different approaches to international relations in a higher synthesis. The penultimate chapter shows how the sociology of global civilizing processes can forge distinctive connections between historical sociology and International Relations, the main objective being to understand the dominant attitudes to cruelty and compassion in different states-systems. The final chapter sets out basic questions that the comparative sociology of global harm conventions should endeavour to answer. The outline of the framework of inquiry which will influence the following two studies of harm in world politics brings together the analysis of the earlier chapters: it integrates the discussion of the concept of harm and types of harm, reflections on a cosmopolitan harm principle, and the discussion of approaches to harm in the study of international relations; it suggests that elements from the writings of Elias and Wight can be usefully combined in a new conception of the sociology of states-systems that analyses their part in promoting global civilizing processes that can benefit the whole species.

1

The concept of harm

All approaches to world politics stress the impact that violent harm has had on the history of relations between states; all recognize the growing influence of non-violent harm in the shape of global environmental degradation or trade policies that disadvantage vulnerable producers. Despite the prevalence of harm, and the various ways in which humans harm and are harmed by others, there has been no attempt to construct a taxonomy of harms in the field. There are compelling normative and empirical reasons for remedying that state of affairs. The quest for a more just world order requires an inventory of the forms of harm that should be eradicated but, for the resources for undertaking that task, one must look beyond International Relations. Turning to works on moral and legal philosophy, this chapter analyses the concept of harm, constructs a classification of the main forms of harm in society and analyses parallels in world politics. But as a prior step, the introductory comments on harm conventions must be taken further, first with respect to intra-group, and then with regard to inter-group, relations.

Harm conventions

No society – not even the most cruel or violent – can survive unless most people internalize the principle that they should not inflict unnecessary harm on other members. Elementary socialization processes that equip infants with an awareness of how their actions can harm other persons as independent centres of experience exist in all societies. No group can survive unless its members have the requisite moral emotions, including sympathy for the victims of harm, and guilt or shame when they violate, or just contemplate violating, fundamental norms. Members are expected to internalize social standards that prohibit forms of violent harm while condoning others such as the punishment of those who violate basic rules, or the use of force to deal with external threats and challenges. In viable state-organized societies, the use of coercion to punish transgressions of rules governing harm is designed to protect society from, amongst other things, any weakening of psychological restraints on conduct. It is inevitable that harm conventions that are supported by a combination of internal and external restraints will reflect prevailing power inequalities,

dominant images of what counts as serious harm, and beliefs about whose suffering, and the kinds of suffering, society ought to prevent. That comment rests
on the assumption that no complex society has yet solved the problem of harm
by ensuring equal security for all members although entirely just solutions are
not absolutely crucial for their survival. Even so, an inability to reach a sufficiently high level of agreement about essential harm conventions, or the state's
unwillingness or inability to enforce them, can result in the decline or collapse
of social systems.

Harm conventions intercede between the capacity to injure and the condition of vulnerability to mental and physical suffering that is also specific
to the human species. On the one side there exist basic universals such as
human frailty (the susceptibility of people as embodied selves to bodily pain
and mental anguish, inevitable physical decline and death). It is important to
add the precariousness of social institutions and their capacity to fail actors,
as well as interdependence between people – their reliance on one another
for the satisfaction of basic needs, and the fact that personal well-being can
be damaged by other people's decisions to violate social conventions (Turner
1993a, 2006). On the other side, there is the capacity for cruelty, and for violent or intimidating behaviour as well as recklessness, negligence or indifference to the adverse effects that actions may have on others; there is, in
addition, the temptation to prey on the vulnerable that has been a feature of
at least all complex societies, and which may never be eliminated entirely.
Moreover, societies use the vulnerability of members to ensure their survival.
By inflicting pain, restricting liberty or causing suffering in some other way,
they use the 'power to hurt' to punish transgressors and to protect members
from injury.

In many societies, the dominant harm conventions are not systematized and
codified but operate informally in everyday life. As part of the modern civilizing process, particular social institutions, domestic legal codes and the international order have constructed elaborate moral codes that formalize duties
not to cause needless harm. The earliest formalization of the harm principle
may have occurred in response to the stretching of social relations across space
with the consequence that interaction increasingly took place between strangers
who lacked close personal affiliations and shared understandings of what they
could expect from each other. One of the first and most famous examples of the
codification of the harm principle in the West was the Hippocratic Oath which
defended the principle, *primum non nocere* ('first, do no harm'). Constructing a
medical ethic in that way was probably a result of enlarging the membership of
the Hippocratic School with the outcomes that have just been noted (Jouanna
1999: 46ff.). Systematic formulations of basic harm conventions have been central features of Western societies that reflect a combination of complex social
ties along with a high degree of reflectiveness about ethical matters that reflect
what Weber (1948a) regarded as distinctive Occidental patterns of societal

rationalization.[1] One example may suffice. Expressing modern commitments, the fourth and fifth Articles of the 1789 French Declaration of the Rights of Man and the Citizen defined liberty as 'the capacity to do anything that does no harm to others', and added that 'legislation is entitled to forbid only those actions which are harmful to society' (cited in Finer 1997: 1539). Of course, there are many other ways of constructing a harm principle. Liberals explicitly rejected earlier versions such as the *malleus malifecarum*, the late fifteenth-century document that proclaimed the need to extirpate the 'dark and horrid harms' of witchcraft. Following the papal bull issued by Innocent VIII, that document was at the heart of European jurisprudence for almost three centuries (Kramer and Sprenger 1971). Codifications of practice have proliferated in modern states as part of the movement to enshrine individual liberties in constitutional frameworks. Ethical concerns about the special vulnerability of the young which may be unusual in the development of more complex societies are also worth noting, as are the various conventions that have developed in the West, especially since the mid-nineteenth century, to end cruelty to animals (Elias 1998; Thomas 1984).[2]

Specific understandings of moral subjectivity, agency and responsibility are evident in the critical space occupied by harm conventions, and not least by systems of punishment – but of greater importance are the particular convictions about the interests and ideals that societies believe they should protect. In many societies, injury to animals that have sacred standing has been high on the moral hierarchy of reprehensible harms. In some ways of life animals have been tried and punished for misdemeanours. Harm to the gods is clearly far more serious for some groups than injury to mere mortals. In such cases, harm conventions that include rules of blasphemy intercede between people and the supernatural realm in order to protect the gods from offence and humans from themselves (frequently from a belief in the afterlife that makes the mundane harms of daily life seem ephemeral). To the surprise of those who thought that secularization was set to continue, political claims that revolve around religious faith have intruded once again into the lives of modern societies.

---

[1] The birth of sociology can be understood as a response to new patterns of interconnectedness that forced humans to confront new questions about how they should be attuned to each other (Mazlish 1989). Smith (1982 [1759]) remains a critical text since it begins with the fact that countless strangers have been thrown together in modern societies. It was unrealistic and inappropriate in his view to expect strangers to behave selflessly towards each other, but they had a right to expect just treatment at the hands of others. At its core, justice required that people should not cause each other unnecessary harm (see Chapter 2 for further discussion). There is a contrast to be made between civilizing processes in early societies where survival depended not just on refraining from harm but on the responsibility to 'share the hunt'.

[2] An example is the UK Children Act of 1989 which defines harm to children as 'ill-treatment or the impairment of health and development' (Adcock *et al.* 1989).

Those points can be connected with Elias's idea of the civilizing process, the process that deals with the question of how people can go about satisfying their elementary needs without 'destroying, frustrating, demeaning or in other ways harming each other time and time again' (Elias 1996: 31). The interplay between sociogenetic and psychogenetic forces – between public institutions or proclaimed social standards, and emotional responses anchored in personality systems – was central to that analysis. As part of a broader study of civilizing processes, the sociology of harm conventions recognizes that the survival of social systems depends on the combined influence of coercive mechanisms and the restraining role of basic human emotions that shape the individual's 'conscience'. All societies depend on universal, or virtually universal, emotions such as guilt, shame, embarrassment and remorse for ensuring high levels of compliance with prohibitions of harm; they also rely on such emotions as indignation or disgust when serious transgressions occur, and on pity or compassion for the victims of unwarranted mental or physical harm. In particular, harm conventions form a core element of every individual's personality structure or 'habitus', and necessarily so because there are no more basic features of human existence (Elias 2000: 365ff.).

Emotional responses to suffering have been extraordinarily diverse in human history, and many seem extraordinarily cruel to the modern eye. Ancient Roman gladiatorial games were public spectacles in which returning, triumphant military leaders and crowd-pleasing emperors celebrated success and displayed their power or prowess by slaughtering those who had been taken captive in war, or dissidents including Christians, and exotic animals acquired through conquest (Kyle 1998). Aztec cosmology demanded the ritual sacrifice and public flaying of captives to make sure that the sun would rise every day (Carrasco 1999). Some societies, including Ancient Israel, have regarded suffering as divine punishment that the faithful must endure. Others, including medieval Christian communities, valued suffering as a test of personal faith or as a way of coming closer to God (Glucklich 2001). Other examples of the tolerance of suffering, and the appetite for violence or cruelty, could be catalogued in a graphic inventory of human inventiveness in diversifying forms of harm such as systems of punishment. Some rationales for suffering are perhaps best regarded as coping mechanisms, as ways in which people reconciled themselves to ordeals that their societies were powerless to control. Medical revolutions in the nineteenth century, including the use of anaesthetic techniques that are now more or less taken for granted in many regions, have relieved large numbers of people from pain and anxiety that their ancestors had no choice but to endure. The use of such technologies in routine surgical practice was not always automatic, and required political intervention.[3] Members of secure liberal democracies are

---

[3] The reference is to the reluctance on the part of surgeons in the United States to administer newly-invented anaesthetics during childbirth because of religious doctrines that valorized suffering (see Rey 1998: ch. 6).

usually spared violence against the body because of those changing sensibilities to suffering and pain (Elias 2000: 1–7).

Most of those who belong to functioning social systems are averse to harming members of the in-group. If internal controls fail, they can be swayed by peer pressure or by the fear of public sanctions to refrain from causing injury or from being complicit in the suffering of others. Psychopaths aside, wrongdoers usually recognize that it is wrong to cause needless harm. Should the balance tilt too far in the other direction, then the survival of the social order may come into question. Harm conventions identify the forms of harm that are permitted and forbidden within a community as well as what is tolerable or prohibited in relations with other groups. In general, the standards that govern relations with other communities have tolerated levels of violence that are taboo in relations within the 'in-group'. At times, they have encouraged acts that are condemned for their cruelty when the victims are members of the same society (Elias 1996: 154ff.; 2007a [1987]: 145).[4]

In ancient empires, the economic gains of enslaving conquered groups, exacting tribute, or reaping the benefits of incorporating defeated forces in the imperial armies often led to prohibitions of mass slaughter that had occurred in earlier eras (see Raaflaub and Rosenstein 1999). Similar self-interested motives have led most societies to regulate warriors' behaviour. Analyses of warfare have stated that the ruling groups usually seek to convince 'socialized warriors' that they have been granted a temporary licence to depart from the usual constraints on force (Bourke 1999: ch. 11; Keeley 1996: 143ff.; Lifton 1974; Liverani 2001; Verkamp 1993).[5] The idea of the 'controlled decontrolling' of violence, a term first used in process sociology to refer to how customary prohibitions on violence are relaxed in physical sports such as boxing (but in a highly regulated way), is relevant here (see p. 170). Societies that need to demonize the enemy in order to justify killing (and many do that to weaken inhibitions against taking life) must be alert to the dangers that may be unleashed when warriors return to society, desensitized to pain and suffering. The 'controlled decontrolling' of violence is essential to reintegrate the returning warrior and to reduce the danger that a 'flood of violent wars' will release 'waves of violence' that may ruin the lives of generations to come (Elias 1996: 461). Examples of the socially destructive consequences of war are the rising levels of violence that followed the return of the crusaders in the late Middle Ages, the destruction that was caused by 'free companies' that roamed Europe as a result of the disbandment of armies at

---

[4] The widespread practice of emphasizing similarities between 'internal' and 'external' enemies reveals the difficulty of separating endogenous from exogenous influences on harm conventions.

[5] As Elias (2006a: ch. 10) stressed in his discussion of the expulsion of the Huguenots from France, states have often promoted core political objectives by harnessing the returning warriors' expertise in violence and intimidation. In that example, 400,000 warriors were used to expel 300,000 Huguenots during the reign of Louis XIV.

the end of the Hundred Years' War, and the higher crime rates that occurred in the aftermath of Europe's wars between the sixteenth and eighteenth centuries (Cohen 1996).[6] Those are examples of a general trend in which the homicide rate, and acts of violence against women in particular, increase sharply at the end of major wars (Martin and Frayer 1997: 14–15).[7]

In some societies, those who have transgressed prohibitions against killing are required to undergo inner cleansing or purification.[8] It may be thought that those who committed or witnessed excessive violence should experience 'traumatic guilt' or publicly acknowledge that they have suffered moral or spiritual damage (Young 1997: 79–80, 125). Perpetrators of excessive violence, or those who have been witness to it, may be consumed by what has come to be known as post-traumatic stress disorder, a relatively modern label coined in the late nineteenth century to describe what may nevertheless be an ancient condition (Edkins 2003; Lifton 1974; Tritle 2000: chs. 3–4). Exactly how widespread that phenomenon is – and how far it varies between societies and historical epochs – are intriguing questions that raise issues about how far the passage from peace to war places enormous psychological burdens on those involved. Referring to that largely unexplored theme, Elias (2007b [1992]: 145) observed that the demands were relatively slight in ancient Athens and in many medieval towns where inhabitants carried weapons, and frequently used them so that 'physical fighting within one's own society (was) much more common than it is today'. Psychological demands and stresses are much greater in modern pacified societies where people do not routinely carry weapons, rarely witness killing, and infrequently encounter the dead or dying (other than as portrayed in the media). In such conditions, extended professional training is necessary to guide warriors through the complex transition from civilian to military life (Grossman 1996).

---

[6] Higher rates of violence had many causes, including the fact that large numbers of returning solders were destitute. See Hay (1992) for a discussion of this theme with respect to Britain, and Cohen (1996) for similar observations with respect to France, at the end of the Hundred Years' War. Significantly, some of the lowest homicide rates in the world are to be found in societies such as Switzerland and Sweden that have not waged wars for decades (Keeley 1996: 32).

[7] Complex methodological questions regarding estimations of crime rates must be placed to one side here. For further discussion, see Johnson and Monkkonen (1996).

[8] Verkamp (1993: 25ff.) notes that 'the pre-Homeric world', like 'the African Zulus, the Eskimos, or the North American Indians', had a fear of 'contamination with contact with the dead'. Post-Homeric Greeks and Romans, and possibly the inhabitants of Ancient Israel, shared that fear, perhaps because of the influence of Zoroastrianism. Many early societies thought it necessary 'to quarantine the (warrior) from the community at large, lest physical contact in itself pollute others'. Verkamp (1993: 25ff.) adds that early Christian notions of 'spiritual contamination' dispensed with that practice (and overcame the fear of 'attacks from the spirits of those whom they had slain in battle'), but they remained convinced of the need for psychological purification.

The discussion has stressed the self-interested motives that groups may have for promoting the 'controlled decontrolling' of violence. The phenomenon of post-traumatic stress disorder serves as a link to other-regarding themes where the sufferer may not only feel guilty for breaching social standards but also, insofar as they can be disentangled, for taking the lives of, or injuring, other humans. Religious ideas have often shaped social attitudes about the moral significance of taking enemy lives. Similar orientations that are now underpinned by international criminal law have an ancient pedigree. The notion of honouring the enemy, which has been a recurrent feature of ideologies of military valour or chivalry, may date back to the first societies (Turney-High 1991).[9] But the general tolerance of greater violence against outsiders reveals that there is no simple passage from the shared condition of vulnerability to suffering to an intersocietal consensus that a cosmopolitan harm principle should govern relations between groups (see the discussion of Simone Weil in Chapter 5). The body can be a source of solidarity, but it can also be the reason for fear and enmity.

International and cosmopolitan forms

Societies have good internal reasons for creating harm conventions that control the behaviour of warriors. Those motives can lead to international equivalents which express what societies agree they should and should not do in peacetime or in war. Self-interested reasons in resolving and avoiding conflict have often provided incentives for exploring the common ground. The institution of 'blood money', where kin-groups relied on compensation for the 'unavenged' loss of life in order to break up cycles of revenge killing, appears to have been one of the earliest methods of conflict resolution (Keeley 1996: 147ff.; Turney-High 1991: 171). Blood money, or resorting to the good offices of third parties, represented a step forward in the level of detachment from disputes that could easily trap societies in spirals of violence that could last for generations (Keeley 1996; Turney-High 1991: ch. 11). Similar ways of disrupting cycles of revenge existed in Ancient Greece, and in the Middle Ages through the practice of *wergild*. They were ingenious ways of controlling violence where anyone who

---

[9] However incomplete, the anthropological record does not suggest that all 'primitive' wars were a 'free-for-all' in which warriors were permitted to indulge murderous instincts (see Chapter 3). Keeley (1996: 143–4), who advances the controversial argument that anthropologists have frequently underestimated the destructiveness of early warfare, argues that there is little evidence that warriors 'revelled in or had a special affection' for violent conflict. Respect for 'accomplished warriors was often tinged with aversion' to killing. Moreover, warriors could be 'spiritually polluted or contaminated' by violence, and they were often thought to be the conduit through which sinister forces, linked with the enemy dead, could enter society with the aim of extracting vengeance (see also Turney-High 1991: 207ff.). On some accounts, many early societies had the equivalent of the modern law of nations that attempts to limit cruelty in warfare (Turney-High 1991: 207ff.).

had been harmed by an outsider had to turn to the coercive power of the group to secure justice.

Elaborate global harm conventions that developed in societies of states would not have developed but for the inventiveness which early societies showed in such domains (although the history of the evolution of such practices has yet to be written). But the achievements of international societies in reaching agreements about the necessity of controlling violent harm have usually been precarious. Given the absence of any higher monopoly of power, fears for national security and survival frequently lead self-reliant states to conclude that there is no choice but to ignore the usual internal prohibitions of violence. More seriously, as Wight (1977: ch. 1) maintained, all previous societies of states were consumed by war as the last surviving great powers engaged in what would prove to be the final struggle for dominance. Even so, global harm conventions in international societies have been important ways of controlling inter-state violence.

As explained elsewhere, those global conventions can be divided into two types: international and cosmopolitan harm conventions (Linklater 2001). International harm conventions are designed to contribute to order by, inter alia, placing constraints on force. As with their constituent parts, societies of states possess civilizing processes that enable political communities to promote core interests without harming each other over and over again (see pp. 127–33). As Bull (1977: ch. 4) maintained, international order may be a primary value since, without it, individuals would be exposed to terrible insecurity and violence. But as his comments on the tension between order and justice emphasized, amicable co-existence is no more than partial progress in international relations. Crucial though they are, international harm conventions have been entirely compatible with indifference to many forms of suffering. Slavery and the slave trade co-existed with principles of international co-existence in the Hellenic states-system, and in the modern society of states until the middle of the nineteenth century (and, to avoid misunderstanding, sexual and other forms of slavery endure to this day but without the approval of international law). Practices that contribute to the maintenance of international order have existed alongside serious violations of individual rights and the ruthless disregard of the interests of small states, and sometimes complete indifference to their survival (Linklater and Suganami 2006b: ch. 4). For those reasons, it is worth recalling the contention that international order must ultimately be judged by what it contributes to world order – a state of affairs in which all individuals enjoy freedom from violence and insecurity (Bull 1977: ch. 1).[10] As defined here,

---

[10] Following Booth (2007: 4–5), the point can be reformulated to stress the importance of ascertaining what international order contributes to 'world security' which refers to 'the structures and processes within human society, locally and globally, that work towards the reduction of the threats and risks that determine individual and group lives'.

world order is the condition in which there is a central role for cosmopolitan harm conventions that have the purpose of protecting individuals and sub-state groups from unnecessary harm whether it is caused by national, international or transnational actors, structures and processes.

The modern society of states has been the site for successive experiments in codifying global harm conventions – international in the shape of collective efforts to promote respect for sovereignty and the principle of non-intervention, and cosmopolitan as in the case of the universal human rights culture, the humanitarian rules of war, and more recent innovations in international criminal law. Cosmopolitan conventions are essential because of the negative consequences of unusually high levels of human interconnectedness, specifically the ability to project military power into the heartland of distant societies and the increased possibility of transnational harm in recent decades. Environmental degradation is a striking contemporary example of transnational harm that travels freely across borders, giving rise to a new moral and political vocabulary, and to limited global harm conventions, that are concerned not with 'national interests' or international order but with the well-being of the species and the fate of future generations. All modern cosmopolitan conventions are heir to codes of conduct that appeared during the first phase of European conquest when the Spanish clergy recognized that the cruelties that were perpetrated by the conquistadores jeopardized the spiritual advances the missionaries hoped for. The Laws of Burgos of 1512 were amongst the earliest efforts to offer protection (however limited) to colonized peoples. At a later stage in the history of overseas colonialism, French and Spanish slave laws such as the *Code Noir* and the *Siete Partidas* limited the powers of slave-owners by forbidding certain forms of cruelty – though, for the most part, without much practical effect (Goveia 2000).

Colonial codes of conduct drew on medieval ideas about the just war (Hamilton 1963) that provided resources for developments in the humanitarian law of war that have occurred in response to the unprecedented levels of destruction made possible by the industrialization of conflict. Especially since the second half of the nineteenth century, various treaties have created legal responsibilities to avoid 'unnecessary suffering' or 'superfluous injury' in military conflicts (Roberts and Guelff 2000). Conventions on torture, genocide and so forth have established the right of the international community to scrutinize and criticize the state's treatment of its citizens, a contraction of 'domestic jurisdiction' that has found novel expression in the evolution of international criminal law since the Nuremberg and Tokyo war crimes tribunals. Those innovations can be linked with the larger project of 'harm reduction' or 'harm minimization', to use expressions drawn from reflections in the 1980s about how national policies could limit 'human suffering' by curbing the use of illicit drugs (Marlatt 1998). Linking such national and global endeavours is the aspiration to reduce or eliminate suffering that is 'useless' or 'for nothing' (Levinas

1998: ch. 8). What is distinctive about national and global movements and organizations that struggled to end slavery and the slave trade, or which have sought to bring about the worldwide abolition of the death penalty, the use of land mines in civil conflicts and so forth is their active involvement in promoting global civilizing processes that replicate the achievements of the most stable modern societies (see Chapter 4).

Most civilizations have developed 'war conventions' which affirmed that non-combatants have a right to be spared pointless suffering. What is unusual about modern variations on that theme is the greater interconnectedness between societies and increasing levels of diverse forms of cross-border harm that have inspired efforts to embed cosmopolitan commitments in global arrangements. The point has been made that some of the principal moral concerns result from 'the industrialization of war' and its destructive effects on civilian populations. However, in the mid-nineteenth century, Marx stressed the emergence of new political problems that stemmed from rising levels of transnational harm that accompanied the globalization of capitalism. For Marx, the radical transformation of the modern world was no more evident than in the steady shift away from the condition in which deliberate, violent harm between societies dominated international relations to a condition in which the life of the species is increasingly shaped by unintended, and often invisible, harm that spreads across national frontiers as a result of the operation of capitalist markets. The distinction between concrete and abstract harm has been coined to describe those developments (Linklater 2002a). Concrete harm involves the intention to make designated others suffer – most obviously, enemies in war. Abstract harm is caused by impersonal forces where people's intentions are less significant than the global structures and processes that push them to act in ways that harm others, though often unintentionally or because of indifference rather than malice. Of course, Marx's predictions of epochal change turned out to be significantly wide of the mark. In reality, abstract harm has been superimposed upon, and become intertwined with, older forms of concrete harm that, contrary to Marx's expectations, reached a new intensity in the first half of the twentieth century.

To turn to E. H. Carr's writings on world politics, one of their main strengths was the call for new forms of political community that could reduce the fears and insecurities that are caused by international harm – the harm that states do to each other – and by transnational harm – the harm caused by market forces (Linklater 1998: ch. 6). Many approaches to global ethics preserve the spirit of that inquiry by distinguishing between 'international exploitation' – 'exploitative exchange that takes place between states' – and 'transnational exploitation' – 'exploitative exchange that takes place between bodies and individuals in different societies' (De-Shalit 1998: 693, fn. 2). Much the same point is captured by separating international justice – justice between states – from transnational justice, which is concerned with reducing global inequities in order to improve the life-chances of the poorer members of world society (O'Neill 1991). Dangers that result from the export of hazardous waste highlight the moral significance of those distinctions. In the past, regimes in Liberia and the Ivory Coast have cooperated with transnational business enterprises to allow hazardous products to be dumped on their territories. The benefits that accrued to business corporations and local elites depended on ignoring the health implications for vulnerable groups. Neglect of their interests is probably best regarded as exhibiting indifference to their welfare rather than a cruel desire to cause suffering (De-Shalit 1998: 707). Thoughtlessness may not attract the same legal and moral sanctions as acts of cruelty but the consequences can be as harmful.[11] An obvious point to make is that, for many people, the main source of insecurity is not the threat or reality of international harm in the shape of violent attack, but one of the by-products of rising levels of interconnectedness, namely exposure to one or other form of transnational harm, such as environmental degradation.

In those circumstances, it is hardly surprising that contemporary struggles to promote cosmopolitan harm conventions have embraced resistance to neo-liberal global economic institutions and strategies as well as efforts to defend principles such as the doctrine of non-combatant immunity in response to modern warfare. In addition, global environmental movements address the wholly unique form of transnational harm caused by global warming. There is no better illustration of the need for 'cosmopolitan environmental harm conventions' to protect people from what is often unintended or invisible trans-boundary harm in 'global risk society', although it is important not to forget that the threats to human security that result from the development of long-distance, aerial bombardment influenced earlier (but largely marginal) arguments in support of moral and political universalism (Herz 1959).[12] Reference has been made to Bull's claim that international order should be judged by the extent of its contribution to world order, the point being that

---

[11] The *Oxford English Dictionary* (*OED*) takes cruelty to mean 'indifference to the pain or misery of others' as well as the 'disposition to inflict suffering'. The *Encyclopaedia* defined cruelty as 'a ferocious passion that contains within it ... hardness with respect to others, incommiseration, vengeance, the pleasure of doing harm out of insensibility of the heart or out of the pleasure of seeing suffering' (quoted in Steintrager 2004: 6, who traces the rise of sensitivities to cruelty during the Enlightenment). The important point is that indifference can rest on pure apathy – on what Arendt (1994) in her discussion of the 'banality of evil' called thoughtlessness – or on a disposition of underlying 'hostility' which can be as 'brutal as hatred and more effective than contempt' (Solomon 1993: 268). The reference to contempt is an important addition to the list of dispositions that can underlie an unwillingness to assist others, or the conscious or unconscious neglect of their interests, or indeed a degree of pleasure in their misfortune, as captured in the notion of *Schadenfreude* (see Portmann 2000). All that need be added is that the distinction between 'killing' and 'letting die' breaks down when cruel indifference based on contempt or hostility is the main reason for failing to rescue vulnerable persons (see pp. 57–9).

[12] See Elliott (2006) on cosmopolitan environmental harm conventions.

stable relations between independent communities are crucially important, but incomplete without global measures to dismantle obstacles to human well-being. Cosmopolitan harm conventions can support the movement towards an international political community in which there is collective support for that ethical ideal. Complementing international conventions, they rest on the assumption that distinctions of citizenship, nationality, race, gender, class and so forth should be stripped of much of the ethical significance they have had in the past – and continue to have in most regions. On that argument, the challenge of coping with 'harm at a distance', whether initiated by states, public or private transnational organizations, or inherent in global market forces or in everyday actions that cause environmental degradation, requires ethical standpoints that transcend familiar insider–outsider dualisms. An example is the belief that the cultural and other characteristics that have separated groups for millennia are not as morally significant as shared human frailties (Rorty 1989: ch. 9). The thesis is that pain, humiliation, exploitation and other setbacks to peoples' interests and aspirations provide a basis for solidarity between groups, or a foundation for global agreements to promote cosmopolitan ethical responsibilities that defend the fundamental obligation to spare other people avoidable harm.

War and conquest have been two of the main determinants of social evolution and two of the principal causes of harm in world politics. They have given insider–outsider dualisms the illusion of permanence in human affairs, although the liberal tenet that 'cruelty is the worst thing we do' (Shklar 1984) might be said to underpin treaties that endeavour to check the effects of such dualisms by establishing universal obligations to refrain from causing other persons 'serious bodily and mental harm'. Global interconnectedness has created pressures to work towards a universal consensus about the urgency of eradicating pointless harm that may not have commanded much support in earlier forms of world political organization. Perhaps that condition will be a catalyst for weakening traditional beliefs that cosmopolitan principles are remote from the exigencies of everyday life, of residual importance because they are not strictly necessary for maintaining order, or utopian because they cannot rival the emotional appeal and influence of immediate attachments. The recent codification of cosmopolitan harm conventions offers hope that such global orientations are beginning to shape the *habitus* that has long stayed within narrower horizons. Recognizing the growing influence of transnational harm, global environmental conventions support a cosmopolitan version of the harm principle that includes duties to avoid damaging the commons (Elliott 2006; Mason 2006). It is of great importance that the emphasis on consideration for the environment does not only stress the obligations of states, or all public and private organizations, but calls on people everywhere to take responsibility for the ways in which routine, everyday acts harm distant strangers and may burden future generations. Arguments for greater reflectiveness with regard to personal 'carbon footprints', for example, are especially notable since they mark the appearance of unusual, if not unique, efforts to build cosmopolitan duties into the individual's *habitus*.

International treaties that aim to protect people from 'serious mental and physical harm' and to limit damage to the environment invite the question of how many forms of harm there are in world politics. As a first step, it is necessary to distinguish between deliberate killing, intended mental or physical injury (both widespread in military conflict) and inadvertent or negligent harm (as in the case of exporting hazards or damaging the environment). The issue of whether the failure to rescue constitutes a separate category is not the least of the reasons for ongoing debates about the meaning of the concept of harm and the scope of the 'harm principle'. As discussions of rescue indicate, the issues are not only philosophical but raise large legal and political questions about the most serious forms of harm that people cause, about what they should be blamed or punished for doing (or not doing as in the case of a failure to rescue), and ultimately about their most fundamental obligations to one another, whether as members of particular societies or as people who are bound together in global networks of interdependence. Such questions lead then to the discussion of what societies should be aiming to achieve in the way of a global civilizing process.

Conceptualizing harm

The modern world may be witnessing a global civilizing process which indicates that societies have reached some measure of consensus about serious harms that should be eliminated from national, international and transnational spheres of interaction. Shared agreements have had to be forged from different moral and cultural starting-points that continue to limit achievements in that domain. In the language of the moral philosophers, societies have not reached a 'view from nowhere' that offers a direct route to a universal consensus about the forms of harm that should be eradicated from domestic and world politics. The sociology of knowledge advises that definitions of harm will reflect the fears and anxieties, as well as the ideals and hopes, of particular groups in distinctive spatio-temporal locations. As noted earlier, modern secular reasoning about the concept of harm is hard to disentangle from concerns about actions that can shorten or disfigure life that have become especially prominent since the Enlightenment. It is abundantly clear that many societies – and quite possibly the majority in human history – have not seen the world in that way (see, however, the discussion of Weil on pp. 222–3). It is certain that every classification of the forms of serious harm will seem strange to some peoples. Or at least some of its features may strike them as puzzling or baffling. Many of the harms that can be included in a modern taxonomic scheme – and reflect contemporary sensibilities – will be perfectly intelligible to other societies. But they do not all attach the same moral importance to such agreed harms or have the same ethical priorities. Deciding what counts as harm is one thing; deciding what counts as wrongful harm is another matter entirely. Most, if not all, societies may have similar views about what is harmful – hence their reliance on similar ways of punishing those who violate social norms (Barry 1995: 141) – but they give different reasons for regarding specific actions as harmful, and they reach different conclusions about what overlapping standpoints mean for the organization of society and for relations with other groups.

To take such discussions forward, it is often best to start with dictionary definitions. The *Oxford English Dictionary* (*OED*) defines harm as 'evil (physical or otherwise) as done to or suffered by some person or thing'. Alternatively, it is 'hurt, injury, damage, mischief' that results in 'grief, sorrow, pain, trouble, distress [or] affliction'. The concept derives from the Old English term, *hearm*, which referred to the 'psychologically defined' experience of 'grief or sorrow' (Kleinig 1978: 27). The *OED* definition highlights key issues, and points the way towards more rigorous analysis. Even when shorn of its theological connotations, the idea of evil which is central to the *OED*, and which has been reworked in recent interpretations of genocide, is notoriously complex. Many approaches call attention to the pleasure that some take in exercising power over others by making them suffer; they emphasize what the *OED* calls 'morally depraved' intentions (Baumeister 1997). On that basis, and as a preliminary step in the process of definition, violent harm can be divided into two broad categories, the first highlighting the motivating influence of the appetite for cruelty, the second emphasizing different reasons for inflicting harm that may include a reluctant use of force in self-defence and a genuine attempt to avoid cruelty and minimize suffering.

Clearly many forms of harm do not involve violence at all. The concept of 'damage' in the *OED* definition includes malicious rumour that harms someone's reputation. A person's material interests can be damaged by theft, extortion or exploitation where physical force is not involved. Despite the saying that 'sticks and stones may break my bones, but words will never hurt me', humiliation, harassment, bullying and so forth can lead to psychological scars that can outlast the pain caused by physical injury. As for the *OED* notion of 'mischief', one might hesitate to use that term to describe the way in which a torturer treats a victim, although one *OED* definition equates the concept with evil. Another definition stresses what may be the more typical, 'milder sense' of the term that includes 'petty annoyance', as in the case of gentle mockery which only becomes a serious matter when it turns into a campaign to damage a person's self-esteem through, for example, systematic bullying or harassment.

References to pain, grief, distress and sorrow in the *OED* definition draw attention to the psychological consequences of physical suffering, the mental anguish that follows the death of loved ones, or feelings of insecurity that result from theft, burglary or vandalism. However, a person can be harmed without experiencing those emotional states – that is without being 'hurt'. A person is harmed by a burglary that takes place while on vacation, but hurt does not enter the equation until the victim discovers the incident (Feinberg 1973: 27). 'Posthumous harm' to reputation is an extreme example of being harmed without being hurt (Feinberg 1984: 79–83). But perhaps enough has been said to indicate that the concept of harm can be divided into many parts that extend from the 'world-destroying' pain of torture (Scarry 1985) to the relatively minor setbacks associated with petty theft or vandalism – and enough has been said to raise questions about what unifies such diverse events and occurrences.

Fortunately, a substantial literature addresses the last problem. *Kakapoeics* is one term that has been coined to describe the exercise of theorizing harm. Others are *zemiotics*, and the equally unmusical and unloveable, *zemiology*, both derived from *zemos,* the Greek for harm. Some prefer the more straightforward label, the 'social harm perspective' (Hillyard *et al.* 2004: 276). All of those terms draw attention to the need for a distinctive sub-field of social inquiry that analyses the problem of harm – or better still, for using such a perspective to integrate approaches and findings that are currently scattered across several disciplines. That there is much more to this inquiry than some have realized is stressed by the architects of 'the social harm perspective' who argue that one irony 'of the apparent triumph of Western liberalism and its rhetoric of rights and responsibilities' is the 'utter indifference it shows to the production of harm' (Hillyard *et al.* 2004: 4). One criticism of orthodox liberal criminology is that it has failed to address the theoretical and political challenges that arise because 'criminal harm forms a very small and largely insignificant proportion of the vast bulk of harms' that occur in everyday life (Hillyard *et al.* 2004: 9). That comment draws attention to harms caused by social and political structures that liberals have often ignored.

Liberal orientations continue to have a leading role in the analysis of the concept of harm, and the following discussion must begin with them. Their central purpose has been to determine the scope of the criminal law. In so doing, they have distinguished between harmful acts that rightly invite state intervention and attract legal sanction, and harmless conduct that properly falls within the sphere of untrammelled personal liberties.[13] For most liberals, the established departure point is the distinction between self- and other-regarding actions that

---

[13] Critics maintain that efforts to ground the criminal law in the harm principle are flawed. They stress that the open-ended nature of the concept of harm makes it easy to extend the criminal law into more and more areas that some groups regard as harming society, thereby reducing personal freedoms. Harcourt (1999) provides a useful account of how the harm principle has been freed from its earlier close connection with liberal progressivism and coupled with socially conservative visions that aim to alter the balance between state power and individual liberties (see also Dan-Cohen 2002: ch. 5). The present work is not concerned with assessing liberal approaches to the scope of the criminal law, but with the related task of discussing structures and actions that generate cosmopolitan obligations because of harm to other persons. But debates about the strengths and weaknesses of the liberal harm principle are clearly important for that enterprise.

underpinned Mill's defence of individual liberty and opposition to legal paternalism (with respect to adults but not children and 'uncivilized' societies). In a
famous claim, Mill (1972: 73) maintained 'the only purpose for which power
can be rightfully exercised over any member of a civilised community, against
his will, is to prevent harm to others'.[14] A person's 'own good, either physical or
moral', he added, is not 'sufficient warrant'. Later elaborations of that principle
have stressed that the violation of personal liberty is an 'evil' – 'the infliction of
a special form of suffering' – that always stands in need of justification (Hart
1968: 22). The presumption in favour of liberty leaves people free to behave as
they please – even if others find their conduct offensive – as long as their actions
do not harm others (Feinberg 1985; Hart 1968: 47).[15]

Mill knew that it was impossible to draw sharp distinctions between self- and
other-regarding actions, but those who think the problems run deeper may
wish to add that actions cannot be classified objectively in that way but always
reflect specific, prior understandings of the right relationship between the individual and society.[16] That said, Mill (1972: 74) stated that 'a person may cause
evil to others not only by his actions but by his inaction, and in either case he
is justly accountable to them for the injury'. The failure to warn someone about
to step onto an unsafe bridge constituted harm, in Mill's view, because it can be
presumed that people want to avoid, and to be warned of, such hidden dangers.
For that reason, the observer 'might seize him and turn him back, without any
real infringement of his liberty' (Mill 1972: 152).

Clearly, normative assumptions about core human interests that can be
harmed by acts of omission or commission underpin such arguments. The liberal
claim is that actions that are 'primarily' or 'chiefly' self-regarding do not harm
basic interests, but actions that are other-regarding do (Feinberg 1986: 56). On
one interpretation of Mill's writings, there is a strong prima facie case for state

---

[14] Mill's reference to civilization invites the comment that the liberal harm principle has been
central to the recent phase of the civilizing process in Elias's technical use of that term. The
influence of the harm principle on contemporary international law, specifically in affirming obligations to refrain from causing 'serious mental and bodily harm' (see Chapter 2),
is testimony to liberal efforts to take the civilizing process forward through such global
initiatives.

[15] Large issues arise about whether it is legitimate for the state to curtail liberties because of
the risk of future harm, and about whether it is necessary to resist efforts to restrict current
freedoms that some regard as essential in order to protect society from unproven threats
(see especially Sunstein 2005 on the precautionary principle). Discussions of such matters
are designed to show that societies have to guard against the danger that the harm principle
will be used to justify major extensions of state power where there is uncertainty about
future trajectories.

[16] Changing attitudes to suicide in the West over the last few centuries illustrate the point.
Suicide was widely regarded as harming society in the Middle Ages. Only later, and particularly during the Enlightenment, did it come to be regarded as entirely a matter of individual
choice, particularly when there was no other escape from debilitating pain (Minois 1995).

intervention when an action harms another person or persons. To rephrase the point, harm to others is a necessary, but not a sufficient, condition for involving the criminal law (Ten 1980: 67). The dominant liberal position is that individuals have an interest in maintaining freedom that may, at times, trump other objectives including the public interest in punishing harm. The question then is how to strike an appropriate balance between personal liberties and prima facie obligations not to cause harm, or between freedom and the criminal law. Some liberals have argued that the balance is best struck by distinguishing between 'serious' and minor harms, by criminalizing only significant harm, and by deterring less severe harms in non-punitive ways (Shue 1981: 117ff.).[17]

Such perplexities are central to Feinberg's magisterial four-volume study of harm and the limits of the criminal law. From that jurisprudential perspective, harm is thought to consist of two main properties: 'it must lead to some kind of adverse effect, or create the danger of such an effect, on its victim's *interests*', and 'it must be inflicted wrongly in violation of the victim's *rights*' (Feinberg 1992: 3–4; italics in original). The second characteristic stresses that a mere setback to an interest does not necessarily justify the involvement of the criminal law. An athlete who loses a competition he or she had expected to win suffers a setback to interests, but the actual winner did not violate that person's rights (Feinberg 1984: 220). According to the principle, *volenti non fit inuria* (to one who has consented, no wrong is done), someone who agrees to be harmed in specific ways, for example in sadomasochistic sex, voluntarily relinquishes the right to secure justice through the criminal law (Feinberg 1984: 115ff.). In such circumstances, harm is caused, but there is no wrong to the consenting person's rights. Because Mill's dichotomy between self- and other-regarding acts is vulnerable to the criticism that all actions affect others to some degree, Feinberg (1984: 12) calls for a restricted definition of harm that limits the state's power to punish what some regard as wrongdoing. The argument is that personal liberties are preserved, and individuals are protected from morally overburdened lives, in that way. A related objective is to ensure that people do not live in fear of legal sanction for causing inadvertent harm.[18] Moreover, the criminal law must be confined to punishing only the most serious forms of harmful wrongdoing if it is not to collapse into legal paternalism.

The analysis raises familiar questions about the relationship between liberty and equality, and particularly about whether supporters of the harm principle

---

[17] Harcourt (1999) argues that the harm principle does not offer a guide to distinguishing between serious and trivial harms, and so liberals must rely on other moral values to decide between punishable and non-punishable harms. Feinberg's position on basic welfare interests recognizes as much (see pp. 46–9), but the critic will argue that this only shifts the debate to the reasons for thinking that some interests are more fundamental than others.

[18] It has been reported that, in the United States, the fear of legal action for causing harm inadvertently is one reason why members of the general public are often reluctant to assist those who, for one reason or another, need medical assistance.

place efforts to maximize personal freedoms ahead of liberty reducing measures
that can reduce gross inequalities. Addressing that concern, Feinberg distinguishes between a 'harmed condition', in which a person suffers at the hands of
another, and a 'harmful condition', in which interests are affected by a handicap or impairment, or by social circumstances where the attempt to establish
personal responsibility for harm is not particularly germane (Feinberg 1992: 6).
This is a grey area. Classical liberals have long been accused of concentrating on
harms that are traceable to individual agency and of neglecting those that result
from inequitable social and political arrangements (Hillyard *et al.* 2004). 'New'
or 'welfare' liberalism responded to the criticism by supporting a redistributive
function for the state and an expanded role for the law with respect to unfair
labour contracts (Richter 1964). Liberals, Feinberg observes, recognize the problem of harmful conditions but, for the most part, they do not think that they raise
issues of criminal responsibility. The criminal law should therefore punish harms
that are 'wrongs'; 'public opinion' can be left to discourage harms that are not
wrongs in the strict sense of the term (Feinberg 1984: 33ff., 135ff.).[19] That stance
may seem to defend a 'nightwatchman' conception of the state with minimum
obligations. It is important to stress, however, that Feinberg (1984: ch. 4) regards
the failure to rescue (when there is little or no danger to potential rescuers) as
harmful wrongdoing that may be a punishable offence under the criminal law
and not, as many other liberals perceive it, as a legitimate exercise in withholding
a benefit (see pp. 57–9). No less important is the claim that, in general, the 'liberal
can be expected to combat harmful conditions of other human beings even when
they are not harmed conditions' (Feinberg 1992: 30).

  Feinberg supports his position on the scope of the criminal law by defining
harm as a wrongful setback to fundamental 'welfare interests' that people must
be able to satisfy before they can hope to realize 'ulterior interests' or promote
more ambitious ends.[20] Basic welfare interests are 'indispensably necessary …
for the achievement of ultimate well-being'; 'one does not usually have much'
when only 'bare minima' are satisfied but, in their absence, 'one cannot live at all'
(Feinberg 1984: 57ff.). What are those 'interests of the most vital kind', and how
universal are they? Feinberg's answer is that they include the hope for

[19] Feinberg cites Macaulay's claim that it is 'desirable that men should not merely abstain from
doing harm to their neighbours, but should render active services to their neighbours';
however, 'in general', he added, 'the penal law must content itself with keeping men from
doing positive harm, and must leave to public opinion, and to the teachers of morality and
religion, the office of furnishing men with motives for doing positive good' (Macaulay
1880a: 255–6).

[20] Students of International Relations will note a parallel with Bull's account of the 'primary
goals' that have to be secured before people can turn to possibly more satisfying personal or
collective ideals, whatever they might be – goals that underpin order, but do not necessarily
ensure justice for individuals or states (Bull 1977: 53–5). For broadly similar approaches,
see Rawls (1971: 62) and Thomson (1987: ch. 3).

the continuance for a foreseeable interval of one's life, and the interests in
one's own physical health and vigor, the integrity and normal functioning
of one's body, the absence of absorbing pain and suffering or grotesque dis-
figurement, minimal intellectual acuity, emotional stability, the absence of
groundless anxieties and resentments, the capacity to engage normally in
social intercourse and to enjoy and maintain friendships, at least minimal
income and financial security, a tolerable social and physical environment,
and a certain amount of freedom from interference and coercion.

(Feinberg 1984: 37ff.)[21]

The 'invasion of a welfare interest' is 'not the only kind of harm a person can
sustain' but when those interests are 'blocked or damaged', the argument is, 'a
person is very seriously harmed indeed' (Feinberg 1984: 37–8). As for the criminal law, its provenance is best restricted to actions that harm welfare interests
(Feinberg 1984: 7–14, 62). Solutions to other forms of harm lie elsewhere, and
not in 'liberty limiting principles' (Feinberg 1984: 7ff.).

As for the universality of such interests, Feinberg (1984: 10–11) makes the
following claim: 'About the property of one class of crimes there can be no con-
troversy. Wilful homicide, forcible rape, aggravated assault, and battery are
crimes (under one name or another) everywhere in the *civilized* world, and no
reasonable person could advocate their "decriminalization"' (italics added; see
also pp. 48–9). As non-controversial as 'crimes against the person' are various
'crimes against property': burglary, grand larceny, and offences such as fraud
and misrepresentation. Criminalized behaviour, such as dangerous driving or
discharging lethal weapons recklessly, have that status not because they necessarily cause harm but because they expose others to an unreasonable risk of
injury (Feinberg 1984: 191).

Feinberg is clearly aware that some religious ascetics have been indifferent
to personal suffering but there is, he suggests, a deeper point to make. For the
most part, decisions to sacrifice a 'welfare interest' for, say, an 'ulterior interest' in promoting a higher ethical ideal can be safely set to one side as unusual
departures from standard practice. There is a parallel with Hart's conception of
the 'moral minimum', or 'minimum content of natural law', that embraces rules
that 'restrict the use of violence in killing or inflicting bodily harm' as well as
principles that prohibit 'mendacity' and 'fraud' (quoted in Feinberg 1990: 44; see
Hart 1961: 189ff.). The main point is that such harm conventions are central to
all functioning ways of life (Feinberg 1990: 44).

---

[21] Honneth (1995: ch. 6) provides a more streamlined and systematic taxonomy based on three
essential human interests – in freedom from assaults on physical integrity, from humiliating practices, and from a lack of moral consideration that deprives persons of opportunities
to make claims against those that have harmed, or might harm, them. For parallel themes,
see Barry (1995: 140): 'welfare corresponds roughly to the absence of harm (i.e. the presence of adequate food, clothing and shelter, freedom from pain and suffering and so on)'.

Notions of the 'moral minimum' are hard to defend given such phenomena as ritual sacrifice in the Aztec world and the cruelties of the Roman games. While prohibitions against murder can be found everywhere, heightened sensitivity to public acts of violence and cruelty is a feature of modern 'civilized' societies, in the technical meaning of the term.[22] But Feinberg seemingly wants to go further by arguing that all societies have some similar ethical commitments. The 'moral minimum', he maintains, 'is not the section of a community's morality that makes it the distinctive community it is', and which 'distinguishes it from other societies with other life-styles and other traditions', but 'the morality the society has in common with all other actual and conceivable societies'. At face value, there is a false dichotomy here between the ethic that is common to all actual or potential forms of life and the diverse customs and traditions that inject colour into particular arrangements (Feinberg 1990: 79).[23] But since some basic constraints on force are necessary for the survival of every society, the ideas that lie behind the notion of a 'moral minimum' cannot be dispensed with lightly. Systems of punishment everywhere rest on common beliefs about the undesirability of death and suffering, restrictions on freedoms and so forth (Barry 1995: 141). The frequency with which societies use violence to settle major differences leads to the same conclusion. Attempts to kill and maim others clearly exist against a background of shared beliefs that, other things being equal, it is better to injure than be injured, to kill rather than be killed. Those points identify virtually universal features of social life as highlighted by Feinberg but without advancing flawed beliefs about a 'true morality' that stands above conventional moralities and that can be used in judgment of them; it recognizes significant common ground between societies while emphasizing the need for the sociological analysis of the historical processes that have led 'civilized' societies to adopt what Feinberg regards as the 'moral minimum'. The relative ease with which many societies have been able to reach agreements about the most basic harms that people can experience is evident in the laws of war that have developed in several civilizations. Such near-universal claims may be unfashionable in some circles, although nothing about them is

---

[22] Feinberg seems committed to this point by arguing that prohibitions against violence are found 'everywhere in the civilized world' which is distinguished from ancient Sparta or Hottentot society where infanticide was tolerated (Feinberg 1984: 10; 1992: 200).

[23] Feinberg's distinction between 'true' or 'critical' and 'conventional' morality rests on a static approach to assessing different customs and practices: 'True morality ... provides the standards and principles by which to judge the actual institutions of any given society, including its conventional morality ... Rights conferred by a universal true morality may also be a part of the conventional moralities of many societies, as the right not to be killed except in defense of self or others, or the right to have what is promised one, are, for example'. Critical morality 'confers a genuine moral right that (may be) unrecognized, indeed explicitly denied, by ... conventional morality' (Feinberg 1992: 200–1). 'Sexual mutilations before marriage' are mentioned as evidence of the tension between specific social conventions and a higher critical morality.

remotely surprising.[24] But it is necessary to turn to sociological investigations of specific civilizing processes to understand particular cultural developments that Feinberg's writings do not explain: they include the heightened sensitivity to pain and suffering in modern societies, the collective efforts that have been invested in defining harm and in classifying its basic forms, and the conviction, which finds expression in Feinberg's liberalism, that certain forms of harm and injury are so undesirable that any 'true' morality must make a stand against them (see the discussion of the civilizing process in Chapter 4).

Classifying harms

Harm conventions must not only distinguish between types of harm but also assess their relative ethical significance because frequently it is not possible to prevent one form of harm without causing another. Societies provide different answers to the question of how many ways there are of harming and being harmed. Beliefs about the moral hierarchy of harms (about the most and least disturbing forms of harm in society, and about preferred trade-offs) vary enormously. Universal significance cannot be claimed for the taxonomy that is set out below; it reflects the modern civilizing process.[25] The classification has been constructed with a view to defending a global version of the harm principle and the cosmopolitan duties that are intrinsic to it – a departure then from traditional reflections on the harm principle which consider the relationship

[24] Several influential strands of post-Second World War anthropological thought argued against ethical universals, preferring instead to emphasize the diversity of morals. However, Malinowski and Radcliffe-Brown focused on cultural universals that stem from the plain fact that societies are shaped by certain basic needs and drives that all people have by virtue of their biological heritage (see Brown 1991 who defends the notion of 'near universals' as a compromise between strict universalism and ethical relativism). As explained above, certain near universals stem from vulnerabilities to harm that are the birthright of all humans. Redfield (1973) remains a valuable survey of critical issues regarding 'human nature' and culturally variable norms, not least by stressing important areas of convergence between different social moralities. Redfield quotes Robert Park's response to Sumner's view that 'the mores can make anything right', but 'they have a harder time making some right things than others', an observation that expresses the position taken here about the prospects for an overlapping moral consensus on the need to eradicate senseless suffering.

[25] Every classification of forms of harm – and every ensemble of underlying concepts such as responsibility, causality and so forth – will reflect the peculiarities of time and place. They are not timeless but bound up with particular social processes. As already noted, the taxonomy set out in the following pages can be explained in terms of the modern civilizing process, and what appear to be the unusual sensitivities to violent and non-violent harm that have developed because of it. The point was made earlier that all taxonomies must be seen in their particular social context, but different societies can recognize parallels between their respective efforts to control violent harm, to restrain anger or aggressive impulses and so forth. All possess civilizing or socializing processes that aim to embed the dominant harm conventions in personality systems from the earliest phases of individual learning. At that level, every society is intelligible to all others.

between state power and personal freedoms in liberal societies, and only rarely discuss the problem of harm in international or world politics (see, however, Shue 1981).[26]

Liberal political thought places the idea of harm at the centre of its theory of the state's restricted right to punish, hence the importance of discussions about whether it is possible to develop a precise definition of the concept that does not expose people to the danger that state power will stray beyond clearly demarcated limits.[27] Issues of definition are no less critical for efforts to define cosmopolitan duties that neither exceed nor fall disappointingly short of the reasonable moral expectations that societies can have of each other. Feinberg's notion of wrongful setbacks to interests informs the following discussion of the prospects for an overlapping global ethical consensus about prima facie cosmopolitan duties to refrain from harming others. The point is that significant cross-cultural support for moral norms that calls for the elimination of such harms is possible despite the varieties of socially constructed hierarchies of harms and clashing, or possibly incommensurable, conceptions of the ultimate foundations of morality. Indeed, a degree of convergence between ethical codes is intrinsic to what there is in the way of a global civilizing process in the modern world (and what there was in earlier eras). That formulation acknowledges the limited nature of that process as well as the scope for sharp, often irreconcilable, disagreements about the most despicable forms of harmful wrongdoing that reflect different social hierarchies of harm, and different accounts of what is serious or trivial. The emphasis here is on the prospects for an inter-societal consensus on unacceptable harms that can enable different societies to make progress in living together more amicably.[28]

Feinberg's writings are a valuable point of departure for the taxonomist of harms. His account of 'properly prohibited behaviour' begins but does not end

---

[26] It is recognized that the members of some groups would be shocked by the absence of 'moral harm' (the harm that immoral acts do to society and the perpetrator) from the following list. Clearly liberal, secular thinking does not accord moral harm the importance it has had in many faith traditions such as the strands of Islamic thought that place it at the centre of the ethical code (Cook 2000). However, the idea of 'moral injury', which results from committing atrocities in war, has a place in the sociological discussion of, for example, post-traumatic stress disorder (see Cunningham 2001: 195). The usual caveats apply about the analytical nature of distinctions between types of harm in the following discussion.

[27] Locke (1960) [1689]: Book II, ch. II, 6) provides the classic statement: 'the Law of Nature ... teaches all Mankind who will but consult it, that being all equal and independent, no ought to harm another in his Life, Health, Liberty, or Possessions'.

[28] All that need be added is that such a consensus is easier to achieve if societies respect major differences between their hierarchies of harm, and recognize the necessity of relying on unconstrained dialogue to explore the prospects for a global agreement. To adopt one of Kant's expressions, part of the challenge is learning how to think from the standpoint of others, and especially the victims of harm. Here, the discussion develops themes set out in Linklater (1998 and 2005).

with 'crimes against the person' and 'against property'. His inventory includes 'reckless' actions that expose others to an unreasonable risk of personal injury (Feinberg 1984: 10–11). Different again is 'public harm' where certain forms of behaviour (such as systematic corruption) erode trust in social institutions. A separate realm revolves around 'public accumulative harm' as illustrated by well-documented examples of environmental harm that result from the fact that millions of people performed what appeared to be trivial, harmless acts on a daily basis for many decades (Feinberg 1984: 227ff.). 'Wrongful gain', or the exploitation of others, is a further instance of harm. Finally, there is the matter of whether harm can be caused by acts of omission rather than commission, and the related question of whether those who are perfectly capable of rescuing others, but chose not to do so, can reasonably be condemned or punished for causing omissive harm.

Building on those points, and recognizing one important lacuna, namely the absence of a discussion of structural harm, the following analysis considers nine ways of harming, and being harmed by, others. They are:

1. Deliberate harm to persons including murder, violent assault, rape, torture, enslavement and threatening behaviour, as well as theft and deception. Those forms of harm are relatively non-controversial, and there is little need to dwell on them here.[29]

2. Humans differ from other species by virtue of their particular vulnerability to pain and humiliation (Rorty 1989). Widely feared, if the anthropological evidence is reliable, are modes of humiliation or stigmatization that cause psychological harm and, in the more extreme forms, shatter personal or collective identity (see Miller 1993, also Goffman 1963).[30] Studies of the 'politics of recognition' have stressed the damage that can be caused by pressures to accept a 'demeaning or contemptible' self-image, or an 'outsider' mentality in relation to the images of superiority found amongst 'established groups in society' (Charles Taylor, quoted in Shapcott 2001: 10; Elias and Scotson 2008 [1994]: introduction). Humiliating strategies can, of course, be directed at the body as well as the mind, as in the practice of branding criminals in classical antiquity, the Nazi demands that Jews wear the Star of David, and the parallels to ancient branding that occurred in the death camps.

An important feature of the modern civilizing process is that many societies believe that additional punishment is warranted when violent acts are linked with a hate campaign against the group to which the victim is presumed to

---

[29] Some forms of harm require more detailed discussion because of debates about whether they are intrinsically less harmful than, for example, killing, or should even be regarded as harmful at all. Omissive harm is the classic example.

[30] See also Primo Levi's testimony on Auschwitz which explained the 'demolition of man' through acts of contempt that included the dismissive refusal to satisfy the most elementary of human requests (Levi 2000: 29; also Gordon 2001; see also pp. 96–7).

belong. In most US states, 'hate crimes' attract additional punishment because they cause 'psychological harm' as well as physical suffering. 'Hate speech' is not only condemned because it causes emotional harm to immediate victims, but because it aims to spread feelings of vulnerability across the group with which victims are identified. Some societies and groups regard such actions as a cause of 'societal harm' as well as injury to stigmatized groups. Punishment may reflect not only outrage at harm to specific victims but indignation at the damage inflicted on public commitments to promote respect for cultural differences (Boeckmann and Turpin-Petrosino 2002; Iganski 2002).

3. Serious harm can occur without any intention to cause suffering. For example, some colonial groups in North America used blankets that were contaminated with smallpox to remove or weaken indigenous populations, but the unintentional transmission of diseases to societies that had no immunity to them appears to have been the main cause of the decimation of South American peoples in the early colonial era (Crosby 1986: ch. 9; McNeill 1979a: ch. 5). Harm by stealth – that is undetected harm – accounts for the worldwide transmission of HIV/AIDs in more recent times. Given their potential effect on the future of humanity, many forms of unintended trans-boundary environmental harm have been at the centre of discussions about the urgency of developing a cosmopolitan response to problems associated with rising levels of human interconnectedness. Notions of 'unstructured collective harms' or 'public accumulative harm' have been used to alert societies to the dangers of remaining wedded to patterns of production and consumption that seemed entirely innocuous only a few decades ago (Feinberg 1984: 227ff.; Kutz 2000: 166). They belong to the larger effort to prohibit or outlaw permissible behaviour the moment there is evidence that the 'sum of imperceptible harms to all victims' has crossed (or is in danger of crossing) the threshold of acceptability (Kutz 2000: 172). In the case of environmental legislation, mounting evidence that a 'harm threshold' has been reached has led states to curtail previous liberties (Feinberg 1984: 226ff.; Kutz 2000: 172). Unusually, such developments were initially concerned with unintended, invisible harm rather than with deliberate injury and, significantly, they have led to expanded notions of what should count as negligent behaviour that must come within the province of the criminal law.[31]

4. Negligence refers to the failure to take reasonable precautions to avoid harming others (Simons 1999: 52–6). When someone is accused of acting negligently, s/he is deemed to have known – or can reasonably be expected to have

---

[31] Discussions about climate change have led to complex issues about the 'permitted share' of global environmental harm, and also about the just distribution of responsibilities to reverse degradation, to compensate victims and to enable poorer societies to advance economically without compounding existing problems (see also Feinberg 1984: 230).

known – that her/his actions created 'unjustifiable risk' for others.[32] In modern societies, exposure to the danger of physical injury has particular importance not only for public morality but also for the criminal law and the law of torts, especially in the case of injury in the workplace (Simons 1999). The law may also address the unjustifiable risk of emotional harm. For example, from the 1950s, social policy governing the welfare of children in Western societies has extended earlier concerns with physical cruelty by focusing on the impact of 'emotional neglect' on long-term personal development (Sznaider 2001: 84ff.). As noted above, harm conventions intercede between vulnerable agents and the actors, structures and processes that have harmed or can harm them. Conventions that deal with negligence intercede between vulnerabilities and the uncertainties that are embedded in the levels of risk which are present in all societies to some degree but in more pronounced ways under conditions of heightened interconnectedness (Beck 1992). One function of those conventions is to establish the precise level of knowledge, foresight and responsibility that society can reasonably expect people to have in the face of predictable and avoidable risks to others.

5. Exploitation is a form of harm in which a person or institution profits unfairly from the vulnerability of others. For classical Marxists, exploitation primarily occurs in the realm of production where, as in the case of capitalism, the bourgeoisie exploit the proletariat by appropriating 'surplus value'. The dominant class benefits from unjust enrichment. Surplus value is a problematical concept but, whatever its strengths and weaknesses, it points to one species of the larger genus of exploitative action. Sexual exploitation is a reminder that exploitation can be non-economic, or sexual as well as economic as in the example of 'sex slavery' (Wertheimer 1996: ch. 6).[33] Underlying the Marxist perspective on labour exploitation is the ethical protest, often muted or suppressed on the spurious grounds that Marxists are engaged in scientific analysis rather than moral reasoning, against the 'exercise of power by some over others to the disadvantage' of the 'less powerful', where disadvantage results in 'extensive harm, domination' or 'oppression' (Nielsen and Ware 1997: xi). Harm conventions that address exploitation respond to the plain fact that many people 'are encumbered with weaknesses or vulnerabilities' – 'physical, psychological, emotional, economic, political' – that the opportunistic, the callous or the desperate have been quick to exploit, and which they will

---

[32] Negligence and recklessness are related and overlapping categories according to the *OED*. It defines recklessness as 'carelessness in respect of the consequences of one's actions', and as conduct that displays a lack of 'prudence and caution'. Its reference to 'heedless rashness' invites the comment that recklessness is a form of negligence that places other people in harm's way (as in the example of reckless or dangerous driving).

[33] Lying and deception can be included under the category of exploitation because they take advantage of another's ignorance, gullibility or other reason for vulnerability to predators.

doubtless continue to exploit in future forms of life though, arguably, the very worst excesses can be eradicated (Wood 1997: 20).

The notion that exploitation takes unfair advantage of the powerless or dependent has long been central to Marxist thought but, in recent years, liberal thinkers have taken the initiative in combining the philosophical analysis of that concept with ethical reflections on duties to 'protect the vulnerable' (Feinberg 1990: 178–9; Goodin 1987; Wertheimer 1996). Two issues have been prominent: first, how far the unequal distribution of costs and benefits is the essence of exploitation; and second, whether a person's overt consent to arrangements from which they will derive unequal rewards undermines any criticism that the relationship is exploitative.

Some theorists have argued that an exploitative relationship always has a 'zero-sum' character: one party gains in direct proportion to another's losses (Wertheimer 1996: 14ff.). But many take the position that different partners can profit from an exploitative relationship. Considering that theme, Wertheimer (1996: 207) marks off 'harmful exploitation', where one side gains and another loses proportionately, from 'mutually advantageous exploitation', where the exploited party also benefits from the exchange. Neither side is worse off in the case of 'mutually advantageous exploitation' (Wertheimer 1996: ch. 7), but by the standards of the time, one person or group may be thought to profit excessively from another's weakness. It should be added that unfairness is clear-cut where, fearing detection and expulsion, illegal migrants cannot protest against 'sweatshop' labour or its equivalent.

Illegal migrants may trade control over everyday life, and allow others to profit from cheap labour, in exchange for non-disclosure. Turning to the second issue that has interested liberals, the question is whether the fact that such arrangements rest on consent rather than coercion is relevant to determining whether the relationship is exploitative, and a matter for the criminal law. Feinberg (1990: ch. 32) argues that unequal gains are not intrinsically unjust if grounded in consensual exploitation. The *volenti* principle frees the dominant party from any legal culpability for causing harm, but it may not escape moral disapproval if third parties judge that the agreement takes advantage of others (Feinberg 1990: ch. 32). The chief beneficiary cannot claim special rights under the *volenti* principle when the consenting party is 'the abnormally vulnerable person' who deserves legal protection 'from unnecessary, deliberate and malicious efforts to exploit his vulnerability' (Feinberg 1984: 217).

The notion of unusual vulnerability is relatively uncontroversial when someone is particularly susceptible to being preyed on by virtue of some mental or physical impairment. The issue is whether that is true where those who occupy socially disadvantaged positions have little alternative but to agree to 'mutually advantageous exploitation'. Marx famously argued that contracts in which workers sell the control of their labour-power are only free in form. Social and political inequalities cast an oppressive shadow over such nominally consensual relations, effectively compelling the labourer to submit to arrangements that are exploitative in the Marxist sense of that term. Social inequalities based on racial or gender differences can also underpin reluctant consent to enter into similar arrangements with stronger parties who are spared such compulsions. Welfare or social liberals reached similar conclusions in the late nineteenth century. The argument was that the fact that parties meet on unequal terms need not be a reason for involving the criminal law (Feinberg 1984: 115ff.), although, as noted earlier, welfare liberals defended state intervention to end unfair labour practices. The issue here is human dignity. As Wood (1997: 21) argues, 'it is an affront to people's human dignity to have their weaknesses used', just as it is 'shameful' to exploit their vulnerability in pursuit of self-interest.

It may be that the harmfulness of such actions should only be a matter for the criminal law in the most abusive conditions.[34] Thinkers on the Left have argued that such discussions reveal the limitations of liberalism, and specifically the failure to support robust measures to change social conditions that expose vulnerable groups to exploitative relations which they are assumed to enter freely but are effectively forced into. From that vantage-point, the larger issue is the obligation to confront structural harm. That observation moves the discussion from debates about the proper scope of the criminal law to broader considerations about the relationship between state power and economic freedoms, and about the extent to which the 'nightwatchman' state stands aside while the powerful use their liberties to take advantage of, and benefit unfairly from, the vulnerable. Ensuing disputes have not only been concerned with how societies should deal with the structural sources of exploitation; they are part of a much broader discussion about the need for greater reflectiveness about social practices, for identifying the hidden causes of exploitation, and for drawing on the most, rather than the least, demanding moral standards to assess them and to chart future directions.[35]

6. Complicity refers to the condition in which people are implicated in the production of harm by virtue of their association with institutions and practices that disadvantage others. The harm caused is mediated rather than directly

---

[34] An interesting example is the 1999 Swedish law on prostitution, specifically the 'prohibition on the purchase of sexual services' which affirms the principle that the seller should not be punished because invariably that person is the 'weaker partner who is exploited by those who wish only to satisfy their sexual drives'. See www.prostitutionresearch.com/swedish.html.

[35] The value they attach to familiar practices often leads societies to endow them with qualities that they do not deserve, or to ignore social problems lest they detract from their flattering self-images. For that reason, Elias suggested that the members of modern societies could acquire critical distance from their mores by contemplating the possibility that future generations might regard them as living in a Middle Ages – and in what was, from their standpoint, a not particularly civilized epoch (Kilminster 2007: 157). To link that point with the current discussion, the importance of heightened sensitivity to involvement in harm has been defended by some moral philosophers, often in response to the fact that powerful

intended (Kutz 2000: 2). The ethical significance of complicity has probably never been greater than it is today where interconnectedness means that 'lives are increasingly complicated by regrettable things brought about through our associations with other people or with the social, economic and political institutions in which we live our lives and make our living' (Kutz 2000: 1).

The related matter of the moral status of what Honderich (1980: ch. 2) calls the wrongs we do in our ordinary lives can be conceptualized in many ways. From one perspective, individual shareholders cannot be held morally and/or legally responsible for harms caused by a business enterprise in which they have investments. Certainly, ending an association with a corporation that causes harm would make little, if any, material difference to the overall level of suffering. Since causal responsibility is minor, it may seem legitimate to deny moral responsibility for harm and to challenge any accusation of blame (Kutz 2000: 113ff.). Such reasoning was evident in Stangl's shocking statement at his trial that he himself had 'never intentionally hurt anyone' during his tenure as Commandant of the Treblinka death camp (Sereny 1995: 365). For some, that defence is not radically different from the thinking of shareholders that have investments in corporations that cause distant harm although, for obvious reasons, parallels between their (often innocent) complicity and Stangl's denial of personal involvement in genocide should not be pressed too far.

Victims of institutional harm may not be persuaded by the argument that the inability to influence organizational behaviour lets the relevant people off the moral hook (Kutz 2000: 186). Even the relatively powerless can be the beneficiaries of harmful practices (Kutz 2000: 45–6). The plain fact that they are implicated, rather than their share of the overall reward, is what matters from that approach (Parekh 1972: 86). To support that argument, Kutz (2000: 129–30, 172) refers to Parfitt's discussion of the apparently oxymoronic notion of the 'harmless torturer' – a hypothetical torturer who does not cause death by his or her efforts alone, but by being one of a thousand torturers who together dispense enough poison to end a victim's life.[36] Kutz concurs with Parfitt's judgment that there is no morally relevant difference between a condition in which one person delivers sufficient poison to end a life, and a condition in which a thousand people cause death 'imperceptibly', but no single person is responsible for delivering the lethal dose. Individuals in those circumstances cannot deny that they

---

groups can profit from the weakness of others, not because they deliberately set out to harm them but because they benefit, more or less automatically, from global structures of power and inequality (see Chapter 2).

[36] The example is not fanciful. At his trial, the SS major general, Otto Ohlendorf, said that he 'never permitted ... shooting by individuals', but 'ordered that several of the men should shoot at the same time to avoid direct personal responsibility' (War Crimes of the Gestapo and SD, Nazi Conspiracy and Aggression, Vol. II, USGPO, Washington, 1946, www.ess. uwe.ac.uk/genocide/Gestapo3.htm).

are causally responsible for killing (Kutz 2000: 143). Each person's imperceptible or low involvement in ending a life does not free the perpetrators from moral blame or legal sanction (although international criminal law may take account of extenuating circumstances such as fear of the consequences of disobeying superior orders). At the very least, the collaborative nature of killing does not excuse the lack of guilt or shame.

On the basis of that example, Kutz (2000: 122ff.) supports 'the complicity principle' – an ethic of accountability in which people are not only responsible for the deliberate injuries they cause but are answerable for being implicated in the collective production of harm. Reference was made earlier to that universal stage of human development in which infants acquire an understanding of their ability to affect others adversely, and where they are socialized into accepting responsibility for harms they cause (Harris 1989). The point is extended in analyses of complicity which argue that people can be connected with each other in highly 'mediated' ways, and which add that self-respect often depends on confronting the moral importance of personal involvement in wrongdoing, even when the individual's influence on others is negligible, or when the decision to step aside from mediated harm may make no tangible difference to the wider world (Hart and Honore 1985: lxxx). Such discussions note the sense of 'unease' that can result from the moral compromises that flow from voluntary association with tarnished institutions (Kutz 2000: 160, 176, 190). They invite people to think from the standpoint of victims, to reflect on responsibilities to those who may be silent and/or hidden from view, and to consider how more demanding ethical commitments to distant others can be built into everyday conduct and relationships (Kutz 2000: 160, 176, 190, 255). In short, they encourage a high level of reflectiveness about the ways in which unprecedented levels of global interconnectedness give individuals a greater moral stake in relations with distant strangers. Adding complicity to a classification of harms reflects such sensitivities to the moral problems which emerge in that way; that may not lead immediately to efforts to alter 'harmful conditions', but it might nevertheless be an important stage in the slow formation of a 'global conscience' that prompts the members of different societies to work together to reduce imperceptible as well as perceptible harm. For that reason, the 'hidden promise of complicity' may well be a global community in which the species anchors 'universal solidarity' and 'cosmopolitan justice' in 'what it deplores' as much as in 'what it prizes' (Kutz 2000: 258–9).

7. More detailed attention must be devoted to the controversial subject of whether serious harm can be caused by acts of omission – or how far, in the words of A. H. Clough's poem, individuals and groups need only observe the principle, 'thou shalt not kill but needs't not strive officiously to keep alive'. Moral and legal philosophers have long debated whether a failure to rescue is inherently less blameworthy than intentional harm. (National legal codes

have reached different conclusions about this matter. For the most part, the Anglo-American tradition has not regarded a failure to rescue as a punishable offence, whereas the Continental European tradition has.) Philosophers have opposed criminalizing the failure to rescue on the grounds that 'negative duties not to kill by commission are … stronger than … positive duties not to kill by omission' (see Moore 1999: 32–3). People violate fundamental 'negative duties' when they cause harm but not when they 'fail to prevent' it or 'omit to save' (Moore 1999: 32–3). Or again, people have 'a moral claim – a right – not to be actively harmed'; what they do not have is an entitlement to be saved (see Katz 1999: 105).

Feinberg (1984: ch. 4; 1992: ch. 7) contends that the position that has just been outlined revolves around a false distinction between harming another and the failure to confer a benefit that 'the law does not compel'. Several moral philosophers have questioned the distinction on very specific grounds, arguing for example that a punishable harm can be caused by failing to secure a vehicle that subsequently spirals out of control, causing death or injury (Moore 1999; also Hart and Honore 1985: 64 on the relationship between omission and negligence). The special obligations that doctors have to their patients mean that a punishable harm is caused by a failure to prescribe or administer essential medication (Feinberg 1984: 179).The controversial question has been whether similarly enforceable duties exist between people who have no comparable contractual obligations. The related legal question is how far criminal codes should include 'bad samaritan statutes' that are designed to punish failures to prevent death or serious injury (Feinberg 1984: 163–5, 186).

Feinberg (1984: ch. 4) maintains that a decision not to assist someone who is drowning must count as punishable harm, particularly when there is little or no risk to the person who is in a position to rescue. Of course, judgments about levels of acceptable risk may not be clear-cut – in which case juries may have to decide what it is reasonable to expect potential rescuers to do in particular circumstances (Feinberg 1992: ch. 7).[37] The key point is that the failure to rescue a drowning person is not self-evidently less blameworthy than pushing a victim into treacherous waters in the first place (Glover 1990: 92ff.). Non-rescuers could only lay claim to complete innocence on the basis of a 'restricted causation claim' that limits accountability to deliberate injury (Feinberg 1984: 165ff.).

The discussion of complicity casts doubt on such notions of limited responsibility. Feinberg (1984: 173–5) argues that one cannot support such a doctrine when a potential rescuer holds another's life in his or her own hands, and

---

[37] Complex issues arise again about the balance between legal duties and personal liberties. Feinberg (1984: 128ff.) maintains that 'bad samaritan statutes' are designed to deal with obligations that arise in exceptional circumstances. They are not about creating more general moral burdens that impose unreasonable restrictions on personal liberties. A similar argument can be found in Bentham (1970 [1789]: ch. 17, part 1, xix).

whatever s/he does will determine the other's fate. Many will 'hesitate', he continues, to speak of the potential rescuer's 'causal role' in another's death in the circumstances that have been described, but the decision to do nothing must be included in any account of the 'causal factors' that resulted in the loss of life (Feinberg 1984: 175).[38] The contention that a failure to assist causes harm by prolonging avoidable suffering is another way of challenging arguments that there is a clear moral difference between causing harm and failing to prevent it, at least where serious injury or death is easily prevented.[39] Also important is the part that failures to rescue can play in engendering feelings of worthlessness in victims or survivors – in producing a sense of abandonment given the evidence that strangers do not seem to care whether they survive or not.[40]

Reflections on the problem of the bystander in Nazi Germany have refined the point. Wiesel has protested that 'remaining a spectator' in the face of terrible violence is 'morally reprehensible' because it effectively sides with the perpetrators (Brown 1990: 54–5). His remarks about the experience of the cold indifference of the spectator's gaze – what Gay (1998: 185) calls a state of 'mortal indifference to their human dignity' – stress that the lack of tangible recognition of the victim's suffering is a source of harm.[41] Levi's testimony on Auschwitz emphasized that small, but not insignificant, ways of displaying 'solidarity with the oppressed' survived even in the death camps (Levi 1988: 138 and 148; Todorov 1999). As already noted with respect to complicity, what is at stake here is solidarity with the victims of harm, and injury caused by withholding displays of sympathy, such as the compassionate gaze or gestures of support.[42]

8. Public harm refers to damage to social and political institutions that have the responsibility for establishing what might be called 'primary' harm conventions. The point is formulated in the light of a distinction between 'primary' rules that regulate conduct, and 'secondary' rules which determine how primary rules are created, administered and enforced (Hart 1961: ch. 5). It is therefore important to distinguish between violations of primary harm

---

[38] MacIntyre (1994) analyses some of the complexities that surround such arguments.

[39] I am grateful to Robert van Vrees for this observation.

[40] That may be precisely the intention. A failure to assist may stem from plain indifference, but it can spring from a cruel disposition that relishes the suffering of others.

[41] One study of how many living near the Mauthausen death camp in Austria looked on with studied indifference at passing labour gangs concludes that the absence of tangible evidence of sympathy caused significant harm in its own right (Horwitz 1991). See also Levinas (quoted in Butler 2004: 131) on the belief that 'the face is the other who asks me not to let him die alone, as if to do so were to become an accomplice in his death', and the contention in Jaspers (1947: 69–70) that 'passivity knows itself morally guilty of every failure, every neglect to act whenever possible, to shield the imperilled, to relieve wrong, to countervail'.

[42] The notion of 'dignitary harm' or 'emotional harm' which has been important in American studies of the law of torts, and also in reflections on transitional justice, is relevant here (see Dan-Cohen 2002: 170, fn. 31; Teitel 2000: 82).

conventions and damage to secondary harm conventions that may be caused by corruption or flagrant breaches of official procedures that erode public confidence in institutions. Public harm so caused is not necessarily deliberately designed to weaken institutions or to disadvantage particular persons, but of course political movements may indeed set out to damage institutions, as in the case of the Nazi assault on constitutional democracy in the Weimar period. Societies can reach a tipping-point when intended or unintended damage to secondary harm conventions outstrips, or is widely perceived to outweigh, violations of primary rules.[43] Functioning societies usually impose severe sanctions on those who weaken the former. A tipping-point may be reached when the will or capacity to impose such penalties breaks down, or when the institutions with the responsibility for enforcing primary conventions can no longer guarantee widespread, and almost automatic, compliance with them.

9. Structural harm exists when individuals or groups are adversely affected by systemic forces that bind them together. Marx saw capitalist exploitation as largely the consequence of social structures rather than individual intentions. Recent explanations of structural harm preserve Marx's critique of methodological individualism (enshrined in the dismissal of bourgeois ideology) that rejects structural analysis on the assumption that all social phenomena are reducible to individual agency.[44] Critics reject methodologies based on the ontological primacy of the individual on the grounds that the 'vast majority of harms are structurally determined' (Tombs and Hillyard 2004: 53). Although 'individuals are responsible at some point', their agency is limited by structural imperatives (Tombs and Hillyard 2004: 53). It follows that many sources of harm cannot be removed by encouraging individual people to modify behaviour; successful strategies must aim for fundamental structural change.

Various interpretations of structural harm have emphasized how capitalist systems of production and exchange cause exploitation in the Marxist sense of the term, but other forms of harm are also relevant to this phenomenon – complicity, for example, as stated earlier. It is important to note a broadening of notions of structural harm over the last few decades that included Galtung's account of 'structural violence'. That concept was less concerned with physical

---

[43] Comparing the level of public alarm in Britain following the decision to invade Iraq, without the authorization of the United Nations Security Council, with media-inflamed public outrage following disclosures of the MPs' 'expenses scandal' provides a reminder that feelings about public harm to national institutions are invariably much stronger than concerns about harm to international institutions that, in some general sense, represent the entire species.

[44] Recent discussions of whether institutions have responsibilities also address this theme, but from a different standpoint (see Erskine 2003).

force or the exploitation of labour than with highlighting the effects of poverty and unemployment, low-quality housing or inadequate health provision on infant mortality rates, educational prospects, levels of social mobility and life expectancy (see Lawler 1994). Other approaches have shifted the emphasis from the social effects of inequalities of power and wealth to the harms that result from patriarchal or racist assumptions that are embedded in various associations and organizations – harms that include assaults on self-esteem, restricted social opportunities, and high exposure to neglect, indifference and discrimination.

The idea of 'institutional racism' is instructive because of its contention that harmful orientations can operate almost invidiously within organizations.[45] The argument is that the term does not only apply to institutions whose members are consciously wedded to racist beliefs, or where all or even most members support views that discriminate against other groups. Rather, the implication is that those who have racist beliefs or underlying prejudices perceive the organization as having a tolerant, lax or indifferent attitude to such attitudes. Those involved see nothing in their immediate environment that suggests that racist views are morally wrong or violate professional conduct. The focus on institutional or structural harm is designed to counter-balance tendencies to concentrate on the harmful conduct of individual actors, or to focus on punitive measures to such an extent that people remain blind to the harmful effects of the ways in which they are locked together, and indifferent to the need for fundamental change to 'harmful conditions'.[46] The implication – which Marx was the first to draw – is that it is essential to move beyond individualistic ontologies in ethics and social-scientific explanations in order to realize the emancipatory potential of what has come to be known as the liberal harm principle.

Applications to international politics

Various forms of harm have been identified: the coercive, the inadvertent, the complicit, the exploitative, the omissive, the accumulative, the negligent, the public and the structural. Causing such harms affects the vital interests of other persons, and can be regarded as prima facie morally, if not legally, wrong. Contemporary international law provides evidence of a degree of consensus about forms of harms that should be prohibited in the relations between states or in world society. Many writings have indicated how that agreement can be

---

[45] The reference is to the 1999 Macpherson Report following the death of Stephen Lawrence in which the London Metropolitan Police Force was found guilty of 'institutional racism' in the shape of discrimination that was caused by 'unwitting prejudice, ignorance and thoughtlessness' as well as 'racial stereotyping' (see Bourne 2001).

[46] Some arguments invariably point the finger at failures of leadership, or at oversights that can be corrected by central efforts to promote institutional change and to introduce new codes of professional conduct.

extended, but just as many have emphasized the improbability of significant global change. Less contentious, but interesting in its own right, is the fact that the modern international system is unusual, if not unique, in facing demands to reduce the extraordinarily diverse forms of harm (some arising, as has been argued, from transnational processes as well as from more traditional geopolitical struggles). Ten forms of harm will be discussed in conjunction with some preliminary observations about the scope of current cosmopolitan harm conventions. The first three forms of harm are variations on the earlier theme of concrete harm (intended harm to others).

1. It is essential to begin with deliberate harm that has been inflicted through acts of conquest, the enslavement of peoples and the seizure of booty; through conducting wars in ways that cause 'unnecessary suffering' to combatants, prisoners of war or civilian populations, and finally through demeaning xenophobic, racial and related interpretations of outsiders. All have been central to international relations for millennia. At times, they have been caused without remorse, and there were few, if any, agreed global standards that placed them in the category of morally scandalous or ethically dubious acts. But shared beliefs that some forms of violent harm are morally repugnant because of the scale of the suffering involved have appeared in many different eras. To focus on the modern world, many developments in the nineteenth century – they include Dunant's initiative in founding the International Red Cross following the suffering that he witnessed at the Battle of Solferino in 1859 (see Moorehead 1998), and the 1899 Hague Conventions that were influenced by the 1863 Lieber Code that was formulated during the American Civil War – were inspired by powerful moral commitments to minimize 'unnecessary suffering' or 'superfluous injury'. No inventory of recent advances with respect to cosmopolitan harm conventions is complete without reference to that radical advance in international law in which the Nuremberg Principles rejected claims that 'acts of state' or 'superior orders' guarantee political and military leaders immunity from prosecution for 'crimes against humanity'. Developments in cosmopolitan law are also evident in the idea of 'universal jurisdiction' which maintains that such crimes can be prosecuted anywhere and everywhere, no matter where the original atrocities occurred (Teitel 2000: ch. 2).

The modern society of states is not unusual in developing such laws of war in response to harm to persons but also to cultural property – and here it is worth recalling that the *OED* definition refers to harm 'suffered by some person or *thing*' (Roberts and Guelff 2000: ch. 37; italics added). Similar conventions existed, for example, in the Ancient Greek and Chinese state-systems, in Ancient Israel, and in the Islamic world. Whether modern international society has surpassed them by creating robust cosmopolitan harm conventions with respect to threats to cultural property is an interesting question. Similar issues arise with respect to 'any advocacy of national, religious or racial hatred that constitutes incitement to discrimination, hostility or violence', as prohibited by Article 20 of the Universal Declaration of Human Rights.[47] It is essential to ask if that involves an unusual advance in promoting respect for cultural differences, albeit one that must be viewed in conjunction with the modern state's unusual ability to organize systematic violence to eliminate, remove or oppress minorities within its territory.[48]

2. Deliberate harm that governments do to their own citizens, whether by torturing them, humiliating them, or otherwise abusing what are now widely regarded as innate human rights has produced various cosmopolitan moral and political responses. Since the end of the Second World War, the proliferation of international legal conventions that prohibit 'serious bodily and mental harm' has demonstrated moral concern with the harm that one section of a society can do to another. Those conventions have challenged classical ideas of state sovereignty that opposed any efforts to make governments accountable to the international community for the treatment of subjects or citizens. Debates about human rights have shown how quickly the limits of agreement are reached in this domain. Disputes about the rights of women stem from major cultural differences about gender roles; they are often entangled with deep resentment of external interference in internal affairs, and with suspicions about the motives of those who assume they are entitled to stand in judgment. The 1993 General Assembly Declaration on the Elimination of Violence against Women condemns so-called 'traditional practices harmful to women', but ever since colonial administrators and missionaries in the early twentieth century tried to end female circumcision/female genital mutilation (FC/FGM) in Burkina Faso, Kenya and Sudan, many groups have opposed what they see as the greater harm caused by external measures to force indigenous 'traditions' to change (Rahman and Toubia 2000: 9ff.).[49] Nevertheless, increased global interconnectedness has led particular strata in different societies to support cosmopolitan conventions that affirm each person's right to live in freedom from such 'crimes against the person'.

The universal human rights culture is probably still in its infancy, as is the defence of humanitarian intervention that represents a major break with the

---

[47] For similar commitments, see also Article 4 of the International Convention on the Elimination of all Forms of Racial Discrimination, and Article 20 of the International Covenant of Civil and Political Rights.

[48] Also important is the question of whether the modern West has been unusual in attaching moral importance to racial differences and in constructing racial hierarchies – matters to come back to in volume 2.

[49] Several governments in recent years have criminalized FC/FGM, or they have made constitutional commitments to protect women from 'harmful customs', while entering significant reservations about human rights treaties (Rahman and Toubia 2000: 59–60).

dominant assumptions about world politics (Wheeler 2000). Those shifts may be features of 'humankind's prehistory' (Elias 2007b [1992]: 156). Sharp differences exist between those who think that international society ought to shoulder the responsibilities of military intervention, particularly when faced with 'supreme humanitarian emergencies' such as the Rwandan genocide in the 1990s (Wheeler 2000), and those who fear that interference will cause greater harm in the long-run by weakening one of the main constraints on force, namely respect for national sovereignty (Jackson 2000).[50] Bystander status is the source of some moral discomfort when societies with commitments to human equality encounter media images of distant suffering. For many, humanitarian war, used sparingly, can help solve the problem of omissive harm. Troubled by the ways in which political means affect ends, others maintain that such humanitarian goals ought to be promoted in non-violent ways that do not jeopardize progress towards perpetual peace (Booth 2001a).

Mass publics in Western democracies have displayed sensitivity to serious human rights abuses in recent years, but the priority remains avoiding unnecessary harm to co-nationals who might be mobilized to serve in rescue missions, and not endangering their lives in foreign adventures that are invariably judged in terms of their importance for vital national interests. Reliance on air power has been one way of overcoming the tension between the obligation to assist and the unwillingness to sacrifice military lives in land campaigns. That approach has shifted the ethical debate to the morality of transferring the human costs of military conflict to civilians in the target societies (Wheeler 2002). The thesis that the harm principle supports the establishment of legally enforceable obligations to rescue, but it does not require co-nationals to place themselves in harm's way in order to save lives, is worth recalling here (see pp. 57–9). At some future point, societies may accept the duties and risks involved in humanitarian intervention. The development of 'cosmopolitan law enforcement' in which militaries are prepared to risk their lives for distant strangers would, however, be a small revolution in international politics (Kaldor 1999). Wherever obligations to co-nationals have priority, the point is quickly reached when the costs of 'saving strangers' are regarded as unbearable.

3. A third category of deliberate harm is caused by non-state actors. Examples include the violence caused by international terrorist groups or transnational criminal organizations that trade in illicit drugs or traffic in women and children for 'sexual slavery', as well as piracy which is as ancient as long-distance

---

[50] From one standpoint, international harm conventions that underpin the society of states need to be amended so that cosmopolitan harm conventions have greater influence. From the other standpoint, the risk is that the imprudent use of force in defence of cosmopolitan principles may endanger international order (which remains the most effective – though imperfect – way of defending people everywhere from the sufferings of warfare, and from the human rights violations that occur in military conflicts).

trade. Those phenomena raise questions about whether ruling strata regarded pirates and enslavers as useful allies, or as instruments of state power, or considered them as *hostis humani generis* – enemies of humankind (Vincent 1986: 104). As for cosmopolitan harm conventions, the issue is whether states had the will and capacity to cooperate so that the dangers posed by non-state actors or transnational groups were reduced as part of a commitment to the pacification of entire regions (Löwenheim 2007).

The emphasis thus far has been on intentional violent harm, but several forms have a different configuration and so the discussion now turns to global examples of types 3–9 on the earlier list, beginning with the following.

4. Unintended or inadvertent harm has come to be most closely associated with damage to the physical environment, whether caused by national governments, business enterprises or private persons, whether unknowingly or 'accidentally', as in the case of the 1986 Chernobyl explosion. That is not a new phenomenon of course. Reflecting on the increasingly global nature of relations of production and exchange, Engels (1969a) stated that rapid technological breakthroughs in Britain could destroy entire livelihoods in China within a single year. That comment reflected Marx and Engels' belief that a new phase of human history had appeared in which future, long-term developments would be shaped less by the customary forms of concrete harm that have been perpetrated by empires or states for millennia than by abstract harm that was an inevitable consequence of the globalization of industrial capitalism.[51] Their observation that world capitalism threw increasing numbers of human beings to the mercy of invisible, impersonal forces was linked with the argument for universal social cooperation to bring unregulated social relations and processes under collective control. The Marxist political economy contained the seeds of more recent forms of cosmopolitanism that anticipate moving beyond sovereign nation-states in conjunction with reconstructing global economic and social relations in order to reduce 'transnational exploitation'. The 'cosmopolitan manifesto' that addresses the manifold problems of the 'global risk society' is heir to those reflections on a possible new phase in the social and political evolution of the species (Beck 2002).

---

[51] The 'great transformation' was not, it should be stressed, one in which a pre-capitalist state of war was giving way to a capitalist peace. According to the first volume of *Das Kapital* (see also Gunder Frank 1978: 39ff.), capitalism was anchored in violence from the beginning. The phase of 'primitive accumulation' was 'anything but idyllic' because 'conquest, enslavement, robbery, murder, briefly force' had played a central part in its development. Capitalism had entered the world 'dripping from head to foot, from every pore, with blood and dirt' (Marx 1970 [1887]: 714, 760). Erasing any memory of its violent past had been one of its remarkable achievements.

Recent ecological approaches, including those that criticize the environmental effects of 'free market capitalism', have stressed the urgency of post-national approaches to unintended trans-boundary harm. Changing ideas about the relationship between sovereign statehood and global responsibilities are perhaps best illustrated by recalling the differences between the 1895 Harmon Doctrine that resulted from a dispute between the United States and Mexico, and the 1941 Trail Smelter Arbitration that followed a similar disagreement between the United States and Canada. Dismissing the accusation that the use of the Rio Grande caused environmental damage in Mexico, the Harmon Doctrine affirmed 'the absolute sovereignty of every nation, as against all others, within its own territory'. The Trail Smelter Arbitration, by contrast, concluded that no 'state has the right to use or permit the use of its territory in such a manner as to cause injury by fumes in or to the territory of another or the properties or persons therein'. That judgment was a major step forward in redefining sovereign rights and duties in the light of new opportunities for transnational harm.[52] Recent developments in environmental law which argue that the exercise of national sovereignty must conform with the principle, *sic utere tuo ut alienum non laedas* – 'one must use one's property so as not to injure others' – are indebted to the Trail Smelter decision (Dobson 2003: 211). Given the fact that the species ultimately depends on the biosphere for its survival, various international legal conventions since the 1972 Stockholm Conference on the Environment have affirmed obligations to avoid harm to other societies and to the global commons (Mason 1999). However, critics of Trail Smelter have argued that its radical potential was blunted by the crucial rider that sovereign rights were only in question when harm was of 'serious consequence', and 'established by clear and convincing evidence' (Bratspies and Miller 2006: 331).[53] Not least because of the precautionary principle, several environmental movements and global legal conventions have called for far-reaching cosmopolitan commitments that embody higher levels of detachment from immediate concerns and greater foresight and self-restraint when there is good reason to suspect that the continued use of certain technologies may have prolonged adverse affects on future generations (see Sunstein 2005 for a critical discussion).

The analysis of the 'world risk society' has emphasized the need for greater 'reflexivity' given the 'universalization' of frequently 'imperceptible' hazards. The argument is that collective learning processes must take the form of

[52] The significance of efforts to reconstitute sovereignty, and to alter the relationship between citizenship and humanity, under conditions of increased interconnectedness, will be considered in volume 2. Preliminary thoughts are set out in the introduction to Linklater (2007a).

[53] See Okowa (2000: 83ff.) on the responsibility for 'due diligence' with respect to the transboundary movement of hazardous waste material which echoes the Trail Smelter judgment that the 'impermissible threshold of tolerable harm' is crossed when, and this is clearly open to competing interpretations, there is a possibility of serious damage.

cosmopolitan responses to unequal exposure to harm, as captured in the idea of the 'proletariat of the global risk society' (Beck 1992: 21ff., 41). An important contribution to green political theory adds that the principal moral issue is justice rather than compassion or charity that do not have the same connotation of the 'obligation to compensate for harm' that must fall most heavily on the societies that have been the main cause of environmental degradation (Dobson 2005).

Obligations of due care are not restricted to what realists have traditionally regarded as 'low politics'. Theorists of the just war were amongst the first to defend such duties when they asserted the responsibility to avoid what has come to be regarded as 'unnecessary suffering' to innocent civilians.[54] Care in the selection of targets in recent military conflicts may signify changing sensibilities in this sphere (Wheeler 2002; see also Thomas 2001). Compensation to surviving family members of civilians who were accidentally killed occurred from time to time during the recent war in Iraq, but major progress in that domain (including published government estimates of the number of foreign casualties in such conflicts) would constitute a new departure in international affairs. Realists are disposed to remind the optimistically minded that such noble considerations are often amongst the first 'casualties of war'. On that argument, there is no reason to think that global environmental networks will avoid the fate of peace movements which have had only limited success in promoting cosmopolitan orientations to the human costs of 'high politics'.[55] The obvious danger is that the belief that the future will closely resemble the past will be self-fulfilling, encouraging traditional national responses to mounting global problems. A great deal depends on how far certain patterns of development that have been prevalent in domestic political systems will be replicated globally. At the national level, closer interconnectedness has often been the spur for the establishment of centralized institutions with the responsibility for coordinating responses to systemic problems (Mennell 2007: ch. 9). Although their scope is limited by struggles between states, similar processes are apparent in the multiplication of global institutions, both formal and informal, that have been established in response to problems that affect all or most societies. One aim has been to promote respect for an ethic of due diligence with regard to the security, environmental and other challenges that may yet weaken national attachments and increase the proportion of politically aware citizens who support a global civilizing process.

5. Negligence occurs when a state, business enterprise or other actor fails to exercise such duties of care by ignoring evidence of possible dangers and

---

[54] As Erskine (2008: 190) notes, innocents are so described because they do no harm (following the Latin term, *nocentes*, non-harming).

[55] Not least where states are preoccupied with 'relative' as opposed to 'absolute' gains (Grieco 1988).

exposing people to the risk of harm. Two examples are 'nuclear colonialism', testing weapons with apparent disregard for the consequences for the health of local populations, as in the South Pacific (Dibblin 1988: 205),[56] and 'environmental apartheid', or exporting hazardous products to societies where health and environmental safeguards are less demanding than in the West (Shiva 2000). In each case, the issue is one of indifference rather than cruel design, although, as stated earlier, the *OED* does not attach much importance to the distinction. As noted earlier, it is important to ascertain whether indifference to the danger of harm is the result of plain 'thoughtlessness' or is anchored in hostile dispositions such as contempt (see p. 39, n. 11).

The gas explosion at the pesticide plant in Bhopal on 3 December 1984 is the most notorious example of harm that has been blamed on corporate negligence, and linked with the 'double standard of morality' that applies in world politics. Underlying the practices of exporting dangerous technologies, or hazardous waste, is the (at least implicit) belief that vulnerable groups are not entitled to levels of health and safety that the more affluent societies expect or enjoy (Shiva 2000; Shue 1981). For such reasons, as Beck (1992: 46) argues, it is unwise to predict that 'a grand harmony will break out in the face of the growing risks of civilization', and reasonable to suppose that 'a variety of new social differentiations and conflicts' will emerge. The impact of class inequalities and status divisions on global risk society provides additional reasons for introducing cosmopolitan harm conventions that grant all people security from basic harms irrespective of race, nationality, class, gender and so forth. The existence of those status divisions and material inequalities is an obvious reason why such conventions do not develop more or less automatically (Barry 1980). Ideas about corporate social responsibility and recourse to the criminal law are two important though still weak responses to such problems (Blowfield and Frynas 2005). Moreover, many transnational business enterprises have been adept at clouding issues of legal liability so that the victims of harm find it virtually impossible to secure justice through the courts, as discussions of the Bhopal incident have shown (Shrivastava 1992). What invariably underlies such strategies is a belief in the sanctity of property rights, and in primary duties to shareholders, that transfers the burden of seeking justice to the victims (Eckersley 2004: 105, 219; Kutz 2000: 236–8). There has been no marked advance in developing a doctrine of 'corporate criminal responsibility in international law' because, from the dominant legal standpoints, multinational enterprises are an ensemble of

---

[56] High cancer rates in the Polynesian Islands have been attributed to French nuclear tests at Mururoa (Vincent 2006). Handl (2006) discusses the Australian and New Zealand claims against France before the International Court of Justice as part of a larger consideration of the role of nuclear technologies in causing trans-boundary harm.

national companies, each accountable to domestic law in the society in which it is incorporated (Crawford 2002a: 112–13).

6. As noted previously, exploitation cannot be reduced to the exploitation of labour but has to be defined more broadly to include the diverse ways in which the powerful take advantage of vulnerable people. Violent forms include sexual exploitation, as exemplified by the Rape of Nanking following Japan's invasion in December 1937, and the case of the 'comfort women' held captive by the Japanese military during the Second World War (Chang 1997; Tanaka 2002). Sex tourism, and the traffic in women and children for use as 'sex slaves', are modern examples of the ruthless exploitation of the vulnerable.[57] In the case of sexual slavery, sexual and economic exploitation are combined in a dark, seamless web. Cosmopolitan law has responded to the phenomenon of sexual exploitation by adding rape in war to crimes against humanity. The Nazi and Japanese slave labour programmes prompted similar measures to outlaw the brutal exploitation of conquered peoples that has been a recurrent feature of war and imperial expansion ever since the first city-states and empires appeared in the Ancient Near East (Kern 1999).

Slave labour is an instance of the broader phenomenon of unjust enrichment which can be direct as in the case of 'Nazi gold', and the profit that companies such as Krupp, Siemens or I. G. Farben gained from exploitation in the death camps, or indirect as in the example of the rewards that accrued to many Swiss banks as a consequence of the Nazi transfer of the property of Holocaust victims (Barkan 2000: ch. 5). Ethical concerns with unjust benefits have argued that continued ownership of artefacts and human remains that properly belong to indigenous groups represents an assault on the collective identities and self-esteem of affected peoples (Thompson 2002: 40ff., 67). Demands for returning stolen artefacts and remains, and claims for compensation for other forms of unjust enrichment such as the profits that resulted from the African slave trade, would appear to be unprecedented in the history of relations between communities. They have led to the observation that such 'restitution cases' represent a sea-change in international morality (Barkan 2000: ix, 301ff.). Demands for economic justice that invite the beneficiaries of undeserved enrichment to settle earlier wrongs include legal efforts to gain restitution from corporations that profited from apartheid (see *Khulumani et al. v. Barclays National Bank*). Such concerns with justice in the Aristotelian sense of 'an excess of the harmful and a deficiency of the beneficial, contrary to the rule of fair apportionment' have arisen in many other spheres of global economic life (Aristotle 1955: Bk. 5, ch. 5). Some examples are public campaigns against the Nestlé Corporation's infant feeding formula (Richter 2001) and, more generally, criticisms of protectionist

---

[57] In this context, see the United Nations Protocol to Prevent, Suppress and Punish Trafficking in Persons, Especially Women and Children.

policies and export subsidies that disadvantage foreign competitors, thereby allowing affluent societies to profit from the vulnerability of producers in the 'developing world'. A related concern is exploitation without intent as in the case of the economic benefits that flow to powerful groups because 'global coercive regimes' act on their behalf (Pogge 2002).

7. Complicity has been defined as the condition of being implicated in 'mediated' harm as a result of association with organizations that adversely affect others. In general, in liberal societies, the accusation of complicity does not have the same moral force as accusations of causing harm deliberately, but much depends on how far those involved are aware of their complicity in injurious actions and how much power they have to influence outcomes.[58]

Different responses to the complaint that present generations are implicated in harms that were suffered, or continue to be suffered, by indigenous peoples clarify the point. One riposte to appeals to make reparations for past injuries, or to apologize for the past, denies that such duties exist, the argument being that the current generations did not cause the relevant harms. The counter-argument is that past harms and their effects form an undeniable part of their collective inheritance. Far from being untainted by associations with the past, the living are 'implicated' in past harms simply by wearing the same 'uniform' and by serving in the same 'team'. 'Only a very narrow individualism would recoil', it has been suggested, at any suggestion that reparations are due (Feinberg 1990: 96–7).

That thesis may rest on claims that current generations enjoy the benefits of unjust enrichment that has its origins in the first settlers' appropriation of 'native' territories. But the contention is entangled with sensitivity to the ways in which the practices that have shaped, and continue to shape, the collective pride and self-esteem of the dominant strata demean subordinated identities. Statements of regret and apology for past injustice can be lampooned as disingenuous public relations exercises. However, reconciliatory mechanisms that are used to build 'relations of respect and trust' may depend on the willingness of dominant groups to acknowledge publicly that their greater power, wealth and status cannot be disentangled from the harmful practices of the past (Thompson 2002: 49–50).

Complicity with respect to unjust enrichment has been described as a missing element in the case for broadening the human rights culture to include the entitlement to be free from malnutrition and starvation (Vincent 1986). On that argument, mutual recrimination and inaction are the predictable outcome of

---

[58] An interesting example is the case of *Tesch, Weinbacher and Drosihn* during the Nuremberg trials. The accused worked for a firm that supplied the gas, Zyklon B, to death camps in Poland. All three knew the gas was used for mass killing. As owner and manager, respectively, the first two were found guilty, while the third, a technician, was acquitted on the grounds that he could neither influence nor prevent the transfer of gas to the camps.

efforts to identify ultimate causal responsibility for the 'resident emergency' of severe deprivation faced by tens of millions of people. The conviction is that the plain fact that other people face extreme hardship should be enough to galvanize the world community to promote the modern equivalent to the early nineteenth-century campaign to abolish the Atlantic slave trade. A campaign of compassion that was less concerned with allocating blame than with alleviating suffering could have the virtue of reducing the gulf between 'north' and 'south', and strengthening international order (Vincent 1986). But the argument did not neglect the contribution that addressing global injustices could make to a more ethical world order. Simply by virtue of their powerful location in the global economy, affluent groups were 'implicated' in global structures and practices that created or perpetuated the deprivation of others (Vincent 1986: 127–8; also Pogge 2002: 142). The moral problem was the failure to care sufficiently about the 'human consequences of our actions' (Chomsky, cited in Vincent 1986: 147).

Those remarks about what has been described as the 'wrong (we do) in our ordinary lives' (see pp. 55–6) were prescient in that ethical concerns about complicity have become more prominent features of public debates – as can be seen from the publicity given to cheap commodities made in sweatshops or to using child labour that forms part of a broader movement to support fair trade, socially responsible investment, ethical tourism and public recognition of the ways in which growth in affluent regions is inextricably connected with environmental harm in vulnerable areas. The issue of complicity in systems of exploitation is raised by each of those examples, the implication being that people are guilty of serious moral omissions as opposed to merely withholding benefits that may have regrettable consequences but is not a major fault. Running through them is the call for greater attentiveness to the diverse causes of harm and the invitation to conduct commercial practices free from self-reproach.

8. Acts of omission raise questions about the relative importance of negative obligations to avoid injury and positive obligations of assistance, along with the issue of whether that is a defensible distinction. Some argue that if a person has the 'power to prevent something bad from happening, without sacrificing anything of comparable moral importance', then there is an obligation to act accordingly, whether or not the person concerned is causally responsible for the predicament of others (Singer 1972: 230).[59] In those circumstances, it has been claimed, 'the traditional distinction between duty and charity cannot be drawn' (Singer 1972: 235). In a related argument, societies are said to breach the negative obligation to avoid harm when they fail to

---

[59] The duty of rescue has been an important part of international maritime law since the 1910 Belgian International Assistance and Salvage at Sea Convention (see Pugash 1977). I am grateful to Abram de Swaan for bringing this phenomenon to my attention.

dismantle coercive global regimes that frustrate vulnerable peoples' efforts to secure a decent life. The precariousness of the distinction between negative and positive duties is underlined by the relatively small sacrifice that affluent groups need to make to end global poverty – on one estimate, no more than around 1 per cent of global aggregate income (Pogge 2002). A 'double standard' of morality has the effect that efforts to promote social justice within national borders have few parallels as far as the 'global economic order' is concerned, the clear assumption being that 'massive and avoidable levels of poverty abroad' is perfectly acceptable (Pogge 2002: 108). Where suffering is remote and invisible, affluent societies are relatively untroubled by the extent to which, in Feinberg's words, they hold the fate of others in their hands (Singer 1972; also pp. 58–9). There is no more striking illustration of how the 'geographical conception of morality' (Burke 1960: 17) blocks the introduction of relevant cosmopolitan harm conventions. Efforts to promote greater reflectiveness about how the instruments of global governance preside over and harm the vulnerable have applied new pressures to old assumptions that domestic and international politics should be governed by different ethical standards.

9. Public international harm is an expression with little obvious relevance for the history of relations between societies. Where levels of global institutionalization are low, states can be criticized when they violate the primary rules they have agreed between themselves, but they cannot be accused of causing harm by breaching secondary harm conventions.[60] The idea of public international harm would seem to have unusual significance in the modern society of states as a result of the enormous growth of international organizations since the end of the nineteenth century, although in Thucydides' account of the Peloponnesian War, one can find disgust at breaches of conventions that had been agreed before the gods. Breaking agreements with other states was not the only reason for revulsion; that was also produced by offences against the gods and by assaults on the civilization of Hellas, for example by violating the sanctity of temples (Price 2001). Clearly, the gods are rarely invoked in criticisms of breaches of secondary harm conventions in the modern society of states. Reference is more likely to be made to harm to global organizations such as the UN that many regard as representing, however imperfectly, international society or as speaking, however obliquely, for the interests and aspirations of the species as a whole. A sense of harming humanity, which is crucial for securing support for robust cosmopolitan harm conventions, remains relatively weak in this society of states although it may be that, in time, concerns about environmental degradation will increase the importance of such orientations. More significant at this stage is the belief that

---

[60] See Buzan and Little (2000: 80–84) on different levels of 'interaction capacity' in states-systems.

certain harms are 'crimes against *humanity*', and the parallel legal notion of universal jurisdiction which expresses the cosmopolitan principle that war criminals and human rights violators can be prosecuted anywhere.

10. Structural harm is no less dependent on high levels of institutionalization that make people vulnerable to the ways in which they are tied together in lengthening social interconnections. As noted earlier, Marxist and neo-Marxist analyses of global dominance and dependence in the capitalist world economy have highlighted harms that have less to do with the intentions of particular people than with structural compulsions and imperatives. One neo-Marxist approach identified the phenomenon of 'unequal exchange' in which the changing terms of trade disadvantage vulnerable producers who are often forced to sell products cheaply on the world market simply to survive, allowing affluent groups to benefit from invisible 'commercial exploitation' (Emmanuel 1972). Other perspectives have stressed the element of design, arguing that over and over again hegemonic powers have secured their ascendancy by creating free trade regimes that disadvantage rivals and block potential challengers with the wider, and possibly unintended, consequence of harming the global poor (Wallerstein 1979). Many welfare liberals have advanced similar concerns about how global economic institutions that were established in response to problems that affluent Western societies faced in the 1920s and 1930s perpetuate 'subjection' and 'deprivation' for 'minor gains' (Pogge 2002: 13, 23–5). Those observations raise questions not just about the responsibilities of those who profit from structural harm but about those who have most influence over the legal and political framework that allows such benefits to exist – the increasingly well-organized transnational bourgeoisie according to some Marxist approaches (van der Pijl 1998). From liberal perspectives, it may be that the concept of indifference or thoughtlessness adequately characterizes the harm caused by global regimes; for Marxists, the preferable concept is exploitation in the technical sense of appropriating surplus value. But perhaps those different analyses can concur that one purpose of highlighting structural harm is to increase awareness of the ways in which certain actors consciously take advantage of the vulnerable while others are complicit, often unwittingly, in perpetuating harmful practices across the globe – and perhaps they can agree that reducing structural harm is one of the main reasons for supporting radical cosmopolitan harm conventions.

Conclusion

The argument of this chapter has been that all societies have harm conventions that stand between universal human capacities that include the ability to inflict pain and similarly universal vulnerabilities such as susceptibility to mental and physical suffering. Most societies have seen the value of international harm conventions either for self-interested reasons or because of moral commitments to refrain from harming outsiders. Such harm conventions stand between the vulnerable and the structures that bind them together in the most recent phase in the history of global interconnectedness. They often mitigate the effects of insider–outsider dualisms, but self-reliance with respect to security and survival has limited their development. The harms that have accompanied the global extension of social and economic relations have led many non-governmental organizations and other actors to attempt to embed cosmopolitan harm conventions in the structure of international society – to place global barriers between vulnerable persons and new threats to their well-being. Unrivalled levels of interconnectedness have had the effect of making the problem of harm in world politics more central to everyday life than ever before.[61] Some of the hazards associated with the 'world risk society', including inter-related threats to health and the environment, create dangers for all people, regardless of class, national, racial, gender and other distinguishing identities. They have driven a small wedge between some social movements and the sovereign nation-state that has been the principal object of political loyalty in recent times. People who are not exposed to equal levels of harm can nevertheless recognize the growing need to support cosmopolitan harm conventions. Increasing interconnectedness places more and more humans in a position where they need to make a moral 'stand' with the consequence that 'the utopia of a world society' may be 'a little more real or at least more urgent' (Beck 1992: 47, 137).

Sceptics will respond that the desire to protect co-nationals from harm is far more powerful than the ambition to ensure that distant strangers enjoy similar forms of protection. Put differently, the discourse of cosmopolitan harm conventions is utopian since it embodies aspirations for equality and impartiality,

---

[61] There is always a danger that such formulations will be interpreted as implying that modern peoples are therefore more morally sensitive to harm than their predecessors were, or that the former are more civilized since they wish to eradicate forms of violent and non-violent harm that peoples in earlier times simply accepted or even enjoyed inflicting on each other. That is not what is meant by the comment that the problem of harm looms larger in the moral lives of modern societies than it did in earlier periods. One need only recall that societies in Ancient Greece or in Renaissance Italy faced internal strife or *stasis* on a regular basis, and that the problem of international order did not exist as a distinctive problem, separate from the challenge of establishing domestic order. Efforts to stabilize an international order, and certainly visions of how to make it conform to principles of humanity, can only arise in relations between social systems that are already significantly pacified. Modern societies therefore face problems, and enjoy opportunities, that earlier societies did not confront, not because they were less civilized but because they were saddled with different predicaments. Modern societies are presented with different problems and possibilities because their relative political stability has led to unusually high levels of interconnectedness that have encouraged a significant minority to think about the well-being of humanity as a whole. More will be said about those issues in the following two volumes.

whereas the language of emotional attachments to family, nation and state is one of inequality and partiality, and necessarily so, as far as states are concerned, because of the relentless competition for power and security. Higher levels of global interconnectedness may create new possibilities for cosmopolitan projects, but whether societies will agree about the varieties of harm that should be eradicated from world society is a different matter entirely. Sceptics may stress the existence of competing notions of harm and the improbability of a universal moral consensus. On the other hand, legal conventions that outlaw 'serious bodily and mental harm' offer some hope that far-reaching agreements will occur in a future phase of global integration – and perhaps not because of a sudden upsurge of international goodwill but from sheer necessity. With that in mind, the next chapter considers what can be said for and against the idea that a cosmopolitan harm principle has become essential for managing current and future global interconnections.

2

The harm principle and global ethics

The prominence of the obligation to avoid serious mental and physical harm in international law prompts the question of whether the modern society of states is making significant progress in harmonizing the duties that citizens have as members of particular communities with the obligations they owe all other people by virtue of shared humanity – alternatively, whether there have been advances in bridging the gulf between the standards that are generally observed in the relations between citizens in stable societies and the principles that govern external affairs (Linklater 1982/1990, 2007a: introduction). In the duty to avoid serious harm, and to cooperate to prevent harm they did not themselves cause, societies may have discovered the solution to the age-old problem of moral obligation in world politics. By agreeing that the most fundamental universal duty of all is to avoid serious harm, the species may be moving closer to answering the question of how separate political communities can co-exist more harmoniously. If so, the harm principle can be regarded as the key element of a long-term global civilizing process.

That approach to the 'citizenship/humanity problem' does not require the sacrifice of legitimate interests – only that societies refrain from promoting their ends by transferring unreasonable costs to outsiders. The antiquity of the theme is evident from its defence in Stoic thought where one first finds the claim that to cause unnecessary harm is to breach the most basic principle that members of humanity should observe in their dealings with each other.[1] Many different ways of supporting the harm principle have been advanced in the history of Western moral and political thought. The first part of this chapter surveys recent lines of defence, and notes in passing how certain formulations in many world religions and non-Western civilizations inspire confidence in the human capacity to place an overlapping moral consensus on pointless suffering at the heart of global governance.

---

[1] Stoic influences are evident in Cicero's comment that 'not only nature, which may be defined as international law, but also the particular laws by which individual peoples are governed similarly ordain that no one is justified in harming another for his own advantage' (Cicero 1967: 144). See Nussbaum (2002) for a critique that stresses the failure to defend duties of assistance.

The second part turns to the argument that the concept of harm is so indeterminate as to rule out an easy passage from supposed 'anthropological constants' to a global agreement about how the harm principle can harmonize obligations to particular groups with responsibilities to people everywhere.[2] An additional objection is that such an approach to global ethics places insufficient demands on moral agents, and is vulnerable to the charge of lacking humanity. The third part argues, first, that the harm principle has an important role – no more than that – in any cosmopolitan ethic and, second, that the issue of whether moral progress has taken place in world politics is largely a matter of how far a 'principle of humaneness' – centred on the harm principle – has been embedded in international society.

Support for any notion of humaneness inevitably raises complex issues about how unjustifiable harm is defined, and about the potential for an intersocietal agreement about an ideal hierarchy of harms, ranging from the relatively trivial to the most reprehensible. Just as complex are the questions that arise when people must cause one form of harm to prevent, punish or deter another. Philosophical debates about punishment, and discussions about the use of force in international relations, have raised central questions about reasonable harm – about harms that may be justified but must nevertheless operate within social constraints that reflect larger concerns about cruel and degrading behaviour or observe proportionality in order to avoid useless suffering. Philosophical discussions of such themes have their intrinsic merit, but they also suggest (though not intentionally) directions for a sociological inquiry into the role of cosmopolitan harm conventions in different international systems. Of particular importance is the question of how far there have been parallels between various philosophical approaches to defending the harm principle and practical responses to the problem of harm in world politics. It is therefore useful to analyse philosophical debates about harm in order to shape the mode of sociological investigation that will be developed in the coming chapters. As discussed earlier, there is no imperative that such an inquiry should be coupled with any specific normative standpoint. However, the argument will combine the strengths of Frankfurt School critical theory and process sociology in order to consider in later volumes how far, or whether, the modern society of states has made progress in embedding a 'principle of humaneness' in its organizing practices.

Defending the harm principle

Moral philosophers have long reflected on the question of whether obligations can be neatly divided into negative duties to avoid injury and positive duties to act benevolently and, furthermore, whether the former take moral priority

[2] The notion of 'anthropological constants' was used by Ernest Mandel (see Geras 1998: 164).

over the latter (Glover 1990: ch. 7; Moore 1959: 218; Pogge 2002: 66–7, 130ff.). It is often argued that people have positive obligations of beneficence to those with whom they have special relationships (such as family members) but no more than negative duties to other human beings. As argued by Cicero amongst others, no prior contract or established social bond is needed to defend the second category of obligations that have the quality of genuine universality (Glover 1990: 134). They comprise what has been called 'natural duties' that do not require formal agreements or implied consent – they are 'the duty not to harm or injure another', 'not to inflict unnecessary suffering', and to assist others in 'jeopardy' as long as there is no 'excessive risk or loss to oneself' (Rawls 1971: 114–15).[3]

It is sometimes thought that the violation of a negative duty such as the duty not to kill is an outrage against society whereas the breach of a positive obligation is a much less serious offence. The former may reflect a psychological desire to harm, and especially reprehensible cruel dispositions, while the latter rests on a simple failure to confer a benefit that may be entirely reasonable given the special obligations that people have to family members, friends or co-nationals, and given their entitlement to pursue their own objectives (Glover 1990: 111). Setting aside the fact that a failure to assist can reveal a vicious temperament, the motivation for causing harm is as important in modern societies as the deed itself.[4] An interesting discussion of someone who is approached for help by two beggars, one of whom s/he has previously harmed, demonstrates that the responsibility for repairing past wrongdoing, or for seeking forgiveness, features prominently in modern ethical codes. As a general rule, the duty to assist the beggar who had been harmed is the greater of the two obligations, assuming it is impossible to assist both simultaneously (Ware 1992: 68).[5] The conclusion to draw is that past harm creates a prima facie obligation of restitution that is prior to general duties of beneficence.

A related issue is whether positive obligations may impose unreasonable burdens on people who, as noted earlier, have pressing responsibilities because of special relationships and the right to pursue their own ends within the restraints laid down by the harm principle. Citizens of affluent societies do not generally blame members of the medical profession for attending to their needs when the

---

[3] O'Neill (1996: 151) distinguishes between the 'special perfect obligations' that parents owe their children and the 'universal perfect obligations' (including the obligation of non-injury) that parents owe all other children, and which should not be sacrificed in the course of promoting the interests of their offspring. I am grateful to Toni Erskine for the references to O'Neill and Rawls.

[4] The contrast is with societies that hold an entire group collectively responsible for wrongdoing that is committed by any one of its members.

[5] The point holds where the two beggars experience equal suffering, but complications set in if the plight of the beggar who was not previously harmed is significantly worse than the predicament of the other person.

utilitarian duty to reduce the aggregate of human misery indicates that there is a greater obligation to assist the desperately ill in the world's poorest regions (Glover 1990: 93–4).[6] The members of modern societies do not usually believe that it is acceptable to enslave or otherwise permanently disadvantage a minority group in order to promote the greatest happiness of the greatest number (Rawls 1971). The belief that a person should be prepared to experience great suffering in order to prevent or relieve an equivalent level of misery to strangers does not command support in liberal societies (Mayerfeld 1999: 9). Of course, an individual may choose to endure suffering for the sake of a family member or friend (by organ donation, for example) or accept the risk of suffering by virtue of enlisting in the emergency services but, as noted in the previous chapter, many liberal societies are unprepared to give obligations of assistance parity with duties to avoid causing harm (see pp. 57–8).

As noted in Chapter 1, many moral philosophers reject the stark division between negative and positive obligations as well as the standard implication that people owe strangers nothing more than the duties that follow from the 'restricted causation model' (see pp. 58–9). But the argument that the responsibility not to cause harm creates an obligation to dismantle 'global coercive regimes' shifts, rather than dissolves, the boundary between negative and positive duties. The difference between observing social expectations to avoid harm and displays of exceptional courage in heroic or 'supererogatory' actions is one reason for valuing that distinction (Urmson 1958). As far as a global ethic is concerned, people might be said to have negative obligations to one another simply as members of a universal moral community (but with more far-reaching implications than is often realized, for the reasons set out in Pogge 2002). They have only limited 'natural' duties to confer benefits on, or to make significant sacrifices for, distant strangers. The main point – more will be said about this later – is not to claim so much for the harm principle that there is a danger of equating it with the whole of morality, or to claim so little for it that people are only required to avoid killing, injuring, humiliating and in related ways harming each other in the course of their interaction.

Various arguments have been advanced in support of the harm principle. The centrality of negative obligations such as 'thou shalt not kill', 'thou shalt not steal' and 'thou shalt not bear false witness' in the Decalogue has been stressed as evidence that duties of 'non-maleficence' are not just 'distinct' from the obligations of beneficence but involve responsibilities 'of a more stringent' kind (Ross 1930: 22). It is further argued that the higher standing of negative obligations is evident from the fact that people generally think that it is unacceptable 'to kill one person in order to keep another alive', or to 'steal from one in order to give

---

[6] It might be added that affluent populations do not usually think they harm poorer societies as a result of the 'brain drain' of skilled medical staff, although the moral issues surrounding active recruitment in those societies do surface from time to time in media discussions.

alms to another' (Ross 1930: 22).[7] Because violations of such principles may be justified in exceptional circumstances, the relevant primary duties have been described as 'conditional' or 'prima facie' rather than absolute. But the licence to breach general principles does not absolve moral agents from the responsibility to observe rules of proportionality and to display appropriate remorse (Moore 1959: 161ff.; Ross 1930: 19–20, 28; see pp. 125–6, n. 25).[8]

Interestingly, Ross did not advance a static model of society in which duties of non-maleficence are guaranteed permanent superiority over positive obligations. He added that compliance with the harm principle over extended periods could prepare the way for public support for more demanding ethical responsibilities including 'recognition of the duty of beneficence' (Ross 1930: 22). He did not discuss how such longer-term processes might unfold, but it may be that studies of the sense of interconnectedness with vulnerable others, as can be found in various writings on the dynamics of individual moral development, cast some light on how they can evolve at the level of personality structures and in the wider realm of social and political affairs (see pp. 145–51).

To explain, there is evidence that infants first learn to comply with negative duties as they become aware of their capacity to injure; only then do they develop an appreciation of the importance of positive obligations along with requisite understandings of their capacity for compassion and care (Aronfreed 1968: ch. 10). Whether or not that is generally true,[9] the evidence is that basic

---

[7] Ross's position resonates with Mill's claim that 'the moralities which prevent every individual from being harmed by others ... are at once those which he himself has most at heart, and those which he has the strongest interest in publishing and enforcing by word and deed' (quoted in Ten 1980: 58).

[8] Urgent considerations may override the prima facie duty not to kill, but Ross (1930: 24) did not think there were obvious 'a priori' methods of ordering conflicting moral obligations (see also Ewing 1959: 141ff.; Frankena 1963: 23–4; Quinton 1973: 107). Arguments about the need for proportionality and remorse when duties of non-injury are violated, however legitimately, have arisen in interesting ways in discussions about the aerial bombardment of German cities during the Second World War. On the central themes, see Grayling (2006) and Sebald (2003).

[9] The socio-psychological dimensions of how individuals learn or do not learn the art of controlling harm is an intriguing subject in its own right. Recent studies of infant development have identified what many would expect, namely that cruelty to animals in the early years is strongly correlated with cruelty to other people in later phases of life. Philosophers have often commented on how adult moral development is influenced by the extent to which infants acquire negative feelings about cruelty to animals. Locke observed that 'if [children] incline to any such cruelty, they should be taught the contrary usage; for the custom of killing beasts will, by degrees, harden their minds even towards men; and they who delight in the suffering and destruction of inferior creatures, will not be apt to be very kind or compassionate or benign to those of their own kind' (quoted in Steintrager 2004: 62; see also Kant as discussed in Passmore 1975). It is interesting that Locke suggests a sequential development of obligations that might be thought to anticipate Ross's general way of thinking. If obligations not to injure animals fail to develop, then similar obligations to other people

moral learning occurs through an awareness of interconnectedness with vulnerable others. Such features of individual development have been at the centre of feminist approaches to ethics, and they have been highlighted by the influential discussion of the distinction between an 'ethic of justice' and the 'ethic of care and responsibility' (Gilligan 1982). Gilligan (1982: 65, 174) maintained that the 'common thread' that runs through the 'different voice' of female moral experience revolves around 'the wish not to hurt others' as well as the desire to resolve conflicts in such a way 'that no one will be hurt'. That morality, which is centred on the ethical 'injunction not to hurt others', often first develops in family relationships – hence criticisms that it may be entirely compatible with parochial loyalties that take little account of the interests of outsiders (Tronto 1994). That is a valid criticism, but there is force behind Gilligan's contention that the sense of responsibility for vulnerable others with whom people are connected represents a moral 'ideal' that can be extended well beyond family relations (Gilligan 1982: 74, 149). Others have applied the theme to world politics – by arguing, for example, that the sense of connectedness is essential if efforts to promote global economic or environmental justice are to succeed (Clement 1996; Robinson 1999; also Dobson 2005 and Young 2006).

It is important to link the last few observations with Ross's remark that compliance with fundamental negative obligations to avoid harm might have the long-term effect of increasing support for positive duties of beneficence. Whether or not it sheds much light on individual moral development, his conception of how obligations evolve sequentially has particular significance for international relations. In general, the central question in world politics has not been whether societies can be cajoled into behaving more altruistically, but whether they can be persuaded to exercise greater control over the power to harm. As far as security dilemmas are concerned, the perennial problem has been whether a state's failure to inflict injury at an opportune moment might strike adversaries as a sign of weakness, or be interpreted as an exercise in self-restraint that encourages others to reciprocate in ways that promote trust over time (Booth and Wheeler 2008: ch. 9; Keohane 1986). As a general rule, states with a history of fear and suspicion must have confidence in each other's implicit or explicit

---

will be jeopardized. Hardening of the heart will make it unlikely that compassionate sentiments will develop. Locke's conception of how obligations develop sequentially may not be wholly accurate. (I am grateful to Toni Erskine for the suggestion that infants often learn how to control the capacity to harm and how to display compassion and care, for example through handling animals, at the same time). Certainly Locke's views led to some peculiar thoughts about the suitability of butchers for jury service. Of particular concern was the fact that sensibilities were coarsened by routine participation in animal slaughter: 'Our practice takes notice of this, in the exclusion of butchers from juries of life and death' (quoted in Steintrager 2004: 62).

commitment to avoid harm before they will take the more radical step of supporting duties of beneficence.[10] Following Ross's approach, one might add that states must have faith in each other's willingness to comply with duties not to injure before concerns with the moral questions that surround failures to rescue, complicity in harm and so forth will materially affect the ways they conduct their external affairs.[11]

The idea of the connected self casts light on how individuals can deepen the sense of moral community so that they are concerned not only with avoiding physical harm but with being free from reproach for causing harm in any of its forms. Connectedness is important for understanding how they can enlarge their images of community to include all those who are affected by their actions. The concept is significant for comprehending how such communities can become more reflective as people develop more complex understandings of how distant strangers are – or can be – harmed by their conduct or disadvantaged by global structures and processes. The conjecture is that Ross's remarks about the sequential relationship between negative and positive duties may be confirmed by analysing the reasons for extending solidarity in at least some historical periods.

Ross (1930: 20, n. 1) maintained that the 'primary duty ... not to harm others' is 'self-evident', and Rawls included it in the list of 'natural duties', but it is important to unpack its foundational quality given its possible importance for understanding past and potential advances in human solidarity. Three lines of argument deserve consideration. The first, which was briefly mentioned in the previous chapter, contends that all societies possess rules of 'forbearance' that recognize their inhabitants' 'vulnerability' to pain and suffering (Hart 1961: 190).[12] Comprising the 'minimum content of natural law', such rules place restraints on killing and maiming, on breaching agreements and on violating property rights that are essential for the survival of society (Hart 1961: 189ff.; see also Moore

---

[10] To explain, a state could try to break a deadlock by offering to assist an adversary that is struggling to deal with the consequences of a natural disaster, but the possibilities for initiating change through such actions may be limited because of the suspicion that accepting aid will be interpreted as a sign of weakness, or the fear that acceptance involves a loss of power or status, or may lead to a state of dependence.

[11] With respect to Ross' understanding of the sequential nature of negative and positive duties, a bridge between the 'stringent' obligation not to inflict physical injury and duties of 'beneficence' can be found in the harm principle, particularly if 'do no harm' is understood to include duties of rescue.

[12] Needless to say, various practices including infanticide are perfectly compatible with the approach. But rules of forbearance reflect the reality that societies are not 'suicide clubs'. The point can be extended by noting that certain biological factors place limits on social organization. No society can organize itself without taking any account of human vulnerability to pain. But the proportion of those who are protected from the forms of suffering that arouse most concern clearly varies enormously – though not, as stated earlier, to the extent of ruling out mutual intelligibility or preventing different cultures from agreeing that certain forms of harm should be eliminated from their international relations.

1959: ch. 5). The universality of those rules, Hart (1961: 191ff.) argued, stems from the need to provide security from violent or non-violent harm, and from the importance of addressing the adverse effects of 'limited altruism', a theme that has been central to a second approach to the harm principle.

Wherever there are 'limited sympathies', it has been stated, there is the prospect of 'active malevolence' either because of an appetite for injuring outsiders or because of a lack of concern 'with the damage so inflicted' (Warnock 1971: 21ff., 80ff., 150).[13] No person is immune from the dangers that result from others' indifference or hostility (Warnock 1971: 150), and all will remain vulnerable until humanity removes the pernicious effects of insider–outsider dualisms. From that perspective, the object of morality is to 'expand our sympathies' or, rather, 'to reduce the liability to damage inherent in their natural tendency to be narrowly restricted' (Warnock 1971: 26). The point is that all people have an interest in global rules of forbearance and in enlarging sympathies to address a shared predicament. The critic may point out that such dangers are greatly 'diminished' for those that are protected by powerful societies (Warnock 1971: 150).[14] Because of unequal vulnerability, people do not have the same interest in establishing cosmopolitan harm conventions that protect them from the effects of their exclusion from other communities – or at least common interests may not extend far. However, the laws of war demonstrate that all people have a stake in mitigating the effects of narrow sympathies where the usual protections that flow from the membership of powerful societies reach their limits, or completely break down – that is when all people can find themselves exposed to the tyranny of warfare, and their state is powerless to help them.

Something rather like Feinberg's idea of welfare interests underlies the two positions surveyed thus far; it is also at the forefront of a third defence of the harm principle that has been advanced in recent theories of justice. 'The paradigm of harm', it has been argued, is 'physical injury, and life goes better, on virtually any conception of the good, in the absence of physical injury' (Barry 1995: 88). For that reason alone, people who profoundly disagree about the 'good' can find some common ground, on lowering their moral sights, in shared understandings about 'the badness of harm' (Barry 1995: 24). The universalism that runs through the approach is supported by widely shared beliefs about effective punishment. Revealingly, 'every society falls back on a quite limited range of punishments such as deprivation of money or property, physical confinement, loss of bodily parts, pain, and death. Unless these were regarded by

[13] Warnock (1971: 86) maintains that the duty of non-maleficence is one of four 'virtues' that are required to cope with the side effects of limited sympathies, the others being non-deception, fairness and beneficence.

[14] I am grateful to Andrew Dobson for this point. Warnock's argument would have been stronger had he followed Hume in emphasizing how the problem of 'confined generosity' is compounded by the struggles that arise because of 'the scanty provision nature has made for [human] wants' (cited in Mackie 1977: 110).

people with a wide variety of conceptions of the good as evils, they would not function reliably as punishments' (Barry 1995: 141–2). Many groups that have perspectives on 'the causation of harm' that clearly diverge from those found in modern societies – the belief in witchcraft, for example – have similar fears that stem from the shared recognition that 'diseases and injuries, destruction or damage of property … and similar misfortunes' are plainly and incontrovertibly harmful (Barry 1995: 142).

Further support for that line of argument can be derived from the evidence that the major world religions have concurred on the ethical importance of a duty of non-injury. Some version of the harm principle is evident not only in Jainism and the Christian Decalogue, as noted earlier, but in many Hindu, Confucian and Islamic texts, but often, it must be stressed, in combination with strong advocacy of duties of beneficence (Bowker 1975, 1997).[15] The examples indicate that Western liberalism is not alone in endorsing a harm principle. The similarities demonstrate that most forms of life have subscribed to some version of 'negative utilitarianism', which is the doctrine that social conventions should at the very least aim to minimize suffering, if not to actively promote happiness (Smart 1973: 28–30).[16] They suggest that there is much to be said for the proposition that 'the hard core of morality' is utilitarian because it is more concerned with the modest goal of encouraging abstention from 'positive injury' than with promoting altruism (Quinton 1973: 69–71).

There is always the danger that claims about the hard core of morality will impute modern concerns to all ethical codes. Mill's statement that the 'moral rules which forbid mankind to hurt one another … are more vital to human well-being than any other maxims … a person may possibly not need the benefits of others; but he always needs that they should not do him hurt' may make perfect sense to the members of contemporary societies (Mill, quoted in Mackie

---

[15] Examples are the Hindu ideals of abstaining from injury (Bowker 1975: 222), and the related pan-Indian concepts of *ahimsa* that stress the vulnerability of all sentient beings to pain or suffering (Harvey 2000: 69, 119ff.), Confucian notions of *ren* or humaneness and *pu jen* (Shun 1997: 49; Yao 2000: 213–14), and the Islamic notion of '*jihad* of the heart'. The following Hindu and Buddhist precepts are especially interesting: 'This is the sum of duty: do not do to others what would cause pain if done to you' (Mahabharata 5: 1517) and 'Hurt not others in ways that you yourself would find hurtful' (Udana-Varga 5: 18). I am grateful to Scott Smith for the last two references.

[16] Smart refers to Popper's contention that all 'moral urgency' has its basis in 'suffering or pain'. The promotion of happiness was, for Popper, much less urgent than the duty to help those that most need it, and to 'prevent suffering'. On that score, the utilitarian argument for maximizing the happiness of the greatest number should be replaced by the maxim, 'minimize suffering' (Popper 1966: ch. 5, n. 6; ch. 9, n. 2). Smart (1973) supported the obligation to promote happiness as well as to minimize suffering, understood as 'misery involving actual pain'. For that reason, he maintained that the principle of negative utility is 'a subordinate rule of thumb', but an important one because often the best that people can do for each other is to try to 'remove their miseries'. That much they can agree on despite substantial differences about the good life.

1977: 135). But most social groups in human history have almost certainly not believed that failures to act benevolently are always less harmful than failures to observe prohibitions of physical injury. Survival in hunting and gathering communities probably depended as much on an unfailing commitment to 'share the hunt' as on compliance with rules forbidding murder, physical assault and so forth. Mill's conception of moral priorities can be seen to reflect a particular stage in the development of society where people are less dependent on the 'altruism' of others for their survival than on one another's commitment to observing elementary principles of justice that are centred on the duty to abstain from harm. That shift in orientation towards other people – and related sensitivities to pain and suffering – are manifestations of the civilizing process which will be considered in more detail later.[17] But for reasons given earlier, the relationship between Mill's argument and quite specific changes in modern societies does not reduce the significance of the harm principle for international politics where the survival and security of communities do not usually depend on the benevolence of others but on the widespread observance of constraints on the power to harm. In relations between such groups, the maxim, '*Do good to yourself with as little evil as possible to others*', although 'much less perfect' than the injunction, 'Do to others as you would have them do unto you', is 'perhaps more useful', precisely because the harmful side effects of parochial loyalties are often dramatically evident (Rousseau 1968 [1765]: 185; italics in original). That maxim does concur with a recurrent theme in the major world religions, which is that the most accessible points of solidarity between strangers are to be found in a shared aversion to basic forms of suffering (Lu 2000).[18] Arguments for the harm principle therefore lean towards the conclusion that an overlapping global moral consensus is most likely to develop if different groups support universalizing the 'disposition to abstain from (deliberate, unjustified) maleficence', as

[17] Mill's contention that people do not require selflessness on the part of others but a commitment to refraining from harm reflects a state of affairs in which strangers have been thrown together, where they are disinclined to rely on each other's kindness, but do think that the least they can expect from each other is a firm commitment to justice. Similar themes can be found in Smith (1982 [1759]). Changes in the wider society that led to such ethical arguments are discussed in Mazlish (1989). All that need be added is that the belief that the harm principle is critical for social organization reflects many of the features of the civilizing process, as discussed by Elias, and not least the fact that people have been thrown together in longer webs of interconnectedness that require them to be better attuned to each other's interests and sensitive to the ways in which they can harm one another. The centrality of the harm principle in so much recent thought, and the interest in classifying the different ways in which people can harm and be harmed by each other, is best understood with reference to the civilizing process. For further discussion, see Chapter 4.

[18] As noted earlier, world religions represented a major breakthrough in integrating diverse groups within the same faith tradition while often insisting on insider–outsider dualisms that blocked further advances in solidarity and often inspired religiously sanctioned violence (see Aho 1981 and Nelson 1973). The argument here is indebted to what Geras (1999) has called 'the view from everywhere'.

well as promoting efforts to ensure that no one is 'excluded' from the scope of moral consideration (Warnock 1971: 80ff., 147).[19]

Turning now to the harm principle and world politics, it has been argued elsewhere that the English School comes closer than any other approach to recognizing its importance for maintaining order and civility between independent political communities (Linklater and Suganami 2006b: part two). All the arguments in support of the harm principle that have been considered thus far surface in the English School account of how radically different societies can agree that the maintenance of international order is essential if they are to protect their populations from the forms of serious harm to which all are vulnerable, though unequally because of asymmetries of power and wealth. The idea of the 'minimum content of natural law' was consciously replicated in Bull's account of the primary goals that make international society possible.[20] Implicit in English School analysis is the belief that the web of formal and informal agreements that constitute the society of states has evolved to control the deleterious effects of limited sympathies (Bull 1977). The thesis that states often find it easier to agree on the bases of international order than on the nature of global justice echoes the standpoint that the 'paradigm of harm' can underpin shared understandings about civility that can enable societies with radically divergent conceptions of the good to co-exist peacefully (Bull 1977: ch. 4). Echoes of liberalism can be heard in the claim that such principles are neutral with respect to visions of justice, and indeed make it possible for societies to pursue divergent normative ideals within their respective territories, largely free from external interference. Finally, in English School analysis, it is possible to detect traces of the view that the common ground of 'negative utilitarianism' is critical for preserving order in world politics. From its perspective, the importance of avoiding 'positive injury' is the 'hard core' of an international morality that is not entirely deaf, however, to pleas for benevolence. Indeed the bedrock of support for negative duties may provide the foundation for future experiments to promote relations that are more strongly influenced by the disposition towards beneficence.[21]

In this context, it is useful to recall Bull's comment that international order should be judged by what it contributes to world order – to arrangements

---

[19] Indeed Warnock (1971: 151) argued that, because they can also suffer, no sentient creature should be excluded from such arrangements.

[20] Bull (1977: 19) maintained that controlling violence, respecting property rights (recognizing sovereign rights) and keeping promises (or complying with treaty obligations) are three primary goals in international society.

[21] It is worth adding that the dominant international ethos supports 'rule' as against 'act utilitarianism' (Wheeler and Bellamy 2001). As noted earlier, Bull (1984), Jackson (2000) and others argue that the benefits of overriding sovereignty in order to achieve humanitarian objectives may be outweighed by long-term damage to international order. The priority of order over justice dictates restraint as well as foresight with respect to the dangerous precedents that may be created by altruistic interventions.

that protect the individual's primary goals in, for example, freedom from vio-lence (Bull 1977: 20–2). Progress in that direction involves, it might be argued, more radical advances in supporting duties of non-maleficence that check the dangers of limited sympathies. More specifically, the sense of belonging to an international society of states can be augmented by a belief in a cosmopolitan community which is united by the Stoic belief that 'superfluous injury' to stran-gers infringes the most elementary laws of humanity. It is unnecessary to look beyond the laws of war that have commanded support in all major civiliza-tions and faith traditions for evidence of how the movement from international towards world order can occur – in short, for evidence of how transnational agreements on cosmopolitan harm conventions that bridge those domains can develop.[22] All English School theory acknowledges that the interests of the great powers are imprinted on international society, while insisting that its arrange-ments are not entirely reducible to their preferences and aspirations. Even the most powerful have to acknowledge that their capabilities are limited, and that they may be unable to protect military personnel who are held captive, and pos-sibly civilians who are denied non-combatant immunity in violent conflict. The levelling effect of force is one reason for the laws of war. A divinely sanctioned belief in the prima facie duty not to injure other humans underpinned the idea of just war in most epochs (Childress 1974; Verkamp 1993: 90ff.). The domin-ant forms of justification may have changed, but commitments to such negative obligations have long indicated how people can reconcile the duties they have as citizens with their responsibilities as human beings. They draw attention to potentials for global agreements about international and cosmopolitan harm conventions that allow societies and individuals to pursue their rival visions of the good, free from injury and its threat.[23] Historically, the realization of such potentials has depended less on the belief that right conduct is its own reward, and more on the recognition of the need for prudence, foresight and self-restraint when societies know that harming others may not be cost-free – in short, when recognition that adversaries will cause at least equivalent levels of

[22] As well as the Christian just war doctrine, examples include ancient Hebraic prohibitions of violence against women and children (Walzer 1996), and Arabic concepts such as *muru-wwa* that set out similar prohibitions on 'unnecessary spoliation' that may have influenced the practice of sparing rather than slaughtering the enemy, and which became a fundamen-tal duty in the later Islamic rules of war (Firestone 1999: ch. 2; Hashmi 1996; Tibi 1996). Crucial to Islamic law was the precept 'do not transgress limits' that was used to defend the rights of non-combatants (Firestone 1999: 55). Ancient Hindu codes of war such as the *Arthashastra* outlawed the murder of civilians, rape and looting, and the destruction of villages (Klostermaier 1996). Similar views informed the pan-Indian (including Jainist and Buddhist) notion of *ahimsa* which was generally opposed to force other than for punitive purposes and in self-defence (Amore 1996).

[23] See also Moore (1972: 1–2) and Lu (2000: 255) on the notion that ethical systems are often divided over 'freedom, humanity, community and security', but broadly united in 'their condemnation of cruelty'.

harm through acts of retaliation pushes them to observe restraints based on the attractions of reciprocity.[24]

Criticisms of the harm principle

The case for thinking that the harm principle provides the basis for fundamental cosmopolitan obligations is insecure if the concept of harm is so indeterminate that it cannot provide a barrier to the random extension of moral responsibilities. Moreover, the principle should be opposed if it is true, as some argue, that it effectively defends conditions in which people are untroubled by high levels of indifference to suffering. To take that point further, there is no doubt that a highly attenuated version of the harm principle informs the neo-liberal thesis that people should be as self-reliant as possible rather than rely on others for the satisfaction of basic needs. A coruscating critique of 'bourgeois individualistic' liberalism rejects its vision of 'possessive and private' persons who resent any demands that go beyond the most basic responsibilities (Parekh 1972: 81). In social systems that uphold 'protective barriers between individuals', the only obligations that matter are those that people impose on themselves: they have no right to harm others – where harm refers to actions that cause physical injury or other serious setbacks to interests – but they have only limited obligations of assistance (Parekh 1972: 84). Pursuing a related theme, an investigation of political theory in the aftermath of the Holocaust states that a moral code is 'plainly inadequate' if all it insists on are duties to 'refrain from harming others', and if it regards the issue of whether or not to help others as a matter for sovereign judgment (Geras 1998: 58). Advocates of the harm principle emphasize the need to protect individual liberties from burdensome obligations. The objection is that its bias towards basic negative duties leads to the standpoint that 'practical indifference to the calamities and suffering of others is ... a legitimate mode of personal conduct' (Geras 1998: 58).

For others, the problem is not that the harm principle lets moral actors off the hook too easily, but that its meaning is so vague that it can be used to defend a confusing medley of obligations. Sceptics have argued that the concept of harm is 'so deeply value-impregnated' that one must doubt whether those with rival conceptions of the good can find some common ground in neutral understandings

---

[24] Parker (2002: 161ff.) contrasts the asymmetrical power relations between European colonial powers and conquered peoples with the condition within Europe where states knew that the safe return of defeated armed forces depended on reciprocity. The 'durability' of such civilizing understandings was conditional on the virtual certainty that the parties would 'meet again' on similar terms. There was very little of that in relations with less powerful groups in the wider world. Elias used the term 'functional democratization' to describe patterns of mutual dependence that created pressures to introduce such civilizing restraints on behaviour (see Chapters 4 and 6 for a discussion of the significance of that concept for responses to distant suffering).

of what is harmful (Ten 1980: 52). From that perspective, harm resembles social constructions of the disgusting which take bewilderingly diverse forms, as Herodotus (2004: Book III, 38) observed in one of the earliest comments on the relativity of morals (see also Corbin 1996).[25] Neutrality claims ignore what is most extraordinary about the social world, namely the rich diversity of customs that have led some groups to decide that infanticide, murdering witches, human sacrifice and so on are rational practices while others condemn their cruelty and barbarism. Most societies may agree that ritual sacrifice is harmful, but that has not stopped some from adopting that practice. Since there is no consensus that the concept of harm should refer simply to acts that result in death or serious mental or physical harm, doubts immediately arise as to whether its meaning can be broadened without 'invoking highly disputable values' and descending into 'arbitrariness' (Ten 1980: 52). Having extended the concept beyond killing and serious injury, one might be forced to conclude that there are no obvious limits to its indefinite expansion (Lucas 1966: 345). Fluidity and indeterminacy pose an immediate problem for the liberal enterprise of carefully defining the coercive powers of the state so that obligations to avoid harm are balanced with rights to individual autonomy.[26] Conceptual open-endedness creates similar difficulties for efforts to identify cosmopolitan obligations that neither fall short of, nor exceed, what is essential for the construction of a just world order. The difficulty is whether such uncertainties undermine all attempts to make meaningful distinctions between negative and positive obligations so that, far from ensuring that cosmopolitan duties are strictly limited in the ways already mentioned, the harm principle turns out to be 'a sink that can drain virtually all of our resources' (Arneson 1998: 85).

There is no agreement about whether there is a 'morally neutral conception of harm' or whether all attempts to identify such notions rest on a prior account of the good.[27] It is impossible to deny that every version of the harm principle has to presuppose a particular conception of subjectivity – some notion of human vulnerability that the principle is designed to protect against. Disputes about the morality of abortion are a reminder that certain highly contested assumptions about the moral subject have to be made before the principle can take effect. The harm principle cannot itself settle disagreements about whether the foetus has the right to live (Barry 1995: 91). Liberals with a 'thin' notion of subjectivity with its protective shell against the encroachment of 'demanding'

---

[25] The reference is to the Greeks' and the Callatiae's astonishment and revulsion at each other's treatment of the dead.

[26] The different conclusions that, for example, Feinberg (1985: ch. 11) and Mackinnon and Dworkin (1997) reach on whether pornography violates the harm principle or merely gives offence highlight the difficulties.

[27] Compare Gray (1996: 135) who rejects the idea of a neutral definition of harm with Barry (1995: 141) who denies that such standpoints have been, or could be, 'backed up by convincing evidence'.

obligations are at odds with religious zealots who harness a 'thicker' conception of the self to the argument that 'sins' should not go unpunished. Those points have been linked with the contention that the idea of harm has 'a spurious air of certainty and definiteness' because of the 'paradigm cases' that include death and physical injury (Lucas 1966: 173). Underlying the seeming plausibility and neutrality of the concept are 'the values of a [particular] community and the ideal patterns of life cherished by it' that decide its exact meaning and significance for any way of life (Lucas 1966: 345).[28] Without such understandings, the harm principle is cut free from essential moorings and unable to guide human conduct.[29]

The importance of egalitarian moral convictions is worth stressing in this context. There is nothing in the harm principle that requires that people should be treated as equals within the same community. A quite independent conception of equal human subjects has to be grafted onto the harm principle before it can contribute to progressive politics of that kind. From that vantage-point, the commitment to equality is at least as, if not more important than, the harm principle. The comment is undoubtedly valid. All that can be stated in response is that shared vulnerabilities create an important path to egalitarian doctrines, one approach to transcending insider–outsider dualisms that has blocked extensions of sympathy and solidarity, and one way of rallying global support for harm conventions with a cosmopolitan purpose.[30]

Pain, suffering and vulnerability

Societies can no more survive without harm conventions than their inhabitants can live without emotional experiences that include attitudes to pain and suffering. Emotions have been described as a point of intersection between nature and society, between somatic and cultural influences. The capacity for fear is part of the biological constitution of the species but, in diverse ways, social forces govern the expression of all 'hard wired' emotions. As with emotions, harm conventions are located at the junction where tensions

---

[28] A similar argument informs the claim that the harm principle is essentially 'a principle of freedom', and is tied to the ideal of 'respect for the autonomy of others' (Raz 1986: 412ff.).

[29] In short, the harm principle is 'communitarian' rather than 'cosmopolitan', diverse in expression rather than uniform, because it depends on particular conceptions of vulnerable subjects embedded in specific social arrangements. See Lucas (1966: 3–4) for comments on the relationship between shared vulnerabilities and moral obligations that are more cosmopolitan than the remarks cited earlier.

[30] This is to take issue with the view that the harm principle is tied up with liberal principles of freedom and autonomy (see note 28 above), or at least it is to stress that it can command the support of people that do not have those ideals or do not couch them in liberal-individualistic terms.

between nature and society, the universal and the particular, are endlessly
played out. On the one side there are certain biological universals that no
society ignores – the susceptibility to pain and illness, the inevitability of
physical decline and death; and on the other, social constructions of the body,
pain, suffering, death and so forth in their remarkable diversity. Harm conventions therefore reflect certain universal properties of the body which are
interlinked with specific cultural influences. But there are limits to diversity. The similarities between harm conventions in different times and places
are unsurprising, even though no one should expect the commonalities to
extend very far.

The continuing tug-of-war between nature and society renders the concept of
harm unstable, and is one reason for the debates about whether the harm principle can serve as a foundation for the criminal law or for some cosmopolitan
ethic. There may be 'no such thing as absolute ethical neutrality' (Habermas
quoted in McCarthy 1998: 148), but that has not prevented societies from wrestling 'approximate agreement' about such 'ultimate ends' as minimizing pointless
suffering from different modes of ethical reasoning. An overlapping consensus
of that kind is all that is needed to maintain 'rational and cooperative moral
discourse' within and between societies (Smart 1973: 26). Particularly important for efforts to explore and reach global agreements through rational deliberation is the idea of 'affectedness' – specifically the condition of vulnerability to
harm by others – which is an intrinsic feature of every social morality (Quinton
1973: 69).[31] The taxonomy of harms developed in Chapter 1 indicates that affectedness takes very different forms, but it is possible to unite them in a global
ethic grounded in the Kantian notion of 'generalizable interests' (see p. 96). To
develop the point, it is useful to begin with the virtually universal susceptibility
to physical pain, and then turn to the other forms of harm that were discussed
earlier.[32]

[31] Questions about how people can affect others in what the wider society regards as morally
offensive ways are left out of the discussion here.

[32] Susceptibility to pain is less than completely universal because of the rare, and usually disastrous, condition known as 'congenital indifference to pain' (Hardcastle 1999: 59–60).
Moreover, cultural and psychological factors can inhibit or intensify the individual's tolerance and experience of pain (Hardcastle 1999: 122ff., ch. 7; Melzack and Wall 1982: chs.
1–2). The impossibility of directly experiencing another person's pain is a recurrent theme
in writings on this subject (Scarry 1985; Wittgenstein 1974: 302–3). It has been a central
element in discussions in the United States about forms of capital punishment that may
cause unnecessary suffering – sometimes imperceptibly – which is illegal according to the
8th constitutional amendment that forbids 'cruel and unusual punishment'. See Kaufman-
Osborn (2001) for further comment. Such debates demonstrate the complexities that surround something as apparently objective and measurable as physical pain, and they reveal
why there are fundamental disagreements about the boundary between tolerable and
unacceptable suffering caused, for example, by capital punishment (see Sarat 2001 for further discussion).

1. Vulnerability and affectedness rest on sentience, which is a condition that humans share with many other species.[33] Nineteenth-century philosophers as diverse as Bentham (1970 [1789]), Marx (1967 [1844]: 326) and Schopenhauer (1995 [1840]: 175–82) placed sentience at the centre of moral and political theory. Recent philosophers have used the concept to support a more inclusive moral community than do standard accounts that appeal to the special characteristics of human rationality. References to sentience underpin protests against 'man's inhumanity to animals' as well as duties to persons who lack or who have lost the capacity to make rational decisions about their lives but who retain rights of equal moral consideration by virtue of the capacity to experience pain, discomfort and distress.[34] Stressing that point, Bentham (1970 [1789]: ch. 17, part one, para 4) argued that the question of how to treat non-human species should focus not on whether they can talk or reason, but whether they can suffer. His contention that sentience 'gives a being the right to equal moral consideration' has long been central to various 'Eastern' religions such as Buddhism or Jainism. Recognizing that fact, Schopenhauer (1995 [1840]: 44, 163, 178) was one of the first European philosophers to stress its importance for countering the exclusionary nature of a Kantian morality that privileged rational capacities. The assault on 'speciesism' – the doctrine that human distress has greater intrinsic moral significance than animal suffering – is part of a larger challenge to the insider–outsider dualisms, or 'established-outsider relations', that have legitimated inflicting pain and suffering in relations within and between communities (Singer 1977: 26–8).

The empirical evidence indicates that the belief that it is morally reprehensible to cause gratuitous pain and suffering to sentient creatures enjoys much higher levels of support in contemporary Western societies than it did two centuries ago.[35] This is a matter to come back to in the discussion of the civilizing process in Chapter 4. Of the many reasons for the shift in emotional attitudes to

---

[33] Lest this seems banal, it should be remembered that deep ecologists reject the claim that only sentient beings can be 'benefited and harmed' (see Bernstein (1998: 89ff. and 180) for further discussion, and for a defence of the view that 'the capacity for undergoing pleasant and unpleasant experiences is necessary and sufficient for moral patienthood'). Also relevant is Singer (1977: 175).

[34] The importance of Montesquieu's assertion that 'it might be better if we thought of men as sentient rather as rational beings' is stressed in Shklar (1984: 23).

[35] The formulation is not meant to denigrate non-Western civilizations. Observations that the 'harshness and cruelty' which existed [in Europe even two centuries ago] was not unusual, and that 'no native of the Asiatic uplands (could have looked) at it without righteous horror', suggest that the West languished behind these regions, and not vice versa (Schopenhauer 1995 [1840]: 177). To my knowledge, there is no comparative account of civilizing processes that puts Schopenhauer's comments to the test, avoiding as far as possible temptations to romanticize some periods and demonize others.

suffering, the most important is the 'secularization of pain' – the belief that no one should be forced to endure physical agony as punishment for wickedness, or as 'a foretaste of the final retribution', or on account of its redemptive or soterio-logical significance for the mortal self, as was supposed in medieval exalta-tions of martyrological suffering.[36] Changing attitudes to pain and suffering in recent centuries have been bound up with modern orientations to the body and health that reject 'dolorist' beliefs about the exalting or dignifying nature of pain (Bowker 1975; Hinnells and Porter 1999; Rey 1998: 318).[37]

Instead of attaching value to suffering, the secularization thesis supported the relief or elimination of intense pain because of its 'world destroying' effects on the 'embodied self' (Rey 1998: 91, 184ff.; Scarry 1985; Turner 1996: ch. 3).[38] Uncoupled from a 'cosmic moral order' with its promise of an afterlife in which suffering is abolished forever, unrelieved pain has come to be seen as entirely 'meaningless'. The 'affirmation of ordinary life' which is one of the main legacies of the European Enlightenment was central to the emerging belief that pain's permanent exile is one of the highest social and political ideals (Taylor 1989: 13ff., 289ff.).[39]

[36] Useful commentaries on religious conceptions of the abomination of the body can be found in Hufton (1995: 332–4) and Sennett (2002: 132). Such constructions of the body – such reminders that so much can be inscribed on it – indicate that there is no direct route from the vulnerabilities of the body to a cosmopolitan harm principle or any other potentially universal moral precept.

[37] Religious conceptions of pain have shaped social action in diverse ways. A 'ruling of the fourth Lateran Council of 1215 threatened medical practitioners with excommunication if they attended anyone who had not first made a full confession, or had at least sworn to do so', the underlying assumption being that 'the sick should provide for the soul before the body' given that sickness 'may sometimes be the result of sin' (see Rawcliffe 1998: 318). Similar ideas survived well into the nineteenth century. Following Jenner's invention of the vaccination for smallpox at the end of the eighteenth century, debates arose as to whether the disease should be treated or endured as divine punishment (see Hinnells and Porter 1999: 271). As noted earlier, in the nineteenth century many Christians were opposed on biblical grounds to alleviating the pain of childbirth (Hinnells and Porter 1999: xi). No one should doubt that those in pain in the Middle Ages sought available remedies for their dis-tress (Hardcastle 1999: 3–4) and see also Rawcliffe (1998) on the medieval hospital. It is not insignificant that the term pain is derived from *poena*, the Greek for punishment.

[38] It is interesting to compare Bentham and Proust with Pascal and Luther on pain. Pleasure, Bentham (1970 [1789]: part 1, ch. 10, para 10) maintained, 'is in *itself* a good – nay even, setting aside immunity from pain, the only good; pain is in itself an evil – and, indeed, without exception, the only evil'. Proust (quoted in Hardcastle 1999: 173) made the wise observation that 'illness is the doctor to whom we pay most heed: to kindness, to knowledge we make promises only: pain we obey'. Opposing those positions was the dolorist view of Pascal: 'Make me truly understand that the ills of the body are nothing more than punish-ment and the complete manifestation of the ills of the soul' (quoted in Hardcastle 1999: 1). Legitimating misery, Luther (quoted in Williams 1973: 90) is said to have responded to the view that happiness is a legitimate goal with the words, 'leiden, leidin, Kreuz, Kreuz' ('suf-fering ... the Cross ...').

[39] Wolin (1960: 325ff.) describes this change in terms of 'the exposed ... nerve ends of modern man', which is evident in 'heightened ... sensitivity to pain'.

To comprehend long-term patterns of social development, it is of course essential to understand how such changes in collective self-consciousness have been linked with progress in remedying pains that people in earlier societies had no choice but to endure, and where coping mechanisms may have involved the spiritual exaltation of 'meaningful' suffering. It is also important to recognize how the moral relegation of pain has been intertwined with the rise of universalistic beliefs that challenged the moral significance of biological, and indeed racial, differences between groups while also lowering the barriers that separate human from non-human life. Bentham was one of many nineteenth-century thinkers who believed that changing conceptions of the ethical relevance of biological and cultural differences were two sides of the same coin.[40] The belief that 'it is wrong to inflict needless suffering' on humans and non-humans alike has won a significant number of new recruits over the last three decades with positive consequences for the civilizing process within, and in relations between, societies (Singer 1977). Very old ideas have been reworked in that development. Recognition of shared physical vulnerabilities underpinned the cosmopolitan orientations of members of the Hippocratic School as well as the Sophists' challenge to supposedly innate distinctions between Greeks and barbarians (Baldry 1965). Such understandings are at the heart of the ethical universalism that now exists amongst 'enlightened' strata in the more egalitarian cultures of the present age.

To use the vocabulary of the modern era, Ancient Greeks did not think in terms of 'generalizability in ethics', an orientation to the moral life that found its most illustrious expression in Kant's claim that the essence of morality lies precisely in its universality – in the belief that moral agents should only act on maxims that all others can freely adopt (Hare 1963; MacIntyre 1967; Singer 1963). Such was the foundation of Kant's defence of cosmopolitan harm conventions and vision of a global civilizing process, but whether the core of morality is to be found in universalizability has been seriously debated, and not least by feminist scholars who have protested against the implicit devaluation of the moral sensitivities that are intrinsic to the 'ethic of care and responsibility'. The main issue is whether Kantian rationalism strayed too far from the worldly triptych of suffering, sympathy and solidarity. The point is best illustrated by the real case that Schopenhauer described in his critique of Kant's excessive rationalism. Referring to the instance of a mother who killed one child by pouring boiling oil down its throat, and another by burying it alive, he maintained that moral repugnance was not aroused by the mother's disrespect for the categorical

---

[40] As he stated: 'the French have already discovered that the blackness of the skin is no reason why a human being should be abandoned without redress to the caprice of a tormentor. It may one day come to be recognized, that the number of the legs, the villosity of the skin, or the termination of the *os sacrum*, are reasons equally insufficient for abandoning a sensitive creature to the same fate' – 'the day *may* come when the rest of the animal creation may acquire those rights which never could have been withholden from them but by the hand of tyranny' (Bentham 1970 [1789]: ch. 17, part one, para 4; italics in original).

imperative, or by the absence of a fear of punishment in the afterlife, but by the depraved mental state that was so 'utterly bereft of compassion' as to inflict such cruelty (Schopenhauer 1995 [1840]: 169–70, 204–5; also Midgley 1992).[41]

Schopenhauer's position finds support in Rorty's contention that Kant 'sent moral philosophy off in the (wrong) direction', albeit 'from the best possible motives' (Rorty 1989: 192–3). By setting 'rational respect' against 'pity and benevolence', such emotions seemed nothing other than 'dubious, second-rate motives for ethical behaviour'; the upshot was that morality appeared 'something distinct from the ability to notice, and identify with, pain and humiliation' (Rorty 1989: 192–3). From such angles, the essence of morality does not lie in dutiful compliance with universal principles, or in the clinical application of cold reason, but in such emotions as compassion that Kant treated with some disdain – and appropriately, it might be thought, because they are not free from the dangers of 'limited altruism' and indifference to outsiders that were noted earlier (Schopenhauer 1995 [1840]: 144, 172ff.).[42] On the other hand, the mother in Schopenhauer's discussion would not be accused of merely lacking tenderness or compassion but would be thought to act unjustly if she harmed other children, albeit in less serious ways.[43] The comment applies to public principles

[41] Cartwright's introduction to Schopenhauer (1995 [1840]: xxviii) notes the parallel between that critique of Kant and the ethic of care and responsibility developed by Gilligan (1982). It is worth adding that Schopenhauer's example reflects the widespread belief in modern societies that female cruelty to children is especially shocking and reprehensible.

[42] The position taken by the neo-Kantian, W. D. Ross (1939: 306) is worth noting in this context: 'And plainly great violence is done to what we really think, when we are asked to believe that ordinary kindness when not dictated by the sense of duty is no better than cruelty'. He had earlier commented that in 'its typical manifestation', duty involves 'a particularly keen sensitiveness to the rights and interests of other people, coupled with a determination to do what is fair as between them; and it is by no means the case that it tends to be divorced from warm personal feeling; it tends rather to be something superadded to that' (Ross 1939: 304). On some accounts, recent Kantians have shown greater enthusiasm for emotions such as compassion precisely because they wish to affirm the importance of 'connectedness' for the moral life (Oakley 1992: 109ff.). Such considerations were not entirely alien to Kant who thought that people should not strain to avoid sites of human suffering. Exposure to the poor, sick and imprisoned could produce 'the pain of compassion' – that impulse which 'Nature' had instilled 'for effecting what the representation of duty might not accomplish by itself' (quoted in Cunningham 2001: 76–7 and 213). Kant's main point was that the philosophical defence of morality cannot be grounded in the emotions. He opted for the greater reliability of 'coldblooded goodness' over the 'warmth of affection' for precisely that reason (see Cunningham 2001: 222). The belief that morality is not simply a matter of acting justly but depends on the motivating force of the appropriate moral emotions is an ancient one that can be traced back at least to Aristotle (1955: Bk II, ch. 6). The following chapter returns to some of the issues raised by Ross' notion of 'sensitiveness' and Oakley's stress on 'connectedness'.

[43] Admittedly, this is not straightforward, but the issue is where the point is reached where it seems more appropriate to accuse a person of acting unjustly than to blame them for a lack of compassion. Influencing such comments are Adam Smith's reflections on the changing nature of the social bond in modern societies, and on a general lowering of the expectations that people have of each other (see p. 31, n. 1).

in general. Their rational and universal character is designed to ensure justice in relations between strangers, or in relations between independent political communities, that do not have special attachments. The aim is to support the principle that it is morally wrong to treat others in ways that would be unfair if positions were reversed. But justice in those relations also depends on the extent to which public principles affirm the virtue of compassion associated with the care ethic, and on how far they state that unnecessary violence should be condemned not only for its injustice but, following Schopenhauer's reasoning, because of its inhumanity.

From Hegel on, thinkers have criticized the generalizability thesis on the grounds that almost any maxim can be universalized, and it may well be that there are few principles that someone has not enthusiastically embraced, however bizarre the consequences. Hare (1963: ch. 9) cites the example of a Nazi who is willing to universalize the principle that all Jews should be exterminated even when his/her own Jewish ancestry is exposed, adding that it is hard to imagine how any appeal to rational debate would persuade such fanatics to think differently. But public principles cannot depend on the approval of the fanatical. Perhaps their legitimacy is best approached by reflecting on interests that are 'generalizable' rather than on principles that can be universalized. Generalizable interests are those that every person can reasonably have in the circumstances of fragility and vulnerability. Expounding the theme, O'Neill (1996: ch. 6, 2000a) argues that moral agents cannot give convincing reasons for the belief that interests in deceiving, injuring and coercing others are generalizable – interests that everyone can legitimately have. Liars, fraudsters and the like only succeed because they can exploit, and are parasitical on, the widespread commitment to honesty, truthfulness and so forth, and act unjustly. An ethic that begins with human frailty and vulnerability therefore inclines towards the conclusion that, other things being equal, interests in avoiding physical violence or humiliating others, in truthfulness and so forth enjoy a special status precisely because of their generalizability. It is a short step to the argument that justice demands the unconditional rejection of any attempt to make 'a *principle of injury* fundamental to lives, institutions or practices' (O'Neill 1996: 165–6; italics in original). The point applies to the other forms of harm that were described earlier.

2. As noted above, the stress on 'affectedness' in the form of physical suffering has been used to highlight the shortcomings of anthropocentric perspectives that do not extend the scope of moral consideration to non-human species (Goodin *et al.* 1997). Human beings may be said to have 'a stronger claim to compassion' because they are also susceptible to 'mental' anguish that results from the 'enhancement of intelligence'; stressing that point, Schopenhauer (1995 [1840]: 192) concluded that animal suffering is 'only physical' and 'less acute' by comparison. There is sufficient merit in that argument to justify the

claim that non-humans deserve 'equal consideration', but not 'equal treatment' with humans (Singer 1977: 22).[44] Distinctive human traits such as a particular vulnerability to humiliation enter the equation at this point. Levi's account of Auschwitz provided an extensive inventory of modes of degradation that could bring about the 'demolition of a man' without causing physical pain. They ranged from public acts of humiliation to passive exercises in withholding recognition that can occur through the most elementary of exchanges between human beings – those that revolve around 'the look and the look denied', and convey the belief in an unbridgeable gulf between the self and other people (Gordon 2001: ch. 1).[45] Similar effects resulted from excluding the other from a second basic mode of interaction between people – answerability in speech.[46] Only humans can be condemned to a world in which pleas to satisfy the most basic needs go unheard, so reducing them to 'bare life' or condemning them to 'social death' (Agamben 1998; Patterson 1982). For that reason, liberals who have proclaimed that 'cruelty is the worst thing we do' have focused on the evils of pain *and* humiliation, noting that the near universal desire for recognition creates a special kind of vulnerability that the malevolent can exploit (Rorty 1989: xv–xvi; Shklar 1984). Opposing a 'principle of injury' requires support for efforts to eradicate the multiple forms of stigmatization and degradation. That project depends on the realization that what counts as humiliation varies between societies; it requires the hermeneutic imagination to understand the inner world of actual or potential victims; it relies on the unique human capacity for extending empathy and sympathy beyond existing cultural horizons that is essential for the advancement of cosmopolitan harm conventions (see Chapter 5).

3. Unintended and negligent harm, exploitation and complicity require more detailed discussion of the importance of the relationship between

---

[44] However, there seems to be no clear dividing-line between humans and non-humans as far as mental anguish is concerned; indeed the boundary is being redrawn all the time.

[45] Levi (2000: 126) describes his first encounter with Pannwitz who tested his knowledge of chemistry before permitting him to work in the Buna laboratory. 'From that day I have thought about Doktor Pannwitz many times and in many ways. I have asked myself how he really functioned as a man … above all, when I was once more a free man, I wanted to meet him again, not from a spirit of revenge, but merely from a personal curiosity about the soul. Because that look was not one between two men; and if I had known how completely to explain the nature of that look, which came as if across the glass window of an aquarium between two beings who live in different worlds, I would also have explained the essence of the great folly of the third Germany.'

[46] One of many examples is the guard's response to Levi's question about the reasons for his refusal to let him grab an icicle hanging outside his window to quench his thirst. The answer, 'there is no "why" here' (*hier ist kein warum*), constituted a denial of membership of the human community (Levi 2000: 29). Other examples of degradation through systematic exclusion from the normal 'circuit of human communication' are discussed in Gordon (2001: 47).

justice and 'complex responsibility' for the development of those conventions. Reflections on who has the greatest responsibility for compensating the victims of rising sea levels (where the probable cause is 'man made' global warming) highlight the significance of injustice in the Aristotelian sense (see p. 69). Echoing Wollstonecraft's claim (quoted in Lu 2000: 262) that 'it is justice, not charity, that is wanting in the world', green political theorists have argued that the duty to compensate, and the primary responsibility for avoiding future harm, fall on those who have enjoyed a surfeit of the beneficial. Theorists have stressed that the duties that arise from the existence of harms that are linked with increasing levels of human interconnectedness should be centred on redistributive or restorative justice rather than on 'an obligation of charity to be met through the exercise of compassion' (Dobson 2003: 28; see Lichtenberg 1981: 87ff.).

Analyses of global environmental justice have emphasized the added difficulty of 'tracking chains of causation and apportioning blame and responsibility' whenever the focus shifts from the paradigmatic examples of mental and bodily harm (Eckersley 2006: 102). In this context, it is worth noting that many transnational advocacy networks, which are organized to deal with 'issues involving bodily harm to vulnerable individuals', have had most success 'when there is a short and clear causal link ... assigning responsibility' (Keck and Sikkink 1998: 27).[47] Even if it was possible to settle debates about the precise extent to which humans have caused climate change, other issues arise about how to allocate causal responsibility and how to determine the just distribution of national obligations (see Grieco 1988). The absence of clear evidence about causal links that leave little doubt about the source and degree of responsibility can limit the effectiveness of transnational advocacy networks. On the other hand, various public and private actors have not suspended discussions about moral and political responsibilities with respect to climate change until exact information about the causal role of different societies or strata comes to hand (not that the most advanced scientific inquiries could deliver incontestable conclusions about such matters). Assessments of future probabilities have led to greater clarity about the urgency of reducing harm to the environment although disputes about fairness may, in the long-run, defer or entirely prevent effective collective action.

---

[47] As Gibney (2004: 48ff.) has shown, complex questions about causal and moral responsibility arise in connection with duties to refugees. Framing that discussion in terms of the harm principle, the argument is that Western governments have often been far more involved in causing refugee problems than they care to admit, not only through military intervention, but, and often less clearly, through the sale or provision of military equipment, or as a result of the 'destabilising effects of neo-liberal economic policies and structural adjustment forced on countries by Western-funded international organizations, such as the IMF and World Bank'. That said, the relationship between the specific harm that any state causes and the scale of its responsibilities are notoriously hard to assess (Gibney 2004: 54).

Considerations of justice are clearly central here. There is growing recognition that generalizing certain interests and lifestyles can lead to devastating consequences for distant strangers as well as co-nationals, and that they may impose unfair, onerous burdens on future generations. Recalling the philosophical differences between Kant and Schopenhauer, it is important to ask if failures to comply with universalizable principles are more serious than a lack of sympathy for the victims of environmental degradation, or more troubling than the absence of emotional investment in the future of the species. The focus on the interests that every person can have – interests that can be promoted without causing unjustifiable harm to other people – generates principles of global justice and suggests how compassion should be channelled.

4. All forms of harm constitute injustice in the sense of an 'excess of the harmful and a deficiency of the beneficial' but, prior to turning now to negligent harm, it is important to note Smith's contention that injustice is a form of harm (Smith 1982 [1759]: 79).[48] That is abundantly clear when people knowingly expose others to the danger of harm. Deliberations about the nature of the harm that is involved in exporting asbestos production capture what is morally at stake (Shue 1981). Following decisions to introduce stringent health and safety regulations in the United States, some business enterprises transferred the relevant technologies to societies with less robust systems of protection. That commercial decision took advantage of a workforce that lacked available information about health issues relating to the industry. Deception occurred as a result of the failure to share knowledge about risks that might have led potential employees to decline to work in the plants, or to accept employment on the basis of informed consent, and on condition that health risks were reduced. In that case, negligence was linked with exploitation – with taking advantage of the ignorance of the vulnerable. The 'generalizability' principle is breached when one person deceives another, or withholds morally significant information, or when the exporting parties, as in the example under discussion, act on a maxim that they would have rejected, had positions with the weaker parties been reversed (O'Neill 2000a: 78–9).[49] Alternatively, the harm of 'being kept in ignorance' (Lucas 1966: 173) constitutes an injustice from the standpoint of an ethic of generalizable interests. For the reasons that were outlined earlier, the dominant parties are open to the accusation of lacking compassion, or of treating

---

[48] The etymological link between the two concepts is worth emphasizing. See Liddell and Scott (1980: 13) on the affinities between *adikeo* (to injure), *adikos* (wrongdoing) and *dike* (justice).

[49] As Ewing (1959: 135) states, deception leads someone to act in ways that could not win their consent – 'otherwise deceit would be unnecessary' – and a person is deprived of the opportunity and right to decide what is in their interest.

others with contempt, when presented with the opportunity to trade others' vulnerability for material reward.

5. Deeper implications are apparent in the case of particular forms of exploitation, specifically unjust enrichment where, for example, the affluent profit from the weakness of vulnerable producers, or when current generations gain from transferring environmental burdens to future generations. Through lifestyle choices that involve, inter alia, paying a 'fair price' for commodities, or reducing carbon footprints, people can register concern with the unintended harms they may do to those positioned further along the global webs of interconnectedness, and in distant places, recognizing that they may have few, if any, opportunities for achieving transnational accountability. But such corrective measures do not go far enough when a certain threshold has been crossed so that individuals benefit not just from occasional, random transactions but from the structures that bind them together in asymmetrical ways. When that point is reached, problems of injustice can only be addressed through systematic changes that are designed to ensure protection for the vulnerable.

Modern reformulations of a Kantian ethic have argued for reforming global political and economic institutions that fail the test of justice, understood as complying with moral principles to which all can give their informed consent (O'Neill 1991: 296–8). An ancient idea, namely the notion in Roman law that 'what touches all should be agreed by all' (*tanget omnes ab omnibus approbatur*) underlies the approach. It informed Kant's cosmopolitan maxim of personal conduct, namely that people should always consider whether their actions can woo each other's consent. Recent variants on that theme link the principle with claims for institutional reform that break with Kant's commitment to territorial sovereignty. On the basis of *tanget onmnes*, all people have an equal right to be represented in decision-making arenas, or in some way consulted about decisions that may affect them adversely; they are entitled 'to refuse or renegotiate offers', and to convey dissatisfaction with the larger political context in which decisions are made (including the existence of global institutions that do not take much account of their interests, and the forms of structural harm to which they are exposed). The corollary is that the dominant institutions and practices should be assessed by the extent to which they are answerable to all those who 'stand to be affected' by them (Habermas 1989: 82ff., 1990; see also Eckersley 2004: ch. 7). Such normative ideals feature in aspirations for cosmopolitan democracy and transnational public spheres that defend taking the achievements of national democracies into the global domain (Fraser 2007; Held 1995; O'Neill 1991: 302). As noted elsewhere, such arguments link the harm principle with a vision of an advanced global civilizing process in which customary insider–outsider dualisms yield ground to cosmopolitan political structures and parallel shifts in moral sensibilities (Linklater 2007d).

6. The character of such an advance becomes clearer by turning to the notions of moral and political responsibility that are linked with the ethics of complicity, and specifically with involvement, possibly despite the best intentions of those concerned, in 'mediated' harm caused by institutions. Rising levels of mediated harm point to the limitations of a doctrine of 'simple' responsibility, and emphasize the need for 'complex' or 'reflexive' responsibility (Davis 2001: 6ff.).[50] For present purposes, simple responsibility requires nothing more than compliance with existing norms. There is no expectation that people should look beyond them for instruction on how to act. Complex responsibility places greater demands on individuals and institutions. It requires them to take the initiative in reflecting on how far their actions, the practices in which they are involved, and the organizations in which they are implicated, cause harm that may not be officially proscribed but should be avoided and reduced wherever possible.[51]

Green political theory and practice have been in the forefront of efforts to promote complex responsibility in the form of greater reflectiveness and foresight with respect to what is often imperceptible, trans-boundary harm. They have defended the transformation of political community with the aim of creating higher levels of global accountability (Eckersley 2004; Mason 2001, 2005). Explorations of complex responsibility also raise issues about personality traits that are no less significant for such designs. Extended notions of the concept take issue with the self-contained self that has been condemned by the critics of liberal individualism and indeed, as noted earlier, by those who deny that the harm principle can support measures to promote global solidarity (see p. 88; Linklater 2006a). They oppose what Elias (1978: 119) called *homo clausus*, the closed self that jealously guards individual freedoms and the private sphere, and makes social responsibilities dependent on irrefutable evidence of a direct causal link between personal conduct and harm to others, or on contracted agreements (Davis 2001: 7–8). Complex responsibility supports a concept of the self that is 'habitually on the look-out' for ways in which actions and affiliations promote personal well-being but 'at the cost of impeding' the interests of people who 'mean nothing to him' (Green 1906: 245). The alternative to *homo clausus*, Elias (1978: 125, 135) argued, is *homines aperti* – more open selves that, in the context of the present argument, may be said to combine sensitivity to connectedness with an orientation towards extended ethical responsibilities that holds

[50] The point holds for unintended harm and unjust enrichment, and for all instances of 'harm at a distance'.

[51] Young (2006) develops a parallel argument pitching what she calls the 'social connection model of responsibility' against the 'limited liability' framework. While the latter is concerned only with transparent causal links between actors and those they affect, the former addresses less obvious ways in which people cause harm, for example by behaving in ways that perpetuate unjust structures.

the key to the progress of cosmopolitan harm conventions (Staub 2003).[52] To return to a point that was made in the introduction to this work, constructions of the self that are open to such cosmopolitan responsibilities are critical for solving the problems that will arise as long as actual social moralities lag behind the mentalities that are needed to control the processes that bind people together in longer webs of interconnectedness, and to govern them so that they can live together without the confinements and constraints of unnecessary harm (Elias 2007b [1992]: 67). Movement in that direction would signify the emergence of a major global civilizing process – a new stage in the social and political evolution of the species.

7. The analysis of complex responsibility, rather like the earlier discussion of omissive harm, sheds light on what it means to follow the harm principle, revealing that it gives rise to more extensive obligations than critics have realized. As for omissive harm, only on a restricted model of causality, it has been noted, can the failure to rescue, when it is a person's power to assist, be regarded as a legitimate refusal to confer a benefit as opposed to a potentially punishable harm (see pp. 58–9). That discussion can be linked with a doctrine of generalizable interests in different ways – for instance, on the grounds that no 'vulnerable agent' can generalize an interest in indifference to suffering (O'Neill 1996: 193–4), or on the related argument that inaction, when another is in need of rescue, risks repayment with similar apathy if positions are ever reversed (Geras 1998), or again because the belief that it is permissible to prolong suffering through inaction cannot be adopted as a 'universal' interest. Debates surrounding Singer's argument for obligations to relieve famine demonstrate that large issues remain about the scale of individual and group responsibilities (Aiken and La Follette 1977). Few seem prepared to assume the obligations that Singer (1972) defends on utilitarian grounds; few are willing to make that commitment on the basis of generalizable interests.[53] But the merit of his ethical position does not stand or fall on the number of people who are currently swayed by such arguments. It is significant that many support humanitarian programmes, fully realizing that it is highly unlikely that positions with the victims are likely to be reversed, and that they will ever be able to repay inaction with equivalent indifference. The reasons that are often advanced for assisting the vulnerable suggest that some sense of complex responsibility – some degree of compassion for people

---

[52] It should be stressed that Elias's distinction between *homo clausus* and *homines aperti* was largely concerned with the failures of methodological individualism in the social sciences and in philosophy, and not with the ethical issues that are under discussion here. But the themes are undoubtedly linked.

[53] The moral imperative being that 'if it is in our power to prevent something bad from happening, without thereby sacrificing anything of comparable moral importance, we ought, morally, to do it' (Singer 1972: 230).

elsewhere – underpins the small advances that have been made in promoting higher levels of solidarity.

8. The importance of generalizable interests with regard to public harm is most evident with respect to the 'free rider' problem. Like deceit, 'free riding' is not generalizable, but is parasitical on broad compliance with public principles that makes defection from cooperative schemes profitable for those involved. Centralized agencies can reduce the attractions of free riding, which is one reason why damage to public institutions (through corruption for example) harms society as a whole. Turning to world politics, many approaches have argued that the 'free rider' problem is especially acute given the absence of a higher power that can ensure 'cooperation under anarchy'. Those perspectives have emphasized that international regimes have a special role in creating incentives to cooperate and disincentives to defect (Keohane 1989). The global equivalent of harm to society occurs when, for example, a state breaches the principle of diplomatic immunity, or damages international organizations that have the responsibility for creating, administering and enforcing primary harm conventions. The former harms the society of states, although people generally may feel that their interests are damaged in the process. In the second case, it is perfectly legitimate to regard damage to global institutions as harming humanity because the prospects for collective responses to worldwide problems are reduced.

9. Earlier remarks about exploitation, complicity and omissive harm are germane to the discussion of structural harm; notions of generalizable interests and complex responsibility are also relevant here. The key point about structural harm is that it has a special relationship with arguments for transforming the way in which the entire species is organized. Marxism has had a critical role in analysing largely unplanned processes of development that affect humanity as a whole, the growth of transnational or structural harm as people have become more closely tied together, and the need for political projects that break free from national horizons and regard the future of humanity as their object – and not least by working towards a condition in which more people can make more of their history under conditions that they have chosen for themselves. The relatively recent idea of structural harm is largely responsible for the development of moral aspirations that are more radical than those linked with restricted, agent-centred or 'national' approaches to harm. The concept has contributed to an awareness of connections between distant strangers, structured inequalities and injustices, and the need for ethical reflections on the ideal rights and duties of people who are, in one sense, far apart, and yet closely tied together by transnational structures and processes.

To conclude this part of the discussion, it is important to consider the relationship between the modest aims traditionally associated with the harm principle and the varied and extensive obligations that have just been outlined. The latter may be thought to conflict with the central purpose of that principle which, for classical liberals, is to establish the primacy of duties to avoid unnecessary harm without imposing burdensome obligations on people. They are not obliged to behave selflessly or heroically – hence the distinction between the 'stringent' duty of non-maleficence, as described by Ross, and supererogatory obligations, or optional duties of beneficence. Compliance with the harm principle, it may be thought, requires little moral imagination; it is no more than what should be expected of 'normal persons' (Warnock 1971: 81–2). For that reason, the main obligations that flow from the harm principle are at the heart of the criminal law in liberal societies (see pp. 43–7). Those are enforceable duties between members of the same society. Considerable merit falls on those who do more than is necessary for the survival of society, especially when they risk personal harm or endanger their lives. Their actions go beyond the realm of binding obligations.

An obvious challenge to the harm principle is that it is hardly a moral achievement to get through the average day without harming other people – though some may suggest that, much of the time, a rather different view applies to international relations.[54] The counter-argument is that ideas of complex responsibility, which are especially relevant to discussions of complicity, unjust enrichment, and omissive or structural harm, demonstrate that there is more to that principle than the ideal of minimum rules of co-existence between people who live behind protective barriers.[55] The contention that support for the harm principle requires 'communication communities' in which the vulnerable can protest against the injuries they have suffered, or may suffer, points to global ideals that are more usually associated with the utopian strands of Western political thought than with more modest liberal ambitions – and particularly with the belief, that was most famously defended by Kant and Marx, that far-reaching changes will be required in the ways in which people are bound together if they are to deal with the challenges of global integration.

The final point in this section is that the harm principle has been criticized because it places insufficient demands on moral agents, while broadening its

---

[54] With respect to everyday life, that comment is plainly true, although broken relationships, private or professional, suggest a different conclusion because, as everyone knows, the relevant skills and sensitivities are often at a premium especially, but not only, when tensions between people arise. Moreover, the question of how to reduce the harm we do in everyday life has acquired new meaning as a result of, for example, concerns about personal carbon footprints or unjust enrichment.

[55] Green's comment on the importance of being 'habitually on the look-out' for ways in which harm may be caused was noted earlier (p. 101). Another English idealist, Bradley (1962: 3–4), advanced a similar view by defining moral responsibility as answerability to others 'for what [the agent] has done, or ... has neglected and left undone', and by supporting accountability in the form of a 'moral tribunal' or 'court of conscience' that can settle accounts. Such ideas are central to the cosmopolitan harm principle.

meaning and implications diverts it from its critical purpose of limiting the scope of the criminal law. Conflicts between obligations will arise, of course, even when the criminal law is confined to punishing what liberals regard as the worst harms. But that problem will be compounded if more extensive obligations are derived from the harm principle, or if it is invoked to support ethical ideals that go beyond the 'moral minimum' that is needed to preserve orderly, 'civilized' societies. Complex questions arise about how humans should act when, for example, prima facie obligations to avoid harm clash, or when it is impossible to prevent one form of harm without causing another. That is familiar territory in international relations theory where realists argue that protesting against human rights violations in another society may harm national security, and that colluding with oppressive regimes may be unpalatable but strategically necessary – or when English School analyses of humanitarian intervention show how different values come into conflict (see pp. 130–1). Such emphases on the tragic qualities of world politics will be discussed in the next chapter. A prior task is to consider ways of thinking about a moral hierarchy of unjustified harms.

A hierarchy of harms?

Harms vary according to the magnitude of the suffering they cause, but few can match the intensity of the pain and anguish inflicted by the merciless torturer. More than anyone else, Montaigne (1965 [1580]: 117; Quint 1998: 52) encouraged a shift in Western moral and political thought by arguing that cruelty should be condemned as 'the extremest of all vices', adding that no vice could be hated more. In recent times, the best-known formulation states that if 'liberal and humane people … were asked to rank the vices', they would not hesitate to 'put cruelty first'; basic moral intuitions express the belief that cruelty is 'the worst thing we do' (Shklar 1984: 44).

The body and pain, often curiously neglected in social and political analysis, stand at the centre of that humanist ethic.[56] It has been suggested that if any experience demonstrates the 'biological unity' of the species, and symbolizes the 'universality' of the human condition, it is pain – the ultimate adversary that people invariably struggle 'with all their energy' to repel (Rey 1998: 1ff.; see

---

[56] Recent sociological thought has rediscovered the body which had been central to the writings of Marx and Elias. When not entirely absent from sociological analysis, the body hovered in the background, exercising an unacknowledged influence, awaiting explication. The same can be said of many approaches to international relations which have been more concerned with the abstractions of states and geopolitical dynamics than with their effect on what Booth (2005: 272ff.) calls 'real people in real places'. Turner (1992: esp. 252ff., 1993a, 1996, 2006) has been centrally involved in recovering the sociology of the body, and in making precariousness and vulnerability central to the defence of universal human rights (see also Nettleton and Watson 1998: introduction).

Bending 2000: ch. 5). No appeal to the controversial subject of universal reason is necessary to establish the most accessible and direct, but far from automatic, route to human solidarity: the widely shared belief that 'well-being' begins with 'freedom from pain' (Montaigne, quoted in Williams and Bendelow 1998: 156). There have been many variations on what has been called the 'vulnerability principle',[57] but here the emphasis is on first-generation Frankfurt School theorists whose reflections on that theme will be connected with process sociology in Chapter 4. Schopenhauer was a major influence on Horkheimer's thinking on that subject. Echoing Montaigne, he argued that of all crimes, cruelty stands out as the most unforgivable; 'nothing shocks our moral feelings' as much as the pleasure some take in causing suffering (Schopenhauer 1995 [1840]: 136, 169). For Horkheimer (quoted in Stirk 1992: 178), 'fear of death and suffering' is the foundation of 'correct solidarity' between 'finite beings' who can sympathize with one another's struggles to improve and lengthen life, and who can broaden such concerns to include all sentient beings.[58] Echoing such themes in his philosophical reflections on ethics after Auschwitz, Adorno (2000: 167ff.; see Bernstein 2002: ch. 8) called for 'a new categorical imperative' that stems from the realization that people 'may not know what is good', but they have acquired a certain clarity about 'inhuman' behaviour and about visions of the 'bad life' that should be unconditionally opposed.[59]

The point of such references to the body and its vulnerabilities has been to show that major cultural differences are no impediment to a global agreement on cruel or 'inhuman' conduct, or to a concerted effort to reject despicable images of the 'good life'. Furthermore, as the idea of an overlapping consensus indicates, it is the possibility of an agreement on such fundamentals that is important rather than the precise philosophical or religious reasons that are advanced for opposing harm – grounds that are invariably divisive in any case.[60] Core features

[57] Freeman (2003: 148) argues that the 'vulnerability principle' has at its core a sense of 'moral responsibility for the known and foreseeable consequences of our actions, and special obligations to those who have been harmed by what we have done, or are vulnerable to future harm from what we propose to do'. Freeman adds that people generally recognize that those who have special relations with them are especially vulnerable to their actions or inactions. However, global interconnectedness has led to new vulnerabilities that demand a 'universalist' response.

[58] Schopenhauer's post-anthropocentric ethic influenced the claim that vulnerability based on the 'shared experience of suffering and creaturely finitude' does not just underpin solidarity with 'the community of men lost in the universe', but is the basis for 'solidarity with life in general' (Horkheimer 1974a: 75 and 1993: 36; also Adorno 2000: 145).

[59] See Geuss (2005) on the emphasis on the abolition of 'superfluous suffering' in first-generation Frankfurt School critical theory.

[60] Three examples may suffice. First, the point has been made that various writings on the world religions have highlighted their reliance on the common experience of suffering to invite the faithful to overcome divisions of language, ethnicity, race, class and so forth. The stress on the divisive role of faith traditions has been rightly emphasized by various responses to the current revival of religion, but it is important to balance that observation

of the human condition create the potential for such a moral consensus but, as stressed earlier, there is no easy route from shared vulnerabilities to a cosmopolitan ethic (Habermas: 1979a: 176–7). Perhaps the claim that only certain interests are generalizable provides the bridge between universal aspects of human experience and cosmopolitan norms without committing 'the naturalistic fallacy' (Moore 1959).[61] The non-generalizability of an interest in cruelty paved the way for agreements about human rights. Described as the first human rights protocols, the 1947 Nuremberg Code outlawed medical experimentation of the kind that occurred in the Nazi death camps, affirming in its fourth provision the obligation to 'avoid all unnecessary physical and mental suffering and injury'. Efforts to abolish torture have their roots in the supposition that most people recognize that no other act creates such 'distance' between persons, or presumes such a steep gradient between self and other (Scarry 1985: 36; Schopenhauer 1995 [1840]: 204–5).[62] The belief that the infliction of pain is 'scandalous' is also evident in Article 4 of the Universal Declaration of Human Rights where it is stated that 'no one shall be subjected to torture or to cruel, inhuman and degrading treatment or punishment' (Asad 1997). Rejections of 'a principle of injury' that authorizes cruelty take account of vulnerability to humiliation as well as

with their progressive role in calling on devotees to take 'suffering seriously' and to extend sympathies to 'the ends of the earth' (Armstrong 2004). Second, others look not to religion but to 'trans-social and trans-historical' experiences of vulnerability to ground a doctrine of human rights. In addition to Turner (1993a, 2006), others who have worked this seam include Butler (2004) and Lu (2000). Following the US military response to 9/11, Butler (2004: xiv, 8–9, 30) posed the question of how public policy and national culture can respond to 'unexpected violence and loss' without promoting its 'further dissemination'. From where, she asks, might the relevant principles emerge if not from the 'apprehension of a common human vulnerability'. Third, eschewing religious and secular foundationalism, others, most notably Rorty, support a 'sentimental education' that enlists 'the stories we tell ourselves' in fictional and other modes of experience to extend sympathy to those whose suffering has long been devalued or ignored because they are outside 'our' community (Morris 1997: 38ff.). Interestingly, Rorty (1989: 192) defends 'moral progress' as movement 'in the direction of greater solidarity' which is not propped up by some notion of 'human essence' or the 'core self', but by the ability to regard 'traditional differences (of tribe, race, religion, customs, and the like) as unimportant when compared with similarities with respect to pain and humiliation'. See Barker-Benfield (1992: 224ff.), Brissenden (1974) and Steintrager (2004) on the rise of such sensitivities during the eighteenth century, and also Moore (1972). Their relationship with the civilizing process is discussed in Chapter 4.

[61] See Habermas (1979a: 176–7): 'In living, the organisms themselves make an evaluation to the effect that self-maintenance is preferable to the destruction of the system, reproduction of life to death, health to the risks of sickness.' But, ethically, nothing follows from the 'descriptive statement that living systems prefer certain states to others'. Referring to moral possibilities that are inherent in 'the structures of ordinary language communication', Habermas adds that 'the *theoretician* does not have the same possibility of choice in relation to the validity claims immanent in speech as he does in relation to the basic biological value of health' (italics in original).

[62] Determination has been stiffened by greater understanding of how quickly 'ordinary' humans can become inured to involvement in torture (Scarry 1985: ch. 1).

pain. In response to genocide, racism and apartheid, modern international society has introduced norms that prohibit 'serious *mental* and physical harm' to the members of other linguistic, racial or ethnic groups. Related changes have taken place with respect to the rights of indigenous peoples. Recognition of the history of assaults on cultural integrity that included displacing and resettling peoples, physical violence and attempted extinction underpin the recent shift from the 1957 International Labour Organisation declaration that saw no harm in assimilating indigenous peoples into mainstream cultures (Thornberry 2002: see p. 135, n. 36).

When seen in conjunction with prohibitions of 'unnecessary suffering' and 'superfluous injury' that were a central part of the Hague Conventions of 1899 and 1907 – and which provided the foundation for the prosecution of crimes against humanity and war crimes at the end of the Second World War – those developments can be regarded as evidence of moral progress in embedding a 'principle of humaneness' in international society. On that principle, a 'culture, society, or historical era' has advanced if its 'laws, customs, institutions and practices' display increased 'sensitivity to', and 'less tolerance' of, 'the pain and suffering of other human beings' (Macklin 1977: 371–2). Assaults on cruelty reflect long-term patterns of change which are not guaranteed to survive, especially, as realists argue, when they clash with national security interests.[63] From other standpoints, progress in reaching agreements about what many regard as natural rights, however hard-won, may not amount to a major advance after all. The objection is that although many societies have similar ideas about acts that are prohibited by 'the principle of humaneness', they do not necessarily endorse the liberal proposition that 'cruelty is the worst thing we do', or they do not support it without major qualifications.[64]

Disputes about the relative importance of civil and political as against social and economic rights are worth noting here. Those debates are open to different

---

[63] Developments since 9/11 demonstrated that support for what had seemed to be a secure global norm can weaken quickly under conditions of actual or perceived insecurity (see Foot 2006). A great deal of attention has focused on the section of Standards of Conduct for Interrogation under 18 U.S.C. 2340–2340A that legitimated coercive techniques as long as injuries did not cause physical pain 'so severe that death, organ failure, or permanent damage resulting in a loss of significant body function will likely result', and as long as psychological suffering did not lead to 'long-term mental harm' (see Greenberg and Dratel 2005: 172–217). See Linklater (2007e) on the relationship between torture and the civilizing process.

[64] Agreements on cruelty are often qualified in important respects. Many national penal codes affirm the individual's right to physical integrity, but deny that the death penalty is cruel and degrading (see Sarat 2001); many defend the right of women to be free from violence while entering reservations about female circumcision/female genital mutilation (Rahman and Toubia 2000: 23–6, 59, 102ff.). As the recent fate of the global norm against torture has shown, agreed rights to personal integrity can be suspended or qualified on the grounds that strategic necessity or supreme national emergency have overriding importance.

interpretations: they may be cited as evidence that a Western liberal hierarchy of harms is rejected by many non-Western societies, or they may seem to indicate that support for some liberal values comes with major concerns about the biases and limitations of the broader liberal project. The belief that cruelty is the worst thing we do can become the basis for self-righteous interference in others' internal affairs in order to end serious violations of human rights. Whether such interventions produce more problems than they solve is clearly a central issue, but the larger question is that the self-congratulatory tone in which some liberals may describe their efforts to protect other peoples from cruelty at the hands of their own regimes can deflect attention from the harmful effects of Western neo-liberal structures and practices, and from the collective failure to take relatively simple steps to address the problem of structural or transnational harm (Richardson 1997, 2000).[65] The idea that global civilizing processes must not be tied to narrowly-defined liberal values stems from the useful reminder that many non-Western groups and societies are not drawn towards the liberal hierarchy of harms, and may be repelled by its casual indifference to material deprivation and economic hardship (Bull 1979a).

Those concerns are reflected in philosophical analyses of the liberal hierarchy of wrongs in which cruelty is regarded as the most reprehensible of harms. The 'common sense hierarchy of immorality' has been accused of acquiescing in social indifference which has been described as 'the greater cause of avoidable human suffering', especially if it is linked with contempt for humanity (Box 1983: 21). An individualistic, agent-centred approach to harmful wrongdoing is seen as freeing actors from the collective responsibility to reduce 'social harm' (Hillyard *et al.* 2004). It is linked with an impoverished public policy, of the kind associated with the classical liberal 'nightwatchman' state where no stand is taken against structures that generate economic and social inequalities (Kekes 1996).

Important questions are raised by the contention that indifference surpasses cruelty as a cause of 'avoidable human suffering'. It may be right that indifference can spring from hostility to humanity, whereas a cruel act may be motivated by a specific desire to harm one and only one person, although the point can be reversed (Box 1983: 21). Those who believe that cruelty is the most extreme of all vices may cite the evidence that 'the suffering of torture victims', just like

---

[65] An interesting twist on this argument maintains that powerful forces in US Administrations in the 1990s argued against humanitarian intervention on the grounds that nothing could be done to assist societies that were consumed by 'atavistic' ethnic violence. The argument was that the distinction between civilized, liberal societies and the barbarism of societies that were still mired in violent conflict conveniently overlooked the part that neo-liberal economic strategies played in promoting economic insecurity and poverty, in widening social and economic inequalities and, however indirectly, in fermenting political unrest that often had an 'ethnic' dimension but was not 'atavistic' at core (Sadowski 1998).

the suffering of rape victims or those who have been held hostage, does not end with 'the termination of violence'. The return to normal life rarely brings 'respite'. Those who have suffered in such ways are 'doubly victims': first, by facing 'extreme violence', and, later, by being 'governed' by 'crueller psychological laws' that may condemn them for the rest of their lives to a 'malevolent fate' (Mayerfeld 1999: 90–1, 151–2).[66] On that argument, the thesis that 'cruelty is the worst thing we do' seems incontrovertible, but great caution must be exercised when constructing a hierarchy of harms with presumed universal validity. Some will question or reject the notion that indifference can cause greater harm, but critics of the liberal approach are right that every hierarchy contains the possibility of overlooking harms that seem less 'serious' from some standpoints, and of deferring efforts to deal with them on the supposition that ending cruelty must come first. Critics stress the limitations of such conceptions of global ethics, particularly when the struggle to end cruelty is not part of a broader project to eradicate needless harm. The claim that there is 'no thing as absolute ethical neutrality' invites the further observation that 'the development of an ethical code governing international relations must evolve by extrapolating values from the ethically relevant but restricted practices of the affected communities' (Margolis 1971: 127). As the discourse theory of morality states, societies must shape that project in a deliberative manner, knowing that the precise character of any global project to end pointless harm cannot be decided in advance by any way of life (Linklater 1998).

Establishing the principle that moral agents have no right to exclude anyone from what O'Neill (1996: 188ff.) calls 'the scope of ethical consideration' provides some guarantee that attempts to create cosmopolitan harm conventions will not be blind to unfamiliar forms of suffering. The crucial point is that all efforts to create global norms should operate on the principle that 'all those affected (must) have an effective opportunity to voice their demands for rights on the basis of concrete experiences of violated integrity, discrimination, and oppression' (Habermas 1998a: 25).[67] Advances in embedding 'the principle of humaneness' in world politics can only occur by following such protocols. In that manner, the duties that people have as members of particular communities can be harmonized with obligations to the rest of the species. The Stoic thinker, Hierocles, observed that people are located in concentric circles of obligation; the question was how to draw the outer circles in towards the centre so that dealings with strangers contain something of the moral concern that is usually reserved for interaction with friends and family members in the inner rings

---

[66] The traumatic effects of violence and cruelty are often magnified in the lives of children whose capacity to trust other people is subsequently destroyed, but a similar sense of social alienation is widespread in adult trauma victims – see Apfel and Simon (1996) and Edkins (2003).

[67] A parallel with the idea of 'thick dialogue' that is 'closely attentive to the sufferings of vulnerable creatures' can be found in Dallmayr (2001: 346).

(Nussbaum 2001: 388). A cosmopolitan harm principle, constructed through open dialogue, is central to the effort to embed that 'civilizing' ethical ideal in global structures.

Conclusion

The Stoic claim that people violate the most basic principles of humanity when they cause unnecessary harm remains central to any cosmopolitan ethic. The question of what the harm principle means for world order is not answered by listing the negative obligations that people owe each other. Positive duties are also involved. Cosmopolitan harm conventions are ways of embedding 'the principle of humaneness' in international relations; they are crucial for moral progress, understood as the reduction or elimination of useless suffering, and as the creation of global institutions that promote respect for the principle that everyone has an equal right to voice concerns about harm and suffering in any decision-making structures that affect them.

The argument has been that the most immediate points of solidarity between strangers lie in common vulnerabilities to mental and physical suffering; therein lies the possibility of an overlapping agreement about 'inhumane behaviour'. Cosmopolitan harm conventions can be said to be immanent in the way in which all societies have been organized, in that all must protect members from superfluous pain and suffering, and all have at least the capacity to extend similar rights to all other persons. The universal human rights culture, augmented by recent developments in international criminal law, is the main contemporary expression of that shared immanent potential.

Classical realists are associated with the view that focusing on such novel features of the modern states-system can blind analysts to the fundamental respects in which international politics have remained the same for centuries, if not millennia. In the anarchic condition, the argument is, states often decide that they can only protect their security by inflicting terrible harm on other societies. No coercive mechanism can enforce compliance with global harm conventions when states decide that core interests require their violation. Those observations suggest that the sociological investigation of the problem of harm in world politics will discover that the similarities between states-systems are greater than the apparent differences, and conclude that international history has been governed by unchanging laws rather than aspirations for moral progress. Those comments do not encourage the view that the role of cosmopolitan harm conventions will increase in future. Other approaches provide their own conjectures about what the sociology of harm in world politics might discover. The next chapter considers the tensions between those views in more detail.

3

Harm and international relations theory

The widening of the circle of those with rights under 'the principle of humaneness' indicates that there have been advances in the moral spheres of international politics, but whether there has been overall progress is another matter. The answer to that question depends on how far such progressions lag behind changes in other areas that restrict their scope, limit their influence, and have the ability to throw them into reverse. The idea of the ambiguities of interconnectedness captures the main issue here which is that advances in learning how to co-exist harmoniously and to assist the vulnerable in distant places have to be viewed alongside the evolution of the capacity to inflict ever more devastating forms of harm on more and more people, and over greater areas. Their relative speed of development – the rates of acceleration or deceleration at different points in time, and the extent to which moral progressions have ever kept pace with revolutions in the power to injure – is a central issue for the analysis of the problem of harm in world politics.

One of the bleaker interpretations of the history of interconnectedness states 'that war is in a sense the habitual condition of mankind, that is to say that human blood must constantly flow somewhere or other on earth; and that for every nation peace is no more than a respite' (de Maistre 1965: 61). Hyperbole no doubt, but that sweeping statement captures the more pessimistic interpretation of the past and future prospects that is usually associated with realism.[1] There is no need to dwell either on its critique of perspectives that assume that geopolitical forces can be bent to the will of the utopians, or on its scepticism towards those who suppose that, even without a balance of power, a condition can be reached in which states 'have power to hurt and will do none' (Shakespeare, Sonnet 94). It is sufficient to note that from the realist standpoint, competition for power and security invariably outruns and undoes any advances that may have occurred in incorporating cosmopolitan harm conventions into international law and morality. Its core assumption is that states refuse to support them when they clash with vital interests, and will abandon restraints on the capacity to injure whenever circumstances demand that course of action. If

---

[1] It was also the starting-point for many Enlightenment views that the purpose of politics is to end misery and misfortune (see Nieman 2002: 37ff.).

realism is correct then the sociology of states-systems will encounter the same dismal patterns over time, and be forced to shed the conceit that the modern states-system is somehow endowed with a unique capacity to break the historical mould.

Few rival positions dismiss realism out of hand. Key debates have revolved around the relative importance of the multiple forces that shape world politics, and on whether the realist supposition that societies may be powerless to alter their future course of development is its great strength or principal weakness. Heeding the lessons of realism, English School interpretations of international societies have highlighted the existence of global civilizing processes that demonstrate that political communities have enjoyed at least partial and short-lived success in building order even in the absence of a higher monopoly of power. In various modulations, the two heirs to the Enlightenment belief in progress – liberalism and Marxism – have proclaimed that the species is not destined to spend its remaining time on earth trapped in competition and conflict. Those rival interpretations of world politics generate their own conjectures about how a comparative sociology of cosmopolitan harm conventions should proceed, and about what it might yield in the way of observations about long-term patterns of development.

The opening section of this chapter focuses on the claim that war is 'the habitual condition of mankind'. Consulting the ethnographic record to make their point, many scholars have concluded that very few societies have lived without the fear or the expectation of warfare which has shaped the main pathways of social and political evolution from the earliest times. Key writings have described how just over five millennia ago, societies first crossed a 'military threshold' and became embroiled in patterns of violent conflict from which there may be no escape. Clearly, the failure to eradicate warfare from relations between communities is a key feature of the human past that no account of cosmopolitan harm conventions can ignore. Over and over again, the ability to contain violence has been put to the test. Little in the historical record encourages optimism that cosmopolitan harm conventions are likely to become the pacemaker of global political development in the foreseeable future. In the light of those observations, the second part of this chapter concentrates on the realist emphasis on the fact that, for millennia, states have been compelled to acquire the power to hurt and 'out-injure' opponents, often just to survive. It notes its emphasis on how the contours of international history have been shaped by critical watersheds or turning-points in states-systems when claims about necessity led the great powers to set moral and legal constraints on the ability to injure to one side.

For neo-realism, that very fact justifies the decision to abstract the international system from the wider totality in which it is located. Abstraction is an end in itself rather than a stage in a larger process of understanding how developments in any specific sphere influence, and are influenced by, other 'levels' in the totality of social forces.[2] The following analysis of different approaches to world politics starts from the assumption that each offers insights into particular dimensions of social and political interaction, but none provides more than a limited account of the overarching structures and processes that have shaped societies and international relations. It is necessary to consider each separately before turning in the following chapter to how their contributions can be combined in a higher synthesis. The argument will be that the analysis of civilizing processes has a unique capacity to forge connections between modes of thought that often have separate paths of development – it has a particular capacity to gather their insights together in a distinctive approach to the sociology of states-systems.

With that objective in mind, the third section considers English School investigations of how independent communities have dealt with balancing self-reliance in the sphere of national security with the aim of reducing the dangers that are inherent in strategic interconnectedness. The section examines their discussion of how shared interests in controlling the power to harm have underpinned efforts to establish civility or civilizing processes in international states-systems. Particular emphasis is placed on English School reflections on tensions between order and justice, and on how maintaining international harm conventions is simultaneously the precondition for advances in introducing cosmopolitan harm conventions, and a major barrier to their establishment.

The fourth section begins with the English School theme that contrasts between 'civilized' and 'uncivilized' peoples have shaped the boundaries of all previous societies of states. Harm conventions were designed to protect the interests of civilized entities within international society, and notions of cultural superiority were employed to justify the conquest of outsider groups. Efforts to remove pernicious distinctions between the 'civilized' and 'barbaric' have been central to the recent evolution of the society of states. They have mirrored larger patterns of change in which greater sensitivity surrounds constructions of 'otherness' and their role in the production of violent and non-violent harm. In particular, the contemporary society of states has witnessed advances in beliefs about how minority peoples should be treated. Sensitivities to the political consequences of invidious self–other distinctions have informed collective understandings that cosmopolitan harm conventions are necessary to protect individuals in their own right as well as the groups with which they identify

---

[2] The contrast here is between Waltz's approach which abstracts the systemic sphere in order to understand recurrent patterns and Elias's position that it is always important to understand what any abstraction has been abstracted from, an orientation that is coupled with the quest for high-level synthesis in the social sciences that is orientated towards providing a comprehensive explanation of how seemingly different spheres of activity are related in long-term patterns of development (see Elias 1978: 63–4, 2007a [1987]: 80, 154–5; Linklater 2009 and Waltz 1979: ch. 1 on what those different methods mean for political analysis).

most closely. The upshot is that identity struggles have influenced efforts to turn the global system into a society of states *and* peoples. How unique that is will be considered in a later volume.

Distinctions between culturally 'advanced' and 'backward' peoples have clearly been a major influence on long-term patterns of social and political development, but they are not always easy to disentangle from a second fault-line, namely class divisions that have been the concern of Marxist inquiries into modes of production. The fifth section considers the significance of their modes of analysis for understanding global harm conventions. Of particular import-ance is the emphasis on the role that coercion played in economic accumulation in pre-capitalist social formations. The belief that it was legitimate to use force to appropriate wealth, which was often accompanied by assumptions about the legitimacy of acquiring wealth by enslaving people, seems to have been the norm in state-organized, pre-capitalist forms of production. What seems to be distinctive about modern industrial capitalism is the apparent separation of the 'economic' and 'political' spheres. According to the dominant ideology, the economic domain consists of relations between equals who enter into osten-sibly free contracts. No longer integral to accumulation, violence largely departs from the scene.

From that perspective, dominant class forces and the prevailing ideologies incline towards prohibiting force against free and equal individuals, but such sensibilities are entirely consistent with the tolerance of, and widespread indif-ference to, the social consequences of structural harm and the 'hidden injur-ies of class' (Sennett and Cobb 1972). Analyses of modes of production draw attention to the biases of cosmopolitan harm conventions in the capitalist world – to the selective protection they afford, and to systematic oversights and omissions. The specific focus on the relationship between class forces, state structures and the constitution of the global political and economic order, including regulatory organizations, therefore sheds light on features of global harm conventions that are usually neglected by mainstream angles on inter-national relations.

The sixth section turns to the ethic of care and responsibility to highlight a separate sphere of inquiry, namely the extent to which shared moral/emo-tional attitudes to harm and suffering have shaped societies of states or, more specifically, how far conceptions of connectedness with vulnerable others have influenced their trajectories of development. Cosmopolitan harm conventions clearly depend on widespread support for such ethical dispositions – on their capacity to shape national responses to strategic necessity, or the challenge of creating civility in the absence of a higher authority, or attitudes to promoting global social justice. Similarly, the fate of harm conventions hangs on the extent to which such sympathies shape collective identities and stimulate efforts to reduce the harmful effects of global relations of production and exchange. The relationships between those phenomena are central to an inquiry into how far a 'principle of humaneness' has influenced the evolution of societies of states, and how far it has generated global civilizing processes.[3]

War and injury

Anthropologists are generally agreed that war and massacre have been 'ubiquitous in the ethnographic record' since the Mesolithic era. Generalizations about the first societies should be treated with caution because little or nothing is known about tens of thousands of (long disappeared) early societies identified by anthropologists (Dawson 1996: 27). However, the broad consensus is that few escaped the ordeal of war. Those that did were usually fairly isolated, often as a result of retreating to remote areas to avoid stronger groups (Goldstein 2001: 32–4; Gregor 1990). Several anthropologists have expressed doubt that 'war' as opposed to 'feuding' is the appropriate epithet for describing violence between the earliest societies, and many have argued that the preferred form of engagement was the ambush or surprise raid that could maximize harm to the enemy while minimizing injury to themselves (Gat 2006: 116ff.). In contrast to the pitched battles of 'advanced' peoples, such conflicts have been compared to highly ritualized sporting contests or 'elaborate games'.

Not only do anthropologists disagree about whether warfare is the appropriate term to describe early inter-group conflicts: they differ about whether 'primitive war' was less destructive than modern warfare. Pointing to evidence that the mass slaughter of adult warrior males as well as women and children was widespread in conflicts between 'band societies', some reject notions of an idyllic peaceful past once associated with depictions of the 'noble savage'. On some estimates, war casualties in distant eras were not only much higher than many have calculated (around 15 per cent of the population and 25 per cent of males according to some estimates), but also greater in percentage terms than

---

[3] The following discussion focuses on particular themes within different theories or traditions, and not on those perspectives in themselves. There is always a danger of suggesting that theories are more compartmentalized and homogenous than they really are. But focusing on internal complexities and overlapping arguments would complicate the discussion unnecessarily. For reasons of convenience, the approach focuses on realist discussions of necessity, English School accounts of order and justice and so forth, but just as the English School recognizes the importance of necessity so do students of collective identity-formation often recognize the value of English School accounts of order and justice. To provide one further example, the issues that are central to the ethic of care run through various areas of inquiry, ranging from classical accounts of the just war, studies of the role of the middle classes in promoting humanitarian narratives in the nineteenth century, and recent approaches to environmental ethics. The five themes considered in this chapter grow out of an earlier discussion of how the interaction between state-building, geopolitics and war, systems of production, the struggle for order and moral-cultural developments have shaped 'the expansion and contraction of community' in international history (see Linklater 1990: 171–2).

in modern wars, the main exception being 'total warfare' where the number of deaths approximates levels of 'pre-state lethality' (Gat 2006: 131–3; Keeley 1996: 64, 108ff., 175).

Some studies of early warfare support the psychological theories proposed by Freud and others in which violence and aggression are regarded as inherent in human nature. Such interpretations of 'primitive warfare' have been criticized on the grounds that complex environmental factors provide the key to understanding early inter-group conflict (Chapman 1999).[4] But however it is explained, the fact that warfare has been prevalent in every phase of social evolution makes optimism about the prospects for perpetual peace hard to sustain. The question of future possibilities has been a major stake in debates about the ethnographic record – and one reason why several anthropologists have denied that 'primitive war' is either as universal or as bloody as gory inventories of alleged atrocities in early inter-group conflicts suggest (Ferguson 1999: 426–7; Turney-High 1991: 186, 226).

Many anthropologists contest the claim that warfare is more 'natural' and universal than empathy and cooperation between groups (Carman 1997: 3ff.; Turney-High 1991: 205, see also 262; also Keeley 1996: 183). But whether war is or is not 'natural' depends on what societies possess in the way of peaceful means of resolving significant disputes. Warfare was often the only way in which early societies could protect themselves from adversaries, and the only mechanism for settling major differences in a condition where there was little to prevent powerful groups from using force, if they wanted to do so, and where hesitating to destroy or weaken an adversary could risk annihilation. For those reasons, societies in distant eras and down to the present day have reserved the right to inflict forms of violent harm on each other that are normally prohibited in relations within the group, at least when there is a stable monopoly of power that can restrain individual action, when mutual trust reduces or removes the need

---

[4] Freud (1939: 85–6) maintained that 'a powerful measure of desire for aggression' is part of the species' 'instinctual endowment'. From a different angle, human instincts may be as strong as those found in other species, but they are far more malleable (see p. 158, n. 6). Humans clearly have a biological capacity for violence, one that evolved as part of the armoury of survival, but whether and how it is expressed depends on environmental factors (Gat 2006: 36ff.). Higher levels of male aggression in most cultures may have biological-genetic foundations, but that is contested (Gat 2006: 77ff.). Uncontroversial is the thesis that males monopolized control of the instruments of violence, and related hunting technologies, at early stages in human history. A virtual male monopoly of war-fighting has been critical for the development of the 'male supremacist complex' (Divale and Harris 1976). No less important is the fact that cultural evolution (which has roots in human biology) has replaced biological evolution as the main influence on social development (Elias 1978: ch. 4). That approach has the merit of stressing the existence of a biological capacity for violence and aggression (which may well be stronger in men than in women) while allowing for the possibility of the eradication of war as a result of collective social learning and advanced civilizing processes (see Chapter 6).

for self-reliance with respect to security, and when people can exercise higher levels of self-control as a result (Elias 2000).

In the absence of such conditions in relations between groups, it is hardly surprising that genuine efforts to limit killing often failed to prevent the escalation of conflict and the significant loss of life (Dawson 1996: 13ff.). Such outcomes are as easily attributed to forces that societies found it hard to control as to bloodthirstiness or an engrained 'pleasure in killing and torturing others' (Elias 2000: 163).[5] Claims that war was 'natural' deflect scholarly attention from important discussions about 'why warfare appears and disappears at different times and places', and also about how societies often succeeded in maintaining peace for prolonged periods – modes of inquiry that suggest that humanity may not be 'doomed to war' after all (Ferguson 1999; Haas 1999: 13ff.). Here the scope of emotional identification is crucial. Dehumanizing representations of outsiders, that seem to have been commonplace in early societies, may explain the incidence and intensity of conflict, although the ethnographic evidence is that such attitudes were not necessarily central to 'primitive' war, which may well have preceded the rise of stark cultural differences between social groups (Haas 1999: 23). Neighbouring societies that believed they were bound together by shared kinship – in a literal or metaphorical sense – may have had greater success in preserving mutual constraints on force (Gregor 1990; Keeley 1996: 65, 85).[6] But presumably warfare bound people closely together while simultaneously promoting their estrangement from other groups – and that was very probably one reason for 'double-bind processes' that engulfed them.[7] The absence of a higher monopoly of power made it difficult to avoid entanglement in warfare and to disrupt cycles of violence that often became deeply embedded in the cultures involved. High levels of self-restraint in relations with outsiders

---

[5] Hallpike (1988: 102–13) may be close to the mark by suggesting that the ubiquity of primitive warfare has less to do with innate aggression than with such phenomena as the absence of mediatory arrangements, low levels of self-restraint in acephalous societies, and the dominant constructions of masculinity. Elias's writings also emphasised that low levels of security in relations between early societies favoured the development of warrior codes that linked male identity with violence and killing (see below, pp. 175–6).

[6] Examples of the constraining effect of 'we-feeling' are provided in various studies of 'primitive warfare'. See, for example, the analysis of the role of 'anti-violence' norms and the role of 'empathy' and 'sensitivity' in the relations of Brazil's Upper Xingu (Gregor 1990). Turney-High (1991: 206) stressed similar themes in an account of the peaceful nature of the Iroquois League.

[7] See Elias (2007a [1987]: 125ff.) for a discussion of that theme. The point about the 'double-bind process' is that group solidarity was necessary for coping with external threats, but the measures that were used to promote group security often generated fear in other groups, which were then obliged to take similar steps to protect themselves – and so on in a spiral of competition and mutual distrust that trapped all concerned in tensions and hostilities that were hard to end. Parallels with the security dilemma will be evident (see Booth and Wheeler 2008). For further comment, see p. 125, n. 23.

have usually been low, hard to develop, and difficult to maintain in conditions where societies have to rely on their own resources for security and survival.

Major social and political transformations occurred with the Neolithic Revolution over ten millennia ago. Small-scale hunting and gathering societies had been the main social systems ever since anatomically modern humans emerged roughly 100,000 to 150,000 years ago (Divale and Harris 1976). Two phases of a transition that took place in the Ancient Near East are worth noting: the emergence of the first settled agricultural communities at the start of the Neolithic period, and the rise of state structures approximately 5,000–6,000 years later. Similar patterns unfolded, probably independently, in other regions including North China, South East Asia, the Mediterranean, Mesoamerica and the Andes in later periods (Scarre 2005). The first city-states in the Ancient Near East, rapidly followed by the first agrarian empires, developed in response to the problems of coordinating the larger populations that could be supported by the agricultural revolution.[8] Their formation created as many problems as they solved, not least by promoting new modes of warfare that pushed societies over the 'military threshold' (Ferguson 2000; Gat 2000).[9] The first 'caged' societies in Mesopotomia from around 3500 BCE acted like a magnet for raiding groups that sought to appropriate their comparatively abundant resources (Mann 1986: ch. 3). Unlike hunting and gathering societies that had the option of migrating to avoid conflict – though how many were mobile is disputed – the former had to stand their ground (Ferguson 2000; Gat 2006: 134). The rise of complex, hierarchical systems that could project their military and political power over larger areas was 'a fateful turning point in human history' that altered war as radically as it transformed social relations.[10] Warfare mutated from 'episodic personal duels, raids and skirmishes to the mass activity that has enmeshed entire societies and bedevilled the human species for the past several thousand years' (Stavrianos 1990: 82).[11]

The emergence of larger territorial monopolies of power with the capacity to wield power over greater areas brought peoples at different levels of technological

---

[8] The momentous nature of the transition 'from village autonomy to supravillage integration' (after tens of thousands of years in which hunting and gathering societies had been dominant) stands out most clearly when it is recalled that the sprawling empires and complex civilizations that would set humanity on an entirely new course emerged within two to three thousand years of that transformation (Carneiro 1970: 736ff.).

[9] Hamblin (2006: 16 and 35) defines the 'military threshold' as 'the point at which warfare has essentially become endemic in a region, and at which all peoples … are forced to militarize their societies to one degree or another', adding that Mesopotamia crossed that line around 3500 BC.

[10] New forms of social stratification emerged along with the rise of institutionalized warfare (Ferguson 1997; Keeley 1996; Vencl 1999). Gender inequalities increased as warrior codes acquired cultural and political dominance.

[11] Inter-city rivalries in Sumer from around the middle of the fourth millennium BCE are the earliest example.

development into close contact, leading to divisions between the 'civilized' and the 'barbarian' that have dominated history ever since. Such divisions have been integral to the collective self-images of all world civilizations; they acquired a particular intensity with the rise of the European overseas empires and the diverse conceptions of racial and cultural hierarchy that developed alongside them. Similar 'natural' hierarchies emerged wherever one civilization emerged as the pacemaker of social development in its region (as in the case of India and China). When equal empires confronted each another, following their respective expansion, they were often obliged to exercise levels of self-restraint that were unpalatable to them, and not least because egocentric worldviews led each to assume that others would yield before displays of superior military power that demonstrated the existence of more advanced, more highly organized, and more destructive ways of life.[12] Where unequals came into contact, such restraints were weaker – if they existed at all.

The upshot is that for several thousands of years after the rise of agrarian societies, world history was shaped by major tensions along the frontier between settled and nomadic societies (Stavrianos 1990: 84ff.). As just noted, throughout that period, divisions between the 'civilized' and the 'barbaric' world became greater and more central to relations between communities. Tributary systems – the dominant modes of political organization for almost five millennia prior to the rise of modern capitalism – expanded into areas that had been controlled by 'barbarian' neighbours, often triggering imitative state formation (Harris 1977: ch. 6; McNeill 1979b: ch. 7, 10). Encounters between the leading-edge polities were not only violent, but were frequently characterized by undisguised cruelty.[13] Violent behaviour that was forbidden within the group (or permissible only in dealings between the upper and lower strata) was not only tolerated in relations with other communities but invariably welcomed as central to the identity of male warriors. Processes of state-formation led most societies to structure themselves in accordance with the Clausewitzian dictum that 'the central activity of war is injuring and the central goal in war is to out-injure the opponent'; and all, bar those that moved away from the principal regions of state-formation, recognized that survival depended on accumulating sufficient military power to force adversaries to bow before the prospect of 'intolerable injury' (Clausewitz 1989 [1832]: 77; Scarry 1985: 12, 63ff., 89).

The social transformations that followed the Neolithic Revolution propelled the species in specific directions that have dominated world history ever since.

---

[12] Such assumptions were central to Roman expansion until, for example, contact was made with the powerful Parthian empire during the reign of Augustus.

[13] Examples are the 'scorched earth' policy adopted by the ancient Egyptians, and related strategies employed by the Assyrian, Hittite and Persian empires (see the chapters by Briant, Ferguson, Gnirs, Haldon and Hassig in Raaflaub and Rosenstein (1999)). Kern (1999) discusses the ruthlessness of siege warfare where quick surrender often resulted in mercy, whereas stubborn resistance could lead to total annihilation.

At their heart was the 'monopoly mechanism' (Elias 2000: 268ff.), as captured in the claim that the dominant historical logic since city-states and empires first appeared in the Ancient Near East has led to an overall 'decrease in the number of autonomous political units' coupled with the long-term trend for the most successful units to 'increase in ... size' (Carneiro 1986). Adorno (1973: 320) described a related feature of that unplanned process when he maintained that history has been a sorry journey from the slingshot to the atomic bomb. The question arises of whether societies could have altered the dominant course of development once they had made the transition to militarized cultures that rarely flinched from inflicting immense suffering to achieve their objectives – and given the rapid diffusion of the means of projecting higher levels of destructive power beyond their frontiers. The more pessimistic responses argue that the possibility of escape may have been lost the moment societies crossed the 'military threshold' (Keegan 1994: 389ff.). The rise of disciplined military forces that aimed to engage and destroy the enemy in open battle has been regarded as the main reason for the 'singular lethality of Western culture at war', a destructiveness that has been described as releasing the West from constraints on force that existed in many non-Western cultures where warfare often revolved around 'ritualistic fighting' and strategies of 'deception and attrition' that were designed to limit violent harm.[14] The 'Western way of war' that subordinated ethical and religious imperatives to military objectives was one reason for Europe's rise to global domination which then promoted the spread of its approach to organized warfare across the world with devastating results (Dawson 1996; Hanson 2002).[15] There is an obvious link with any inquiry into the fate of cosmopolitan

---

[14] Keegan (1994: 214–15) maintains that highly ritualized, chivalrous forms of combat, influenced by the Confucian belief that the mark of superiority was the ability to prevail 'without violence', survived for longer in China than in most other major civilizations. Along with Hanson (1989) and Keegan (1994), Dawson (1996: 6–8) argues that the West was unusual in releasing warfare from moral and religious constraints to the degree that it did. Both India and China subordinated war to the higher norms that were embedded in the Brahman caste and in the Confucian ethos. Even in the age of the Chinese warring states, it has been argued, there was little support for the Western style of offensive warfare; the preference was to triumph with as little fighting as possible. In an important qualification, it is acknowledged that, in that period, attitudes to war and strategy came closer to the Western way of warfare that emerged in ancient Greece, and were aimed at 'strategies of annihilation' as against strategies of 'exhaustion' (see Dawson 1996: 9, fn. 4). Those are matters to return to in volume 3.

[15] Keegan (1994: 388ff.) maintains that Western modes of warfare need to recover the commitment to 'subordinating the warrior impulse to the constraints of law and custom' that existed in Confucian China. His comments on the battle between Ch'u and Sung in 638 BC, which was an example of war conducted according to 'the manners of the duel', are especially interesting in this respect Keegan (1994: 173); see also Walzer (1980: 225) who refers to the same conflict and Neiberg (2001: 13 and 19)). With regard to early Muslim debates about the use of force and duties to non-combatants, Firestone (1999: ch. 3, 67–8) maintains that the 'very large numbers of exhortations calling Muslims to engage in battle

harm conventions. The emergence of larger 'survival units' equipped with increasing levels of destructive power and wedded to 'insider–outside divisions' outpaced efforts to use 'anti-violence' norms or a 'principle of humaneness' to bring the central dynamics of international history under control (Carman 1997; Haas 1990: 13ff.; also Chapter 4). Dominant patterns of cultural evolution were free from the moral inhibitions and constraints that existed within stable communities. Whether societies could have altered the balance of power between those forces is the question that is posed by the forces that were released at the beginning of the Neolithic Era. Whether, even now, they can develop systems of universal cooperation that can alter the main course of development is still the central issue. The following discussion of how leading theories approach the problem of harm in world politics proceeds with those questions in mind.

The forces of necessity

Classical realists generally lamented the dominance of power politics and agonized over the tensions between ethics and force. They advised great caution in thinking that the species will ever escape the tragic consequences of successive waves of state-formation and geopolitical competition. They maintained that great powers invariably refuse to be bound by international legal and moral conventions that clash with vital interests. Beyond the problem of persuading the strong to comply with global norms lay complex issues about whether universal ideologies seem destined to be captured by the dominant powers and distorted to serve or dignify their egotistical aims. From that perspective, every cosmopolitan vision, including those that long for the globalization of the harm principle, is likely to be a utopian irrelevance, or to be hijacked and harnessed to serve the material interests of the great powers.[16]

Deep pessimism about the prospects for global change is evident in the contention that 'more and more rigorous rules' with respect to the conduct of war have emerged over roughly the last century along with 'less and less observance'

---

against their enemies suggest that significant portions of the community were not inclined to do so ... Militant groups promoting aggressive behaviour towards opponents of Islam eventually won the day'. Klostermaier (1996: 230–1) refers to the *smrti* works in Hinduism that insisted that 'under no circumstances were civilians to be brought into the war ... it would have been unthinkable to kill women and children as part of the planned operations'. Indiscriminate warfare would have seemed 'demonic' to ancient Indians. He adds that the 'kind of warfare introduced by the Muslim conquerors was something totally new to India', and that earlier conquests had been 'rather tame' by comparison.

[16] Carr's critique of utopianism underpins those remarks (see Carr 2001: ch. 2), as does Mann's comment that early empires often seized control of universal ideologies that had brought some unity to 'multi-actor systems' (Mann 1986). Moral universalism has been linked with projects of reforming international society, but it has often been incorporated within imperial ideologies that maintained that empire provided an escape from incessant warfare.

of restraints in violent conflict (Wright 1964: 364). An important comment on the prospect for any global civilizing process states that 'the tendencies of modern civilization have been accompanied' by the 'decreasing frequency' but 'increasing seriousness' and deadliness of warfare (Tilly 1993; Wright 1964).[17] That remark was made in response to the evolution of the modern laws of war from the 1856 Paris Declaration Respecting Maritime Warfare to the 1949 Geneva Conventions, but it resonates with the more sweeping historical observation that, time and time again, the laws of war have been modified to legitimize using new instruments of force that initially seemed to be incompatible with the dominant moral or religious commitments of the era (Price 1997: 2).[18]

The realism that is under discussion here does not worship violence or exalt in cruelty – it is not the kind that defends war on account of its medicinal properties – because of its contribution, in Hegel's phrase, to 'the ethical health of peoples' (Hegel 1952 [1821]: 210). Nor is it the kind that announces that princes will enjoy success if they earn a reputation for unstinting ruthlessness.[19] Attention is focused instead on the moderate versions of realism that pose a major challenge to the utopian temperament while supporting the Augustinian theme that societies should strive to suppress the cruel dispositions that invariably find an outlet in war (Mapel 1996: 54; Verkamp 1993). As the last point indicates, the milder forms maintain that states, including those with the highest moral intentions and aspirations, are often blown off course by the forces of necessity. They conclude that a politics of limits and self-restraint is more prudent and responsible than a politics of perfectibility, less prone to generate violence and domination, but difficult to sustain (Williams 2005).[20] From that standpoint,

---

[17] It has been said that, because of their greater destructiveness, modern wars do not last as long as their predecessors did, needlessly prolonging suffering. As Walzer (1980: 129ff.) observes, Sidgwick argued on utilitarian grounds that efforts to civilize warfare would be counterproductive. The fewer the restraints on warfare, the more likely states would try to avoid it. The point has found advocates beyond the province of philosophers. Seth Low, a US delegate to the 1899 Hague Conventions, spoke against trying to place constraints on warfare for precisely that reason (see Price 1997: 40–1).

[18] As Clausewitz (1989 [1832]: 76) maintained, 'the invention of gunpowder and the constant improvement of firearms are enough in themselves to show that the advance of civilization has done nothing practical to alter or deflect the impulse to destroy the enemy, which is central to the very idea of war'. To adapt Marxist terminology, the material basis of international society – the instruments of violence and the forms of military organization that develop around them – constitute the foundation on which the global legal and political superstructure is erected.

[19] Machiavelli (1950 [1532]: 528) advanced the classic formulation of that point when he claimed that no consideration should be given to 'justice or injustice, humanity or cruelty, nor of glory or of shame' when the safety of the country is at stake. The prince had to embrace 'wholeheartedly' any course of action that would 'save the life and preserve the freedom' of the state.

[20] Williams (2005: 209–10) discusses Foucault's endorsement of a politics of limits that aims to ensure that 'the games of power' are played with 'as little domination as possible'.

reflections on the prospects for cosmopolitan harm conventions must not lose sight of the reality that all experiments in international cooperation take place in 'a world that is competitive at its core' (Mearsheimer 2001: 46ff.).[21]

The question of necessity is usually discussed in connection with those circumstances where 'national' interests are believed to clash with the idea of the just war. With regard to *ius ad bellum*, realists argue that occasions often arise when the 'strict observance of legal and moral prohibitions against aggression' will 'compromise the state's security and survival'; with respect to *ius in bello*, they add that even those wars that are fought for limited ends and with limited means contain a high risk of violating 'the principle of double effect' through the deliberate killing of innocent people (Mapel 1996). The supposition that military necessity dictates that states are free to breach such limits in extreme circumstances is not only central to Western realism but has appeared in conceptions of the relationship between ethics and politics in many other civilizations (Mapel 1996).[22] The common ground is the belief that tragic circumstances often dictate moral compromises for the sake of the relevant bounded community.

A process or developmental approach can usefully extend the argument that there is no place in political life for those who are unwilling to acquire 'dirty hands' by using the state's 'power to hurt' to force adversaries to submit. In his account of the *Peloponnesian War*, Thucydides described how military leaders responded with increasing ruthlessness to immediate threats, whether imagined or real. A foreshortening of temporal horizons was evident in the recurrent failure to assess the likely consequences of ever more violent behaviour – and specifically the inability to foresee how the application of maximum force without regard for the customary moral constraints would rebound on the cities involved. In tandem with the upward spiral of violence and counter-violence, older distinctions between what was necessary and what was simply advantageous broke down (Pouncey 1980). Thucydides argued that those who called for prudence, moderation and restraint were outflanked by opponents who condemned their lack of courage, protested against effeminacy, and made uncompromising ruthlessness central to notions of fitness for rule.

The project of developing cosmopolitan harm conventions operates along similar lines (Linklater 2002b). There is nothing in the version of realism which is under discussion here that is hostile to, or dismissive of, that aspiration. Indeed, its logic is support for a political architecture that is 'designed to prevent people from doing too much harm' to each other (Isaiah Berlin, quoted in Williams 2005: 132–3), coupled with an awareness of the obstacles to achieving a global consensus about such matters, and to securing widespread compliance with the relevant negative obligations.

[21] If one keeps that in mind, the realist will argue, the dominant international trends over the last few thousand years will make perfect sense.

[22] As an example, the idea that 'necessity overrides the forbidden' has been an important theme in certain Islamic conceptions of international relations (Tibi 1996: 133).

The analysis of how increasing fears for security can quickly lead to justifications of actions that had been regarded as injudicious or impermissible has enormous significance for cosmopolitan harm conventions. For realists, such conventions are precarious because of temptations to enlarge the meaning of necessity in the context of heightened fear and insecurity, thereby weakening what existed in the way of self-restraint.[23] Such observations about obvious threats to harm conventions of any kind do not demonstrate the impossibility of preserving the space for moral deliberation even with the pressures of warfare. In a celebrated discussion of the ethics of aerial bombardment with reference to the Second World War, Walzer argued that a supreme national emergency would have justified the British policy of directly targeting civilian populations, but no such danger existed when the case for the bombing campaign was made between 1942 and 1945. Nor did the United States face such a crisis when it decided in August 1945 to use the atomic bomb against Hiroshima and Nagasaki (Walzer 1980: ch. 16). The conclusion of that probing analysis of 'the realm of necessity' was that the US Administration had scope for moral deliberation and agency, but also duties to the Japanese people to whom it 'owed ... an experiment in negotiation' (Walzer 1980: 268). But the moral issues extend well beyond immediate responsibilities to civilian populations.[24]

Walzer does not oppose the realist thesis that leaders have special responsibilities to their national communities that can override obligations not to harm outsiders and that may even justify terrible violence against them in extraordinary circumstances.[25] But the argument lends support to the idea that necessity

[23] One need look no further than recent discussions of torture for evidence of how security fears and necessity claims can quickly unravel prohibitions on violence that appeared to be central to the self-image of the liberal powers (see Foot 2006 and Levinson 2004).

[24] A decision against using the atomic bomb would also have been significant for the 'double-bind process' (see pp. 177–8). On that argument, even defensive means of promoting national interests can sow the seeds of insecurity in relations between actual adversaries. But they can intensify distrust and competition between states *more generally*, and lock them into processes that they are unable to control. The larger point is that the use of force, such as occurred in the final stages of the war against Japan, invariably has much broader political implications, although the preoccupation with immediate interests can rule out forms of restraint that may help to create a more general climate of trust. Realists argue that obstacles to exercising self-restraint arise because adversaries may interpret any hesitation to press home an advantage as a sign of weakness, whereas ruthlessness may well remove any doubts about the adversaries' resolve, albeit with destructive long-term consequences for all involved (see Booth and Wheeler 2008: ch. 9 on trust and world politics).

[25] Walzer (1980: 262) maintains that responsible parties should openly acknowledge the killing of the innocent since such actions are a 'blasphemy against our deepest moral commitments'. The idea has distant origins. Medieval conceptions of the just war stressed that killing, however justified, is an evil that should be accompanied by remorse and the quest for atonement (Tooke 1965). That general sensibility surfaces in many different ways. During the recent war in Iraq, the argument was made that coalition forces should have expressed remorse over the loss of civilian lives, for example by publishing estimates of the number who had been killed (see Taylor 1998: ch. 9 on the more general issue of the

claims should always meet with suspicion lest they 'give weight and finality' to judgments about the relationship between means and ends that should remain open to 'criticism and re-evaluation' (Childress 1974: 481). Those reflections on 'state of nature situations' aim to demonstrate that there is scope for ethical agency in warfare where the temptation to enlarge the meaning of necessity may produce moral chaos (Kern 1999: 80ff.; Singer 1963: 152ff.). Attitudes to war in early Hebrew, Assyrian and Greek cultures, and particularly prohibitions of the indiscriminate killing of women and children, registered those dangers, as has the contention in the modern law of warfare that strategic necessity does not condone savagery and cruelty.[26] Related discussions arose in conjunction with the defence of 'civilized' torture in the 'war against terror'.[27]

Realists do not deny that states can mitigate the effects of security dilemmas by recognizing the legitimacy of each other's core interests, or by curbing the impulse to seize every opportunity to exploit an advantage. But they have generally rejected the belief that the scope for moral agency can be greatly expanded while anarchy exists. The related contention that few, if any, ancient or medieval states were 'free from war' has clear implications for any account of the possibility of strengthening cosmopolitan harm conventions, the argument being that pressures to ignore such practices are often unstoppable in military conflicts where self-restraint usually depends on little more than the fragile reed of reciprocity (Ferguson 1999: 427; Schelling 1966: 138ff.). The analysis draws attention to the tragic dimensions of international competition, and is generally designed to promote empathy and understanding between actors who are locked in struggles that prove hard to control. The approach maintains that

vanishing body). An interesting overview of the ethical issues involved in overriding the prima facie duty not to cause harm can be found in Ewing (1959). The argument is that the relevant authorities should acknowledge that basic moral principles have been compromised, even though there were good reasons for setting them to one side. He maintained that compromises should be influenced by prior obligations such as the prima facie duty not to harm. Wherever possible, the latter should 'modify in some respect the way in which the act is performed'; it should continue to have influence long after harm has been caused, for example, by encouraging expressions of regret, or acts of reparation, or some other way of communicating a 'special feeling of responsibility towards those who have suffered' (Ewing 1959: 110, 136). Ewing did not apply that reasoning to relations between states, but some of his comments on the just war suggest that consideration be given to displays of remorse for the accidental killing of civilians (Ewing 1959: 110). Larger issues arise about the role of apology and forgiveness in promoting civilizing or 'recivilizing' processes (see Blomert 2002), but they go beyond the present discussion (see also Murphy 1990).

[26] Article 16 of the 1863 Lieber Code (the manual circulated to military personnel during the American Civil War) stated that 'military necessity does not admit of cruelty – that is, the infliction of suffering for the sake of suffering or for revenge, nor of maiming and wounding except in fight, nor of torture to extort confessions' (quoted in Price 1997: 20).

[27] The reference is to efforts to reconcile torture and civilization by suggesting that necessity claims could be subjected to, for example, ex post facto judicial assessment that considers whether violations of civilized norms were justified (see Levinson 2004; Linklater 2007e).

such conflicts often lead to an unintended coarsening of sensibilities and to the increased tolerance of excessive force. The realist might therefore suggest that the sociologist of cosmopolitan harm conventions should not be surprised to find that the similarities between states-systems are much greater than any differences, and not least because of the decisive impact that great power rivalries have on their long-term development.

It would be foolish to dismiss the realist's point out of hand, but perhaps unwise to suppose that the sociology of states-systems is almost bound to discover that there is 'nothing new under the sun'. War may have been a permanent feature of human development, but its ferocity and frequency have not been constant across the millennia (Ferguson 1999: 427). Wars can be classified according to the intensity of violence,[28] but the detailed study of the social forces that have encouraged or prohibited acts of cruelty as part of larger structures of self-restraint has yet to be provided.[29] Such an inquiry can proceed from the Kantian belief that the species may yet undergo collective learning processes that bring it closer to perpetual peace. That conviction would seem to be incompatible with realism. But when coupled with the idea that international political progress will never be complete, and can always be reversed, it is entirely compatible with the combination of realism and universalism that can be found in, for instance, the writings of Morgenthau (1971: ch. 30) and Herz (1959). Along with Kant, they point to the difficulty of altering the dominant trends of the last six millennia, while insisting that the possibility of unparalleled suffering in warfare requires a systematic reassessment of social practices that may well have brought humanity to 'the end of the road' (Elias 2010: 3).

The attractions of society

A bridge between the realist focus on recurrent geopolitical rivalry and the Kantian vision of a world community can be found in the comparative 'sociology of states-systems' in English School writings (Wight 1977: ch. 1). Its aim is to understand past and present achievements in establishing order in the unpromising world of anarchy. The emphasis has mainly been on international harm conventions that tame, but do not end, the competition for power in anarchical societies. The analysis also takes account of pressures to give concrete

---

[28] Quincy Wright's four-fold taxonomy of societal orientations towards violence remains useful. The main distinctions were between 'unwarlike peoples' for whom force has an entirely defensive purpose; the 'moderately warlike' who fight for 'sport, ritual, revenge, personal prestige'; the 'warlike' who use force to capture booty or slaves; and the 'most warlike' who 'fight for political purposes', and are motivated by the desire to seize territory, to achieve political domination, to acquire military supremacy and, in such ways, bolster 'the authority of rulers' (Wright 1964: 37).

[29] See Collins (1974) for an important contribution to the social theory of cruelty.

expression to the belief in a universal moral community, for example by promoting respect for the humanitarian laws of war.

As noted elsewhere, English School writings on international society refer,
albeit tangentially, to two themes at the centre of the current investigation: a
global harm principle and the interconnected notion of the 'civilizing process'
in the technical meaning of the term (Linklater and Suganami 2006b: ch. 4).[30]
Of particular importance is the emphasis on the precariousness of global civilizing processes that limit violent harm. Struggles for power and security are
moderated rather than suspended – hence the reason for thinking that Elias's
remark that civilizing and decivilizing processes always develop in tandem
(the question is which is dominant at any moment) would be a useful motto
for English School inquiry (Linklater and Suganami 2006b: 210ff.; see also pp.
172–5). As befits the idea that the history of modern international society consists of a 'succession of hegemonies', the fundamental role of the great powers is
never far from the centre of the discussion. Their ambiguous presence means
that they alone can enforce compliance with the rules of international society
but, at the same time, they pose the greatest threat to their survival.[31] Although
Wight did not use the term, he placed the 'monopoly mechanism' at the heart of
his account of long-term patterns of development in international societies. All
previous examples had experienced the same fate – the gradual concentration of
military might in the hands of a smaller number of great powers that finally col-
lided in a terminal struggle for dominance (Wight 1977: ch. 1). Perhaps, Wight
argued, all are condemned to the same destiny which is to be replaced by a universal empire, whether through the victory of one or other of the great powers,
or because political division and military exhaustion gives a predatory neighbour the opportunity to impose its will on the entire system.

The precariousness of order is a consequence of the ease with which the dominant powers can dismantle agreements and unravel compromises that have
been forged over long intervals in the face of enormous political difficulties. But
in the main, English School theory has been less concerned with the destructive

---

[30] There is no reason to repeat the argument here. Suffice it to add that the distinctiveness of
English School analysis has been said to be its emphasis on the importance of the duty to
minimize injury for the political project of building and preserving order (Donelan 1990: ch.
4; also Jackson 2000: 154 and Wight 1966b: 128–9). The idea that international society is
the manifestation of a global 'civilizing process' can be found in Butterfield (1953: ch. 7)
and Watson (1982: 20). There is no evidence that Elias's writings influenced the choice of
terminology. The common ground is that the civilizing process embraces mutual respect
and understanding, forms of self-restraint that check the pursuit of short-term national
gains because of a longer-term interest in the preservation of order, and the use of diplomatic dialogue to find acceptable solutions to major disputes and differences (Linklater and
Suganami 2006b: 206ff.).

[31] Wight (1991: 130) stressed, and was in agreement with Toynbee on this matter, that the
great rather than the small powers have usually been responsible for the breakdown of
order (see McNeill 1989: 160ff.).

dimensions of world politics than with analysing, in a way that leaves some scope for optimism, the collective labour that has led to significant achievements in creating order and in controlling violent harm. Nothing more than enlightened self-interest is required to dispose states to support the institutions of international society, but other phenomena such as the idea that the constituent communities belong to a common civilization have had a moderating influence. In early modern Europe, for example, natural law conceptions of a universal community provided intellectual resources that states could harness for the purpose of constructing the new discourse of international society (Bull 1977: 82).

That universalistic heritage has allowed states to do more than reach agreements about principles of co-existence. It has underpinned diplomatic efforts to convert the belief in a universal moral community into humanitarian laws of war and, in more recent times, into human rights conventions that establish global expectations about how states should treat their citizens. Societies of states therefore face pressures from the 'systemic' forces analysed by realists and from humanitarian movements that aim to make international society conform to their visions of world unity. The upshot for the sociology of cosmopolitan harm conventions is that societies of states are faced with mediating between those competing forces – with finding a compromise between political realism and moral universalism. The quest to maintain order is never so advanced that states can devote all their energies to humanitarian objectives; nor is it always so confounded by geopolitical tensions that universalistic ideals are entirely ignored. But because of the fear that international rivalries will boil over in generalized war, order has usually had priority over justice. English School theorists insist that stability has intrinsic value, adding that there is little possibility of promoting humanitarian ends without it (Bull 1977: ch. 4).

Wight maintained that tensions between 'systemic' forces and 'societal' principles usually have greater influence on the development of societies of states than do the conflicts between the dominant international institutions and struggles to transcend them that appeal beyond international society to an allegedly higher world community (see however the discussion of revolutionary movements in Wight 1977: ch. 1). The 'most conspicuous theme in international history', he argued, 'is not the growth of internationalism (but) the series of efforts, by one power after another, to gain mastery of the states-system – efforts that have been defeated only by a coalition of the majority of other powers at the cost of an exhausting general war' (Wight 1978: 30). That was not to rule out the possibility that some vision of human unity might exercise more influence at some future date, or to dismiss visions of internationalism as epiphenomenal. The comment reflected Wight's pessimistic stance on 'revolutionist' ideals in which states eradicate the use of force, as well as his belief that widespread internationalist convictions are not essential for the maintenance of order. Recognition of common interests rather than attachments to any global political ideology or

ethical belief-system was all that was required of states. Bull expressed similar views while emphasizing the importance of internationalist thought for
addressing the challenges that have arisen as a result of the admission of a large
number of non-Western states into the modern society of states, and specifically
because of the need for major global reforms to ensure that the first universal
society of states commands the respect of the world's poorer peoples (Bull 2000;
Bull and Watson 1984).

The extent to which the sense of belonging to a 'higher' civilization has contributed to the maintenance of international order has already been noted. In
the case of the modern states-system, that civilizational identity led to the conviction that 'barbarian' outsiders do not have rights to political independence,
or the elementary rights to be free from conquest and violence that sovereign
states have conferred on one another. Atrocities that were committed during
successive waves of European expansion are a reminder of how ideas of 'cultural
differentiation' from, and superiority to, outlying peoples resulted in forms of
violent harm that were banned from 'civilized' international society (Hanson
2002: 303ff.; Kiernan 1998; Wight 1977: 34–5). The dark side of that society
was expressed in 'frontier decivilizing processes' that were unleashed when
Europeans encountered 'savages' that blocked their 'rightful' expansion (Keal
2003; Mennell 2007: 201).

At times, the language of necessity influenced the view that Europe's civilized compliance with the laws of war would give 'barbarians' an unfair military advantage (Wight 1991: 50ff.).[32] But civilized self-images were inherently
contradictory as they generated collective doubts about whether excessive force
in relations with 'savages' compromised claims to moral superiority and pride
in refinement and civility. The debates that attended the Spanish conquest of
the Americas remain instructive. Reflections on the place of 'the newly-discov-
ered Indians' produced, amongst other things, the belief that Christian international society should embrace the 'backward' and the 'unbelievers', albeit as
junior partners, and on unambiguously unequal terms (Wight 1991: 69–70).
That development rejected the 'principle of injury' that was mentioned earlier
(see p. 96), as did later struggles against the Atlantic slave trade and slavery, and

---

[32] Representing Britain at 1899 Hague Conventions, Admiral Fisher expressed the widely
held view that 'a restriction on the invention and construction of new types of arms would
place civilized peoples in a disadvantageous position in time of war with nations less civilized or with savage tribes' (quoted in Price 1997: 42). See also Mill in Tunick (2005) on the
belief that the principles of 'civilized' warfare did not apply to such peoples who could not
be trusted to comply with rules of reciprocity. It was often supposed that 'savages' combined
an appetite for cruelty with a tolerance of physical pain that was not found amongst refined,
civilized peoples. In short, the former's lower rationality and lack of self-restraint entitled
the 'civilized' to ignore the moral and legal principles that were widely observed in relations
between 'advanced' peoples in international society. Clearly, related attitudes influenced
the 'war against terror'.

the other cruelties of colonialism, that drew on the Enlightenment critique of domination and violence. In such ways, universalistic ideas played a valuable role in paving the way for the expansion of international society, and for globalizing the right to be free from senseless harm. The influence of those ideas illustrates the English School thesis that competition for military power and security is shaped – to a greater extent than realists recognize – by conceptions of international civility and, at times, by images of a world community.

It has been suggested that modern international society has survived because the constituent parts have been persuaded that their separate long-term interests will suffer unless they restrain ambitions to export rival conceptions of justice beyond national borders (Bull 1977: ch. 4). The belief that efforts to promote 'solidarist' ideals may jeopardize the 'pluralist' international order has been a recurrent theme in the English School analysis of how humanitarian intervention may cause more harm than good not only by weakening hard-won constraints on force but also by jeopardizing the advances that have occurred in agreeing to subordinate the global promotion of rival ideals to the quest for pluralist co-existence (Bull 1984a; Jackson 2000; Mayall 1999; Vincent and Wilson 1993; Wheeler 2000). But echoing Bull's claim that international order should be judged by what it contributes to world order (see pp. 36–7), some English School members have observed (or did so at the turn of the millennium) that the time may be ripe for incorporating new principles of intervention in the constitution of international society, at least when faced with incontrovertible evidence of a 'supreme humanitarian emergency' (Wheeler 2000). An earlier, and related, approach to the pluralist conception of the relationship between international society and world community held that global social justice is not just an end in itself but is crucial for ensuring that international order wins the support of the poorest communities (Vincent 1986).

Analyses of global moral standards have extended that mode of analysis by examining how 'transnational moral entrepreneurs' press national governments to collaborate to alleviate the suffering of the world's vulnerable peoples (Edelman 1990: 524ff.). Such investigations observe that social movements that support universal values may accomplish little without the backing of sympathetic states that use their power and authority to promote compliance with demanding global norms. Through such alliances, international society and world society have come to enjoy a certain complementarity (Clark 2007; Edelman 1990). Also important, though less tangible, is the influence that those standards have on conceptions of international legitimacy, on emotional responses to violent and non-violent harm, and on general attitudes to what is tolerable and what must be forbidden in a 'civilized' international society. Inquiries into those dynamics suggest how ethical principles can acquire sufficient autonomy from material interests to influence long-term trends in world politics, and not least by encouraging levels of self-restraint that partly solve the classical problem of how to maintain 'cooperation under anarchy'. They suggest that national and transnational movements in global civil society may yet acquire the ability to steer the society of states in a more cosmopolitan direction – though no member of the English School would conclude that such developments reveal that abolishing the struggle for power and security is about to become any easier (Edelman 1990: 524; Hurrell 2007; Raymond 1997: 231ff.).

The previous section ended with some comments about the importance of the realist focus on necessity for the sociology of cosmopolitan harm conventions, noting that the historical evidence might force analysts to conclude that the similarities between states-systems are greater than the differences. Analyses of international society converge with realism when they point out that certain long-term processes appear over and over again in states-systems – so much is obvious from observations about the sequence of hegemonies in the modern states-system, and the probable violent fate of all anarchical societies. However, the approach moves beyond realism by incorporating the analysis of the destructive potential of systemic forces within a more comprehensive inquiry into how the principles of international society and visions of world community influence the competition for security and power.

English School theorists are as reluctant as realists to state that there has been overall progress in world politics, but all recognize that international societies are a major diplomatic achievement, that they constitute an advance in global civility. As Bull and Watson (1984) argued, the expansion of international society is an example of progress in creating a universal legal and political framework that spans diverse cultures and civilizations. There is a parallel to draw with approaches to world history that observe that despite the 'numerous back-eddies and local breakdowns of civilized complexity, (there) has been an ineluctable expansion of the portions of the globe subjected to or incorporated within civilized social structures' (McNeill 1983: 10). The point to make is that the expansion of international society has been influential in shaping 'the contours of *the* civilizing process of humankind at large' (Goudsblom 2006: 14).[33] To rephrase that comment, the 'convergent evolution' of social systems has led to global harm conventions that reveal that independent communities have made some progress in creating a universal framework of moral and legal restraints (that may yet enable them to co-exist with significantly lower levels of violent and non-violent harm).[34] It is important that the sociology of cosmopolitan harm conventions incorporates such insights in its organizing framework of analysis. The key questions which will be set out in the last chapter therefore

---

[33] A similar point can be found in Jackson (2000: 181) where it is maintained that the society of states is the most successful form of world political organization that has appeared thus far in reconciling the desire to live in independent political communities with the need for order.

[34] See Sanderson (1988: ch. 3) on the idea of 'convergent evolution'. Also relevant is the general theme of cultural convergence and divergence in world history as discussed in Northrup (2005). These are matters to come back to in volume 3.

express the need to transcend realism on two scores: by analysing civilizing forces in different states-systems, and by considering how far the complementarity of international and world society – exemplified by the human rights culture and developments in criminal law – demonstrates that modern international society is breaking new ground. The question is how far 'convergent evolution' towards support for a cosmopolitan harm principle represents the development of 'civilized social structures' that may yet contract the dominion of violent and non-violent harm.

The perils of collective identities

If it is to succeed where its predecessors failed with respect to establishing cosmopolitan harm conventions, then modern international society will need to weaken harmful identities that rest on invidious distinctions between insiders and outsiders. Such dualisms have been intrinsic to relations between groups from the earliest times, but they may have intensified during the first wave of state-formation. In the ensuing conditions of insecurity, emotional ties to particular 'survival units' have invariably been inimical to extensions of solidarity that are, in principle, possible because of the vulnerabilities that people have in common.[35] International societies are intriguing forms of world political organization because the constituent parts need to have acquired some level of detachment from parochial standpoints in order to reach agreements about principles of co-existence. As previously noted, inter-state understandings have often rested on shared assumptions about collective superiority over outlying regions that justified acts of violence, seizures of territory and so forth that were deemed impermissible in relations between 'civilized' states. Political communities that succeeded in moving beyond a fixation with cultural differences in their dealings with one another often assumed they had the sovereign right to commit terrible acts of violence against domestic minorities. Significantly, over the last few decades, such assumptions and actions have often been condemned by key elements of the world community and international society.

Disagreements exist about whether cultural differences are increasing in political importance after several centuries in which the opposite trend seemed to be taking place (Brown 1988). What is beyond doubt is that, in many states, the politics of recognition are at least as important as the politics of redistributive justice that was spearheaded by the Left (Fraser 2000). It is also clear that moral sensitivities to the dangers that reside in constructions of 'self–other' relations, and to actual instances of harm to collective identities in the form of violence, humiliation and exclusion, have moved to the centre of modern political theory and practice, and possibly to a greater extent than ever before. That may be a

---

[35] Several chapters in Raaflaub and Rosenstein (1999) discuss the violent consequences of collective social identities based on pernicious distinctions between insiders and outsiders.

distinctive feature of the modern or 'post-modern' world, and clear testimony to 'civilizing' influences. It is up to the comparative sociology of cosmopolitan harm conventions to ascertain whether there have been major progressions in recognizing the relationship between insider–outsider dualisms and the long history of violent and non-violent harm, and also in confronting the formidable task of dismantling the pernicious distinctions between self and other that have dominated human affairs for millennia.

The expansion of international society to include the former colonies as sovereign equals required the weakening of earlier hierarchical conceptions of world order in which the 'higher civilizations' saw themselves as surrounded by 'barbarians' or 'infidels' (Bull and Watson 1984). Support for a multiplicity of civilizations, none standing above the others, gained ground in this period, but the society of states has made limited progress in ensuring cultural justice for all peoples (Shapcott 2001). From the standpoint of many indigenous groups, the decolonization process that brought sovereign independence to new states did not end their plight as colonized minorities within, for example, 'white settler' societies. Until recently, the dominant strata in those social systems believed that 'pre-modern' or 'tribal' identities would wither away as social evolution followed its 'natural' course of securing their assimilation within 'advanced' cultures. As with earlier struggles to be free from imperial domination, indigenous peoples have rejected distinctions between the 'civilized' and the 'barbarian' along with related assumptions that the former are entitled to judge other societies on their terms (Keal 2003). But few if any indigenous groups have the resources to establish sovereign states. They have been largely concerned as a result with ending violent and non-violent harm, with gaining restitution for past injustices, and with acquiring forms of self-government that enable them to preserve 'traditional' values that 'mainstream' society no longer regards as inferior or holds in contempt.

Indigenous groups call for the establishment of an international society of states *and* peoples or, more accurately, for its re-establishment under post-colonial conditions. In the first phase of contact, European states recognized the separate status of African principalities but, in the four centuries following the conquest of Mexico, there was a broad retreat from the practice of acknowledging that non-European political systems possessed sovereign rights or their equivalent (Bull 1984b: ch. 7). The now-discredited legal concept of *terra nullius* (uninhabited land) was one example of how more inclusive notions of an international society that had embraced European sovereign states and non-European polities were destroyed by that infamous justification of colonial rule that resulted in genocide, the seizure of land and the destruction of indigenous identities (Keal 2003: 20, 51ff.).

Greater sensitivity to indigenous demands is one of the most interesting normative shifts in international relations since the end of the Second World War. Changing ethical sensibilities have led to substantial change in only a handful of cases, but developments in international law have addressed one aspect of 'the moral backwardness of international society' by adding group rights to a human rights culture that reflects the biases of Western individualism (Keal 2003; Thornberry 2002).[36] What can be regarded as an innovative approach to bridging the gulf between international and world order – namely the global recognition of group rights – is deeply controversial in many societies where there is a fear that such concessions will lead to social and/or political fragmentation. For their part, many liberals have expressed concerns that recognizing group rights may result in a dangerous contraction of the rights of individuals and in their subordination to the interests of collectivities. But as the earlier discussion of 'hate speech' noted (see p. 52), support for minority rights acknowledges that many people have suffered violent and non-violent harm at the hands of others who are not concerned with their personal characteristics and actions as such, but are motivated by contempt for the stigmatized groups with which they are associated. For that reason, cosmopolitan harm conventions must balance respect for individual liberty with the collective 'recognition and protection' of subordinated peoples (Thornberry 2002: 378ff.).

Parallel demands have been advanced by minority nations that have been victims of assimilationist strategies promoted by modern states.[37] Global standards are also now more favourably disposed to their plight, although national governments have failed to agree on a definition of 'minority people' (Thornberry 2002: 52ff.). Even so, changing principles of legitimacy with respect to minority groups provide evidence of some movement, however qualified,

---

[36] The main example is the shift from the worldview that informed the 1957 International Labour Organisation Convention No. 107 on Indigenous and Tribal Populations. The Convention referred to 'semi-tribal' groups that were 'in the process of losing their tribal characteristics', but which were 'not yet integrated into the national community' – a process that was regarded as progressive as long as it did not use 'force or coercion' to bring about 'the artificial assimilation of these populations' (Article 1, paragraph 2; Article 2, paragraphs 3 and 4 in Thornberry 2002: annex 1). Reflecting a change in global standards, the 1989 ILO Convention and the 1993 United Nations Draft Declaration on the Rights of Indigenous Peoples defend the rights of indigenous peoples to 'maintain and develop their identities, languages and religions, within the framework of the States in which they live' (Preamble, in Thornberry 2002: annex 2). As part of the more general 'right of all peoples' including minority nations 'to be different', and to 'consider themselves different', the 1993 Draft Declaration states that indigenous 'peoples are equal in dignity and rights' to all others (Preamble, in Thornberry 2002: annex 3). That Declaration defends indigenous rights to exercise 'control … over developments affecting them and their lands, territories and resources' so they can more effectively 'practise and revitalise their cultural traditions and customs' and protect 'sacred places, including burial sites' (Preamble and Articles 12–13, in Thornberry 2002: annex 3).

[37] That is not to suggest that all minority nations look favourably on indigenous groups in the same society, or that indigenous peoples can conclude that they will also profit from the former's success in increasing power and prestige.

towards re-creating a society of states and peoples.[38] For over four centuries, sovereign rights and the duty of non-intervention usually overshadowed
concerns about the well-being of national or religious minorities. Until quite
recently, the expulsion of peoples was an accepted practice in the European system of states (Elias 2006a; Rae 2002). With respect to the Ottoman treatment
of Armenians at the end of the nineteenth century, 'the Great Powers peti-
tioned the Sultan on their behalf, but rarely went further than this'; following
the Armenian genocide in 1915, the European powers pleaded with Ottoman
rulers to respect 'changing international norms of legitimate state behaviour',
and threatened, but subsequently failed, to hold the regime accountable at the
end of the First World War (Rae 2002: 161). After the Treaty of Lausanne in
1923, the great powers presided over the mass movement of Greeks and Turks;
approximately 1.5 million Greeks left Turkey for Greece, and 400,000 Turks
moved from Greece to Turkey with little choice in the matter (Jackson Preece
1998). States that encouraged such population transfers effectively condoned
'ethnic cleansing' as it has been called since the Yugoslav wars of the 1990s.
The relationship between sovereignty and minority rights has undergone radical change in the second part of the twentieth century. Mass deportations and
genocide were condemned as criminal offences at the end of the Second World
War as part of a major 'normative shift in international attitudes' (Jackson
Preece 1998). Later conventions prohibiting 'serious bodily or mental harm' to
national, ethnic, racial and other minorities are a further example of how sovereignty has become increasingly conditional on 'the responsibility to protect'
in the intervening period (Crawford 2002a).[39]

Such 'civilizing' ideas are not universally welcomed. An influential critique in
the immediate aftermath of the Second World War raised the alarm that respect
for group rights could undermine stability and encourage secession in the newly

---

[38] Sharp contrasts between historical eras should be treated with caution. Rae (2002: 245)
argues that the protection of religious minority rights under the Peace of Westphalia was
a significant 'normative shift in the system' since no 'international norms regarding the
internal constitution of the state' existed when Ferdinand and Isabella embarked on creating 'a homogeneous state' in Spain in the late fifteenth century. In the early seventeenth
century, many (including Cardinal Richelieu) regarded Spain's expulsion of Muslims, who
had only recently converted to Christianity, as barbaric. Louis XIV maintained the sovereign could behave as he pleased towards religious minorities, but his standpoint 'was widely
rejected across Europe' (Rae 2002: 81, 121 and 161).

[39] See Article II of the 1973 International Convention on the Suppression and Punishment
of the Crime of Apartheid that prohibits harm to 'the members of a racial group or groups'
whether by infringing 'their freedom or dignity, or by subjecting them to torture or to cruel,
inhuman or degrading treatment or punishment', and similar formulations with respect
to harm to 'national, ethnical, racial or religious groups' in the 1948 Convention on the
Prevention and Punishment of the Crime of Genocide, as well as Articles 4–7 of the 1993
Statute that established the tribunal that was authorized to prosecute persons responsible for
violating international humanitarian law in the former Yugoslavia (see Evans 1994: 36–7,
218 and 393).

independent societies (Claude 1969).[40] Strategic alliances that depend on stable allies that are involved in suppressing minorities are worth emphasizing here. The more general belief that states contribute to international order by preserving internal stability – often at the cost of individual and group freedoms – is also influential (Bull 1979a; Keal 1983: 203–4). Demands for group rights effectively ask modern societies to reverse long-term processes of development that often led to a strong sense of national solidarity that many continue to cherish. Modern states acquired supremacy over rival forms of political organization in early modern Europe by monopolizing control of the instruments of violence and the right of taxation, and by weakening sub-state and transnational loyalties until the point was reached where citizens regarded the nation as the 'natural' object of emotional identification (Linklater 1998). Incessant geopolitical rivalry and warfare encouraged such 'totalizing identities'. The question arises of whether the decline of force in relations between the major industrial powers has created unusual opportunities for the resurgence of loyalties that are both 'higher' and 'lower' than the nation-state. Many societies face pressures to recognize multiple identities as groups struggle for the recognition of sub-state loyalties and/or build transnational solidarities in response to global issues such as environmental degradation. Perhaps they herald the emergence of new forms of political community that will observe restraints in relations with minority groups and outsiders that did not exist in the period in which 'monolithic' national identities were ascendant.[41]

Interest in the difficulties involved in creating 'post-national constellations' is not confined to the analysts of developments within modern states. It runs through studies of the relationship between sub-state, state and transnational loyalties in emergent supranational organizations such as the European Union. The larger issue is how far people can combine 'old' and 'new' loyalties in new systems of identification that respond to the problems that result from being forced together in longer webs of interconnectedness, and that may be impossible to solve without new centres of power and authority which, on current evidence, offer little 'emotional warmth' to large numbers of those involved (Elias 2000: 551; Mennell 1994). Within many nation-states, an enormous labour is required to reconcile identities and loyalties that are in conflict because of past failures to address injustices between established groups and outsiders. As, if not more, complex is the challenge of weakening insider–outsider dualisms,

---

[40] That concern remains powerful in multi-ethnic societies where sovereignty was acquired only recently, and where the fear of liberal imperialism, which Kosovan independence will have done little to dispel, runs high.

[41] Evidently, national loyalties can be recharged by anxieties about levels of migration. Increased security fears in recent years as a result of terrorist attacks aroused public concern that 'multicultural' policies ignored problems of social integration with the result that the societies involved are now exposed to the threats posed by Islamist transnational politico-religious affiliations.

and the perils of collective identities, in the context of increasing interconnect-edness when major institutional innovations are needed in response to inter-twined global problems. Evolving interconnectedness has highly ambiguous consequences. On the one hand, the pressures to become more sensitive to the interests of other people over greater distances encourage people to develop more realistic understandings of one another; on the other hand, encroaching threats to power, status and autonomy often promote counter-movements that rely on hostile and demeaning representations of outsiders.[42] But that has long been a feature of 'double-bind processes' between states.

Realist reflections on the logic of anarchy warn against assuming that soci-eties are poised to develop the multiple identities that are critical for develop-ing cosmopolitan harm conventions that promote cultural justice within and between states. The English School analysis of international society adds that the goal of preserving order and stability has often outweighed any interest in the plight of 'sub-national' peoples. But as advocates of that approach implicitly recognize, the expansion of international society has been accompanied by a degree of detachment from exclusionary cultural or civilizational standpoints – by important advances in 'thinking from the standpoint of the other' that have made it easier for radically different societies to come together within the same universal diplomatic framework. The rise of the human rights culture provides evidence of changing global assumptions about sovereignty. Legal responsi-bilities to refrain from exercising sovereign power in ways that cause serious bodily and mental harm to various 'sub-national' groups appeared shortly after international obligations to minimize 'unnecessary suffering' and 'superfluous injury' in war (see pp. 37–8). The result is an increased awareness in some circles of the importance of 'post-national' communities that display great sensitivity to cultural differences, and which are skilled at easing tensions and resolving conflicts that emerge from, and/or accentuate, pernicious self–other distinc-tions within and between states. Studies of identity politics have drawn atten-tion to the role of such dualisms in unleashing violent and non-violent harm in the modern society of states. The sociology of cosmopolitan harm conven-tions can broaden the inquiry by comparing the typical responses to pernicious

---

[42] The potentials for combining diverse loyalties including those that support cosmopolitan harm conventions have clearly varied across human history. As Elias (1991: 139) stated, 'societies, as they are constituted today, have several interwoven levels of integration. The kin group, the tribal level, the state level, the continental level, and finally the level of humanity, they all are steps in the ladder. Observers of the contemporary scene may notice a very pronounced difference in the power chances available to representatives of differ-ent levels of integration at different stages of humanity's development'. Elias (2001a: 164–5) also argued that 'integration-disintegration tensions' – conflicts between the processes that force people together into longer webs of interconnectedness, and the new divisions and distinctions that spring into existence almost simultaneously – look certain to continue well into the future.

dualisms in different states-systems, and by asking whether the current order has witnessed forms of collective learning in that domain that augur well for future efforts to control the processes that have forced radically different groups together without relying on political strategies that stigmatize, humiliate, and in other ways withhold respect.

The vagaries of class

The clear implication of the class analysis of history and politics is that economic exploitation has long blocked the introduction of cosmopolitan harm conventions that protect vulnerable, lower strata from dominant social groups. A related theme is that specific subordinate classes and 'counter-hegemonic' movements have a distinctive role to play in creating cosmopolitan arrangements. Those comments need to be seen in conjunction with a central dimension of the materialist interpretation of history which is usually ignored by mainstream criticisms of its failure to understand the impact of war and geopolitics on the history of relations between societies – namely, its interest in the long-term trend from small, isolated communities to territorial states and empires, and the growing global interconnections that Marx was amongst the first to analyse. Mainstream approaches to international relations which argue that economic forces and rising levels of interdependence are subordinate to the divisive consequences of geopolitical rivalries have failed to deal with Marxist claims that those domains have been inseparable for much of human history.[43] An additional point is that conventional theories have concentrated on violent harm whereas historical materialism has been more preoccupied with understanding the increasingly important phenomenon of non-violent harm and its relationship with global structures. The link between rising levels of interconnectedness and structural harm is the basis then for a distinctive historical-materialist approach to cosmopolitan harm conventions.

That panoramic historical overview has inspired analysts that lament the decline of studies of long-term processes while rejecting materialist accounts of the 'globalization of human society' (Elias 1994: 144ff.; Mennell 1990a). A recurrent theme, which is evident in realist critiques of liberal and Marxist theories of interdependence, is that expansions of economic activity have not been as important as the growth of state power and the role of geopolitical rivalries in promoting human interconnectedness. One response to that criticism points

---

[43] Curtin (1984: ch. 1) argues that merchants in the first trading settlements were amongst the earliest 'cross-cultural brokers' to develop harm conventions. It may be that international societies emerged in regions that had already witnessed significant commercial integration and attendant forms of cross-cultural brokerage (see Wight 1977: 33). In any event, the evidence is that early states and empires were usually the driving-force behind longer trading networks that may nevertheless have prepared the way for those outcomes (Thomas 1979: 55–6).

to Marx's recognition that early societies relied on force to protect communal resources from seizure by outsiders. In short, warfare was one of the crucial 'conditions' of production (Marx 1973 [1857–58]: 474). An additional core element of Marx's theory of history was that war and conquest were inherent in pre-capitalist systems of production; force was integral to the accumulation of wealth; more fundamentally, state power was class power. The importance of those themes is probably best illustrated by the prominence of state-organized slavery in world history.

Marx emphasized that conquest and enslavement (which, as noted earlier, greatly increased with early state-formation) drew more and more people into wider networks of mutual dependence. Of course, his principal focus was on industrial capitalism which, because of its inner compulsion to expand to new areas in the quest for untapped markets and new forces or relations of production, was the revolutionary force that accelerated the trend towards the universalization of social and economic connections. Global transformations were evident in the conquest of distance, and in the related phenomenon that the effects of capitalist crises and major technological breakthroughs could be felt all over the world, more or less simultaneously. For the first time, understanding the history of the social and economic integration of the species and the processes that had come to influence peoples everywhere was placed at the centre of social and political inquiry. Marx's inquiry identified two main phases in the evolution of connections between societies, and envisaged a third era that was thought to be unfolding in the womb of the capitalist system.[44] Early societies were organized around relations of personal dependence in which individuals were tied to specific groups like 'herd animals', or shackled to particular slave owners, feudal lords and similar agents of (concrete) labour exploitation. The rise of industrial capitalism replaced those ties, but unprecedented levels of personal independence left people at the mercy of uncontrolled global market forces. What was tracked in the narrative is the increasing role of structural harm in human subjection, and its central importance for any project of universal emancipation.

Traditional critiques of historical materialism are not exactly wide of the mark when they emphasize its general neglect of the impact of ethnicity, nationalism, geopolitics and war on the course of human development – and, more specifically, the failure to understand how they would bar the way to an envisaged condition in which relations of personal dependence and independence would finally give way to the condition of 'socialized humanity'. In that future state, the assumption was, people would be associated as equals in a universal system

---

[44] There are clear parallels with Elias's claim that what changes in history is the way in which people are bound together, and with his contention that the purpose of sociology is to analyse long-term developmental processes that have come to affect the entire species (Elias 2000: 402).

of cooperation that ended not only labour exploitation but geopolitical strug-gles, fear and distrust between societies, and all pernicious insider–outsider dis-tinctions. Realists have long stressed that Marx erred in predicting an epochal transformation in which the injuries caused by major wars would decline or disappear while harm caused by structural forces would increase, encouraging new transnational solidarities and movements between subordinate classes. But many non-realist approaches have advanced accounts of global transformations that run on parallel lines to Marxist predictions of a broad, overall change in the relationship between concrete and abstract harm, and between international and transnational harm – which is not to imply that they have necessarily been influ-enced by, or are sympathetic to, historical materialism (see pp. 38–9).[45] There is also a major difference between approaches that describe those changes in posi-tive terms (as forces for pacification) and Marxist and neo-Marxist approaches that emphasize connections between structural harm, new opportunities for transnational exploitation, and growing global inequalities of power and wealth (that the dominant strata will protect, if need be, by physical force).

Before proceeding further, it is important to consider Marxist responses to the accusation that they fail to recognize the autonomy of war and geopolitics. The counter-claim, as noted earlier, is that pre-capitalist systems of production did not separate coercion from the accumulation of wealth. Modern capitalist societies, and the ideologies that have legitimated uncoupling markets from the supposed irrationalities of state interference, took the unique step of separating 'politics' from 'economics', although Marxists argue that the divorce between those spheres is more apparent than real. Politics and economics are profoundly interconnected, but the illusion of forming autonomous spheres legitimates capitalist social relations which are portrayed as the outcome of free contracts between equal people (Rosenberg 1994; Teschke 2003).

Marx was mainly concerned with demonstrating that such contracts were not free and equal, but of greater importance for present purposes are his reflections on how the separation between economics and politics has shaped modern attitudes to permissible and impermissible harm. Given the dominant ideol-ogy of freedom and equality, it is unsurprising, from a historical-materialist perspective, that capitalist societies emphasize the importance of, and celebrate achievements in, prohibiting physical harm, that the liberal harm principle lies at the heart of the criminal law, and that the notion that 'cruelty is the worst thing we do' has come to enjoy widespread support – possibly to a greater extent than ever before. Nor is it odd that 'bourgeois' reformist movements in the

---

[45] Two illustrations may suffice – the liberal account of how the 'trading state' has been a pacifying force in world politics (Rosecrance 1986), and the discussion of how changes in sector integration, specifically the growth of economic interdependence, have moderated the competition for military power and security (Buzan and Little 2000: ch. 16). The second approach is much closer to realism, but critical of the ahistoricism of Waltz's structural realism.

nineteenth century were largely preoccupied with the brutalities of slavery and empire, with violence against women and children, or with cruelty to animals. Those observations resonate with accounts of the formation of a new middle-class identity with 'refined' ethical sensibilities that was established through measured contrasts with the 'rougher' dispositions of the 'lower' strata (and the violent character of the aristocracy).[46] Marx's contempt for bourgeois freedoms reflected their embodiment in a specific project that proclaimed the virtues of liberty and equality while neglecting the class inequalities and modes of exploitation that were intrinsic to capitalist social relations. There is no need to pause to consider whether classical Marxists failed to appreciate that subordinate classes also had a long-term interest in sharing bourgeois freedoms. The critical point was that it was necessary to transcend liberalism in order to bring an end to distinctively modern forms of structural harm.

The 'social harm' approach has emphasized that the separation of 'economics' and 'politics' has exposed vulnerable groups to 'setbacks' that lie outside the classical 'paradigm' of harm with its focus on physical injury, mental cruelty and so forth (Hillyard *et al.* 2004; see pp. 43–6).[47] To vary the theme, the use of labour-power had to respect the prevailing prohibitions of force, but that left ample scope for structural harm, exploitation, negligence or complicity – a level of discretion that has been challenged as a result of modern sensibilities to the ways in which harm can be caused by indifference, or without the intention to cause suffering, as in the earlier example of 'exporting hazards' (see p. 99; also Nichols 1997: ch. 5). But such sensibilities are largely confined to philosophical engagements with the problem of indifference to harm in world politics; practical measures to deal with distant harm lag behind.

Marx stressed that force had been central to the first phase in the global spread of capitalist relations.[48] But as violence came to be regarded as incompatible

---

[46] An extensive literature deals with the relationship between 'campaigns of compassion' and the nineteenth-century middle-class culture of refinement. Barker-Benfield (1992: 55ff., 224ff., 231ff.) provides a useful overview. Haskell (1985) offers a controversial account of how capitalism generated new humanitarian sensibilities that influenced the struggle to abolish the Atlantic slave trade and slavery (see also Crawford 2002b). Thomas (1984) maintains that opposition to 'barbaric' aristocratic and working-class blood sports was at the heart of constructions of a 'civilized' bourgeois identity. Those perspectives suggest that historical materialism can shed light on how capitalist social relations and modern attitudes to cruelty and violence are internally related. But such aspects of the civilizing process have not been central to materialist forms of inquiry (see pp. 199–207).

[47] A new ethic of indifference that was enshrined in the commercial tenet – 'I can only gain by hurting you' – appeared in the seventeenth and eighteenth centuries, displacing earlier Christian ideas of charity and altruism. Engels referred to 'social murder' to describe the structural qualities of modern harm (see Harris 1974).

[48] For example, British rule in India led to 'unspeakable cruelties' and to 'the massacre of the population of large towns, with no other consideration bestowed upon them than on natural events' (see Warren 1980: 41 quoting Marx's 'The British Role in India'). Warren (1980: 21) added that 'the period of cruellest exploitation in the history of English industrial

with, and indeed as a hindrance to, the 'natural' functioning of markets, Marxist and neo-Marxist theories focused their attention on the global structures, and on alliances between elites in core and peripheral societies, that created the conditions in which markets could operate freely and in which transfers of wealth could take place without the reliance on coercion – through, for example, such phenomena as 'unequal exchange' (Emmanuel 1972). Other perspectives have analysed the interplay between state structures, class forces and global international organizations that underpin the worldwide exploitation of labour. As in the case of studies of 'transnational class formation', they criticize neo-liberal ideas about the unrivalled efficiency of free market forces, showing how those arrangements are anchored in global power structures, and prone to crisis and instability that can seriously harm the interests of vulnerable peoples across the world (Robinson and Harris 2000; van der Pijl 1998). Such discussions run parallel to left-liberal accounts of the harmful consequences of 'global coercive regimes' which show, from rather different premises, how powerful groups profit from the exploitation of others – not in the Marxist use of that term but in the liberal sense of 'taking advantage of the vulnerable' (see pp. 53–5). The liberal discourse therefore highlights the moral deficits of global relations of dominance and dependence that have often been muted in the structural forms of Marxist political economy – specifically the phenomenon of unjust enrichment that exposes affluent groups to charges of complicity in profiting from systematically generated vulnerabilities.[49]

Third World neo-Marxist approaches toppled the Western proletariat from its position as the key instrument of universal emancipation,[50] a development that was part of the larger move towards a more detached understanding of world history, one that was freed from triumphalist assumptions about capitalist

capitalism', the era between 1780 and 1814, 'is remarkable as much for its brevity as for its cruelty'. Usually missing from such accounts is a detailed discussion of changing attitudes to force – of how the dominant views of what was tolerable and what should be permitted changed as part of the 'civilizing process' (see Chapter 4).

[49] Such normative themes were rarely encountered in structuralist Marxist accounts of the capitalist world economy that had their heyday in the 1970s and 1980s. However, one work from that period – Emmanuel (1972) – is worth recalling because of its influence in highlighting the extent to which the Western industrial proletariat profited from, and was complicit in, unequal exchange. In the terms that were used in Chapter 2, the working classes did not cause deliberate harm, but profited from unjust enrichment, and were complicit in 'mediated' harm. That is to employ ethical terms that were rarely used in those discussions, or which were masked given a peculiar aversion to moral philosophy on the part of the founding figures of historical materialism.

[50] The reference is to Marx's bizarre contention that 'the whole of human servitude is involved in the relation of worker to production', that all other 'relations of servitude are only modifications and consequences' of the miseries associated with the productive process, and that the proletariat would release all humanity from suffering in the course of its emancipation (Marx 1967 [1844]: 299). Such biases stood in the way of a comprehensive theory of social harm that dealt with, amongst other things, race, ethnicity and gender.

modernity, and from the conviction that its spread beyond Europe would bring unprecedented rewards that non-European societies could not hope to secure by themselves. The collapse of the European overseas empires was one reason for the break with such egocentric worldviews. In particular, leading neo-Marxist approaches to the world economy in the 1960s and 1970s combined a belief in the progressive role of Third World nationalist movements with new understandings of global dominance and dependence over the last few centuries. Their aim was to develop a more 'global' perspective on the rise and development of the capitalist world economy – one that did not see history as culminating in modern Europe, but which linked greater awareness of Europe's role in promoting the servitude and subordination of other peoples with the commitment to a more genuinely internationalist or cosmopolitan political practice (see Burke 2003; Hobson 2004).

Marxist analyses of class structures raise distinctive questions for the sociology of cosmopolitan harm conventions. That is partly the result of Marx's critical method which analysed tensions between dominant ideologies and the social practices they legitimated, and which coupled that inquiry with visions of alternative social relations that were thought to be immanent within existing arrangements. None of the other approaches that are discussed in this chapter matches its perspective on the transformation of social and political relations.

But the broad fate of that inquiry raises interesting issues for the sociology of cosmopolitan harm conventions. On the one hand, there is the Marxian focus on the tensions between the dominant capitalist ideology with its affirmation of freedom and equality, and the realities of economic exploitation. There is, in addition, the critique of bourgeois freedoms and (implicitly) the focus on the shortcomings of a liberal harm principle that mainly focuses on the problem of violent harm and ignores the problem of exploitation – a shortcoming that has already been noted in critical discussions of the liberal tenet that 'cruelty is the worst thing we do' (see pp. 105–6). Those considerations point to tensions between ideology and practice that can lead to struggles to reduce the level of violent and non-violent harm. On the other side stand the approaches to global power structures that stress the absence of immanent alternatives and potentials. An example is the study of the transnational capitalist class that presides over global patterns of change that uproot individuals from traditional communities and expose them to structural harm while depriving them of opportunities – which democratic liberalism regards as their right – to participate in decision-making processes that can protect them from exploitation (Robinson and Harris 2000). Such approaches resemble realism in suggesting that strong parallels exist between different eras. All contentions that there has been significant progress in human history are treated with suspicion given the permanent reality of class domination and labour exploitation, and its current worldwide manifestations. The break with systems of production in which force was an accepted method of accumulating wealth remains a revolutionary development, in that the theory and practice of freedom and equality hold out the promise of entirely new global relations: they help explain why the development of a more cosmopolitan international society is possible. But the focus on the iron cage of 'market civilization' or 'disciplinary neo-liberalism' points in a different direction because it suggests that the future belongs to global political and economic structures that will create poverty, exploitation and subordination, and that will leave the affluent with a strangle-hold on the life-chances of uprooted and divided, vulnerable peoples (Bowden and Seabrooke 2006; Gill 1995). A comparative sociology of cosmopolitan harm conventions cannot ignore that interpretation of the blighted achievements of capitalist modernity which, at its best, preserves the Marxian focus on the tragic consequences of the evolution of the species from the small-scale societies of earliest times to the global condition that exists today (van der Pijl 2007).

The potentialities for care

How the tensions within capitalist modernity are resolved may depend on how far notions of care and compassion are extended beyond borders, and how far they keep pace with universalizing processes that are tying more and more people together. To consider that point in more detail, it is necessary to turn to one of the most innovative developments in late twentieth-century social and political theory – the idea of the 'ethic of care and responsibility'.

The analysis of that ethic arose in the attempt to demonstrate the gendered nature of mainstream psychological studies of individual moral development – applications to international relations occurred much later (Robinson 1999). Those developments are relevant to the investigation of cosmopolitan harm conventions, and specifically to an inquiry into the extent to which moral attitudes to vulnerability and suffering have influenced the long-term development of states-systems. Of course, the ethic of care is not the only perspective surveyed in this chapter that considers such questions about the relationship between power and morality. All of the approaches endeavour to shed light on the extent to which societies may succeed in living together with the minimum of suffering (Moore 1972: 102).[51] What the ethic of care adds to those

---

[51] That is explicit in the critical-theoretical offshoots of Western Marxism that aim to 'lend a voice to (the) suffering' and to promote solidarity as 'universal compassion among all suffering creatures' (Adorno 1973: 17; Horkheimer, quoted in Bohman 1999: 196). Studies of self–other relations (or identity and difference) have a similar interest which is directed at destabilizing pernicious distinctions and their harmful effects. Advocates of mainstream approaches to international relations are often hesitant to foreground moral claims, or they avoid them because of a commitment to dispassionate analysis, but they often state that one of the purposes of social inquiry is to understand how people can co-exist with lower levels of suffering. As already noted, Bull's defence of 'neutrality' was combined with a muted defence of world order, a condition in which people would be free from dangers to life and security (Bull 1977: xv). Partly because it is an example of the influence of Christian values

discussions is a particular emphasis on the significance of the sense of connectedness with vulnerable others for social and political life. That theme emerged
as part of a socio-psychological analysis of specific ethical skills that women
acquire – often to a greater degree than men – as carers in traditional families.
But as already noted, their importance extends beyond that domain, and has
particular relevance for reflections on the moral challenges that have arisen as a
result of increasing interconnectedness.

As is generally known, Gilligan's study of the ethic of care and responsibility
was a critical riposte to Kohlberg's claim that the highest level of individual moral
development is to be found in the disposition to think in terms of universalizable principles of justice. That essentially Kantian standpoint was challenged
for privileging the traditional male experience of the importance of impersonal
principles for organizing relations between strangers in the public domain. The
male orientation towards ethics was criticized for downgrading the values that
reflect the 'different voice' that has been especially central to the lives of women,
but which they have not monopolized.[52] Gilligan stressed the equal value of that
form of moral experience, adding that it could be combined with an ethic of
justice to ensure that heightened sensitivities to the existence or danger of violent and non-violent harm governed the public and private spheres (Gilligan
1982: 174; also Clement 1996; Larrabee 1993; O'Neill 1989). Such sensibilities
could offer protection from ethical positions in which an insistence on complying with principles of justice could lead to a lack of humanity – to a fetish for
obeying abstract rules that were divorced from considerations of actual needs
and circumstances.[53]

In the care ethic, considerable importance is attached to the nature of emotional identification with specific others – the dependent and vulnerable others
with whom women in particular are often intimately 'connected' (Dillon 1992;
Gilligan 1982: ch. 3). The discussion has led to the question of how far the

on classical realist and international society perspectives, it is also worth citing Butterfield's
comment that 'because the infliction of suffering is so terrible a thing, it is our duty to prevent or to stop it where we can without adding to it; but it is not a virtue to avenge if we open
the gates to a further realm of suffering and atrocity' (quoted in Murray 1997: 117). As Foot
(2006: 131) has observed, Carr's writings made the link between scholarship and alleviating
suffering abundantly clear, reflecting the influence of certain humanistic themes in radical
social inquiry on his version of realism.

[52] Fletcher (1995: 283ff.) argues that as early as the sixteenth century in the West, and especially
between 1660 and 1800, such sensitivities to the needs of family members were thought to
reflect a tenderness from which men were largely immune. The belief that women were
naturally disposed to care for specific others was often used to justify their subordination
especially up to the eighteenth century, at which point sentimental fiction began to regard
female sensitivity to suffering as a necessary antidote to male hard-heartedness and the cold
rationality of the public sphere (Barker-Benfield 1992: ch. 1, 66ff., 215ff.).

[53] Kant's position on the unconditional duty not to lie is frequently cited in discussions of
deontological moral systems that suffer from precisely that defect.

qualities that Gilligan found in female interviewees (including 'the wish not to hurt others' and the desire to resolve differences without harming anyone) can shape all realms of social and political interaction (see p. 81).[54] The scale of the challenge is evident from the determining role of the 'power to hurt' in international relations, and from the implicit assumption in realist thought that the ethic of care is best regarded as a morality that is suited to the private sphere rather than an ideal that can be applied across all human relationships (Gilligan 1982: 149; also Clement 1996; Dillon 1992).

But realist criticisms are too quick to dismiss the importance of the care ethic for governing patterns of interconnectedness so that people are spared unnecessary harm. Crucial here is feminist advocacy of 'interactive universalism', a standpoint that concentrates on the 'networks of dependence and the web of human affairs in which we are immersed', and which argues that attention to the 'vulnerabilities' of those affected should govern the moral compass (Benhabib 1993: 189; also Robinson 1999).[55] That is not just an ethical ideal however. Analyses of the struggle to abolish the Atlantic slave trade have stressed the role that women played in publicizing sexual violence, physical brutality and the deprivation of family life, not least through empathy with the suffering of female slaves (Ware 1992: 60ff.).[56]

References to slavery invite discussion of dimensions of the West's encounter with non-Western peoples where one conception of the ethic of care (though not the version that has been advocated in feminist writings – the differences are revealing) led to disastrous forms of paternalism. To illustrate, Australian

---

[54] To rephrase the point, support for the ethic of care is not about dignifying moral dispositions that reflect women's traditional confinement to the private sphere, but about harnessing particular ethical sensibilities that can be found across different social strata, albeit in varying degrees, in order to try to reduce violent and non-violent harm (see Clement 1996: 2–3, 89 for a related defence of a 'public ethic of care').

[55] As noted, Gilligan's position was that the traditional male experience of the public world breeds a high level of detachment from the specific needs of particular persons. A related contention is that the predominant ethic is largely centred on 'negative' obligations, and on low levels of solidarity (Clement 1996: 113; see Chapter 2). Conventional female socialization processes, by contrast, are said to stress the importance of high levels of involvement in promoting the well-being of specific others. The ethic of care and responsibility has been influential in suggesting how connectedness, interactive universalism, and responsiveness to the needs of particular people can promote higher levels of social solidarity, or alter what Elias (1978: 122ff.) called the 'We/I' balance in modern society and politics (that is, the relationship between individual interests and collective purposes).

[56] With their refined sensibilities, women were expected to play a special role in humanizing or 'civilizing' male attitudes to slavery (Ware 1992: 66ff.). The notion that women are more peace-loving than men may owe much to their participation in nineteenth-century 'compassions of campaign' to alleviate the suffering of slaves, and to end cruelty to animals and children (see Ware 1992: 66ff.). It is important not to essentialize, however. As Connell (1995) argues, the traits that are associated with the dominant forms of masculinity or femininity in any epoch are usually spread across the gender divide, albeit unequally.

missions that moved aboriginal groups from traditional lands in the nineteenth century may have thought they were saving imperilled souls, securing endangered communities from settlers with murderous intent, and guaranteeing the survival of groups that faced serious hardship and persistent drought. They almost certainly cared about their wards – at least about their spiritual welfare – without necessarily anticipating the harm that would be caused by uprooting people from 'tribal lands' (Rowse 1998; Stevens 1994). Interventions of that kind are a striking example of how notions of care – whether anchored in religious zeal or cultural condescension but always uncoupled from the responsibility to engage others as equals in open dialogue – can lead to suffering or domination (Bauman 1993: 96–7, 103; Shapcott 2001). Critics of the care ethic have asked whether a morality that has its basis in relations between people who are intimately bound together can support a strong sense of moral responsibility to distant strangers where no such connections exist (Clement 1996: 84). Others have raised the question of whether the ethic is necessarily linked with moral parochialism (Tronto 1994). For those reasons, critics have argued that a care ethic has to be elevated by a commitment to universal moral principles, and specifically by a dialogic ethic that provides a safeguard against harms caused by 'limited altruism' or cultural condescension (Benhabib 1993: 150ff., 181ff.; on limited altruism, see pp. 82–3).

The reference to Australian missions underlines the significance of dialogue for the ethic of care and responsibility. That ethic and the discourse theory of morality have been said to be at odds with each other – especially because the latter is associated with the notion of exercising 'public reason' to determine impartial principles of justice that govern relations between relatively autonomous strangers. For some, the discourse standpoint is a gendered one that devalues the skills and sensitivities that are involved in caring for the needs of concrete others. But the earlier argument about how the ethics of care and justice can be combined in a higher synthesis indicates that it is a mistake to drive a wedge between those two positions. Discourse ethics affirms the principle that all human beings have the right to be consulted about decisions that may affect them. Due attention is paid to tangible and intangible connections between people, to their vulnerability to each other's actions or to the harmful effects of social structures, and to the importance of answerability to others under conditions of mutual dependence. The notion that, ideally, 'public reason' should lead to rules of justice that demonstrate great sensitivity to diverse forms of suffering is suggested by the argument that all who stand to be affected by the actions of others are morally entitled to advance demands that reflect their experience of 'violated integrity, discrimination, and oppression' (Habermas 1998a, see p. 110). By 'lending a voice to suffering', the politics of dialogue supports a 'progressive expansion of horizons' in which no one is regarded as 'inferior' (Habermas 1998a: 25, 388; also Linklater 2005). Similar themes are evident in that defence of the ethics of care which states that particular responsibilities arise because those who are 'closer to us will *tend* to be more vulnerable to our actions and choices than those distant from us', but which immediately adds that there are also 'special obligations to care' for distant strangers who are 'particularly vulnerable to our actions and choices' because of their position of weakness in the structures and processes that bind people together (Clement 1996: 73; italics in original).[57] The ethic of care and the discourse theory of morality can therefore play a complementary role in defending cosmopolitan harm conventions that have the function of protecting the vulnerable.

Some comments are required on the affinities between the care ethic and a cosmopolitan harm principle. It was noted that the ethic of care and responsibility has been associated with the desire to avoid harming others and with resolving conflicts in such a way that no one is hurt, or hurt needlessly. How far such sensibilities have shaped the long-term development of states-systems is a central question for the sociology of cosmopolitan harm conventions, as is the question of whether their influence is any stronger in the modern world than it was in earlier times. All of the approaches to world politics that have been considered in this chapter have important positions on those questions. Some implicitly recognize the importance of care, albeit within narrow limits. Realist perspectives recognize that mutual sensitivity to legitimate fears and interests is essential if adversaries are to control the potential to harm each other; English School perspectives stress that some level of empathy, mutual understanding and self-restraint is critical for preserving international society. Indeed, some members of the School have argued for greater care over how actions affect not just states as abstractions but individual people. As noted earlier, the issues have arisen in discussions of complicity in perpetuating global injustice and with respect to serious violations of human rights.[58]

Mainstream perspectives have usually argued that such commitments have little more than a marginal influence on the overall course of events. (Marxist approaches to structural harm often display the same pessimism.) To return to the first section of this chapter, realism maintains that warfare is the litmus test of an ethic of care; it is the domain in which moral concerns about connections with vulnerable others do not extend beyond an interest in the well-being of co-nationals or, when they do, invariably yield to considerations of strategic necessity and calculations of military advantage. But Walzer's arguments about the scope for moral deliberation in warfare share many of the concerns that run through the ethic of care and responsibility. There is common opposition

---

[57] Clement (1996: 73) adds that 'we have special obligations to our family and friends because we can affect their interests to a great extent. But many people beyond our family and friends are *also* potentially vulnerable to our actions and choices, and thus the ethic of care and responsibility has implications beyond our sphere of personal relations'.

[58] Vincent's sympathy with Chomsky's emphasis on caring about the consequences of 'our' actions has influenced later thinking about complicity with regimes that are guilty of serious human rights violations (see p. 71, and Wheeler and Dunne 1998).

to destructive masculinities in which pleasure is derived from inflicting suffering that exceeds what is defensible even in the name of military necessity.[59] The
desire to control violent masculinity has an ancient pedigree that can be traced
back to the first formulations of just war thinking. Indeed, in their efforts to
tame the male warrior they defended moral qualities that are now celebrated by
the care ethic.[60] An example was Augustine's claim that the greatest evil in warfare is taking life from 'motives of hatred and cruelty rather than reluctantly and
in obedience to law', and without the loss of 'human feeling' (Mapel 1996: 64).[61]
Also noteworthy is the fact that various articulations of just war theory down
the centuries have affirmed the duty to 'evaluate social life *from the standpoint*
of the suffering', and to ensure that *humanitas* (common humanity) moderates
the conduct of war (Elshtain 1987: 123; italics in original).[62] An emphasis on
shared vulnerabilities underpins such notions of military valour that obviously
clash with destructive masculinities that do not waver when opportunities arise
to make 'a principle of injury' central to relations with enemies (see p. 96). The
key moral dispositions have long been enshrined in formal and informal codes
of honour and chivalry that influenced thinking about the laws of war which,
interestingly, has been linked with the prima facie duty to avoid unnecessary
harm which was considered in the preceding chapter (Childress 1974; Norman
1995: ch. 1).[63] An important question for the sociology of cosmopolitan harm

---

[59] Ember and Ember (1997) state that the skeletal remains from early warfare indicate that
    young adult males were the main perpetrators of violence. The point can be generalized
    across human history.

[60] The fact that 'there are cultures ... where rape is absent, or extremely rare', and societies
    where it is 'authorized by an ideology of supremacy' (Connell 1995: 47, 83) reveals that
    masculinity can be constructed in very different ways, some more sensitive than others to
    the sentiments conveyed by the care ethic, some entirely dismissive or contemptuous of
    them. A similar point underpins the distinction between warriors that respect rules of chiv-
    alry and warriors that find pleasure in killing (Walzer 1980: 134).

[61] Anyone who contemplates the evils of war without 'heartfelt grief' compounds its agonies
    'because he has lost human feeling' (Augustine 1972: Book XIX, 7). Johnson (1992: 71)
    notes that Christian warriors in the early Middle Ages were required to undergo penance if
    they had killed 'out of malice toward the enemy rather than with a feeling of regretful duty
    in the service of justice'.

[62] Elshtain (1992: 103) gives the example of the 1983 US Catholic Bishops' Pastoral Letter on
    War and Peace, *The Challenge of Peace: God's Promise and our Response*, which states that in
    waging war, it is 'of utmost importance in assessing harms and the justice of accepting them
    to think about the poor and helpless, for they are usually the ones who have least to gain and
    the most to lose when war's violence touches their lives'. Elsewhere, Elshtain (1987: 126) has
    argued that it is important to trace such attitudes back to efforts to promote the '*feminiza-
    tion* of (early) Christian ideals of fellowship and community' (italics added). They endeav-
    oured to apply the concept of *agape*, which referred to 'the mother's unconditional love for
    her child', to society and politics more generally.

[63] The so-called 'naked soldier' phenomenon, as described by Walzer (1980: 138ff.), refers to
    taboos that are mentioned in many war memoirs against killing unarmed enemy personnel.
    Such acts of forbearance or 'kindness', based on the recognition of the shared humanity of

conventions is how far such displays of 'human feeling' restrained the use of force in different states-systems – and here it is important to recall that the dominant theories of international relations continue to neglect the role of the emotions (see Chapter 5). No less central is the question of whether, because of rising levels of global interconnectedness, the ethic of care has become more important than ever for the organization of world politics – and whether the greater awareness of interconnectedness with vulnerable others creates entirely unprecedented opportunities for weaving cosmopolitan harm conventions into international affairs. If that is true, then the ethic of care may finally come into its own.

Conclusion

Leading theories of international relations offer various conjectures about what the sociology of cosmopolitan harm conventions should examine, and what it might discover. They invite a more detailed analysis of how far societies can alter the general patterns of development that were set in motion by the rise of the first states and empires in the Ancient Near East between 3,000 and 5,000 years ago – and then by similar long-term processes in other regions. The idea of the ambiguities of human interconnectedness summarizes those overall directions. On the one hand, many societies have acquired levels of collective power that have led to extraordinary levels of control over the natural world and to extraordinary wealth for many people. On the other hand, the principal dynamics of the last few millennia have produced astonishing breakthroughs in the ability to use destructive military power over larger areas. To the ability to destroy total populations must be added the contemporary threats to security and survival that result from global warming and climate change. For those reasons, many have suggested that the particular forms of social and political organization that emerged around five centuries ago may be reaching 'the end of the road' (Elias 2010; see pp. 261–3).

Whether societies can alter the overall pattern of development of the last few centuries or millennia – and how they might do that – are questions that divide the principal theories of international relations. Many have identified obstacles that may be impossible to overcome: geopolitical competition and war, struggles over material resources, and pernicious self–other distinctions. Many have stressed achievements in responding to the ambiguities of interconnectedness so that people are spared unnecessary harm: they include success in creating

the enemy, have preserved, Walzer (1980: ch. 9) argues, the distinction between murder and war. Bourke (1999: 63, 148) gives the example of 'fraternization' at the front during the Easter and Christmas ceasefires in the early part of the First World War, as well as various memoirs of the First and Second World Wars, that expressed a degree of identification with the enemy which was often based in reciprocated admiration for courage and skill in combat, and in the 'civilizing' appreciation of a common plight.

international order, and in constructing, in the recent period, a universal society of states with commitments to protecting human rights; efforts to reduce harmful distinctions between peoples; the emergence of cosmopolitan standards that universalize the right to freedom and equality; partial success in replacing 'totalizing' loyalties with multiple identities in which duties to the state are located within a complex web of attachments to groups and organizations 'above' and 'below' the national community; global applications of the harm principle that largely reflect liberal values and preferences, but equip subordinate groups and their representatives with the moral resources with which to contest relations of domination and exploitation; and, finally, more realistic understandings of other people that have developed alongside lengthening webs of interconnectedness, and which find expression in the recognition of shared human vulnerabilities that is central to arguments for globalizing the ethic of care and responsibility.

The sociologist of cosmopolitan harm conventions can analyse the interplay between those phenomena in different states-systems, secure in the knowledge that the relationship between them will almost certainly decide the fate of future efforts to protect all people from senseless violent and non-violent harm. An 'empirical research programme' that reflects those considerations – and which integrates earlier comments about the concept of harm and the harm principle – will be set out in the final chapter. That project brings together various themes that often exist in relative isolation in different literatures. Analyses of harm have been the preserve of students of criminology and jurisprudence; reflections on the harm principle have been confined to specialist investigations in moral and legal philosophy where the influence of liberal political thought is especially strong. Discussions of harm in international relations proceed without much engagement with those analyses (which in turn rarely discuss world politics). Different approaches to harm in international relations theory also frequently develop in isolation. English School analyses of international society have been notoriously unwilling to engage with Marxist studies of global dominance and dependence; realist approaches to geopolitics and war rarely take much note of the literature on identity politics, and so forth. There is a need to consider how the strengths of different approaches can be integrated in a higher theoretical synthesis.

To develop that further, it is necessary to turn to the sociology of 'civilizing' and 'decivilizing' processes which has succeeded in reaching a level of synthesis that is rare in the humanities and in the social sciences, and not least by placing the relationship between macro- and micro-sociological developments (including state-building and warfare, higher levels of interconnectedness, and emotional responses to cruelty and violence) in long-term perspective. But it is not only the scope of that analysis that can help turn the arguments of the last three chapters into an empirical research programme that is concerned with cosmopolitan harm conventions in different states-systems. The substantive claims that are central to the sociology of civilizing and decivilizing processes also have particular importance for the analysis of harm. The main reason is that the approach has not confined its attention to changes within social systems. A major goal has been to show how 'internal' change has been linked with struggles between states and with long-term trends towards higher levels of global interdependence. A related aim has been to understand the prospects for a global civilizing process which, in the terms used in the present discussion, enables people everywhere to live without the burden of unnecessary harm. The next two chapters show how such ideas can underpin new connections between historical sociology and International Relations.

4

The sociology of civilizing processes

Thus far the discussion has analysed the various ways of harming and of being harmed within specific societies and in world politics. It has considered how a cosmopolitan harm principle can promote the humane governance of increasing interconnectedness. Attention then turned to leading theories of international relations, noting major differences about how far societies have progressed – or are likely to progress – in embedding the 'principle of humaneness' in global arrangements. Those theories offer competing interpretations of the prospects for, and constraints upon, such a development; they have discrepant accounts of the dominant forms of harm and their ultimate causes, and divergent interpretations of how to ameliorate or solve the problem of harm in world politics. The point has been reached where it is possible to begin to integrate earlier themes in a higher synthesis that aims to understand civilizing processes in international relations.

The importance of analysing such processes has been recognized by those English School writers who have referred to levels of 'civility' – and even to 'civilizing processes' – in world affairs (p. 128, n. 30). As far as the latter term is concerned, they have not engaged with the perspective that contributes most to such an inquiry – the standpoint of process sociology which was pioneered by Elias and developed by a small but increasingly influential body of scholars who have built on his work in recent years.[1] The next part of this discussion therefore turns to Elias's explanation of long-term patterns of change in Western European societies over approximately the last five centuries. This chapter and the following one will develop an approach to global civilizing processes that links process sociology (which has been broadly opposed to partisan scholarship) with Frankfurt School influenced critical international theory.

This chapter is in five sections. The first section discusses Elias's use of the idea of the 'civilizing process' to analyse the diverse ways in which societies have

---

[1] English School theory generally lacks Elias's focus on how the rise of European international society was part of the larger transformation of social and political relations. On the other hand, Elias's account of the civilizing process paid insufficient attention to the development of global civilizing institutions such as international law and diplomacy. The issues are considered in more detail in volume 2.

dealt with universal body functions as well as different methods of controlling the human capacity for violent and non-violent harm. The second section summarizes his account of the European civilizing process with its emphasis on the relationship between the rise of state monopoly powers, internal pacification, lengthening chains of social and economic interaction, the internalization of constraints on aggressive impulses, changing attitudes to cruelty and violence, and the growth of 'emotional identification' between members of the same society. The third section discusses Elias's argument that civilizing processes always develop in tandem with 'decivilizing processes', a thesis that was advanced in the course of an investigation into the 'breakdown of civilization' in Nazi Germany, but which is also significant for his reflections on international relations which are considered in the fourth section.

It is important to add that Elias was unusual amongst sociologists of his generation in arguing that relations between societies must occupy a central place in the sociological investigation of long-term processes of social and political development.[2] Whether it is meaningful to speak of civilizing processes in international relations is a recurrent question in his writings. At times, they maintain that the European civilizing process with its reduced tolerance of violent harm has barely influenced foreign policy. Repeatedly, precarious taboos against force have been weakened when societies are anxious about their security. Solidarity between insiders strengthened, and divisions with outsiders usually intensified, in such circumstances. Parallels with realist arguments about the logic of anarchy will be apparent but, for Elias, such reactions to external threats have to be considered in conjunction with the 'compulsions of interdependence' that require self-restraint, foresight and other dispositions that English School writers associate with the existence of a society of states.[3] But one of the limitations of his examination of the civilizing process is the lack of a detailed discussion of

---

[2] That said, Elias did not produce a specialist work on international relations, although Elias (2010) does provide an extended discussion of the dangers of nuclear war, but without referring to major works on strategic studies and world politics. Comments about the importance of relations between communities are scattered throughout his writings and often appear in unlikely places – for instance, in works devoted to changing conceptions of time, the evolution of the human capacity for language and symbolization, the relationship between involvement and detachment in human development, and attitudes to death and dying in modern societies. The scattered nature of Elias's comments on relations between societies indicates that he believed that an examination of any social trend or practice had to take account of international politics. In his writings there is an implicit assumption that the study of international relations has no claim to be regarded as 'a domain apart', and that the false separation of sociology and International Relations blocks the path to a deeper understanding of human affairs. The present work is similarly dissatisfied with the division of labour between the two disciplines, and with most attempts to bring them closer together (see Chapter 5).

[3] A rare reference to 'the state's changing position within the developing *society of states*' can be found in Elias (1978: 171; italics added).

the institutions of international society. He focused on growing interconnect-edness in order to consider how far central 'realist' dynamics in world politics might yet be weakened. The question was whether more universal social and economic ties confronted different peoples with the challenge of learning how to become attuned to one another's interests over longer distances – a variation on the pressures that had taken place earlier within sovereign states as part of the civilizing process that might lead to closer international cooperation. But those worldwide trends did not guarantee higher levels of self-restraint, or the widening of the scope of emotional identification, which had occurred within many political communities. Global disintegration could prove stronger than global integration because of the tensions that resulted from a widespread fear of the loss of group power, status and autonomy.

Those observations suggest new directions for the sociology of states-sys-tems, or for the comparative investigation of global civilizing processes. They highlight the importance of analysing the higher tolerance of violent harm in relations between states than in relations within them; they invite discussion of how far the tolerance threshold may decline as a result of pressures to exer-cise higher levels of self-restraint in the face of more universal social and eco-nomic connections; they draw attention to questions about the extent to which those relations lead more people to think about the well-being of the species as a whole, and not just about the interests of their 'survival unit'; and they raise the issue of whether continuing struggles for power and security, and anxieties about the effects of global interconnectedness, will perpetuate a condition in which the restraints on force that exist within civilized communities make little impression on world politics (see Kaspersen and Gabriel 2008 on 'survival units' in process sociology).

The fifth section provides a brief assessment of some of Elias's claims about the European civilizing process – one that recognizes the need to compare it with what may seem to be the principal rival account of long-term trends in modern society. For many, the main alternative is Foucault's account of discipline and punishment, and its claim that the reduced tolerance of public violence had less to do with advancing humanitarian sensibilities than with the growth of new instruments of disciplinary power and the intensification of self-monitoring. The two approaches converge in attempting to explain linkages between changes in the organization of public authority and transformations of the emotional life; they emphasize the importance of higher levels of self-restraint in pacified modern societies. But if Elias's perspective has 'the right of way' over other per-spectives (Kilminster, cited in Mennell 2007: x) that is not just because it cov-ers a significantly longer time-frame than most (roughly five centuries in the study of the civilizing process, and the whole of human history in Elias's later writings) but also because it provides a more comprehensive explanation of the main dynamics in those centuries and indeed across history as a whole. In the case of the civilizing process, the investigation was centred on relations between the rise of larger territorial monopolies of power, the closer interweaving of the lives of members of relatively pacified societies, and changes in sensitivity to the needs of others, and in the scope of emotional identification with other people. Humanitarianism was not the driving-force behind shifting attitudes to violence and suffering in those centuries; nor was it epiphenomenal. Foucault's writings contain an explicit assault on the belief that modern people are more compassionate and less cruel than their ancestors. Elias's interest in locating humanitarian sentiments in larger processes of change had a similar demystifying or debunking purpose since it was designed to show that moderns are not civilized as a result of their natural endowments; rather they have become civilized (as they define it) in largely unintended ways as a result of the pressures they have faced by virtue of being forced together (Elias 1978: 154–5). Elias and Foucault therefore attempted to develop interpretations of modern societies that rested on more detached understandings of how people have become what they are, including less accustomed to acts of violence. The final section considers the significance of that aim for connections between process sociology and critical international theory.

Civilizing processes

It has been said that 1939 was hardly the most propitious moment to publish a book on the European civilizing process, but that comment would only hit its mark if Elias had firmly believed in the superiority of Western civilization.[4] His aim was not to reinforce and justify Europe's flattering self-images but to explain the development of collective understandings about its civilized nature and assumed supremacy over other ways of life. A related ambition was to expose the delusions of 'civilized' and 'civilizing' worldviews. By the end of the nineteenth century, Europe's civilized state was widely thought to be a permanent condition rather than a largely unplanned, and far from inevitable or irreversible, long-term process of change – and just as civilization was believed to be the innate property of advanced peoples, so was savagery considered to be the natural lot of the inferior 'races'. The idea of multiple civilizations, none more valuable than the others, has gained ground since the end of the Second World War; the belief that European civilization is surrounded by peoples which it must civilize has fallen into disgrace in many circles (Wallerstein 1991: chs. 14–15). Elias's claim that every society possesses its distinctive civilizing process is closer to the view that has triumphed in that period, although he maintained that the modern civilizing process has provided levels of personal security which are

---

[4] Elias's major work on the civilizing process was published in German in 1939 by an obscure Swiss publisher. It was first published in English in two volumes in 1978 and 1982. A revised edition was published in 2000 (Elias 2000). The definitive version will be published by University College Dublin Press in the near future.

not the historical norm. But before making more detailed comparisons, it was necessary to explain the development of Europe's unwavering faith in the universal significance of its mode of social and political organization, and belief in its right and destiny to remake other societies in its own image.

In the 1930s, at the time when Elias was working on his magnum opus, there were major disputes about whether modern civilization was 'the acme or nadir of the human social achievement'; the emphasis on the levels of psychological suppression that were intrinsic to 'civilized' ways of life was not uncommon (Elias 2000: 375). Given his influence on Elias, it is important to cite Freud's remark that modern civilization requires the 'renunciation of instinctual gratifications' and the inevitable forfeiting of personal happiness (Freud 1939: 63).[5] Crucially, Freud (1939: 142, 1998 [1932]) stated that he had not succumbed to the delusion that modern civilization is 'the most precious thing that we possess or could acquire', and is guaranteed to 'lead us to undreamt-of heights of perfection'. Similar themes are evident in Elias's claim that modern Europeans had deluded themselves into thinking that they enjoyed a natural state of civilization, and in his assertion that the lack of an historical appreciation of the long formative process of civilization helped explain the collective failure to understand that their way of life was always imperilled.[6] Unfounded confidence that the survival of civil arrangements could be taken for granted left modern peoples unprepared for the assault on civilization that occurred during the 1930s. Barbarism of that kind was assumed to be a characteristic of distant eras or typical of 'savages'. Modern Europeans were assumed to be incapable of falling from a state of grace.

Those comments indicate that Elias's aim was to provide a detached understanding of modern European civilization at a time when the Nazi assault on its constitutive practices and principles had already begun to transform the

[5] Freudian themes are evident in Elias's belief that civilization generated its own distinctive pathologies and also in Foucault's thesis that 'civilization, in a general way, constitutes a milieu favourable to the development of madness', at least in its peculiarly modern forms (Foucault 1973: 217). Elias maintained that the flight from the constraints of civilization often led to the search for happiness in compensatory fantasy worlds. Various tensions between groups have been diminished, only for 'the battlefield' to be 'moved within', in a struggle between basic drives and the 'super-ego' (Elias 2000: 375).

[6] How far Elias shared Freud's belief that the 'mental constitution' of peoples contains something of 'unconquerable nature' that condemns them to the disastrous effects of aggressive dispositions and the potential for self-destruction must be passed over here (Freud 1939: 44, 85–6). In an afterthought to a critique of the doctrine of innate aggression, Elias (1978: 178–9) criticized the tendency 'to confuse the greater plasticity of human instinctive behaviour, which implies a greater ability on the part of man to control the instincts, with mankind as a species possessing weak instincts'. Elias added that there is 'no proof at all that human instincts are any weaker than those of lions, apes or sparrows', but they appear to be more 'malleable' and 'most amenable to control' – hence the need to recognize that the history of the species is one in which cultural evolution has replaced biological evolution as the main pacemaker of development.

continent – but his orientation also emphasized the 'civilized' world's enduring failure to make progress in solving the problem of force in international relations. The idea of the civilizing process has led to suspicions that Elias was an apologist for European modernity, but he made it perfectly clear that the project had 'not been guided ... by the idea that our civilized mode of behaviour is the most advanced of all humanly possible modes of behaviour'; nor was it designed to cast a 'slur' on other societies (Elias 2000: xiv, 2008a: 113–14).[7] In the course of arguing that every society has its civilizing process, he maintained that there is never a 'zero point' with respect to civilization – no decisive moment in which a civilizing process emerges as if from nowhere, and drives a society beyond a state of unvarnished barbarism (Elias 2007b [1992]: 119). Certain features that are shared by people everywhere are integral to that standpoint. Elias (1978: 118ff.) observed that every human has the same point of departure, namely total dependence on others for care and survival, and the need to learn how to control 'animalic needs' and biological impulses. Every person is required to internalize the dominant social standards with regard to 'outward bodily propriety', and the relevant modes of self-regulation with respect to basic drives that include the potential for anger, aggressive behaviour and violence. In recognition of such universals, *The Civilizing Process* analysed various 'manners books' between the thirteenth and eighteenth centuries that had offered guides to such daily routines as urinating, defecating, spitting, washing, undressing, eating, and the other aspects of body management that remind people that they are only partially divorced from nature.[8] To understand changes in civilized conduct that the manners books had promoted, or reflected, it was important to comprehend how state-building, domestic pacification and extended networks of interdependence led to new ideas about the sources of shame and embarrassment, and to new conceptions of what should arouse repugnance and disgust. The civilizing process referred to the interconnections between those long-term patterns of social and psychological change.

There is a close relationship between the civilizing process and the problem of harm. All societies have such processes because all must address the question of how their members can go about satisfying their most basic needs without 'destroying, frustrating, demeaning or in other ways *harming* each other time and time again' (Elias 1996: 31; italics added). To repeat, Elias's perspective on the civilizing process dealt with a modern variant on a universal theme since no viable society is uncivilized in the sense of lacking conventions for regulating violent and non-violent harm, or socializing institutions that instil respect for

---

[7] Elias attached the last point to the observation that in Ancient Greece, the tolerance of killing and wounding was much higher than in modern European society. But there was no desire to 'cast a slur' on the Greek world which had produced extraordinary achievements in philosophy, art, politics and so on, often under conditions of insecurity that people in modern civilized societies rarely face.

[8] Elias (2000: 142ff.) added that controlling the sex drive is no less important.

basic standards of behaviour as well as the socially valued patterns of individual self-restraint and emotion management, or coercive mechanisms that can be brought into play when the mechanisms that deal with 'drive formation' fail to secure compliance with relevant norms.[9] From there, it was a short step to the claim that it is possible to compare processes of civilization at different points in the development of any society, and to compare civilizing processes in different ways of life. Social comparisons had to be made in a non-evaluative manner, and specifically without supposing that 'we are good', whereas 'they are bad' (Elias 2008a: 114). To proceed otherwise would be to assume that other societies had faced a clear choice between 'their' values and 'ours', and had somehow taken the wrong course (Elias 2008a: 115). Analysts had to strive to understand the beliefs and practices that had emerged as societies responded to the particular challenges that confronted them, rather than try to measure their achievements and failures by using an ethical yardstick that reflected the circumstances of the contemporary era. Observers had to remember that their 'civilized' era had its origins in earlier forms of life that often had fewer opportunities (because of higher levels of violence, endemic insecurity, and permanent exposure to uncontrolled natural forces) to engineer social change or plan future developments. From that standpoint, the achievements that had occurred in the face of severe constraints were all the more impressive (Kilminster 2007: ch. 4);[10] moreover, modern accomplishments were less obviously grounds for collective self-congratulation, and no reason for collective indulgence in feelings of superiority. It was also important to recognize that familiar social practices are not frozen in time, but are unfinished products of long-term patterns of change that are constantly evolving, and which never escape the possibility of sudden reversal.

In Elias's emphasis on long-term developments, one can find some sympathy with the ambitions of nineteenth-century social and political theorists who tried to create a universal history, albeit with the limited, ethnocentric resources at their disposal, and often with a flawed belief in the inevitability and irreversibility of human progress (Elias 1994: 132). Twentieth-century thinkers had been right to cast historical teleology aside – the supposition that history culminated in modern Europe had to be jettisoned – but 'the baby (had) been thrown out with the bath water' as sociologists deserted inquiries into long-term horizons (Elias 2000: 468).[11] The investigation of civilizing processes therefore

---

[9] In the following pages, comments on the civilizing process refer to the European example, unless stated otherwise.

[10] See Elias (2009a) for the claim that every era is equally important for efforts to comprehend human struggles to satisfy basic needs in the face of social and natural constraints and pressures.

[11] Elias (1994: 119, 144–7) singled out Marx's focus on long-term trajectories as one of those 'indispensable' hypotheses that cannot be 'bypassed', and added that in some respects its vision of a comprehensive theory of society has yet to be equalled, notwithstanding biases

involved the recovery of unfashionable historical sensibilities in the face of what Elias (2009b [1986]) described as 'the retreat of sociology into the present'.[12] Investigations of long-term processes inevitably raised questions about whether it is possible to identify specific tendencies and directions, and indeed whether it is meaningful to speak of progressions in particular spheres of activity, while eschewing notions of overall progress (Elias 2007b [1992]: 156).

With respect to Western Europe, Elias (2001a: 48) stated that it is not always realized 'that physical security from violence by other people is not so great in all societies as in our own'. Domestic pacification had been inextricably connected with unplanned patterns of state-formation that led to a combination of internal and external constraints on violence and aggression that do not exist (or do not exist to the same extent) where individual people and groups must rely on themselves for their security. In short, relatively high levels of personal safety were not the result of natural peaceful inclinations that elevated Europeans above intrinsically belligerent societies. Other pronounced trends that had hardly been 'consciously planned' included 'a progressive reduction in inequality between and within countries since the end of the eighteenth century' (Elias 1978: 154). By contrast, the dominant strata in pre-industrial societies usually tried 'to exploit their power chances to the last' in ways that demonstrated that they were 'relatively unconcerned about the destiny of subordinate people', although they were often willing, as befitted their conception of rough justice, 'to put up with the same thing when fortune turned against them' (Elias 2008b: 21). The evidence was that, during the twentieth century, the 'power gradient' in relations between men and women, parents and children, European societies and the former colonies and, 'with qualifications', between rulers and the ruled had decreased as a result of the efforts of various 'emancipation movements' (Elias 1996: 24–5). Indeed, 'the conscious, planned concern with improvement of the social order and human living conditions – as inadequate as it is – has never been greater than it is today' (quoted in van Krieken 1998: 70).

Changing power balances had been critical for the partial success of emancipation movements. In particular, 'functional democratization' in modern societies was the key to equalizing tendencies. That was the process by which members of the dominant strata became increasingly dependent on the lower strata for the satisfaction of their needs, in which the fate of powerful and weaker groups was intertwined, and in which the subordinate strata came to

and misinterpretations that were the product of its political involvement in the outcome of class conflicts.

[12] There is a rough parallel between Elias's lament about the tyranny of short-term perspectives and the critique of 'presentism' in International Relations (see Buzan and Little 2000: 18–19). The parallel is not an exact one because Sociology has its origins in analyses of 'the great transformation' that led to European modernity, whereas the focus on current affairs (often divorced from the examination of long-term developments) has long been the dominant tendency in International Relations.

enjoy unusual opportunities for extracting significant concessions from higher strata that were obliged to treat them with greater respect. That emphasis on the consequences of functional democratization did not deny that humanitarian sensibilities had influenced the course of social development, but the point was that such orientations have rarely had much impact under conditions of greater inequality, and will almost certainly have less influence if or when steeper 'power gradients' return.[13]

Some of those comments may generate concerns that, despite his protestations, Elias had not entirely expunged all trace of nineteenth-century European triumphalism. There is evidence that he concluded that 'overall, humanity was ... progressing' but, if so, that judgment came with major qualifications, and not least because of the continuing failure to end cycles of violence between communities (van Krieken 1998: 69). Any lingering suspicion of a progressivist bias should be dispelled by noting his contention that civilizing tendencies are 'always linked to counter-trends' or to 'decivilizing processes' that can, in a relatively short time-span, gain the 'upper hand' (Elias, quoted in van Krieken 1998: 69–70). His observations that the Third Reich had not only reversed the civilizing process but also expressed potentials for domination that may be built into modern civilized societies are noteworthy in this regard. Elias stressed that the possibility of large-scale intra-state violence had not been brought to an end; potentially decivilizing distinctions between established and outsiders clearly persisted; and the threat and use of violent harm continued to govern world affairs. That has led to the judgment that Elias supported an essentially ambivalent attitude to the idea of social progress (van Krieken 1998: 69).

---

[13] Mennell (2007: 311) argues that the increasing social inequalities that are the consequence of the expansion of free market capitalism may bring an end to the recent phase of emancipation struggles. It is worth adding that Elias devoted a major work to the subject of 'the loneliness of the dying' in modern societies. The old and the dying were increasingly hidden 'behind the scenes', and denied the comfort of 'extended' family ties that existed in earlier periods of European history and in much of the rest of the world (Elias 2001a). Elias's discussion of that less than progressive feature of the civilizing process drew on his broader analysis of distinctions between the 'established and the outsiders' in all ways of life. From that standpoint, the old and dying are 'outsiders' in relation to 'established' groups; the benefits of functional democratization that have accrued to many lower strata are not always enjoyed by those who have entered the final stages of the life-cycle. Elias maintained that one of the main features of the civilizing process is the effort to screen what has come to be regarded as distressing or disturbing from public view. Powerful forces lead people to conceal everything that they feel has an 'animalic' character, including unsettling reminders of the inevitability of death. The concealment of animal slaughter was another example of the desire to protect the self from disturbing scenes (see also pp. 170–171, also p. 95, n. 42 on Kant's belief in the 'civilizing' role of arenas of suffering). There is an interesting parallel with Foucault's discussion of the practice of isolating the insane in order to protect the 'rational' members of modern societies from the shocking experience of the *animality of madness*' (Foucault 1973: 78, 223–4).

The belief that 'the civilization of which I speak is never completed and always endangered' was part of the motivation for explaining the civilizing process (Elias 1996: 173). Thus far, the process of civilization had largely developed in an 'unplanned' and 'haphazard manner', as an outcome of the way in which people had been thrown together; it had barely influenced international relations, and there was no guarantee that it ever would (Elias 1998: 145, 2001a: 81–2). The goal of sociological investigation was to equip people with higher levels of understanding of the social world which they could then use to advance the more positive aspects of the civilizing process – specifically progress in taming violence and in widening the scope of emotional identification between people, in relations within and between states (Kilminster and Mennell 2003: 189). Elias's confidence in the capacity of sociology to provide knowledge that could be employed to bring social relations under control so that all humans could enjoy security and happiness reveals the influence of nineteenth-century grand narratives that were developed by Comte and Marx (Kilminster 2007). Moreover, something rather similar to the aspirations of Frankfurt School social theory is evident in his contention that the purpose of sociological explanation is to enable people to distinguish between 'restraints' that are essential 'for complicated societies to function', and constraints that have been 'built into us to bolster up the authority of certain ruling groups' (Elias 1978: 153–4). Elias insisted that such hopes for the species should not compromise the detached search for 'reality-congruent' knowledge; the fear that partisan inquiry would jeopardize that enterprise – that it would generate false beliefs about human potentials, or simplistic accounts of how largely unplanned processes can be brought under control – led to an uncompromising argument for non-partisan sociological inquiry that could one day rival the greater detachment of natural-scientific inquiry and emulate its achievements in explaining extraordinary features of the 'external world' (Elias 2007a [1987]: 65, 78, 83).[14]

The European civilizing process

Elias offered a multi-causal explanation of the reconfiguration of politics, economy and society in Europe between the fifteenth and twentieth centuries. The approach considered the reciprocal relations between the formation of the state's monopoly control of the instruments of violence and right of taxation, the rise of urban centres and marketized, money economies, longer trade networks and the more intensive social interdependencies that required people to learn new ways of relating to each other (as in the guidance to conduct that was provided

---

[14] See Kilminster (2007: ch. 5) for an explanation of the ascetic nature of Elias's sociological vocation, and for the defence of a mode of inquiry that combines explicit normative commitments with the rigorous quest for 'reality-congruent' knowledge.

by the manners books). Of particular importance for the present work, the analysis also explained changing orientations to cruelty and violence that involved the fundamental reorientation of emotions such as shame and embarrassment. The inquiry into unplanned long-term processes that brought people together in new social figurations was unusually synoptic because it did not just explain large-scale social-structural changes but also analysed their relationship with the reorganization of personality traits. The inquiry straddled distinctions between macro- and micro-level processes, materialist and idealist modes of explanation, agency and structure and so forth; developments at any of those 'levels' could not be understood without explaining broader processes of societal transformation.[15]

The point of departure was the emergence of new monopolies of physical violence from the 'elimination contests' between rival power centres that had been locked together in struggles for territorial control in the Middle Ages. Internal pacification permitted the rise of flourishing urban centres and market economies. The greater wealth that flowed into state coffers led to the further increase in territorial concentrations of power that could maintain social order. Additional economic growth and prosperity resulted, permitting further advances in the development of state power. People became tied together in a complex social division of labour that demanded higher levels of self-restraint. Deepening social connections required greater sensitivity to the actual and potential behaviour of other actors, near and far. Gradually but unevenly across society, the balance of power between internal and external constraints on conduct changed. Self-restraint began to operate like a 'second nature' that exercised growing influence on the regulation of conduct, although the state did not surrender its role as the foundation of civil order, and the application and fear of external, coercive sanctions remained critical for the survival of society (Elias 2007b [1992]: 124ff.). A crucial element in that multi-dimensional pattern of development was the 'taming of warriors', firstly within the aristocratic feudal courts and then across all social strata. 'Martial fervour' that had dominated feudal society, and which had been central to the acquisition and maintenance of 'prestige' amongst male nobles, was slowly dethroned and replaced by the disciplined pursuit of monetary

---

[15] This is the appropriate moment to mention Elias's disdain for dualisms that were responsible for much squandered effort in the social sciences (see Dunning 1986: 7ff.). The metaphor of the dance was employed to explain specific figurations in which people are interlinked in ways that theoretical dualisms often fail to comprehend. Each dancer is influenced by others' movements in a figuration that none controls, which is clearly more than the sum of the actions of all those involved, but which cannot be said to exist apart from, or outside, those involved (Elias 2000: 482–3). Elias (1978: 128ff.) provides a detailed explanation of how the idea of figuration can solve various problems in social analysis, many resulting from false dichotomies between 'individual' and 'society' (or between 'agent' and 'structure' in contemporary parlance).

success and by the search for status through commercial accomplishments (Elias 2000: 405ff.).[16]

New forms of self-restraint first appeared among the secular upper classes in what Elias (2006d) called 'court society' where elaborate codes of etiquette and propriety separated the higher, 'civilized' groups from the lower strata.[17] The social and psychological distance between the French court – which was Elias's principal example – and other social strata was eroded in some measure by links between the monarchy and the commercial classes that were formed to balance the power of the nobility and, in turn, by alliances between the nobles and the bourgeoisie that were forged to check the power of the king (Elias 2006d: ch. 7). Growing social interdependence modified the effects of asymmetries of power, forcing groups to acknowledge each other's disruptive capabilities, to display greater consideration for the members of other strata, and to anticipate how actions that had adverse effects on others could rebound on the instigators – in short, pressures mounted to develop personality structures that valued the capacity 'to think from the standpoint of the multiplicity of people' as part of an emerging regime of more rigorous self-control (Elias 1994: 140). Regarding

[16] In his explanation of the 'taming of the warriors', Elias described the shift from dominant and destructive masculinities in the Middle Ages. He observed that 'unconcealed male dominance' and violence towards women was prevalent in the Middle Ages, and stressed that the shift from the warrior to the courtier involved a civilizing or disciplining process that applied 'not least to the relation between men and women', and revealed that women 'had far greater power at court than in any other formation in this society' (Elias 2006d: 260–61; 2000: 155ff., 245ff.). He added that women were also involved in perpetrating acts of violence, although Fletcher (1997: 187, n. 9) suggests that may have been uncommon (Elias 2000: 163). Interestingly, at some point before 1971, Elias worked on a manuscript on 'the balance of power between the sexes' that was lost for the reasons discussed in Mennell (1998: 25). Other process sociologists have provided important insights into the gendered dimensions of the civilizing process. Dunning has made 'masculinity norms' central to the analysis of the civilizing of sport. His inquiries into football violence discuss the influence of conceptions of 'manliness' that 'are reminiscent in many ways of the masculinity norms which were general in British society at an earlier stage of its development'. They can be traced back to 'medieval and early modern forms of segmental bonding' that were linked with 'aggressive masculinity and comparative inability to exercise self-control' (Dunning 2008: 238ff.). It is worth adding that constructions of idealized female roles that have also been integral to the civilizing process may explain why many regard the violence of women – and particularly violent harm to children – as especially shocking (see also the earlier discussion of Schopenhauer on pp. 94–5). References to the rules governing 'feminine bodily comportment' (including different rules for men and women with respect to touching) are also relevant to a more gender-sensitive interpretation of the civilizing process (see Young 1990: ch. 8). For further reflections, see Liston (2007).

[17] There are parallels between Elias's discussion of the 'spirit' of courtly rationality (see Elias 2006d: 120ff.) and the study of 'mentalities' spearheaded by the *Annales* historians in France, on which subject see Burguiere (1982). As for Elias's perspective, many have asked whether the focus on the 'secular upper classes' underestimated the influence of religious organizations, ideas and practices on the civilizing process. For further discussion, see Goudsblom (2004).

psychological developments, Elias (1996: 109, 460) stated that there was more to the civilizing process than 'the non-violent coexistence of humans'. More 'positive characteristics', involving 'the extent and depth of people's mutual identification with each other', and the capacity to 'empathize' or 'to feel for and sympathize' with others in the same society, emerged alongside internal pacification (Elias 1996: 109, 460).[18]

Those comments on equalizing tendencies recognized the continuing importance of asymmetries of power and influence in relations between 'the established and the outsiders'. But the 'compulsions of interdependence' made it more difficult for the dominant strata to promote their sectional interests in the face of opposition from the lower ranks. They came under considerable pressure to moderate feelings of social superiority, and to refrain from 'intolerable displays of arrogance or self-aggrandisement', such as the unrestrained public humiliation or open stigmatization of others (Wouters 1998: 134). As noted earlier, increasing interconnectedness gave subordinate groups the opportunity to extract concessions from more powerful strata, despite the latter's frequent resentment of, or deep ambivalence about, the loss of prestige and autonomy. Alongside that development, lower ranks begin to shed their 'outsider' status and the feelings of social inferiority that had been evident in earlier practices of admiring and/or emulating the behaviour of 'established' groups, and in creating 'within themselves a "super ego"' that internalized the social standards that were found amongst the upper classes (Elias 2000: 430). The diffusion of courtly manners occurred as a result of such shifts in the power balance between groups whose lives were increasingly and inextricably chained together. Those changes did not take place within societies that were hermetically sealed from each other. The social integration of Europe's 'courtly aristocracy' ensured that new conceptions of civility spread freely, but unevenly, across frontiers (Loyal 2004: 130–1). The French court played a major role in articulating the idea of 'civilization' as a

---

[18] Haskell (1985) offers an account of the relationship between markets and changing sensibilities that is sympathetic to Elias's perspective. He maintains that marketization encouraged actors to cultivate a reputation for integrity but also humanitarian orientations that later influenced the struggle to abolish slavery. It is not clear that the argument succeeds in identifying the causal link between marketization and the growth of humanitarianism (see Mennell 2007: 110ff.). For Elias, humanitarian sensibilities are not only anchored in moral concerns for other people; they emerge along with the patterns of self-restraint and mutual attunement that are forced on them by the compulsions of interconnectedness. Such civilized self-controls led people to feel uneasy about seemingly unnecessary violence or cruelty. To suggest that they had become more humanitarian is to ignore the pressures that pushed them towards certain moral sensibilities that may seem autonomous markers of their civilized state (as they themselves often wanted to think). Rather than assume they were chosen voluntarily by people separately, and in isolation from each other, the sociologist had to explain how those sentiments emerged as part of major social transformations that can go into reverse at any time, at which point 'civilized' people could desert those ethical sensibilities quite quickly in response to new dangers and new constraints upon them.

mark of its distinction from the more impulsive and less-restrained lower orders. Its belief that the civilizing process was incomplete, and had 'to be pushed further' in relations with societies that were in need of 'improvement', exercised enormous influence not only on individual European neighbours but on collective attitudes towards 'inferior' peoples that came to include the belief in a mandate to conquer and civilize (Elias 2000: 39–41).[19]

Describing differences between the medieval and modern eras, Elias maintained that people became 'increasingly constrained' by the process of civilization 'to settle conflicts in non-violent ways, thus pressuring each other to tame their impulses towards aggressiveness and cruelty' (Wouters 2004: 199). One effect was that people came 'to identify more readily with other people as such, regardless of social origins' as part of the 'long-term civilizing trend towards more even and more thorough control over the emotions' (Elias 1978: 155). The rise of humanitarian sensibilities played its part in shaping those developments but, as noted earlier, it would be a mistake to think that they had causal primacy. Their influence on the civilizing process had to be understood in conjunction with the practical difficulties that people faced in living together as a result of the growing entanglements that had been made possible by the state's monopolization of physical power – entanglements that would not have developed otherwise. The absence of a higher monopoly of power in the Middle Ages, the importance of a 'self-help' principle for warriors in unpacified societies, the celebration of martial virtues in the *habitus* of the nobles, and low levels of functional democratization in the relations between social strata, explained the higher levels of violent and non-violent harm in that period, and the thinner veneer of inner restraint and emotional self-control. Modern peoples would not have become 'civilized', or come to portray themselves in that way, but for such patterns of social and political change. The latter formed the precarious foundation for the collective delusion that civilization demonstrated higher rationality and greater moral sophistication. Such orientations were 'process reducing' (Elias 2000: postscript). Internal pacification had led to new levels of mutual dependence; functional democratization encouraged more realistic appraisals of other people and begrudging admiration for them; in that context, humanitarian sensibilities were more able to develop.

Differences in the everyday lives of people in medieval and modern societies were considerable. In a characteristic observation, Elias observed that 'if members of present-day Western civilized society were to find themselves suddenly transported into a past epoch of their own society, such as the medieval-feudal

---

[19] Elias (2000: part one) discussed the development of the idea of civilization out of earlier notions such as 'courtesie' and 'civility', and maintained that the German notion of *Kultur* which stressed national differences (in contrast with the more inclusive notion of civilization developed by the French) had immense significance for their respective trajectories of development, particularly in the first half of the twentieth century.

period, they would find there much that they esteem "uncivilized" in other societies today'. '[D]epending on their situation and inclinations', he added, they would either be 'attracted by the wilder, more unrestrained and adventurous life of the upper classes in this society, or repulsed by the "barbaric" customs, the squalor and coarseness ... encountered there'. They would encounter a world in which public displays of extreme emotional responses were commonplace. In feudal society, where the use of force was an accepted way of settling differences, the warrior 'could use physical violence if he was strong and powerful enough; he could openly indulge his inclinations in many directions that have subsequently been closed by social prohibitions'. No external power stood in the way of the desire to hurt, humiliate or exploit. But the warrior 'paid for this greater opportunity of direct pleasure with a greater chance of direct fear', including 'an extraordinary degree of exposure to the violence and the passions of others'. In that world, 'both joy and pain were discharged more freely'. Rapid shifts between 'great kindness' and 'naked cruelty' were more common in the Middle Ages than in modern Europe where the emotions rarely swing as violently between the extremes but tend to converge around the middle of the spectrum (Elias 2000: ix, 372, 2001a: 15).[20] With 'rare exceptions', everyone who was in a position to do so 'abandoned himself to the extreme pleasures of ferocity, murder, torture, destruction and sadism', and to all manner of 'unimaginable emotional outbursts'. Killing was a 'socially permitted pleasure' in war, as was physical torture. Indeed, the whole 'social structure ... pushed its members in this direction, making it seem necessary and practically advantageous to behave in this way' (quoted in van Krieken 1998: 97).

The civilizing process involved the curtailment of pleasures derived from committing and witnessing violent harm (and also non-violent harm in the shape of displays of contempt towards 'inferiors'). Opposition to 'the old warrior custom' of duelling – a practice that had been anchored in the male honour code that underpinned the nobility's resistance to states' efforts to abolish private force, and fuelled its resentment at the encroachment of the impartial rule of law – was an early instance of the 'lowering of the threshold of repugnance' with respect to the appetite for using force against others in the same society (Dunning 2008: 225).[21] The appearance of less violent, more 'civilized', systems

---

[20] Elias clarified the argument by suggesting that the level of self-restraint is as great in modern societies as it is amongst 'less civilized' peoples. But in the latter case, it often exists alongside a tendency for emotional displays to swing between the extremes.

[21] Huizinga (1970: 116) maintained that the duel had been conducted in a civilized manner, the point being to satisfy honour by wounding and not necessarily by killing. But such exercises of force came to be regarded as uncivilized, and duelling was abolished in England, the Scandinavian countries and the Swiss cantons by the mid-nineteenth century. It virtually disappeared across the rest of Europe in the following decades. The main exception was Germany where duelling retained its 'lethal character' (McAleer 1994; also Elias 2006d: 107–8 and 1996: 44ff. for a discussion of the influence of surviving elements of the aristocratic male warrior code on German politics and society in the inter-war years).

of punishment also revealed changing sensibilities. Men, women and children had been drawn in large numbers to open spectacles of violent punishment for what would later be regarded as minor offences (see the discussion in Banner 2002: ch. 2). Towards the end of the eighteenth century, public execution fell into disfavour throughout Western Europe as a result of changing notions of disgust that included growing revulsion against the public display of cadavers (Spierenburg 1991: 212–13). From then on, people would no longer look forward to seeing others 'hanged, quartered [and] broken on the wheel' for 'Sunday entertainment' (Elias 2001a: 2). Various modes of punishment such as blinding, amputation, whipping and branding were gradually swept aside in the course of such mutations of public taste and decency.[22]

However, changing conceptions of the repulsive were linked with higher levels of 'identification with other people' and a greater sense of 'sharing in their suffering and death' than had existed in the ancient or medieval worlds (Elias 2001a: 2). The effects were evident in virtually every sphere of life. The principle 'that under no circumstances should men hit women' became 'more deeply anchored in the feelings of individuals than it ever was in previous centuries' (Elias 1996: 176). Similar developments transformed understandings about how adults should behave towards children. As Elias (2008b: 36) noted, a 'heightening of the taboos against violence in relations between parents and children … is one of the many examples of the complexity of the civilising movement in our time'.[23] Reports of 'infants thrown on to dung heaps or into rivers' were prevalent

---

[22] See, in particular, Corbin (1996) on the changing 'delicacy of the senses'. 'To separate the abode of the dead from that of the living', Corbin (1996: 58–9) argues, 'became an incessant demand' from the end of the eighteenth century, and not least because of the association of death with disease. A related development during the second half of the eighteenth century was the relocation of cemeteries outside urban centres (Spierenburg 1991: 154). The influence of concerns about disease on the course of the civilizing process raises larger issues that cannot be discussed here. Mennell (2007: 68) claims that Elias's position was that arguments about improving public hygiene usually followed efforts to impose new forms of social control and self-regulation. The former were employed to convince others that complying with 'higher' standards was in their interests. But whatever future avenues of research may disclose, the emergence of more 'civilized' sensibilities was usually linked with sharper contrasts between 'civilized' upper and 'uncouth' lower strata (Corbin 1996: 39, 71). Decisions to place executions behind the scenes owed a great deal to elite revulsion at the lower orders' indulgence in the carnivalesque on such occasions (Banner 2002: 144ff.). Gatrell (1994: 266ff.) supports that thesis by arguing that revulsion towards those who found a debauched pleasure in witnessing executions played a greater role in ending state-authorized killing than did concern for the suffering of the victims. The significance of such comments for Elias's position is considered on p. 171, n. 26.

[23] Changes in the level of violence between men and women, and between adults and children, have been interpreted as evidence of the greater importance of family life in the eighteenth century. Spierenburg (1991: 287) stresses the increased reliance on the family as a sanctuary at a time when growing 'depersonalization and self-control … had come to characterize the relations between people in other areas of life'. Elias (2000: 159–60) regarded the separation

in Greece and Rome where, in the main, public opinion 'regarded the killing of infants or the sale of children – if they were pretty, to brothels, otherwise as slaves' as appropriate (Elias 2008b: 18–19). Not until the late nineteenth century did laws against infanticide find their way into the pages of Europe's statute books. The fact that 'no-one noticed that children required special treatment' revealed that 'the threshold of sensibility among people in antiquity – like those of Europeans in the Middle Ages and the early modern period – was quite different from that of the present day, particularly in relation to the use of physical violence. People were used to being violent to each other' (Elias 2008b: 18–19).

Additional insight into the civilizing process could be derived from understanding changing orientations towards the social standards governing sport. Sporting competitions permitted the 'controlled decontrolling of restraints on emotions' – a partial cathartic release from the dullness of everyday routines, and from associated 'civilized' inhibitions and prohibitions (Elias and Dunning 2008a: 77). They provided an outlet for combative or aggressive impulses that modern moral codes and the imperatives of social interaction had largely suppressed. New standards that defined civilized behaviour towards animals were integral to that inquiry. Changing understandings of activities such as fox-hunting illustrated the 'growing internalization of the social prohibition against violence and the advance in the threshold of revulsion against violence, especially against killing and even against seeing it done'. It was revealing that 'in its heyday, the ritual of English fox-hunting, which prohibited any direct human participation in the killing, represented a civilizing spurt'; it marked 'an advance in people's revulsion against doing violence'. But 'with the continued advance of the threshold of sensitivity' many thought it was 'representative of an earlier civilizing spurt and (wanted) it abolished'.[24] Other (more recent) examples of the impact of the civilizing process on other areas of life are easy to identify. Public concerns about bullying in schools, smacking children, harassment in the workplace, humiliating army recruits and so forth also reveal how the reduced tolerance of violent and non-violent harm has spread across most spheres of social interaction in the recent period, reflecting the prevalent standards and the expectations that people have of each other in those areas.

The peculiar nature of the civilizing process is captured by the observation that practices that violate standards of decency have often been moved 'behind the scenes' as opposed to being abolished. Their re-entry into the public domain could not be discounted. Slaughtering animals behind the closed doors of the abattoir is an example of the concealment of what has come to be seen as

---

of the private and public spheres – and the enhanced role of the family in providing emotional satisfaction – as key elements of the civilizing process.

[24] Contrasts with earlier times are further underlined by the ritual practice of cat-burning that was prevalent in Paris and in other parts of pre-industrial Europe, usually because of associations between cats and witchcraft (Elias 2000: 171ff.; also Darnton 2001).

disgusting or distasteful.[25] Another illustration is screening the execution of criminals from public view in, for example, those US states where the death penalty has not been abolished. As noted earlier, the 'loneliness of the dying' is linked with the 'civilized' desire to avoid or minimize witnessing unsettling or disturbing occurrences (Elias 2000: 102, 159ff.).[26] All those examples suggest that there has been much more to the civilizing process than the appearance of a higher moral 'conscience', and also that references to higher levels of 'emotional identification' with other people, and to compassionate feelings towards the suffering, do not capture its complex layers, ambiguities and hypocrisies. Alongside the more positive associations that the former terms denote arose powerful, privatizing urges to insulate the self from encounters with the 'vulgarities' of existence (see Elias 2001a: 10–16 on assessing the 'costs' and 'gains' of 'civilization').[27]

The social trends that have been discussed were not inevitable; they did not evolve in a unilinear manner, free from detours, reversals and interruptions; nor did they spread evenly across all social sectors, as if pre-ordained. Elias concluded his study of court society with some remarks about the violence of the French Revolution that may seem to sit uncomfortably alongside the thesis that five centuries of development can be summarized by Caxton's remark in the late fifteenth century that 'what was once permitted is now forbidden' (Elias 2000: 70–1).[28] A major social gulf appeared between 'privileged elites' and

---

[25] Spierenburg (1991) maintains that it is not butchery as much as its visibility that is shocking (also Elias 2000: 102). Methods of killing can arouse feelings of disgust but, as a general rule, animal slaughter in itself does not.

[26] Gatrell (1994: 12ff., 226–7, 232ff., 265ff.) argues that the abolition of public execution may have had less to do with humanitarian consideration for prisoners than with 'decorum' and with a general revulsion against public displays of the 'squeamish' or unsightly. Garland (1990: 245) develops a similar argument about the relationship between the civilizing process and the 'privatization' or 'sanitation' of capital punishment in the United States. Halttunen (1995) claims that the eighteenth-century culture of sensibility regarded pain as morally unacceptable, but abolitionism was greatly influenced by fears about the coarsening of sensibilities and anxieties about the possible social consequences of fuelling the public appetite for violence. That formulation invites further discussion of how established groups have combined humanitarian and pragmatic arguments to promote social change. See also the reference to the interplay between considerations of morality and hygiene in note 22 above.

[27] US debates over the death penalty are revealing in this context. The shift from hanging to the use of lethal injections was designed to reconcile the death penalty with 'civilized' norms (Banner 2002: 170ff.). Complex legal debates continue about whether or not 'medicalized' execution violates the constitutional amendment that prohibits 'cruel and unusual' punishment. Disagreements have centred on the methodologies that are used to assess the intensity of pain caused by 'civilized' executions (Sarat 2001). Nothing better illustrates the contortions and convolutions of the civilizing process. Similar issues surrounded efforts to defend constitutional or 'civilized' torture following the terrorist attacks on 9/11 (see Linklater 2007e).

[28] The reference was to Caxton's late fifteenth-century treatise, *Book of Curtesye*.

'rising groups' as a result of the former's inability to adapt to the changing balance of forces. Ascending groups turned to violence to seize what they regarded
as their right to share political power (Elias 2006d: ch. 9). The analysis revealed
how unresolved differences between 'established' and 'outsider' groups can lead
to open conflict, how the civilizing process can be reversed, and how society can
descend into violence. Despite the terror, the French Revolution had the longer-
term effect of extending the civilizing process by abolishing elite privileges. But
Elias's postscript on the Revolution provided a reminder that no account of that
process is complete unless it investigates contrary trends and the latent possibility of sporadic violent outbursts and, in exceptional circumstances, social
upheaval and the collapse of public institutions.

Decivilizing processes

Many Enlightenment thinkers believed that history was not destined to unfold in
a progressive direction; disruptive forces that could throw it back on itself could
surface at any moment (Hampson 1968). Citing Mirabeau's fear that civilization
will not endure unless ruling groups act to protect it, Elias (2000: 39ff., 1996: 308)
observed that as of the Napoleonic conquest of Egypt, European peoples surmised that civilization was their natural birthright rather than a hard-fought
and precarious accomplishment. The result was that they were ill-prepared for
the rise of National Socialism and genocidal politics – 'the deepest regression
into barbarism in the twentieth century' that shattered the myth that violence
on that scale was no longer possible in the civilized West (Elias 1996: 308). Nazi
attempts to exterminate the European Jews were the most shocking demonstra-
tion of the 'vulnerability of civilization', and of how counter-trends can be set
in motion when civilized societies face economic and political crisis. As noted
earlier, any suspicion that Elias subscribed to a progressivist interpretation of
history should be removed by his comment that the civilizing process consists
of 'two directions', one leading in a forward, the other in a backward, direction.
In short, civilizing processes always 'go along with decivilizing processes'; the
question is which trend has the 'upper hand' in any juncture or era (quoted in
Fletcher 1997: 83; also Mennell 1990b).[29]

On the Nazi atrocities, Elias (1996: 303–4) stressed that it was not only important to understand what was distinctive about German history but also essential
to recognize that 'the highly organised and scientifically planned extermination
of whole population groups' like 'scientifically conducted mass wars', does not
seem to be 'entirely out of place in highly technicized mass societies'. It was crucial to explain 'the *social* conditions which have favoured barbarians of this kind

[29] In a similar vein, Goudsblom (1996: 26) maintains that it 'may not be a bad rule of thumb
and not an unsound research strategy to assume that for any given trend a countertrend
may be found, operating in the opposite direction'.

and which might favour them again in the future' given that such outbreaks of savagery 'might stem directly from tendencies inherent in the structure of modern industrial societies', and might well reappear at some future date (Elias 1996: 303–4; italics in original). It was essential to account for the 'civilization of barbarism' rather than fall back on idealized portrayals of modern societies that assume that systematic killing is incompatible with the civilizing process, reflecting for example unique features of German society (van Krieken 1998: 174).[30] One critique of revisionist histories of the Third Reich that deny that the death camps existed, preferring instead to explain mass killing as sporadic outbreaks of bloodthirstiness among the Wehrmacht and the SS in 'the aftermath of battle', underlines the importance of Elias's account of the long-term trend towards the intensification of civilized self-restraints. Revisionists, the argument is, miss the important point which is that *'far fewer Jews would have been killed'* had extermination techniques depended on *'Angrifflust'*, or 'pleasure in attacking' (Mennell 1998: 249; italics in original). Supported by many studies of 'industrial killing', the thesis is that the Holocaust owed less to such outbursts of mass hatred and collective frenzy than to advances in collective social power that result from bureaucratic domination.

Those arguments locate the Holocaust in the broader trend in modern societies that is also evident in contemporary wars that 'depersonalize' violence so that 'ferocious cruelty' is no longer a structural requirement (Collins 1974: 436). The contention is that those societies appear to be 'more humane'; however 'dangers of callousness' and 'cruelty without passion' have actually increased (Collins 1974: 432ff.).[31] A critical development is the bureaucratic division of specialized, seemingly harmless routine tasks that can have devastating cumulative effects but, conveniently from the vantage-point of role

---

[30] Bauman's influential study of the relationship between modernity and the Holocaust appears to be deliberately set against Elias's idea of the civilizing process although there is no real engagement with the latter's argument (Bauman 1989). This is a matter to come back to in volume 2.

[31] It is necessary to leave to one side the controversial 'Goldhagen thesis' that anti-Semitism was prevalent in German society and that large numbers of people knew about, and condoned the existence of, the death camps (Goldhagen 1996). The general point stands that highly sophisticated, mechanized instruments of violence have led to depersonalized killing. More civilized applications of the 'power to hurt' – more civilized because they do not always require those involved in the 'war machine' to hate adversaries or to have blood on their hands (quite literally) – have increased the number of people that can be killed in a single moment without anger. Passionless killing on such an unprecedented scale is possible because of 'civilized' demands to subordinate personal feelings or 'conscience' to the imperatives of bureaucratic systems. The notion of the 'desk murderer' to describe the large number of officials who routinely administered the Nazi genocide captures the key point. It might be added that 'civilized' publics may be more likely to tolerate the use of force as long as it is distant, and does not intrude into everyday existence, although it is important not to underestimate the influence of beliefs about 'unnecessary suffering', attitudes to proportionality and so forth on modern attitudes to the conduct of war.

occupants, unburden the conscience by diffusing responsibility for violent outcomes. No less important is the phenomenon of long-distance harm in which perpetrators do not necessarily encounter adversaries or witness the suffering they inflict.[32] In short, longer social webs have encouraged the dampening of aggressive impulses. One consequence is that those who harm invisible victims through depersonalized violence can be spared the psychological turmoil that often affects those who personally witness killing and suffering (Garland 1990: 223).[33]

Those points suggest that the process of civilization has given rise to contradictory tendencies. Disgust at cruelty and repugnance towards violence are pronounced trends. Functional democratization has increased the level of sensitivity to others' interests, and emotional or 'humanitarian' identification between people (in the same society). But the revulsion against certain practices may not lead to their abolition; standards of public taste can be met by placing them 'behind the scenes'. State-building and lengthening connections have led to the 'individualization' of people who face pressures to adopt a more detached and reflective position towards the world, as if viewing it from outside (Smith 2001: 21ff.; see also pp. 226–7). As a result, the civilizing process cannot be reduced to a single dynamic such as the growth of humanitarian sensibilities – but it would be a seriously flawed interpretation that contended that they were no more than rationalizations for actions that spring from sinister motives.

Nietzsche may have been right that 'pleasure in cruelty is not really extinct today; only, given our greater delicacy, that pleasure has to undergo a certain sublimation'. Garland (1990: 63–4), who quotes that passage in conjunction with a discussion of modern attitudes to punishment, adds that due weight needs to be given to the impact of 'sympathy and compassion' as well as 'anger and indignation' on the recent history of punitive regimes. Tensions within the civilizing process are possibly best captured by the notion that 'modern sensibilities display a definite selectivity' in their targets (Garland 1990: 243). People 'are highly attuned to perceive and recoil from certain forms of violence, but at the same time they have particular blind spots, or sympathetic limitations, so that other

---

[32] Orwell (1970) captured the point perfectly. 'As I write', he observed in 1941, 'highly civilized beings are flying overhead, trying to kill me. They do not feel any enmity against me as an individual ... They are only "doing their duty", as the saying goes. Most of them, I have no doubt, are kind-hearted, law-abiding men, who would never dream of committing murder in private life. On the other hand, if one of them succeeds in blowing me to pieces ... he will never sleep any the worse for it. He is serving his country which has the power to absolve him from evil'. Orwell stressed the power of patriotism, but the emphasis was also placed on how killing without guilt or remorse is facilitated by what Bauman (1989: 26) calls the 'invisibility of victims'.

[33] As noted in Chapter 1, exposure to such psychological damage may be greater for those who have been brought up in civilized societies with little direct experience of violence, death and dying. But dangers can be reduced by 'harm at a distance'.

forms of violence are less clearly registered and experienced'.[34] The upshot is that public indifference to violence or suffering can survive as long as it remains 'discreet, disguised, or somehow removed from view' (Garland 1990: 243).[35] Large questions remain about what decides whether the tensions that lie at the heart of the civilizing process are resolved in favour of emotional identification with the victims of suffering or are reconciled in the shape of indifference – or, perhaps more accurately, about what determines the relative power of the different emotional responses that violence or suffering may produce in modern populations. It is far from clear that Elias's writings provide a satisfactory answer to that question – but his aim, it must be stressed, was to take the 'first steps toward an explanation' of the civilizing process that later work could amend and refine (Elias 2000: xiv).

A global civilizing process?

The civilizing process was not a series of separate tendencies within different states that later discovered they had been travelling along similar trajectories of development. It spread from the French court to other court societies through practices of imitation and dynastic inter-marriage that bound together the ruling strata. An aristocratic code that 'tempered to a certain degree' the 'unrestrained pursuit of competitive self-interest' influenced relations between the absolutist courts. The belief that force was legitimate as long as it was used 'in a gentlemanly fashion' (rather like the etiquette of duelling) had some effect on reducing the contradictions between the principles that ruling groups followed within their territories and 'the code they observed in inter-state relations' (Elias 1996: 138–9). Civilizing processes occurred within an aristocratic international society but their influence, it will have been noted, did little more than moderate the pursuit of self-interest. Their relative weakness reflected the 'janus-faced' nature of societies – the conjunction of 'inward pacification' and

---

[34] Since Elias discusses fox-hunting, one might note that in Britain in recent years modern sensibilities have been more concerned with the fate of the fox than the plight of the battery hen, although that may now be changing. It has been pointed out that more parliamentary time was devoted to discussing the moral issues surrounding fox-hunting than to debating the case that was made for invading Iraq. Such peculiarities are evidence of what Elias called the contradictions in the modern civilizing process that will be discussed in the next section.

[35] The history of international relations contains many examples of selectivity in the moral domain. Western publics have not been especially vociferous in opposing the detention or torture of terrorist suspects as long as the consequences are hidden from view, but published images of the degradation of the detainees at Abu Ghraib aroused concern. The cynic might suggest that publics do not wish to be reminded of the relaxation of the usual taboos against violence and the curtailment of liberties which many quietly condone when personal and national security appear to be at risk, and they do not care to view images that contradict their sense of being highly civilized.

'outward threat' that is a recurrent feature of human history (Elias 2001a: 4). Most people in the present era and in earlier periods have lived with 'two different', invariably 'contradictory codes of conduct' (Elias 2007a [1987]: 145). A condition of internal pacification has been that the use of force to kill others in the same society is either prohibited or highly regulated, as in the case of specialist state officials that are licensed to use violence within the constraints of the rule of law. The insecurities that exist when societies are not answerable to a higher coercive authority lead to a higher probability and expectation of force. The 'vicious circle' of 'mutual distrust', and the 'unbridled use of violence' when leaders 'expected an advantage, and were unafraid of retaliation', have been 'very general' or almost 'normal throughout the ages' (Elias 1996: 137–8). At times, conflict was moderated by a 'fear of retaliation by superhuman agencies'. Only rarely have societies realized 'that if they want to live without fear of each other ... they can only do so by imposing certain common rules of conduct and ... corresponding restraints upon themselves' (Elias 1996: 137–8).

What were the grounds for contending that 'we are basically still living exactly as our forefathers did in the period of their so-called "barbarism"' in that force and cunning are, in the last resort, the decisive influences on the course of international affairs (Elias 1996: 176).[36] The explanation mirrors the account of the reasons for state-formation in early modern Europe. Princes in that era attempted, often for defensive purposes, to control strategically significant territory adjacent to their own lands rather than to extend their power as far as possible. The unplanned and unforeseeable outcome of series of such manoeuvres was the emergence of the modern European system of states. In an essentially realist approach, Elias referred to 'elimination contests' in which

---

[36] Lest there is any doubt that this was his position, see the following comment in Elias (2007b [1992]: 128–9). 'There is, in fact, not very much to choose between the torment which people threaten to inflict on each other as a result of radiation poisoning – the slow and painful death in the aftermath of an atomic battle – and the torment American Indians in the heyday of their independence continuously threatened to inflict upon each other. The difference is that the personality structure of the great majority of people forming the kind of state-societies that threaten each other with the wholescale destruction – the mass killing and mass poisoning – of a nuclear war, is entirely geared to peaceful pursuits ... The pattern of self-restraint characteristic of ... Indian warrior(s) is very different. For one thing, his whole life, at least during the years of his manhood, is entirely dedicated to the pursuit of war ... (Warriors) have to pay a heavy price for the enormous pleasure, promised to them by their social code, they may feel while torturing their prisoners to death in the most horrible manner. They can not only expect to be tortured in the same way by others, if they are unlucky and one of their campaigns miscarries. They also have to prepare themselves for that eventuality from childhood.' Continuities between old and new forms of violence are stressed by the observation that what changes 'in the way in which people maim, kill and torture each other in the course of their power struggles' are 'the techniques used and the numbers of people concerned', though the citation above indicates that rising levels of mechanized force have been accompanied by a decline in the thirst for violence and appetite for killing (Elias 2007a [1987]: 175).

weaker 'survival units' were amalgamated in larger territorial concentrations of power. The 'monopoly mechanism' that led to European states had been a central influence on the whole course of human history, and might indeed continue to dominate international relations until such time as humanity falls under the dominion of a world state that proceeds to pacify the globe.[37]

To explain the monopoly mechanism, Elias referred to the 'double-bind process' in which political-military units acquire the instruments of violence, often for defensive reasons, only to discover that others do exactly the same, and engulf them all in a spiral effect of accumulating deadly weapons linked with fear, uncertainty and suspicion that none can bring under control (Elias 1996: 176–7, 1978: 30). A central concept in realism – the 'security dilemma' – immediately comes to mind (Booth and Wheeler 2008). The 'double-bind process' referred to specific security dilemmas and their cumulative effect on the overall development of society; but it discussed that phenomenon in conjunction with similar trends in relations between human groups and the natural world. Linking those analyses was an emphasis on highly 'emotive' responses to threats, low levels of detachment from immediate, pressing concerns, the failure to acquire 'reality-congruent' knowledge, and the consequent lack of control over natural and social phenomena that seemed to be unalterable (Mennell 1998: 166ff.). Referring to a 'kind of circularity' that 'is by no means rare in the development of human societies', Elias (2007a [1987]: 112) maintained that 'high exposure' to danger 'tends to heighten the emotivity of human responses'. That, in turn, 'lessens the chance of a realistic assessment of the critical process and, hence, of a realistic practice in relation to it'. In the case of security dilemmas, responses to danger that are governed by 'strong affects' encourage others to behave in a similar manner; through action and reaction, all become trapped in 'modes of thought governed by fantasy' that reduce the chances of bringing social processes under collective control.[38] The double-bind process refers to a failure to achieve detachment from challenges to security and survival, and the tendency to impute hostile intentions to others that are not based on realistic understandings of their circumstances but on the high fantasy content of worldviews; the

---

[37] Elias (2000: 254) maintains that we 'may surmise that with continuing integration even larger units will gradually be assembled under a stable government and internally pacified, and that they in their turn will turn their weapons outwards against human aggregates of the same size until, with a further integration, a still greater reduction of distances, they too gradually grow together and world society is pacified' (but see also the more sceptical tone of Elias 2010). Mennell (1990a) emphasizes that Elias believed that over and over again in human history the destruction of small powers was followed by a final struggle for dominance between the surviving great powers. There is a clear parallel with Wight (1977: ch. 1) who added that the result of such struggles has been the replacement of states-systems by empires. Parallels also exist with Wendt (2003).

[38] See Elias (2007a [1987]: 107ff.) on how recourse to 'fantasy' in the face of danger simply reproduces threats and further encourages 'modes of thought governed more by fantasy than by reality'. The themes are also central to Elias (2010).

upshot is an inability to understand shared predicaments and to find a way to collective solutions.

At the heart of Elias's writings is a tragic conception of world politics that is in harmony with classical realism (Lebow 2003; Mearsheimer 2001). The direction of modern European history reflected a more general pattern that runs through human development as a whole – the paradox that 'the number of *internally* relatively highly pacified states (has) diminished in number and increased in territorial size' while 'the scale of wars *between* them increased' (Mennell 2007: 172). On Elias's argument, it is hard to envisage an end to that process that does not involve the creation of a worldwide state as a result of some final bout of 'elimination contests'. The absence of a power monopoly that has underpinned civilizing processes within sovereign states has left societies with little effective choice about how to provide for their security. Lacking evidence of realistic alternatives, individuals have identified with specific 'survival units', ensuring the persistence of insider–outsider dualisms with a high fantasy content that make it difficult to break out of double-bind processes. The higher level of tolerance of violence in relations between societies seemed certain to endure. The implication for the civilizing process was perfectly clear. Belief in progress tended to ignore the reality that 'a curious split runs through our civilization' because of the 'duality of nation-states' normative codes'. The term referred to the gulf between the 'civilized' social standards that people regard as central to their lives within pacified communities and the more permissive attitudes to harm that govern orientations towards international relations (Elias 1996: 154ff., 177, 461).

Elias (1996: 143) argued that modern states have yet to make much progress in establishing 'a common code of norms' that checks the pursuit of self-interest, or in reaching a civilized condition in which 'individual self-restraint' is not largely dependent on the fear of others. He added that it is 'possible' but by no means certain that 'humankind is approaching the end of elimination contests in the form of wars' (Elias 1996: 3–4). Whether that comment reflected faith in the pacifying role of nuclear weapons is unclear.[39] Considering what, in the absence of a world state, might promote the globalization of internal restraints and common norms, process sociologists have argued that the balance of terror can be regarded as the 'functional equivalent' of a higher monopoly power; the fear of nuclear war has encouraged levels of self-control and foresight that have some similarities with the changes in personality traits that occurred as part of the civilizing process (Mennell 1990a; van Benthem van den Bergh 1992: 35ff., ch. 6).

It would be curious if the process of civilization had not made some impression on how societies conduct their external relations, and indeed Elias made

---

[39] Elias (2010) sets out the case for thinking that the species may be nearing 'the end of the road' and may face the prospect of a 'return to the cave'. Nuclear war could not be ruled out, but the sense of danger could encourage levels of detachment and foresight, coupled with breakthroughs to collective responses, that have been rare in the history of relations between human groups.

several comparisons between pre-modern and modern world politics that confirm that thought. For example, transitions from peace to war are now more
complex and protracted than they were in Ancient Athens or in medieval towns
where internalized inhibitions against violence in everyday life were lower than
they are today (Elias 1996: 210; 2007a [1987]: 145; 2008a: 125–6).[40] Across 'all
warrior societies (including, for example, ancient Athens), proving oneself in
physical combat against other people', and killing them if necessary, were critical
'in establishing a man's standing' (Elias 1996: 51). By contrast, the 'present-day
military tradition seeks to limit training in the use of physical violence as far
as possible to violence against people who do not belong to one's own state-
society' (Elias 1996: 51).[41] The civilizing process requires warriors to conduct
themselves in ways that reflect the broader character of their social condition.
Pleasure in killing is discouraged. Military codes and legal conventions create duties (although they are not always honoured) to fight with appropriate
restraint in order to minimize the unnecessary suffering of enemy and civilian
populations. Cruel deeds, or witnessing actions that transgress the boundary
between murder and legitimate killing in war, can result in serious personality
disorders; they can arouse repugnance and opposition in societies that pride
themselves in their level of civilization (Lifton 1974).[42]

[40] Certain parallels with Freud's thought are striking. Corresponding with Einstein in 1932,
Freud (1998 [1932]: 145–6) maintained that war 'is in the crassest opposition to the psych-
ical attitude imposed on us by the process of civilization' with the result that 'sensations
which were pleasurable to our ancestors have become indifferent or even intolerable to
ourselves'. Freud added that war now seems repugnant to many because 'everyone has a
right to his own life, because war puts an end to human lives that are full of hope, because
it brings individual men into humiliating situations, because it compels them against their
will to murder other men, and because it destroys precious material objects which have
been produced by the labours of humanity'. He continued that modern warfare no longer
provides 'an opportunity for achieving the old ideals of heroism', adding that the time is fast
approaching when a war might involve 'the extermination of one or perhaps both of the
antagonists'. See Verkamp (1993: 61) on Freud's comments on the fact that modern warriors
are not constrained, however, by the savages' fear of the souls of dead adversaries.

[41] Participation in violent sport made it easier for ancient warriors to undergo the transition
from peace to war. The ancient Greek *pancration* – a form of ground wrestling in which
it was permissible, but regrettable, to kill an opponent – demonstrated that 'the threshold of sensitivity with regard to the infliction of physical injuries and even to killing in a
game-contest' was very different from what it is today (Elias 2008a: 118ff.). As for modern
attitudes to violent harm and the transition from peace to war, Elias (2001a: 51) observed
that 'how the personnel of the concentration camps adjusted psychologically to the daily
mass-killings is an open question that would merit closer investigation'. That is a matter to
come back to in volume 2.

[42] Efforts to develop 'combat pills' that can deaden the warriors' senses and reduce the risk
of post-traumatic stress disorder provide an interesting illustration of how the civilizing
process leads societies into entanglements that did not exist, or did not exist to anything
like the same extent, in earlier eras (Elias 2000: xiv). One of their purposes is to inhibit
guilt in killing, but the danger is that serious violations of the laws of war may occur more
frequently as a result of the suppression of inhibiting emotions. For further discussion, see
Baard (2003).

According to Elias, the prevalent emotional attitudes to genocide in different eras provide further insight into the global significance of civilizing processes. In antiquity, the level of moral repugnance against mass atrocities was 'decidedly lower', and 'feelings of guilt or shame' in the minds of perpetrators were 'decidedly weaker' than they are 'in the relatively developed nation-states of the twentieth century' (Elias 2008a: 126). Indeed, parallels to modern inhibitions to mass killing may have been 'entirely lacking' (Elias 2008a: 126). By comparison, even during the Second World War, 'certain minimum rules of civilized conduct' were observed with respect to the treatment of prisoners of war. Notwithstanding the exceptions, 'a kernel of self-esteem which prevents the senseless torturing of enemies and allows identification with one's enemy in the last instance as another human being, together with compassion for his suffering', did not entirely collapse (Elias 1996: 309). None of that survived in the Third Reich's policy towards the Jews – which was why its genocidal behaviour was 'regarded with spontaneous feelings of horror' (Elias 1996: 445). Some faith that a global civilizing process was emerging could be derived from the superpowers' competition to affirm the individual's right to be protected from laws that are 'inhumane'. Such developments could mark 'the early stage of a long process' during which 'humankind as the highest level of integration may gain equality' with sovereign nation-states (Elias 1991: 140).[43] In support of that argument, it might be added, present-day observers can point to the evolution of international criminal law, and to the steps that have been taken to punish warriors who are found guilty of violating the humanitarian law of war. Those developments are not universally welcomed, but they were probably unimaginable, or at least unrealizable, in earlier epochs.

Modern nation-states differ from Antiquity and the Middle Ages where there was little 'identification of person with person', and where the 'idea that all people are equal' barely existed, even on the 'horizon', although today strong attachments to specific 'survival units' allow only weak identification with other people (Elias 2000: 175). The ascending bourgeoisie in the nineteenth century spearheaded efforts to convert progressions in mutual identification into universalistic and egalitarian principles of world political organization, but they had little success in overcoming the tensions between the duties of humanity and the obligations of citizenship, and in reducing the gulf between the principles that apply within and between communities. Despite radical setbacks, the bourgeois ethic pointed to the problematical nature of the dual standard of morality that tolerated forms of harm in international relations that were prohibited within civilized groups (Elias 1996: 160).[44] Egalitarian and universalistic

---

[43] Other approaches have emphasized the existence of regional civilizing processes at the level of the European Union (Kapteyn 1996, 2004; Linklater 2010).

[44] There were clear national differences in this area. Greater emphasis on the gulf between domestic and international morality existed in Germany than in Britain in the nineteenth century (Elias 1996: 160ff.). There are interesting parallels between Elias's account of the

moral principles had acquired a foothold in international society, and they were not easily swept aside even in the absence of global systems of enforcement. Evidence that civilized constraints did not collapse altogether during the Second World War, and that 'pleasure in killing' was partly contained, indicated that a return to 'brutalization and dehumanization … in relatively civilized societies always requires considerable time'. However, the conflict had also shown that 'sensitivity towards killing, towards dying people and death' can evaporate quickly under conditions of fear and insecurity (Elias 2001a: 51). Global civilizing processes were a remote possibility as long as international relations remained anarchical. But enthusiasm for any advances had to be balanced by the strong possibility that in the coming decades, 'the armour of civilized conduct' will crumble rapidly if the insecurities that existed during the Second World War 'were to break in upon us again, and if danger became as incalculable as once it was. Corresponding fears would soon burst the limits set to them today' (Elias 1996: xv).[45]

Throughout his writings, Elias stressed the difficulties that states face in promoting a global civilizing process that can allow them to live together without 'destroying, frustrating, demeaning or in other ways harming each other time and time again' (see p. 159). But as with relations within states, the compulsions of interdependence have forced them into devising ways of restraining the ability to inflict violent and non-violent harm. There are strong pressures to learn how to adapt behaviour to the interests of other people over greater distances. Moreover, states are not entirely autonomous but form 'part of another less highly organized' and 'less well-integrated system' that has the capacity 'to regulate its own course' (Elias 2007a [1987]: 101). The reference was to the global 'balance of power system' which 'constitutes the highest level of integration and organized power' that can promote a variant on the combination of internal and external restraints that emerged with the civilizing process. There is a parallel with the English School claim that the balance of power may be crucial for the existence of international society (Dunne 2003), and there is the same recognition that such 'steering mechanisms' are fragile and prone to collapse.[46]

---

development of bourgeois conceptions of international politics and the analysis of the decline of 'aristocratic internationalism' in Morgenthau (1973) and the discussion of the nationalization of political community in Carr (1945).

[45] The civilizing process may have suppressed the 'joy in killing and destruction' that Elias (2000: 170) regarded as central to warrior codes in earlier eras, but that did not alter the fact that 'in a period of incessant violence in inter-state affairs … internalized defences against impulses to violence inevitably remain unstable and brittle' (Elias 2008a: 133).

[46] Elias did not engage with – and may not have been aware of the existence of – English School writings on civility or civilizing processes in international society. Potentials for synthesis are discussed in the next chapter. Volume 2 addresses the extent to which the French court, which was a model for other court societies, encouraged others to embrace principles of 'civilized' diplomacy.

As noted earlier, Mennell (2007: 247) has pointed to a general trend within pacified societies in which the power of centralized institutions has increased in response to the problems and challenges created by rising levels of interconnectedness. That comment reflects Elias's conjectures about how humanity may deal with similar challenges that have emerged as a result of the closer interweaving of societies. The discussion of such global pressures marked a break with the 'methodological nationalism' of much social science in the period in which Elias was writing. Sociologists, Elias (2001b: 163) argued, can no longer close their 'eyes to the fact that in our time, in place of the individual states, humanity split up into states is increasingly … the framework of reference' for those who wish to understand 'many developmental processes and structural changes'. It had become essential to shift focus to 'long-term social processes' that affect 'in the last resort, the development of humanity', understood as the totality of all societies (Elias 2009c: 178).[47] The case for switching the 'field of vision' from 'the level of intra-state relationships to that of humankind' did not simply allude to the fact that sociologists had tended to ignore relations between societies. The deeper point was that changes in the internal organization of society and in the structure of international relations are always inseparable, but 'concept formation' in the social sciences is only now beginning to reflect that reality (Elias 1991: 138ff.).[48]

[47] Mennell (1998: ch. 9) discusses the significance of the shift to humanity as the central frame of reference in Elias's later work, and notes how it was linked with a focus on the significance of the capacity for symbolization, cognitive detachment and time-measurement for the evolution of the species. See Elias (2007a [1987] and 2007b [1992]) for further discussion. Kilminster (2007: 144) stresses that, for Elias, the point was not just to widen the horizons of social inquiry to focus on processes that have come to affect humanity as a whole, but to guard against 'the intrusion of national self-images into concept formation' at that level. The challenge of moving towards a higher level of synthesis in the social sciences was linked with the problem of reducing the influence of flattering collective self-images with a high fantasy content on the production of knowledge (Kilminster 2007: 136). The quest for higher-level synthesis was integral to Elias's interest in the generation of 'reality-congruent' knowledge that could improve the species' prospects of regulating processes that are in danger of spiralling out of control.

[48] One could not hope to 'understand the development of Germany', Elias (1996: 179) maintained, without analysing its 'position in the inter-state framework and correspondingly in the power and status hierarchies of states. It is impossible here to separate inter-state and intra-state lines of development; from a sociological standpoint, intra-state and inter-state structures are inseparable even though the sociological tradition up till now has involved a concentration mainly, and quite often exclusively, on the former. The development of Germany shows particularly clearly how processes within and between states are indissolubly interwoven'. Those observations have clear implications for the study of international relations although Elias was not concerned with that matter. The point is that the analysis of struggles for power and security, and the study of international society, should form part of a larger inquiry into the transformation of society, and specifically into rising levels of human interconnectedness with all their ambiguities (Linklater 2009).

The synoptic approach that was developed in Elias's writings highlights relations between these phenomena: the emergence of ever-larger territorial monopolies of power in human history; the various technological revolutions and social and political transformations that have drawn more and more people into longer (now global) chains of interdependence; the pressures to become orientated to the interests of radically different societies; and changes in the scope of emotional identification so that humans now identify with millions, or hundreds of millions, of people in the same society – and even with all other members of the species, although that has not occurred to anything like the same extent (Elias 2007a [1987]: 65ff.). States have been at the centre of all of those processes. They have been a driving-force behind the long-term trend towards the 'globalization of human society' (Mennell 1990a). That process cannot be understood in isolation from the competition for power, from the tendency for people to identify strongly with the relevant 'survival unit', and from their commitment to pernicious insider–outsider dualisms that have prevented them from cooperating to address global problems or which have blocked the path to new forms of political community that combine loyalties 'above' and 'below' the state.

The upshot of those remarks is that concept-formation within more synoptic modes of social-scientific inquiry needs to cast light on 'integration and dis-integration tensions' within world society, and to try to ascertain whether the former may yet prevail in ways that promote a global civilizing process (Elias 2008c: 86ff.). A clear trend was the need for the 'attunement of human conduct over wider areas and foresight over longer chains of action than ever before' (Elias 2000: 379). More people are aware that their lives are inextricably bound together with people thousands of miles away. Functional democratization – which is still rudimentary in world politics – pushes some to try to adapt to others' needs and interests, without the restraining hand of a higher monopoly of power. 'Unions of states' in some regions demonstrate an awareness of the need for higher 'steering mechanisms'; in time, they may even replace 'individual states' as 'the dominant social unit' (Elias 2001b: 164–5).[49] But many people do not care for invitations to divide loyalties between traditional 'survival units' and 'unions of states'. The process of European integration revealed how the changes associated with coping with global interdependence can come as a 'shock to the traditional national self-images' of people; as a result of the dominant 'natiocentric socialisation of children and adults', many of them could see the wisdom in creating new transnational political structures but, when pressed, they would confess that they held little 'emotional significance for them' (Elias 2000: 551).

---

[49] See Kapteyn (1996), Linklater (2010) and Smith (2001: 130–1) on the relationship between European collaboration and the civilizing process.

The power of 'survival units' was one reason for a dominant trend in world history, namely for the 'social *habitus*' (everyday patterns of behaviour and the corresponding emotions) to lag behind 'global integration' (Elias 2007a [1987]: 67). It is indeed possible that 'the immense process of integration' that the species is going through may be followed by a 'dominant disintegration process', and by a decivilizing 'counter spurt' in which attachments to particular 'survival units' become even stronger (Elias 2001b: 165 and 222; 2008c: 70). For many people, global integration brings unwelcome encroachments on traditional ways of life and threats to power, social standing and independence that must be firmly resisted. It was important not to fall into the trap of thinking that rising levels of interconnectedness must simply erode such fears and weaken parochial loyalties. The analyst had to remember that

> the need to elevate oneself above one's fellow humans, and thus the need to find something to look down upon in one's fellow creatures, is so widespread and deep-rooted that it is hard to discover any single society ... that has not ... found the opportunity to use another society as an outsider society, as a kind of scapegoat for its own shortcomings.

> (Elias 1990: 226ff.)

It was important to think about 'integration–disintegration tensions' in long-term perspective. The current phase of global integration belongs to 'an early stage in the development of humanity', indeed to what might be regarded as 'humankind's prehistory' (Elias 2007b [1992]: 128). Until the last few thousand years, Elias added, humans lived in relatively small, isolated communities with populations of a few dozen; their incorporation into larger groups has taken place over several millennia, during which time they have repeatedly failed 'to understand and ... control the social dynamics' that drove 'the rulers of different states' to settle conflicts by force (Elias 2007b [1992]: 128). For reasons that were outlined earlier, they have not been particularly successful in achieving significant detachment from familiar worldviews, in thinking from the standpoint of others, and in learning how to co-exist with the minimum of violent and non-violent harm. Even in the current phase of global integration, the idea of humanity is a 'blank area' on the 'emotional maps' of large numbers of people (Elias 2001b: 168, 202–3, 232). It was possible to identify an increase in the sense of responsibility 'for the fate of others far beyond the frontiers of (our) own country or continent' that is connected with the larger process of 'widening of identification between person and person' (Elias 2001b: 168, 202–3, 232). More people than ever before know 'that an enormously large part of humanity live their entire lives on the verge of starvation' (Elias 1996: 26). Even though 'relatively little is done' to solve that problem, the 'feeling of responsibility which people have for each other' has 'increased' to some degree, just as 'conscience formation ... changed in the course of the twentieth century' (Elias 2001b: 168, 202–3, 232). During the remaining period in which the sun is able to sustain life on earth, he added, it should not be beyond human ingenuity to learn how to create a tolerable life for people in all parts of the globe, assuming they survive 'the violence of our age' (Elias 1991: 146–7). As noted above, humans might be more likely to cooperate to that end if they could see themselves from a future vantage-point in which they appeared to be 'late barbarians' living in the Dark Ages (Elias 1991: 146–7; Kilminster 2007: 157). The argument of this work is that collaboration to promote cosmopolitan harm conventions is central to future success in creating a social *habitus* that no longer lags behind global integration; it is one way in which societies can deal with the fact that they will not earn the right to call themselves civilized until they finally learn how to live together with no more than socially necessary, minimum levels of violent and non-violent harm (Elias 2000: 446–7).

Process sociology and critical theory

Most works devoted to Elias's account of the civilizing process have explained the nature of his long-neglected contribution to sociology, or they have shown how his central thesis can be applied in different ways or developed further. Rather less attention has been given to assessing his preliminary observations about the civilizing process, and there is still much to do to establish how far they are valid (Fletcher 1997; van Krieken 1998; see, however, Mennell 2007). A significant body of historical work, some of which makes direct reference to Elias's writings, supports his overall thesis. Some confirm the argument that the civilizing process led to new forms of body control that are evident in changing modes of self-restraint with respect to physical gestures or the governance of emotions (Bremmer and Roodenburg 1991); some endorse the contention that the changing threshold of shame and embarrassment has pushed the unpleasant, unsightly or disgusting behind the scenes as part of the growing separation between private and public life (Aries 1974; Perrott 1990; Stone 1979);[50] some have suggested that the rise of 'civil conversation' supports claims about the appearance of new forms of orientation between people and related concerns about avoiding offence (Burke 1993); more fundamentally, many argue that the current evidence endorses the claim that (at least until recently) there has been an overall long-term decline in the level of interpersonal violence that is linked with the appearance of stronger internal restraints on aggressive impulses (Johnson and Monkkonen 1996; Stone 1983, 1985; also Garland 2000 and Mennell 2007: ch. 6); and finally, many works are broadly supportive of the thesis that the growing aversion to pain and suffering (as exemplified by

---

[50] See also the references to Corbin (1996) in note 22 above, and Foucault (1973).

the struggles to abolish slavery, severe punishment, domestic violence and animal cruelty) have been defining features of European societies, at least since the Enlightenment.[51] On the other side of the equation, there are disagreements with many aspects of Elias's work, but especially with his belief in the greater violence of the Middle Ages.[52]

For many the principal issue may not be whether the processes that Elias described actually occurred, but how far they took place because of changing attitudes to suffering and as a result of increasing emotional identification between persons. What may be the main alternative interpretation of the development of modern society explained the decline of violent punishment in terms of the emergence of new forms of social discipline and control. Foucault famously contrasted the gory public execution of Damiens in 1757, which was designed to demonstrate the sovereign's absolute power over the body, with the rise of new forms of panoptical power as expressed in the rise of the modern prison. Incarceration moved punishment behind the scenes, and replaced inflicting physical pain with reforming and rehabilitating the criminal, allegedly because of the humanitarian ethos of the Enlightenment. The emergence of 'civilized' punishment had less to do with moral sensibilities than with the progress that states made in the period between 1770 and 1810 in learning how 'not to punish less, but to punish better; to punish with an attenuated severity perhaps,

---

[51] See Davis (1970) on slavery, Sznaider (2001) on cruelty to animals and children, Thomas (1984) on animal suffering, Rey (1998) and Sarat (2001) on changing notions of pain, Banner (2002), and Gatrell (1994) and Silverman (2001) on punishment.

[52] A few illustrations may suffice. In his account of the history of capital punishment in Germany, Evans (1997: ch. 2–3) takes issue with Elias's observations about the greater cruelty of earlier European societies. Rather than being simply 'orgiastic celebrations of cruelty', or means of re-establishing the solidarity of the community in the face of transgressions of fundamental norms, public execution was linked with hopes for the redemption of the criminal, and with some sympathy for malefactors. But the fact remains that social tolerance of physical pain was greater than it is today. Banner (2002: ch. 1) argues that Americans displayed solidarity with offenders prior to the late eighteenth century because of the belief that wrongdoers had succumbed to evil dispositions from which no mortal was immune. Identification with offenders declined in the nineteenth century as the criminal came to be regarded as a social outcast, as someone whose breach of the community's values signified, for example, some kind of psychological defect. Gatrell (1994: 37) argues that with the privatization of capital punishment, the wrongdoer lost some of the sympathy that had been part of the public spectacle of witnessing the pain and suffering that was inflicted on a still redeemable life. Sennett (2002: 299ff.) makes a similar point with respect to the practice of concealing execution from public view in revolutionary France. Those analyses do not take issue with Elias's comments about what now seems to be the greater physical cruelty of medieval and early modern European societies, but they raise the question of whether Elias emphasized the extent to which, for example, violence against the body was combined with care for the immortal soul. That said, Elias's account of the importance of combat in the lives of medieval warriors finds support in Thomas (2009: ch. 2) which also shows how the older martial virtues went into decline with the rise of professional standing armies and the long-term trend towards the 'civilianization of the population'.

but in order to ... insert the power to punish more deeply into the social body' (Foucault 1979: 82).[53] Far from explaining the revulsion against cruel punishment, the 'humanitarian explanation' has given modern people the flattering assurance that they are living in a progressive age that has left behind the violent practices of the 'ruder nations' (see also Banner 2002: 100ff.).

One purpose of Foucauldian critical theory was to shatter such delusions. Before discussing how far similar themes are central to process sociology, it is important to note how much Elias and Foucault had in common. They were agreed that growing 'self-reflection' and self-discipline had become central to the ways in which people are now locked together, although, as noted earlier, Elias traced the emergence of civilized self-restraint farther back in time – to the court societies of fifteenth- and sixteenth-century Europe (Elias 2000: 372–3). They were both drawn beyond traditional histories of politics and economics to explore what Elias regarded as new internal controls on fundamental drives and what Foucault called 'the history of feelings, behaviour and the body' (Turner 1991: 17; also Finzsch and Jutte 1996). But there were important differences in their explanation of the driving-forces behind modern social arrangements.

Foucault's thesis that the decline of violent punishment can be explained in terms of changing forms of power and control rather than as an outcome of an upsurge of sympathy for its victims has been accused of reductionism. The main criticism has been that too little attention is paid to developments in the moral-cultural sphere.[54] Elias's approach advises against trying to ascertain whether 'power' has been more influential than 'morality' in shaping modern society; the issue is how they evolved together as part of the reconfiguration of social bonds (Spierenburg 2004). Monopolies of coercive power, domestic pacification, longer chains of interdependence, the increasing role of self-restraint, changing forms of orientation, and attendant shifts in the scope of emotional identification evolved together in an intertwined manner. From that approach, changes in moral orientation – new emotional responses to pain and suffering, for example – are not epiphenomenal, but they need to be understood as elements in a larger process of social transformation which is always suffused with relations of power. Tensions between the established and the outsiders have shaped the demands that people have made of each other in the course of being brought

---

[53] Sharpe (1990) advises against assuming there was a sharp break between the more and less cruel phases of modern history. See also Spierenburg (2004) for a critique of Foucault's belief in a major rupture in modes of punishment in the main European societies.

[54] Habermas (1987: 287ff.) criticized Foucault's practice of concentrating only on 'processes of subjugation', or on 'contexts of more or less consciously strategic action' that led him to exclude 'values, norms and processes of mutual understanding'. 'Moral-practical learning processes have to present themselves to him as intensifications of processes of empowerment' with the resulting failure to analyse 'the development of normative structures in connection with the modern formation of power' (Habermas 1987: 289–90). Elias, by contrast, cannot be accused of analysing normative structures in that way.

together in longer social webs. Two aspects of that process were mentioned earlier: the mechanisms by which dominant values are transmitted to other strata (through for example emulating 'superiors') and the changing fortunes of subordinate groups when, as a result of 'functional democratization', they acquire new opportunities to improve their social position (Elias 2000: 392, 400).

Many discussions that have been influenced by Foucauldian themes shed light on how the civilizing process developed in conjunction with decivilizing trends.[55] As noted earlier, government decisions to place executions behind the scenes may have owed more to elite revulsion towards the behaviour of the unrefined lower orders than to sympathy for the victims (p. 171, n. 26). Middle-class efforts to differentiate themselves from aristocratic harshness and the unruliness of the 'lower elements' appear to have been powerful elements of campaigns to abolish public execution (Gatrell 1994: 232). In nineteenth-century England, when middle-class groups embarked on outlawing blood sports that were enjoyed by the lower orders, they may have been as concerned with imposing new forms of social discipline as with ending animal suffering (Thomas 1984). The new sensitivities to cruelty that underpinned remonstrations against the 'barbaric' customs of upper and lower groups seem to have been central to the construction of a distinctive bourgeois identity (see also Malcolmson 1973; Elias 1996: 136, 140).

Complex issues surround the relationship between civilization and punishment. Foucault's explanation of the rise of the prison would appear to be at odds with Elias's account of the civilizing process. As already stated, one question is how far the rise of the prison can be reduced to innovations in disciplinary power or should be explained in conjunction with a genuine shift in emotional attitudes to suffering (Garland 1990: chs. 7 and 10; Spierenburg 1991). Some argue that, towards the end of the eighteenth century, sympathy for the prisoner was a significant consideration in the struggle to abolish capital punishment (Banner 2002: 108ff.). Prisons reduced the need for violence against the body,[56]

---

[55] Social and political theory was robbed of the planned discussion between Habermas and Foucault due to the latter's premature death. Less well-known is the fact that Elias invited Foucault to a conference at Bielefeld but Foucault's final illness prevented his attendance. Interestingly, Foucault translated Elias's book, *The Loneliness of the Dying*, for his personal use towards the end of his life (Spierenburg 2004: 611).

[56] Their establishment led to the disappearance of the body as the main target of penal repression (Foucault 1979: 8). A related theme is that reliance on inflicting pain was a consequence of the available methods of punishment rather than any desire to cause or witness physical suffering – see Banner (2002: 48, 72ff.) who maintains that spectators do not seem to have been moved by the offender's agonies which included disembowelment while still alive. Public displays of the bodies of dead criminals (often gibbeted) invariably drew large crowds. Sennett (2002: 298) maintains that the Ancien Regime rarely decapitated offenders because death occurred rather too quickly, disappointing public expectations. See also Braudel (1982: 516ff.) on the relationship between publicly approved spectacles of suffering and domestic pacification.

but their establishment seems to have owed something to a 'growing distaste' for executions for relatively minor offences, as well as to the sympathetic consideration that the naturally virtuous had been corrupted by environmental forces that they may have been unable to control.[57] Reform and rehabilitation could be accomplished behind the prison gates (Banner 2002: 99ff.).[58]

Elias and Foucault were not at odds on how civilization involves high levels of psychological repression, but Elias did not share Foucault's opinion that relations of power are all that have changed over recent decades and centuries (see Garland 1990: chs. 6–7, 9). For some, the narrative that sees one system of domination replace another overlooks the influence of 'campaigns of compassion' on British and American society in the nineteenth century. Whether with respect to slavery and torture, prison and hospital reform, or improvements in the lives of children and the eradication of animal cruelty, those campaigns gave expression to the categorical rejection of the 'unjustifiable affliction of pain' that many regard as the hallmark of modern humanitarianism (Sznaider 2001: 9). It is acknowledged that the relevant social movements often wedded compassion to efforts to extend social control, but the stress on 'top down' reconfigurations of power is criticized for ignoring subordinate group initiatives to promote change.[59]

A central theme in the study of the civilizing process is that the fate of 'campaigns of compassion' is tied up with the level of 'functional democratization'. On Elias's account, the 'functional dependence' of more powerful groups on the lower strata was one reason for the influence of emancipatory movements. The

[57] Banner (2002: 107ff.) maintains that the movement to abolish public execution might not have won the day but for the fact that prisons provided an alternative form of punishment, but 'sympathy' was as important as considerations of 'utility'.

[58] Several works have stressed the 'cult of tender-heartedness', and the kindred notions of the 'Man of Feeling' or the 'Man of Sentiment', that emerged as important cultural influences because of the Enlightenment. Sentimental novels such as Richardson's *Pamela* introduced humanitarian narratives that defended new conceptions of masculinity which broke with aristocratic conceptions of the male ideal. That genre also highlighted the civilizing role of 'the fairer sex' (Barker-Benfield 1992: 139–40; Fletcher 1995: ch. 16; Hufton 1995: 441ff.; Stone 1979: 162ff.; Thomas 1984: 173ff.).

[59] Sznaider (2001: 1–2) may be overzealous in stating that 'it is in the nature of modernity to instil compassion … What they see as discipline, I see as compassion. Where they see power, I see moral sentiments' – 'they' being Foucauldians. Sznaider supports Haskell's thesis that capitalist markets played a major role in the rise of modern humanitarianism (also Barker-Benfield 1992). Markets, it is argued, led to personality types that 'attended to the remote consequences of [their] acts'; they promoted 'new levels of scrupulosity in the fulfilment of ethical maxims' including respect for 'promise keeping' (Haskell 1985: 551ff.). But, as noted earlier, it is not clear why humanitarian concerns should have developed alongside an appreciation of how longer chains of interdependence bound people more closely together, or how the rise of business scrupulosity led to a moral concern for the victims of slavery (see Ashworth 1987; Mennell 2007: 110–12). Other works that analyse the reasons for changing attitudes to cruelty include Burke *et al.* (2000) and Gay (1994).

approach recognizes that moral ideas have more than a 'halo effect' that satisfies the need for flattering self-images; there is more to them than the surface manifestation of deeper power relations; they are not just instrumental in conferring legitimacy on existing social arrangements; they are inextricably connected with the challenges that people face as a result of how they are bound together in specific forms of life, and they can become an obstacle to adapting to new conditions such as the contemporary problem of controlling the social and economic processes that now tie all peoples together.[60] Under such circumstances, societies are pulled in two directions: on the one hand, there is the morality that is peculiar to a specific way of life, and which affirms the special rights and responsibilities that members have to each other; on the other hand, there is an ethic that reflects the realities of their interconnectedness (see Chapter 2). It is an ethic that grows out of the practical necessity of agreeing on moral and political principles that are, to some extent, 'independent of time and space', an ethic of impersonal rules and universal principles that has the effect of '(making) room for a morality of humanity' (Durkheim 1993: 100–1). The idea of equality has gained ground in that context, exercising an influence that may be unprecedented in the history of international relations but, of course, it frequently clashes with the 'natiocentric' morality of the sovereign state (Buzan and Little 2000: 340; Elias 1996: 154ff.).

Elias devoted more attention than did Foucault to analysing the relations between intra-state and inter-state processes, and to reflecting on the challenges that are inherent in the globalization of society. A central theme in his writings is that sociology has the task of providing knowledge that societies can employ, at some point in the future, to steer future global trajectories of development. The point of debunking self-images with a high fantasy content was that it could equip people with a degree of detachment from their ways of life and with an ability to think from the standpoint of others that can improve their prospects of living together more amicably. Though less engaged with problems of world politics, Foucault may seem more vocal in his defence of an international citizenry that 'promises to raise itself up against every abuse of power, no matter who the author or the victims' may be (quoted in Keenan 1987: 20–4). But the differences are illusory.

---

[60] Marxist theories have often been criticized for reducing moral ideas to power relations, but the argument that notions of equality are integral to the ways in which people are interconnected in capitalist societies is closer, at least in form, to Elias's approach to the civilizing process (see pp. 141–2). But Elias did not devote much attention to the relationship between capitalism, bourgeois notions of freedom and equality, and the civilizing process. Some Marxists – an example is Warren (1980: 18ff.) – emphasize that societies with commitments to equality become caught up in tensions from which others are largely immune. The discourse of equality constrains powerful groups, and it provides resources that subordinate forces can use to contest domination and exclusion (see Linklater 1998 for further discussion of those themes). There is no space here to consider how those developments influenced the role of emancipatory struggles.

Elias did not anchor his sociological perspective in such normative commitments, his assumption being that the pursuit of detached knowledge holds the key to understanding how the species can reach the condition mentioned earlier (Mennell 1998: 171–2). But he did not conceal his moral preferences. Reference has been made to his claim that all people should be regarded as having an inalienable right to live as long as possible, if that is their wish, and that those who violate their efforts should be treated as 'criminals or insane' (see p. 23). There are unmistakable parallels between Elias's humanism and the idea of solidarity based on universal vulnerabilities that Horkheimer and Adorno defended (see p. 106). On some occasions, Elias seemed to have a vision of critical social science that has clear affinities with Frankfurt School theory (see p. 163). That parallel invites discussion of how process sociology and critical theory can be combined in a higher synthesis than the one that Elias defended – a more comprehensive standpoint that provides an explicit defence of ethical commitments (such as those considered in Chapter 2) while maintaining the belief in the detached quest for vital 'reality-congruent' knowledge (see Bogner 1987; Kilminster 2007: 129–30). That is the standpoint taken here. The assumption is that such an investigation is orientated towards understanding how societies can use the cosmopolitan harm principle to alter the relative influence of power struggles and humanitarian objectives in the coming phase of global integration (Linklater 2007a: introduction).

Conclusion

Elias's perspective advanced a distinctive approach to the place of international relations in the great transformation of society that occurred in Western Europe between the fifteenth and twentieth centuries, a transformation that has influenced all parts of the world. Although this was not Elias's intention, the approach offers a way of combining the modes of inquiry that were considered in the previous chapter into a more synoptic standpoint that analyses global civilizing processes in different international systems.

To begin with realism, there are parallels between that approach and Elias's comments about 'double-bind processes' and elimination contests that have led to larger monopolies of power. There is a broad similarity between the realist emphasis on the importance of military necessity and Elias's observations about how fears for security and survival can quickly weaken the prohibitions on force. Both approaches underline the obstacles to embedding cosmopolitan harm conventions in world politics. There are all too few references in Elias's writings to the civilizing idea of international society, and little confidence that societies of states can do more than moderate the competition for power and security. There is implicit recognition that states-systems and balance of power arrangements comprise the highest 'global steering mechanisms'. Their existence indicates that societies can achieve a level of detachment from both parochial interests and short-term advantages to cooperate to restrain the use of force. But success is hampered by continuing loyalties to 'survival units' and by insider–outsider dualisms that can intensify whenever peoples are forced together in ways that threaten their autonomy. Elias devoted little attention to class inequalities but the focus on 'established–outsider' relations includes their role in frustrating efforts to establish cosmopolitan harm conventions that deal with increasingly prominent non-violent forms of harm (see Chapter 1).

The question is whether other possibilities are already immanent within existing social arrangements. Elias maintained that global social and economic relations have created some pressures to emulate the civilizing process. The compulsions of interdependence have led to some advances in controlling the capacity for violent harm, and in learning how to become better attuned to others' needs and aspirations. But economic and political inequalities – or the lack of functional democratization – stand in the way of the significant widening of the scope of emotional identification. Highly pacified societies may no longer find pleasure in killing, but one of the paradoxes of their condition is that all have been exposed to the danger of nuclear war in an era when military conflict may depend not on hatred or anger but on a dispassionate use of technological expertise and compliance with organizational imperatives. The species may nevertheless have reached the extraordinary state of affairs in which 'elimination contests' are coming to an end, at least in the relations with states that possess the most destructive instruments of violence.

A central theme in process sociology is that high levels of interconnectedness and functional democratization create imperatives to acquire more realistic understanding of other societies – to discover that insider–outsider dualisms obscure the fact that in some respects all people are much the same (de Swaan 1995). It has become somewhat easier to grasp the moral and political significance of the reality that all individuals have the same departure point in life. Given their dependence and vulnerabilities, all must be cared for in their early years; they must also learn to care for others, though they have often been encouraged to think that no such responsibilities exist towards those in other 'survival units'. Such features of the social *habitus* impede the development of regional and global 'steering mechanisms' that deal with the problems associated with rising levels of interconnectedness. Some consolation can be found in the fact that global integration is still in its infancy, assuming that the species does not suffer the calamity of global nuclear war or an equivalent catastrophe in the future.

Most people remain attached to specific bounded communities even when many spheres of social interaction operate on a higher plane – at the level of humanity as a whole. The most highly-pacified societies cannot avoid moral questions about how they should behave towards distant strangers located further along the global webs of interconnectedness. Concerns about human rights are an outgrowth of their civilizing process. They are the chief manifestation of the ability to widen the scope of emotional identification to include all people for no other reason than that they have common interests in avoiding pain and suffering. As their lives become interwoven with other peoples, many feel an obligation to reflect on how they cause harm to others in any of the ways discussed in Chapter 1. Their orientation and behaviour might be said to spearhead efforts to place a cosmopolitan harm principle at the heart of global interaction – to weave an ethic of care and responsibility into social relations at all levels (see Chapter 2, and also pp. 146–51). The challenge for the comparative examination of states-systems is to ascertain how distinctive those orientations and actions are, and to determine how unusual the modern era is. The challenge is to compare global civilizing processes, and specifically degrees of success in creating the conditions in which people can satisfy basic needs without 'destroying, frustrating, demeaning or in other ways harming each other time and time again'.

5

Historical sociology and world politics: structures, norms and emotions

The discussion now turns to the significance of the explanation of the civilizing process for recent efforts to build bridges between International Relations and historical sociology. Dissatisfaction with neo-realism – and specifically with its belief that the 'propelling principles' of relations between states have not changed for millennia – has provided the impetus for investments in linking the two fields. Critics of neo-realism have emphasized the differences between states-systems in at least two ways: by focusing on global normative frameworks that reflect the changing moral purposes of the state, or by tracing the impact of modes of production on the supposedly unchanging realm of world politics (Reus-Smit 1999; Rosenberg 1994). Those approaches demonstrate that efforts to forge new links between historical sociology and International Relations follow different pathways, some inclining towards analysing the ideational, and others the material, dimensions of human interaction. For reasons discussed in Chapter 4, a more complete account of world politics should aim for a higher level of synthesis that integrates those 'levels of analysis'; and it should transcend them by considering domains that have been central to process sociology: namely developments in collective emotions that include attitudes to violence, cruelty, humiliation, exploitation and other ways of inflicting violent or non-violent harm on the members of other societies.

Leading developments within historical sociology over the last twenty years have attached greater importance to international politics than ever before. Breaking with the once dominant endogenous accounts of social change, they have made the analysis of global political and economic structures central to understanding the development of modern societies (Giddens 1985). The majority of approaches have taken a broadly materialist approach to relations between states; nowhere is that more pronounced than in world-systems theory which maintains that commodity exchange within the global capitalist system holds the key to understanding state-formation and external action.[1] A recurrent criticism has been that it underestimates the impact of the relatively

---

[1] As Kilminster (2007: 158) argues, the great achievement of world-systems theory is its 'detachment from natio-centric thinking'; its principal weakness is the lack of a 'civilizational-socialization component'.

autonomous domain of geopolitical competition and war on the evolution of the modern world-system. Other works cannot be criticized for neglecting military power and physical coercion. Anderson, Giddens, Skocpol and Tilly pioneered the trend towards overcoming their absence from mainstream sociological analysis, invariably stressing in the process the fatal tendency in Marxist thought of regarding state power and geopolitical rivalry as side effects of allegedly deeper social forces: modes of production, property relations and class conflict. For Giddens (1985), for example, historical sociology had to incorporate the main strengths of historical materialism within a more comprehensive, multi-causal explanation that acknowledged that politics between communities possess a degree of autonomy from three other phenomena that have shaped long-term processes of social change: the rise of state power, capitalism and industrialization. That account challenged the reductionism of classical realism as well as Marxism.

In the main, the shift towards a higher synthesis marked by multi-causal analysis has been wedded to the belief that material forces are the principal determinants of domestic and global political and economic structures.[2] An exception to the more general rule is Mann (1986) who focuses on the interplay between economic, political, military *and* ideological forces to explain long-term trends in the accumulation, organization and projection of collective power over larger areas during the last five and a half millennia. That perspective has been criticized for subscribing to Weber's position that ideas are like 'switchmen' that only influence the tracks along which pre-existing material interests travel. Constructivists have argued that Weberian ontology has ignored the co-constitutive relationship of identities and interests (Reus-Smit 2002).[3] Be that as it may, Mann's position directed the sociological investigation of long-term patterns of change closer to the line of inquiry that will be defended in this chapter. Not the

---

[2] Anderson (1974) highlighted the importance of strategic interaction in the transition from feudalism to capitalism; Skocpol (1979) analysed the interplay between geopolitical rivalry, growing state demands on the wealth of the dominant strata, and class conflict in triggering modern revolutions; Tilly (1993) argued that the interaction between the growth of coercive power and capital accumulation allowed territorial states to displace competing forms of political organization in early modern Europe, namely small city-states and aspiring empires; as already noted, Giddens (1985) highlighted four different forces to explain the nature of modern societies. Giddens' later work explored developments in the emotional life with respect to the transformation of intimacy. None of those approaches attached much importance to the moral and cultural dimensions of world politics.

[3] Mann has been criticized for regarding ideology as an instrument that dominant groups use to consolidate power and authority (Reus-Smit 2002). That is true of what Mann calls 'immanent' ideologies that bolster the position of dominant groups. 'Transcendent' ideologies, including world religions that have not been captured by states, have a different role such as providing modes of orientation for those who have been caught up in perplexing, and often unpredictable, social change, and who may also resent or resist prevailing power structures. See Mann (1986: chs. 10 and 11) on the role of Christianity in the Roman Empire, and on world religions more generally.

least of his innovations was stressing the importance of interaction between the members of 'multi-actor systems' – or states-systems to use the preferred term in International Relations – for macro-sociological approaches to very long-term developmental processes. The approach addressed two sides of the triangle of forces that should lie at the centre of the historical sociology of international politics – the increasing scale of territorial concentrations of power, and the development of higher levels of human interconnectedness. Rather less was said about the scope of emotional identification, although Mann's comments about world religions contain much that is important for any exploration of the third side of the theoretical triangle.[4]

It is hardly surprising that the developments in historical sociology that have stressed the impact of war and geopolitics on social and political structures have attracted the attention of students of international relations who are, however, often guilty of ignoring 'home-grown' approaches, and particularly Wight's essays on the comparative 'sociology of states-systems' that predated the recent interest in building links with historical sociology by over three decades.[5] With societies of states as the level of analysis, Wight advanced compelling insights and conjectures about how geopolitical rivalry and war, support for international institutions such as diplomacy and the balance of power, and visions of a latent or potential universal moral community have affected the evolution of those rare, and short-lived, forms of world political organization. Curiously, Wight's analysis of culture, community and communication in different systems of states has not had much impact on English School writings that view international politics from the perspective of world history.[6] Its influence has been more evident in work bordering English School investigation – for example, in

---

[4] With respect to the Roman Empire, Mann (1986: ch. 10, esp. 301–2 and 307) argues that disaffection with economic and political structures, and widespread feelings of anomie, created the conditions for the emergence of Christian visions of a moral community that offered alternative, potentially more 'cosmopolitan', normative attachments that were organized around the promise of eventual 'relief from earthly sufferings'.

[5] That is not to suggest that Wight considered the significance of the writings by leading historical sociologists for his project on states-systems. The failure to engage with classical sociologists (Comte, Marx, Weber, Durkheim and so forth) partly explains his lack of influence on historical sociology, and his invisibility from leading surveys of that field, but that is also symptomatic of the general neglect of the International Relations literature in the social sciences (see Buzan and Little 2001).

[6] The reference is to the focus on 'the pendulum effect' (the rise and demise of concentrations of coercive power in the history of international relations) in Watson (1992), although that orientation to changing configurations of political power was influenced by Wight's claim that the modern states-system has been a succession of hegemonies (see p. 128). The analysis of the structural qualities of different states-systems in Buzan and Little (2000) draws on English School writings to overcome the deficiencies of neo-realism, but there is little discussion of the moral and cultural forces that interested Wight (but see Buzan 2010). Buzan (2004) develops what might be called a structuralist English School approach to the relationship between international and world society.

studies of the evolution of principles of international legitimacy in the modern states-system and in reflections on harm in world politics (Clark 2005, 2007; Linklater 2002b; Linklater and Suganami 2006: part two).

Studies of the moral and cultural dimensions of world politics are often set against the neo-realist belief that material interests are 'determining in the final instance', although the former clearly recognize that cultural forces have to be understood in conjunction with power structures. Modes of investigation that focus on norms in world politics run parallel to forms of historical sociology that have analysed such phenomena as the importance of 'brotherhood' in the social and political ethics of the major world religions (Weber 1948b: 329–30). They share some of the features of neo-Weberian writings on 'civilizational complexes and intercivilizational relations' that focus on the extent to which answerability to others has featured strongly in the 'structures of consciousness' of major civilizations (Nelson 1973). Such inquiries rely on a 'thicker' conception of the self than is to be found in materialist approaches to historical sociology. That has been taken further in analyses of collective emotions that have only recently attracted the attention of students of international politics (Bleiker and Hutchison 2008; Crawford 2001). They are all critically important for the comparative examination of 'civilizing', cosmopolitan harm conventions.

This chapter considers the significance of those developments for the sociology of global harm conventions. The first part provides a brief account of leading 'materialistic' and 'idealist' approaches to historical sociology and international relations, while the second makes the case for linking the two approaches with insights drawn from 'historical psychology' or 'historical social psychology'. As shown in the last chapter, that synthetic approach was central to Elias's claim that an account of the bonds between people should analyse the linkages between 'sociogenetic' forces (the organization of physical power, the structure of economic life and so on) and 'psychogenetic' forces (the social habits, emotions, internal constraints and so forth which are embodied in representative personality structures). The approach emphasized the importance of a 'thicker' conception of the self – one that does not regard people as bundles of interests, or even as influenced by norms as well as interests, but which emphasizes the extent to which individual and collective behaviour is shaped by relatively autonomous emotions. As such an exercise in considering people 'in the round' (see Kilminster 2007: 22), process sociology has shown how emotional responses to violence and cruelty changed in conjunction with the pacification of modern societies and the need for greater responsiveness to the interests of others in lengthening social webs. Modern attitudes to unnecessary suffering in world politics – and specifically contemporary revulsion against genocide and serious human rights violations – were seen as part of the transformation of social structures and individual drives over the last five centuries. Part three discusses how the case for 'historical social psychology' has been constructed in recent years, and specifically in the approach to cultural history known as 'emotionology'. Building on Elias's conjectures about the possible relationship between the coming phase of global integration and insider–outsider dualisms, the final section considers one aspect of process sociology with particular importance for the sociology of global harm conventions, namely 'the scope of emotional identification' and the configuration of 'we images'.

The process-sociological analysis of those forces represents an advance beyond the better-known approaches to historical sociology, but it has yet to feature prominently in the discussion of how to build links between those perspectives and International Relations. The interest in a genuine synthesis of the two fields leads to a central issue for the present discussion which is the role of 'cosmopolitan emotions' in different states-systems, and the extent to which emotional identification with outsiders affected dominant attitudes to violent and non-violent harm (Nussbaum *et al.* 2002: introduction). It is clear that such emotions must be viewed in association with the compulsions of interdependence and their effect on the material power and social standing of different groups; key emotions must be considered in conjunction with the pressures to become better attuned to others, and with opposing trends in which communities and specific strata try to insulate themselves from external influences, or struggle over the costs and benefits of growing entanglements. It is necessary to understand their material context and linkages with social norms while rejecting any temptation to regard them as epiphenomenal, and therefore incapable of shaping the course of events in their own right. As for the analysis of the problem of harm, the assumption is that cosmopolitan harm conventions will have limited effect unless they are part of larger socio- and psycho-genetic changes that promote cosmopolitan emotions – emotions such as compassion, indignation, revulsion, guilt and shame that have been monopolized by the dominant 'survival units' in world history but which can be wrenched from them, and cultivated in the lives of people who can be drawn into associations that represent a move to higher levels of social integration.[7] The final point to make at this stage is that the analysis of relations between the 'power to hurt' in world politics

---

[7] Elias focused on monopolies of force and taxation but, as argued elsewhere, it is important to add monopolies on political loyalty, and on rights to represent communities in international affairs and to commit them to obligations under international law (Linklater 1998). Monopolies with respect to loyalties are as important as the first two power concentrations for the survival of national communities – and their erosion is crucial for the movement towards higher levels of social and political integration. To explain, such innovations as the International Criminal Court have created opportunities for shaming people before the whole world, and for promoting in all societies feelings of cosmopolitan shame and guilt, as well as cosmopolitan indignation when presented with evidence of grave injustice. Advances to 'post-national' communities will not occur unless large numbers of people believe that negative emotional responses to violent and non-violent harm to outsiders are incumbent upon them simply as fellow humans, world citizens, Europeans and so forth – alternatively, unless sympathy for the victims is part of their *habitus*. The analysis of 'embodied cosmopolitanism' in Linklater (2007d) deals with related issues.

and actual, or potential, normative restraints on that capacity requires the integration of several, one-sided conceptions of historical sociology which can be achieved by taking the standpoint of process sociology.

Historical sociology and international relations

Historical sociology emerged as a distinctive field of inquiry in the nineteenth century as part of an attempt to understand the transformation of European societies. Its main architects had a predilection for viewing social change through the lens of 'evolutionary or endogenous models of social development' (Giddens 1985: 22ff.). Their approach was linked with the prediction that non-European societies would eventually follow Europe's unique evolutionary pathways. Many believed that the diffusion of the latter's practices and norms would bind different societies together in a global commercial or industrial society that contained the promise of replacing war with peace. Reflecting the belief that the world is governed by less benevolent forces, recent historical sociology has addressed earlier failures to consider the impact of war and geopolitics on relations within and between societies. Several influential approaches over the last three decades have characterized international politics in realist terms, often ignoring trends within International Relations that are highly critical of the structural forms of realism, and inclined to head in rather different intellectual directions (Hobden and Hobson 2002; Linklater 1990).

That is not to suggest that approaches to international politics that build links with historical sociology in reaction against 'presentism' have been unsympathetic to realism or opposed to incorporating its core themes in their analytical frameworks (Buzan and Little 2002).[8] As noted earlier, the continuing importance of realism is evident in the thesis that the history of the modern states-system is a 'succession of hegemonies', and in the exploration of the 'pendulum effect' – the tension between monopolistic trends in states-systems and struggles for political autonomy within imperial orders that can be traced from the first phases of state-formation in the ancient Near East down to the present day (Watson 1992: 251ff.). In the course of defending 'structural realism', a perspective that is indebted to neo-realism but is critical of its lack of sensitivity to historical change, Buzan and Little (2000, 2002) investigate different 'interaction capacities' over roughly 40,000 years of international history. That

---

[8] An example is Fischer's reply to Ruggie's critique of Waltz's neo-realism in which Ruggie (1983) argued that the latter failed to explain one of the crucial transitions in world politics over the last few centuries – the shift from the medieval to the modern system with its distinctive notions of territoriality and sovereignty. Fischer (1992) maintains that neo-realism has the advantage of being able to explain the propelling principles in both epochs and, by implication, to be uniquely placed to account for the entire history of relations between communities that have been forced to deal with the constraints and compulsions of international anarchy.

analysis of shifts in levels of societal interconnectedness, and changes in the dominant forms of 'sector integration' (specifically whether or how far societies are bound together by geopolitical ties or economic processes), identifies recurrent patterns of geopolitical struggle across human history; but it draws attention to significant variations between different states-systems, and especially to the increased prominence, and possible transformative role, of economic as against geopolitical sources of sector integration in the contemporary society of states (Buzan and Little 2002).

That approach has some similarities with Elias's analysis of rising levels of human interconnectedness and changing social bonds, but it does not combine the long-term trend towards the monopolization of power, demands for higher levels of attunement between societies, and the significance of those developments for the scope of emotional identification within a single, conceptual framework. As with structuralist approaches more generally, the discussion is largely limited to two sides of the triangle mentioned earlier. However, the important comment that 'the widespread acceptance of a universal norm of human equality' represents a 'wholly new departure in human history' recognizes the importance of the third side, even though, in that work, it does not receive the same attention (Buzan and Little 2000: 340). That observation about equality arises in conjunction with the observation that structural realist explanation can usefully draw upon English School analysis. It provides a bridge to the latter's exploration of the significance of moral and cultural factors for two dimensions of international society: for the development of the constitutive rules that govern membership of that society, and for the evolution of the regulative principles that shape dominant conceptions of right conduct, and moderate struggles for power and security (Clark 2005, 2007; Wight 1977: ch. 6). Exemplary is Watson's observation that modern states have not only been concerned with rules for maintaining international order, but have also been involved in a quest for 'ethical standards and codes of conduct which span more than one cultural frame'; they have been engaged, in other words, in a diplomatic dialogue to explore how far they can agree on 'transcultural principles', or standards of acceptable behaviour, in the first universal society of states (Watson 1987, 1992: 308).[9]

Constructivist writings on global legal and moral norms have influenced English School reflections on the relationship between power and principle (Buzan and Little 2000: 104–5). The former have added methodological

---

[9] Heeren's observation that the modern states-system surpasses its predecessors in its 'maturity and refinement' with regard to the balance of power and other basic institutions, as well as in its commitment to 'the mutual independence of its members, however disproportionate they may otherwise be in regard to physical power' has been emphasized by Watson (1992: 209) and also by Buzan and Little (2002: 201). The emergence of 'transcultural values' can be regarded as evidence of a global civilizing process that extends beyond the search for principles of orderly co-existence to the quest for universal organizing principles in a states-system that is witnessing unprecedented levels of human interconnectedness.

sophistication to the discussion through a detailed critique of the neo-realist argument that material capabilities can be separated from normative structures that can only influence them, as if from 'outside', although constructivists recognize that the impact of norms is usually constrained by such phenomena as geopolitical struggle and global capitalism (Kurki and Sinclair 2010). The claim that norms constitute interests clearly rejects approaches that restrict inquiry to assessing their relative 'external' influence on the course of events, as in the case of Weber's 'switchman' metaphor (Reus-Smit 2002). Constructivist writings have therefore been particularly interested in the analysis of the role of specific norms in world politics, a mode of inquiry that complements English School theory and is highly relevant to the study of global civilizing processes although connections have yet to be made with that literature (see Kratochwil 2008 and Reus-Smit 2009 for example).

It is important to pause to consider the significance of some Weberian themes for the sociology of cosmopolitan harm conventions. Criticisms of the 'switchman' metaphor should not deflect attention from particular aspects of Weber's sociology of world religions that have immense importance for any explanatory project that is concerned with the ethical dimensions of relations between groups, whether or not the primary focus is on the problem of harm. Of special significance are Weber's reflections on the role of 'the dualism of in-group and out-group morality' in early religious worldviews. Time and again, the ethic, 'As you do unto me I shall do unto you' had restricted social application, and was thought to be a central rule of conduct only in the relations between those who belonged to the same exclusionary faith community – likewise, the 'principled obligation to give brotherly support in times of distress' was not extended to all people, but was confined to 'the association of neighbours' (Weber 1948b: 329). Different again were the 'ethically rationalized religions', such as Islam and Christianity, where visions of 'universal brotherhood' lifted some restrictions on the scope of the 'do unto others' principle. Universal ethical orientations that addressed the senselessness of much suffering led to extensions of *caritas*, or 'love for the sufferer *per se*', to all persons – and in some cases, a variant on what has come to be known as the ethic of care governed relations with enemies (Weber 1948b: 329–30; see above pp. 145–7). The relevance of that discussion for attitudes to harm conventions and their scope of application – that is, the extent to which they govern relations with other peoples, including adversaries – will be evident.

In his reflections on the ethics of the world religions, Weber did not simply argue that norms play a relatively independent role in fashioning social structures and trajectories of development; the deeper point as far as building links between historical sociology and International Relations around the study of harm conventions is concerned, was that particular ethical orientations were an integral part of the rationalization of modern societies. The idea of societal rationalization referred, amongst other things, to the more reflective orientations to reality and systematized modes of thinking that have distinguished modernity from other epochs, not least by increasing human power over nature (Kalberg 1980). Weber's dispute with historical materialism partly revolved around its failure to recognize that modern capitalist forces and relations of production were one element of a larger process of societal rationalization that encompassed all spheres of human interaction – with no single domain, whether economic, political, military and so on, so causally fundamental as to justify the distinction between the material base and the legal-political superstructure that Marx used to describe the structure of society. It is well-known that Weber's explanation of the rise of modern capitalism attached particular importance to the rationalization of the ethical-religious domain, and to 'elective affinities' between economic and religious orientations towards the world (Gerth and Mills 1948a: 61–5). Through a comparative analysis of faith traditions, Weber set out to show that the transformation of Europe was in some measure dependent on particular forms of ethical rationalization, and specifically on the emergence of universal dispositions that transcended 'barriers (between) societal associations, often including that of one's own faith' (Weber 1948b: 330).

The notion of elective affinities indicates that ethical commitments do not alter social arrangements on their own but must, in some way, be carried along by specific interests that are engaged in inventing new modes of orientation towards the world – the apparent corollary is that interests have no greater causal significance in their own right, but must be linked with social struggles and movements that defend and disseminate new collective identities and ideals. There are parallels with the process-sociological explanation of changing relations between competitions for power and the 'social standards of self-regulation'. Rather than impute causal primacy to one or other of those forces, it is important to understand how they evolve together as people come to be associated in specific figurations, or patterns of mutual dependence, and as they acquire new patterns of orientation in response to the challenges of everyday life and the problems of co-existence. In his examination of those relations, Weber focused on the peculiar character of the Occidental city which, it might be added, is rather like an international states-system in microcosm in that the amicable co-existence of diverse groups depends on what Watson described as ethical standards and codes of conduct that can span different cultural frameworks. The point can be rephrased to claim that social stability rests in part on how far different groups acquire significantly 'detached' or 'decentred' worldviews – which, for reasons given earlier, will depend on the extent to which people have to rely on their skill and resources for their protection, are caught up in 'double-bind processes' that escape their control, or enjoy the security that a stable, higher monopoly of power can provide (see pp. 177–8).

Without pausing to consider the details, suffice it to add that Weber (1948c: 402) believed that the medieval city promoted unusually high levels of 'fraternization', a theme that influenced later discussions of the development of unique rationalization processes in the modern West. Of particular interest for present purposes is the claim that the dissolution of 'invidious dualisms' between insiders and outsiders in Western Europe set it on a different course from Ancient India and China where 'restrictive particularisms' in the form of caste distinctions or kinship obligations blocked the way to 'wider universalities' of thought and action (Nelson 1976). As explained elsewhere, Nelson differed from Weber by arguing that those dimensions of European civilization had not been determined entirely by endogenous (intra-European) forces (Linklater 1998: ch. 5). Pre-empting more recent work in this area, he stressed the need to investigate how inter-civilizational relations had shaped the distinctive universal structures of consciousness that first emerged in the West (see Hobson 2004). In particular, European encounters with the rationalizing tendencies that were pronounced in Islamic philosophical theology in the twelfth and thirteenth centuries had a profound and lasting impact on the dominant conceptions of the relationship between faith and reason in Western Christendom. A chain reaction was released in which more systematic, reflective orientations towards nature and society acquired cultural dominance, and propelled Western civilization in unique directions. It was one reason for its rise to parity with other civilizations, and for its eventual dominance of them.[10]

It may be that emergent conceptions of a European civilization were not accompanied by a sense of cultural superiority over other peoples, but the longer-term narrative has to explain the transition from the condition in which Europeans regarded African polities as equals or as approximate equals, or expressed astonishment at China's technical and other achievements, to that state of affairs in which they looked down on other peoples, portraying them as 'savage' or 'barbarian' when measured against the nineteenth-century 'standard of civilization' (Bull 1984b; Gong 1984). For much of that period, the cultural breakthrough to universality, that Nelson emphasized, had a limited effect on Europe's relations with the wider world; its precise influence largely depended on the level of functional democratization that existed between European and non-European peoples (Mennell 2007: 153–4). At their height, the former were able to force China or the Ottoman Empire to retreat from hegemonic conceptions of world order that were offensive to Europeans. Only with the 'revolt against the West', and the obvious costs involved in holding onto the overseas colonies, did the European powers begin to shed elements of their own hegemonic worldview, and to abandon cherished accounts of their racial or cultural superiority (Bull and Watson 1984: introduction). Only as a result of such pressures and demands did they begin to relax the 'restricted particularisms' that were intrinsic to their

---

[10] The twelfth-century European renaissance set a course in which confidence in secular reason, as expressed in the rise of philosophical theology, the development of the medical and natural sciences and other modes of experience, transformed Western structures of consciousness and social practices (Nelson 1973).

traditional conceptions of international relations, to confront the 'undesirable privileges and prerogatives of the past', and to move towards more 'universal rationales' and 'communities of discourse' that embodied post-colonial expectations of 'answerability' between groups that now faced each other as moral equals (Nelson 1973: 89, 102).

Nelson's reflections on changing relations between 'restrictive particularisms' and 'universal rationales' raise interesting issues for the comparative analysis of global civilizing processes. There are interesting parallels between his perspective and more recent discussions of levels of detachment from traditional worldviews that societies must achieve if they are to agree on morals and principles that bridge different cultural frameworks. Critics may argue that Nelson's analysis of universals of language, logic and consciousness reversed the biases of materialist approaches. In short, cultural phenomena were privileged. It is unclear whether Nelson believed that European civilization enjoyed certain potentials for breakthroughs to universal rationales that other civilizations did not have, or could not so easily realize because of the forces that Weber analysed – for example, because of the power of caste identification in India and kinship loyalties in China. Those questions must be left to one side here. More important for present purposes is the analysis of the conditions that favour the development of social and moral universals as found, for example, in Weber's account of how new patterns of interdependence within the Occidental city led to solidarities that supported higher forms of social integration.

Similar ideas are evident in those explorations of early state-formation that show that the survival of new political structures depended on peoples' capacity to combine traditional kin-based loyalties with broadened conceptions of solidarity and responsibility. That such wider cultural frameworks were critical is clear from the archaeological evidence that many early states succumbed to the influence of centrifugal processes after a period in which unifying and centralizing tendencies had been pre-eminent (Sherratt 1995). Inquiries into such phenomena point to a central weakness of structuralist forms of historical sociology, as highlighted by Habermas's claim that historical materialism developed a highly original account of how many societies had freed themselves from the domination of natural forces, but then failed to analyse the equally important challenges that people have faced in learning how to create and maintain viable social systems (Habermas 1979a: chs. 3–4).

To summarize, the more synoptic forms of historical sociology span the discussion of coercive power, the structures of economic life, and cultural forces or belief-systems. They recognize the relative autonomy of those phenomena, including the role that moral principles play not only in enabling people to live together, but also in providing them with cultural resources with which to contest social arrangements and imagine alternative possibilities. But the search for a higher synthesis cannot end there. There is a need to move to more synoptic frameworks with 'thicker' conceptions of the self and a more 'rounded' conception of people.

Again, Weber's writings are crucial. The rationalization of different social spheres in Western civilization had not taken place without significant parallel changes in personality traits.[11] Weber gave the example of the part that legal-bureaucratic systems of domination have played in replacing personal loyalties in feudal society with compliance with impersonal rules that required those involved to expunge 'anger' as well as 'love, hate … and all purely personal and irrational forms of feeling' from relations with each other. The standpoint is echoed in Elias's account of the shift from medieval society, where rapid fluctuations between emotional extremes were commonplace, to modern civilized societies where emotions tend to be more tightly controlled and to remain in the middle of the spectrum (Goudsblom 2004; see p. 167). There are parallels between Weber's reflections about how social demands for particular forms of self-discipline expose people to new dangers, and Elias's comments about the relationship between the social need for high levels of self-restraint and emotional self-control and modern systems of bureaucratized or industrial killing.[12]

The logic of the inquiry is that no explanation of material and ideational factors is complete without analysing the influence of collective emotions on social life. Elias's writings on that matter concur with Freud's observation that the threat and use of force may be all that is needed to preserve order for a short interval, but the long-term survival of social systems requires not just external constraints but the inner compulsions that result from identification with others (Freud 1998 [1932]: 142). Those writings register a central theme in recent approaches to the emotions, namely that they play a vital role in binding agents and structures together – and in separating them from outsiders (Barbalet 2002: introduction). In Elias's language, emotions play a vital role in converting social standards into 'second nature' – in embodying norms, quite literally, in psychological drives so that compliance is more or less automatic, more or less instinctive (see pp. 164–6; Harré and Parrott 1996: ch. 1).[13] His writings

---

[11] The idea of 'characterology' has been used to describe Weber's approach to the relationship between the disciplined Calvinist self and modern capitalism (Turner 1993b: conclusion). The analysis of changes in character distinguishes that mode of historical sociology from the structural or materialist approaches that were considered earlier. There are clear parallels with Elias's analysis of how developments at the sociogenetic level are combined with shifts at the psychogenetic level, and specifically in alterations of 'modes of conduct', 'consciousness' and 'drive structures' (Elias 2000: 408, 412–14; Goudsblom 2004).

[12] Nelson (1971b: 167, 170) described Weber's bleak references in *The Protestant Ethic* to 'specialists without spirit, sensualists without heart' as 'warnings against the further expansion of the domain of conscienceless reason', and as 'prophecies about the menacing shape of things to come'. See also the analysis of the relationship between modernity and organised violence in influential works by Arendt (1994) and Bauman (1989).

[13] Lyon and Barbalet (1994: 48) refer to 'embodied sociality' (to how social norms are incorporated in the emotional lives of agents), and Greenspan (1995: 194–5) discusses how

explained how basic social standards governing bodily comportment and the management of gestures, or the control of aggressive impulses and emotions such as anger, or the regulation of the ability to injure and in other ways harm other people, become part of the *habitus*. For that reason, the exploration of the civilizing process did not end with the discussion of state-formation and pacification, or lengthening social networks, or the subsequent pressures to become more sensitive to the interest of other persons, but emphasized parallel changes in fundamental emotions such as shame and embarrassment, as had been revealed by the 'manners books' (Elias 2000: 114ff.). In so doing, the analysis of the process of civilization highlighted a crucial feature of the emotions which is their location at the intersection between the biological and social worlds.[14]

To conclude this section, it is important to draw out some of the implications of the present discussion for the sociology of cosmopolitan harm conventions. The main strength of materialist approaches to power and production is the focus on territorial monopolies of physical force, on extensions of economic and political relations that have increased the influence of structural constraints on human conduct, and on the part that sectional interests play in shaping the distribution of material resources and meaningful social opportunities. The 'systemic' forces that chain people together are invariably reflected in binding moral and cultural frameworks, but it falls to other perspectives to account for them. The discussion has stressed that analyses of normative codes overcome at least two major lacunae in materialist approaches: the general neglect of the insider–outsider dualisms that restrict solidarity to members of the same 'survival unit', and the failure to consider the universalistic dimensions of social standards that create pressures to lift restrictions on sympathy and solidarity for other groups. Those normative features of the economic and political ties between people are crucial for understanding cosmopolitan harm conventions in different states-systems.

emotions can 'provide a kind of moral knowledge that short-cuts beliefs in some cases' and supplies agents with precise 'reasons for acting'. The importance of collective emotions is made clear by the frequency with which violations of fundamental social standards lead to collective anger or indignation, and to demands for punishment or retribution. Viable societies rely on such collective responses for their survival while at the same trying to ensure that the outpouring of emotions does not run out of control with potentially disruptive consequences. Societies enter periods of great danger when the seam between the principal rules and standards, and their emotional counterparts comes apart.

[14] Harré and Parrott (1996: 1) make the important point that emotions 'are at once bodily responses and expressions of judgments, at once somatic and cognitive. They seem to have deep evolutionary roots yet they are, among human phenomena, notably culturally variable in many of their aspects'. By way of illustration, social norms shape emotional responses to pain, and specifically how pain is experienced and communicated to others. However, social constructions of pain are not infinite, but are restricted by biological imperatives that people have a limited ability to control. Elias (2009c) places the somatic and cultural dimensions of the emotional life in long-term perspective.

Enormous labour is involved in building emotional commitments to such conventions. Societies have to overcome insider–outsider dualisms that have been integral to their physical survival and self-esteem. They have to develop ways of thinking from the standpoint of others that require critical detachment from cherished and uplifting worldviews, and a break with feelings of group superiority; many have to find ways of reducing levels of fear, envy and suspicion that are rooted in a history of violent conflict before they can begin to widen the scope of emotional identification and enlarge the circle of moral consideration. Conceptions of historical sociology that focus on struggles for power or wealth are better at explaining constraints on advances in solidarity, or the compulsions of interconnectedness that may force societies to re-examine traditional orientations towards other peoples, than at understanding where the potentials for breakthroughs to higher levels of universality lie. The analysis of 'fraternization' that weakened 'the dualism of in-group and out-group morality', and the discussion of universal structures of consciousness that overcame 'restricted particularisms', shed more light on the substantive issues. Such inquiries point to under-researched questions about why some moral codes are more universalistic than others, or less resistant to enlarging the scope of ethical concern. To answer them it is important to focus not just on the reasons people give for believing that acts are virtuous, commendable, reprehensible or intolerable, but also on basic dimensions of the emotional life such as attitudes to violence, the level of compassion for victims of relievable suffering, or the place of shame or guilt in maintaining conformity with the social standards that prohibit certain forms of violent and non-violent harm. The question is how far universal or near universal emotions create the potential for extensions of human sympathy on which the progress of cosmopolitan harm conventions ultimately depends (see also the discussion of Schopenhauer on pp. 94–5).

Historical social psychology

Elias (2000: 406ff.) called for a new approach to the social sciences that analysed the typical 'personality structure' in any civilizing process. He referred to 'historical psychology' and 'historical social psychology' to describe a 'science that does not yet exist', one that would erase 'the sharp dividing line' between history and psychology with the aim of understanding how personality types and traits change with transformations in the bonds between people.[15] As shown in Chapter 4, Elias developed a holistic approach to long-term social processes in which state-formation, urbanization, marketization and so forth were viewed in conjunction with changing 'drive structures' and everyday emotions (Elias

---

[15] The approach is evident in Elias's study of the court society which showed how 'basic personality characteristics' reflected the 'spirit' of the court people and the dominant 'mode of expression' (Elias 2006d: 120ff.).

2000: 414). Part of the impetus was humanistic – to ensure that the focus on abstractions such as states and markets, or explorations of directions of social and political change, consider their effects on everyday experience. As noted earlier, a related task was to promote a deeper explanation of the social world that could enable humans to become better attuned to one another, to identify with each other simply as persons, and to integrate traditional attachments with loyalties to higher-level political associations that allowed them to plan their lives together more effectively.

Elias was not alone in contending that the social sciences had to develop ways of analysing elusive developments at the level of the emotions. Two years after the appearance of *The Civilizing Process*, the *Annales* historian, Lucien Febvre, published an essay devoted to 'sensibility and history'. Subtitled 'how to recon- stitute the emotional life of the past', it called for 'a vast collective investigation to be opened on the fundamental sentiments of man and the forms they take' (Burke 1973: 24).[16] Febvre lamented the fact that 'we have no history of pity, or of cruelty', 'no history of love', 'no history of death', 'no history of joy', and not much more than 'a rapid sketch of the history of fear' (Burke 1973: 24). To solve the problem, he envisaged a new sub-field that analysed how far collective men- talities have changed across the generations, and which aimed to reveal whether there have been 'sudden about-turns' in the emotional life that are perhaps most evident in the lurch from 'hate to clemency, from the most savage cruelty to the most touching pity' (Burke 1973: 17). Questioning the validity of Huizinga's portrait of dramatic swings between the emotional extremes in the Middle Ages, Febvre asked if the accumulated historical evidence would support the conclu- sion that 'the emotional history of humanity' can be divided into discrete peri- ods, distinguishable from one another by the extent to which there was 'more cruelty than pity', or more hatred than compassion (Burke 1973: 17–18).[17] Those observations raised questions that have been at the centre of the explosion of interest in the emotions over roughly the last two decades: they include assess- ing the importance of particular emotions such as pity on any phase of social and political life, and trying to identify, given that evidence may be contradict- ory or incomplete, the prevalent emotional dispositions or representative emo- tional traits in earlier epochs. It is important to consider each question in turn before considering their significance for the sociology of cosmopolitan harm conventions.

A useful starting-point is Elias's rejection of psycho-analytical assumptions that the 'id' or some fragment of the 'unconscious' has been fixed throughout

---

[16] In 'History and Psychology', Febvre described historical psychology as an approach to reconstituting 'the whole physical, intellectual and moral universe' of preceding gener- ations, and to equipping the social sciences with 'a detailed inventory of the mental equip- ment of the men of the time' (quoted in Burke 1973: 9).

[17] Huizinga was an important influence on Elias's account of the Middles Ages which will be considered in volume 2.

history. Elias (2000: 409) argued that some emotions are biological, and apparently unchanging, while others are as diverse as the cultures in which they exist. Without exception, societies have imposed 'structures of control' that lay down the paths along which all impulses are 'channelled in each person through his or her relations with other people from birth onward' (Elias 2000: 409).[18] Archaic emotions that are governed by the most primitive part of the human brain (the cortex) have to be distinguished from emotions regulated by the neo-cortex (Elias 1978: 178). Recent research supports the argument by stating that, far from being acquired as a result of social pressures, 'basic' emotions such as fear and anger are 'universal and innate' properties of 'human nature' – they seem to be anchored in the amygdala, thalamus and other parts of the limbic system that were the first regions of the brain to evolve.[19] Those emotions have been distinguished from 'higher cognitive' emotions such as love, shame, guilt and embarrassment which are linked with the neo-cortex, the area associated with logical thought that developed later than the cortical regions.[20] 'Higher' emotions seem to be more culturally diverse and malleable than the most basic forms (Evans 2001: ch. 1).[21] In related discussions, some observers have argued that support for a 'universal language' of the emotions can be derived from the evidence that different cultures have mutually intelligible facial expressions that communicate happiness, sadness, anger and so forth. But this is controversial territory. Critics have questioned the existence of emotional universals, pointing to the ethnocentrism of imputing emotional expressions that are prevalent in North America, where the bulk of the empirical research on the emotions has been conducted, to people everywhere.[22] Others, most notably Brown (1991), maintain that it may be more accurate to think in terms of 'near universal' emotions. Disputes about whether there is a 'universal language' of the emotions look set to continue. But many analysts agree that, in the rush to underline cultural differences between

---

[18] Elias (2000: 409) added that 'nowhere, except perhaps in the case of madmen, do people ... find themselves face to face with psychological functions in their pristine state ... The libidinal energies which one encounters in any living human being are always already socially processed ... The more animalic and automatic levels of people's personality are neither more nor less significant for the understanding of human conduct than their controls'.

[19] LeDoux (1998: ch. 6) maintains that the amygdala provides early warning of danger by triggering fear; the higher cortical regions then assess whether threats are apparent or real.

[20] Reference was made to reports of research on drugs that may reduce the dangers of post-traumatic stress syndrome. The drugs are directed at the amygdala which controls emotions such as fear. Evans (2001: ch. 1) provides a useful overview of efforts to classify the emotions, and introduction to debates about how many basic emotions exist.

[21] As Darwin and others have argued, fundamental emotions such as fear are clearly not monopolized by humans.

[22] Ekman sought to control for that problem by studying the Fore of Papua New Guinea who had not previously encountered Westerners. Ekman and Friesen (1998), Evans (2001), Wierzbicka (1999) and Oatley and Jenkins (1996: ch. 2) provide useful overviews of ongoing controversies about the universal language of the emotions.

peoples, many of the dominant voices in post-Second World War anthropology overlooked significant common ground, including certain basic emotions that are the result of a shared biological inheritance (see Brown 1991; also p. 49, n. 24).

The notion that the mind is a tabula rasa at birth has been replaced by the view that some emotions are 'hard-wired' and linked with very specific physiological reactions.[23] There has been solid support in recent years for the idea that cultural parameters are shaped by an 'emotional repertoire' which is similar in all societies (Evans 2001: 11; see also pp. 222–3). However, in the main, even hard-wired emotions are 'socially processed'; the lens must be directed at the governing conventions (including harm conventions) that configure and channel them in authorized directions. 'Emotion scripts' or 'display rules' that govern the expression of basic drives or impulses are the main objects of analysis. If anger is a universal emotion (and that is not agreed), then it is unsurprising that every society has developed an appropriate script that defines when it is and is not legitimate to feel anger, and steers its expression along particular pathways that reflect group understandings of what is permissible, or indeed necessary, and what is unacceptably threatening or disruptive, or unbecoming of those involved (Harris 2001). References to emotion scripts invariably add that feelings such as guilt, shame and sympathy have a cognitive or evaluative component (Parrott and Harré 1996; also pp. 205–6, n. 13). They encapsulate normative judgments about how people should behave towards others – about what is and is not allowable or appropriate according to the prevailing social standards of self-regulation (Solomon 1993). As noted earlier, agents and structures are not separable, but are bound together when the relevant norms are embodied in individuals' emotional lives. They may be so closely tied together – rules may be so deeply embedded – that a way of life seems entirely natural to its members whereas the dominant practices in other societies appear completely alien, and may arouse revulsion or disgust. When they understand that socialization processes define what is natural or unnatural in different societies – and when they see others as human just like themselves engaged in struggles to satisfy basic needs – then they can move somewhat closer to the realization that their attachment to a particular group need not be a barrier to sympathy with others' quests for meaning and happiness, and with efforts to ward off threats to security and survival. But that realization may not be enough to erase historical feelings of enmity or suspicion, or to weaken feelings of collective superiority that may have developed as a result of power competitions.

Political theorists from Aristotle and the Stoics in the ancient world to Hume, Smith and Rousseau in the eighteenth century, and Hegel and Marx in the nineteenth century, knew that emotions play a vital role in maintaining the

---

[23] The principal physiological change is hormone secretion – for example, noradrenaline in the case of anger, and epinephrine with respect to anxiety (Barbalet 2002: 3).

bonds between the members of society and in providing the impetus behind collective action. In one sense, modern writings have simply rediscovered the emotions, but they have gone beyond proto-sociological approaches that regarded them as part of an unchanging human nature.[24] To establish the claim that emotions should be taken seriously as objects of social inquiry, they have had to overcome significant resistance. Emotions have often been regarded as 'primitive' attributes whose influence will diminish with the progress of reason. Long associated with femininity, emotions have had the negative connotation of subjection to impulsive forces, or they have been regarded as a threat to the rational, rule-governed, organization of society (Bleiker and Hutchison 2008: 120ff.; Fischer 2000; Lupton 1998).[25] Game-theoretical or rational choice approaches that regard interests as the key determinants of human conduct display a bias against analysing anything as fleeting or immeasurable as emotions, and they doubt or deny that any methodology can provide a rigorous test of hypotheses about their causal influence that can match studies of the impact of interests on individual and collective behaviour (Bleiker and Hutchison 2008: 124ff.; Elster 1999; Scheff 1994). The hegemony of interest-based explanation in the study of international relations which fails to consider people 'in the round' goes some way towards explaining the long-standing neglect of the emotions in that particular field (Crawford 2001; p. 197).[26] Approaches to the moral dimensions of world politics have often fared little better, failing to realize that 'most of what is morally interesting about human life is played out in the domain of the emotions' (De Sousa 1987: 17).

As a pioneer in the sociology of the emotions, Elias (2000: 414ff.) attached special importance to shame and embarrassment, which were 'inseparable' components of the civilizing process. More recent writings on emotions maintain that, by experiencing shame, a person conceives him/herself as 'inferior' to others, and as facing the prospect of losing 'the love or respect' of those whose approval matters (Elias 2000: 414–15). Shame sets up a tension between certain inner drives and the part of the self that represents 'social opinion'. There are parallels, therefore, between Elias's focus on the role of shame in promoting

---

[24] Hume and Smith regarded empathy and benevolence as natural sentiments (see p. 214) while Rousseau (1968 [1765]: 182) believed there was an *'innate* repugnance at seeing a fellow-creature suffer' (italics added).

[25] Philosophers from Plato to Kant argued against allowing the emotions to intrude into the public domain since they are inherently 'pathological' and corrupting – an aspect of 'nature' that is most evident in 'less rational' subjects (Solomon 1993: 9ff., 133).

[26] English School approaches recognize the importance of empathy for the preservation of order (see Linklater 2004). Classical realist and neo-realist perspectives may assume that emotions have the potential to rival ideological convictions in complicating the quest for global stability. However, a specific demand for 'emotion management' underlies the belief that 'rational' foreign policy should concentrate on the reciprocal accommodation of others' legitimate interests, and resist any temptation to descend into an 'irrational' indulgence in ideological competition.

social conformity and more recent writings on the productive role of the emotions.[27] Some analysts have finessed the discussion by arguing that shame and guilt serve different purposes. On some accounts, feelings of shame arise when a person believes there is a 'relatively enduring' flaw in the 'global self', whereas guilt expresses the conviction that a wrongful act is simply 'out of character' rather than the manifestation of an engrained personality fault (Tangney and Dearing 2002: ch. 2). The corollary of shame, it has been argued, is the desire to conceal evidence of the tainted self,[28] whereas with guilt it is open acknowledgement of social transgression, remorse and apology or some other attempt at reconciliation with the victim(s) that can restore self-esteem. In short, shame has a powerful other-regarding dimension that is centred on the fear of humiliation, while guilt is directed inside the self and occurs when a person violates, or is tempted to violate, the warnings of an inner conscience (Tangney and Dearing 2002).[29] On some accounts, guilt has a stronger empathetic content but, for many, shame may play a greater role in securing conformity with social standards. The 'inhibiting presence of other persons', along with the fear of discovery and disapproval, and the desire to protect self-esteem, can exercise a decisive 'restraining influence' when the dictates of 'conscience' are insufficiently strong (Greenwald and Harder 1998: 227ff.; Harris 1989: ch. 2).[30] For such reasons, shame has been described as the 'primary' or 'master' social emotion (Scheff 1988).

Whatever their relative influence and general effects, it is widely agreed that shame and guilt are key regulators of conduct in modern societies (Greenwald and Harder 1998).[31] There is strong empirical support for the argument that parental efforts to instil the sense of shame in connection with anti-social behaviour are fundamental elements of the first stages of infant moral development,

---

[27] Cooley's idea of 'the looking glass self', a term that draws attention to the restraining role of imagining how others judge one's behaviour, is a major reference-point in recent discussions (see Cooley 1998: 20–22; Harris 1989: 92ff.).

[28] Gilbert and Andrews (1998: 142) state that shame is thought to derive from the Indo-European word meaning to hide.

[29] Tangney and Dearing (2002) add that shame can have a negative effect because the accompanying sense of 'worthlessness' may lead people to avoid blame by holding others responsible for their moral shortcomings. Guilt is more often linked with pro-social dispositions, and specifically with empathy with, and responsibility towards, others. Ahmed *et al.* (2001) and Gilbert and Andrews (1998: chs. 1, 6 and 12) consider the issues in more detail. See Deigh (1983) for a different approach, and Lu (2007).

[30] Tangney and Dearing (2002: 193–4) advise that those claims should be treated with caution because shame has a low empathic content. With reference to sentencing policy, they argue that shaming the criminal can foster feelings of humiliation that may rebound on society whereas imposing community service, for example, can have a 'restorative' effect that flows from recognizing a duty to 'repair the harm' that was inflicted on others. See also Ahmed *et al.* (2001).

[31] Issues raised by the distinction between shame and guilt cultures go beyond the present discussion.

and indeed that the capacity to experience shame appears before the ability to feel guilt.[32] Equipping infants with the 'pro-social' capacity to empathize with those they have harmed is a related, and seemingly universal, feature of early socialization processes (Hoffman 2000).[33] Empathy should be distinguished from sympathy however. Torturers can use skills in empathizing with victims to identify the most effective ways of extracting information. The capacity to sympathize is a quality that training programmes seek to eradicate or suppress (Scarry 1985: ch. 1). That they have to be expunged at all is a reminder that, if they are to become functioning members of society, infants need to develop an understanding of their power to cause harm; they must learn the skill of empathizing with others as independent centres of experience, and they must acquire more complex moral traits that include the capacity to sympathize with others, and to feel compassionate towards them.[34] Such qualities and all the emotions that attend them are fundamental to the ability to identify with others in the first, immediate social circles, and to the unique potentiality for widening the scope of identification to include 'outsiders', and potentially all other people. Attachments to more inclusive associations (that weaken insider–outsider distinctions that people acquire through elementary socialization processes) depend on a widespread belief that violations of the norms that integrate people at 'higher' levels should produce counterparts to the feelings of shame or guilt that occur in the 'lower' spheres. What did not arouse shame (or guilt) in earlier behaviour towards outsiders has to become shameful in a process in which actions that were once permitted lose legitimacy, and are forbidden. Materialist forms of historical sociology that often excel in explaining structural constraints usually devote little attention to the cultural transformations and psychological changes that accompany the movement towards identification with others in more inclusive forms of community such as world religions or states (see pp. 204–6). The social sciences will be ill-equipped to reflect on how people can meet the challenges of current and future levels of global integration until there is a deeper understanding of how they unlearn socially inherited prejudices towards outsiders (over long-term processes that often require the passing of

[32] There is evidence that infants display signs of the capacity to feel shame from about the age of two; the ability to feel guilt, which involves more complex social capabilities, appears, on some accounts, around the age of eight. See Tangney and Dearing (2002: 6), Harris (1989: ch. 4) and Schore (1998).

[33] According to Hoffman (2000: 120–1), 'empathy-based guilt' develops specifically between the ages of four and eight as infants acquire 'more elaborate representations of others' ranging from an awareness of how specific actions cause harm and suffering to the more complex realization, around the age of ten to twelve, that harm is caused by violating principles of justice.

[34] Nussbaum (2001: 301ff.) argues that compassion should be regarded as a step beyond sympathy because it usually involves more intense feelings about the suffering of others (see also the discussion of passive and active sympathy on pp. 223–4).

many generations) and how they build relations of trust and solidarity with former adversaries or strangers.

Eighteenth- and nineteenth-century philosophers such as Rousseau, Hume, Smith and Schopenhauer were right that basic moral emotions are crucial for the survival of social bonds, but mistaken in thinking they were part of human nature rather than the outcome of long-term patterns of biological and cultural development. 'Human nature' claims sidestep fundamental sociological questions about how to explain the unequal distribution of emotions such as shame or compassion in any society, or important differences between groups.[35] Precisely such a sociological perspective on the emotions is evident in feminist writings that argue that women in traditional Western families are more likely to have the emotional skills that are essential for performing the tasks associated with the ethic of care and responsibility (see pp. 146–7; Hoffman 2000: 123). No society can survive unless a significant part of its population has that emotional repertoire, but clearly its distribution across society – or across humanity as a whole – is uneven.[36] It is safe to assume that the same is true of most, if not all, fundamental emotions.

Thus far, shame and guilt have been considered with reference to the expectations that people have of each other as members of the same society, but they can also influence behaviour towards outsider groups, and can arise, for example, as a result of inflicting unnecessary suffering in war. They may be linked with damage to personal esteem and/or the loss of social approval. The ultimate cause may not be compassion for the victims as much as remorse at infringing taboos against violent harm that the relevant society supports for reasons of self-interest, or because civilized self-images dictate restraint towards enemies (see Chapter 1). But compassion is almost certainly crucial for linking guilt and shame to emotional attachments to wider communities – compassion

---

[35] Elias (2000: 410) referred to the importance of comparing different levels of restraint in the conduct of foreign policy, as influenced by the relevant civilizing process.

[36] Some studies of gender differences have argued that empathy is stronger among girls than boys from an early age, the standard explanation being that boys are compelled to control emotions as part of the transition to the 'restrictive emotionality' of traditional constructions of masculinity that discourage public displays of weakness and vulnerability. A possible exception is anger which men are more likely to report, and which may at times reflect habits of suppressing or failing to communicate other emotions. On such accounts, girls are taught to be more emotionally communicative, and to regard emotional expression as integral to social bonding. Moreover, men have been reported to be less likely than women to admit to shame, guilt, fear and sadness – which does not mean that such emotions are experienced less frequently or less intensely than in the lives of women. The greater importance of connectedness may be one reason for women reporting higher levels of guilt and shame. The evidence for that thesis, and indeed for gender differences with respect to feelings of guilt or shame, is disputed however. It has been argued that such differences may be less pronounced or significant in many non-Western cultures where 'collectivist' rather than 'individualistic' social standards prevail. Fischer (2000) provides a useful overview of the central issues.

rather than pity which, it is often argued, can stem from satisfaction in knowing that others are suffering, or which can be connected with feelings of superiority where, for example, the victim's own folly is regarded as the reason for his or her plight (see Blum 1980; also Nietzsche 1956 [1867/1872]: preface, v). Pity does not bridge the gulf between self and other by fostering identification with victims. Compassion makes the important breakthrough in extending the boundaries of community because it is linked with the sympathetic recognition of how individual or collective plans and purposes can be brutally ruined by vulnerabilities that people are often powerless to avoid (Nussbaum 2001: 314–15). The imaginative reconstruction of the suffering of others is all that is needed to deal with feelings of separation that pity does not bridge (Snow 1991).

For that reason, many philosophical approaches to enlarging the scope of mutual identification have focused on promoting the capacity to imagine oneself in the place of others. They include warnings against hubris that emphasize that no one is permanently immune from the levelling effect of a cruel fate (Snow 1991).[37] A related approach invites people to convert such imaginative capacities into an insurance scheme that is based on the principle that every group has a (generalizable) interest in assisting those in distress, assuming it is able to do so, and not least because of the possibility that, at some future point, roles could be reversed (Geras 1998). That point invites the observation that the willingness of people to enlarge the scope of emotional identification almost certainly depends on their confidence that others (former outsiders) will assist them if they are in distress.[38] But advances in enlarging the sense of community cannot be reduced

---

[37] Rousseau's *Emile*, quoted in Nussbaum (2001: 315–16, 350) provides a striking illustration of the approach. 'Why are kings without pity for their subjects? ... Why are the rich so hard to the poor? It is because they have no fear of being poor. Why does a noble have such contempt for a peasant? It is because he will never be a peasant.' Rousseau proceeded to argue for the need to inculcate a sense of 'compassion without hierarchy', based simply on the 'common vulnerability of all human beings'. The argument might be interpreted as an exercise in moral exhortation in the context of low functional democratization (see pp. 161–2). It called for levels of self-reflectiveness and identification with others that are more likely to develop under conditions of mutual dependence where it is easier (and also necessary) for people to imagine themselves in others' shoes, confronting a similar fate. 'Do not', Rousseau urged, 'accustom your pupil to regard the sufferings of the unfortunate and the labors of the poor from the height of his glory; and do not hope to teach him to pity them if he considers them alien to them. Make him understand well that the fate of these unhappy people can be his, that all their ills are in the ground beneath his feet, that countless unforeseen and inevitable events can plunge him into them from one moment to the next. Teach him to count on neither birth nor health nor riches. Show him all the vicissitudes of fortune'. The challenge was to imagine a condition of functional democratization when one clearly did not exist, by Rousseau's own admission (see also pp. 229–30).

[38] Such arguments implicitly recognize that functional democratization may not be high enough to encourage people to assist distant strangers, but they try to circumvent the problem by extending the time-horizon and by inviting people to imagine circumstances in which they may become dependent on those they are currently able, but disinclined, to assist.

to calculations of self-interest, although pragmatic considerations are undoubtedly important; the successful transition to 'higher' levels of integration also depends on the influence of emotions such as shame and guilt. Schopenhauer (1995 [1840]: 150) identified one important motive, which is keeping oneself 'free from the self-reproach of being the cause of another's suffering' – free from the shame or guilt that may result from failing to help others. As is well-known, those considerations are usually much stronger between those who belong to the same 'survival unit', but public appeals to assist distant strangers raise the question of how far the desire to assist others, and to avoid self-reproach, find expression (however inconsistently or fleetingly) in relations between communities (see the discussion of cosmopolitan emotions on p. 222ff.).[39]

Rousseau's remark that educators cannot expect to arouse feelings of 'pity' where people find the suffering of others 'alien' to their own experience has obvious relevance for international relations where many societies believe that actual or potential adversaries will not assist them, or suspect that they will exploit their vulnerability to gain an advantage over them. Under such conditions, it is hardly surprising that several recent approaches to the extension of solidarity have followed Rousseau's lead by concentrating on the need to build compassion around common vulnerabilities.[40] The idea of a 'sentimental education' that promotes the belief that 'they' are not fundamentally different from 'us' is one such response to countering the role of insider–outsider dualisms in fostering indifference (Rorty 1989: ch. 9). From that perspective, a cosmopolitan project can replace an exaggerated emphasis on cultural diversity with a focus on common aversions to pain and humiliation.[41] That approach to enlarging

---

[39] The most basic forms of compassion based on shared vulnerabilities partly explain the largely unprompted public charitable donations following the 'Asian Tsunami' of December 2004. A degree of familiarity with the region and identification with the people (as a result of mass tourism) may also have exercised some influence. The main point is that members of the species have a unique capacity to enlarge the circle of mutual identification to include all others. The compassionate, imaginative reconstruction of the suffering of those they will never meet, and whose fate they may never actually experience, is the unique psychological trait that makes extensions of moral community possible – although that potential must find expression in, and be cultivated by, collective symbols and shared belief-systems, and it may not develop far without functional democratization (see also pp. 229–30).

[40] Such appeals are not uncomplicated however. Smith (1982 [1759]: 9–10) argued that emotional identification with the victims of suffering depends on the capacity to imagine oneself in their place. But, it should be added, media images of distant suffering can have contradictory effects. They may well prompt action, but they can provide unsettling reminders of vulnerability and mortality that many would prefer to avoid. There is a parallel here with Elias's remarks about civilized attitudes to keeping disturbing phenomena behind the scenes (see pp. 170–1).

[41] Rorty (1989: ch. 9) argued that an appreciation of common vulnerabilities was a less powerful motivation for rescuing Jews during the Second World War than the belief that national or similar ties bound helpers and victims together (see also pp. 107, n. 63). Geras (1995) provides a different account of the motives of many rescuers, but both agree that the project

the sense of 'we-feeling' has clear significance for any approach to the historical sociology of international relations which is especially concerned with the processes that have shaped the expansion and contraction of moral communities, and which have influenced collective beliefs about who has rights to be protected from unnecessary harm.[42]

Emotionology and emotional identification

Febvre's query about whether 'the emotional history of humanity' can be divided into discrete epochs in which cruelty exceeded kindness raises important questions about the accessibility of the emotional life, and about whether any sources can provide definitive insights into such elusive 'mental phenomena' as the emotions (Barbu 1960: 17). Problems of understanding arise in conjunction with what has been called 'collective emotionality' or 'emotional climates', terms that describe the 'complex of feelings' or 'pattern of emotional dispositions' that influence group identities, interests and behaviour (Barbalet 1998: 159; Barbu 1960: 12, 43). It is useful to recall that Elias found that manners books provided evidence of how the basic emotions of shame and embarrassment were reconfigured as part of 'the rationalization of human relations' in the early stages of the civilizing process (Barbu 1960: 197). The task of the historical social psychologist who pursues a similar quest is to uncover and investigate the conventions that legislate in the area of emotion management. The relevant behaviour codes advise on appropriateness in two inter-related spheres: they identify the emotions that people would 'normally' be expected to experience in particular circumstances (emotions such as grief, sadness, joy, shame, anger, compassion and so forth); and they distinguish between acceptable and unacceptable modes of expression (excessive anger or grief, inadequate displays of shame or remorse, and so on).

Uncovering and understanding the governing conventions is no easy task – and then analysts confront the challenge of assessing the extent to which the relevant social standards were embodied in the individual's *habitus*, and how far they influenced action. Difficulties arise in estimating levels of compliance with emotion codes – in judging whether people embraced them with enthusiasm, or complied begrudgingly because they feared the consequences of antagonizing more powerful strata, and also in determining whether pragmatic acceptance was the surface-manifestation of deeper levels of norm-contestation and

---

of enlarging community involves altering the balance of power between the ethical significance of cultural or differences and the perception of widely shared vulnerabilities.

[42] In International Relations, Deutsch's influential analysis of security communities remains unusual in providing a theoretically informed analysis of the scope of 'we feeling' (Deutsch 1970; also Adler and Barnett 1998). For a discussion of the related theme of 'we images' in process sociology, see de Swaan (1995) and Mennell (1994).

struggles for power that contained the possibility of new social structures and relationships.[43]

To consider those matters in more detail, it is useful to turn to emotionology which has wrestled with the methodological issues that arise when trying to understand the social role of the emotions (Stearns and Stearns 1985). The concept refers to the study of 'the attitudes or standards that a society, or a definable group within a society, maintains towards basic emotions and their appropriate expression' (Stearns and Stearns 1985: 813). A core assumption is that the analyst lacks direct access to the inner world of the emotional life, but it is possible to identity 'collective emotional standards' in particular societies or eras, mindful that there is no automatic match between 'official' norms and actual behaviour.[44]

Working from such premises, many social and cultural historians claim to have identified significant changes in emotion management in modern Western societies over the last few decades. For example, studies of the 'increase in familial affection' in the seventeenth and eighteenth centuries, and changing attitudes to animal suffering, tend to confirm what Elias called the changing threshold of repugnance with respect to violence and cruelty – in both the public and private spheres. In a related development, process sociologists have investigated the recent phenomenon of 'informalization' – the relaxation of conventions that required, inter alia, greater deference to 'authority' than exists today (Wouters 2004). As in the case of Elias's study of manners books, emotionologists can examine codes of conduct that enabled people to become more effectively orientated towards each other, or that tried to guide their behaviour in particular directions so that they complied with what the dominant strata regarded as 'civilized' behaviour.[45] At times, changes in public policy may occur as a result

[43] Crossley (1998) provides an interesting discussion of how inter-subjective understandings about appropriateness develop, and are contested, in social life.

[44] The ambition is to identify emotion scripts that are expressed in individual or collective experience in that they influence psychological responses to violence, cruelty and so forth, and shape behaviour. Emotionologists recognise that 'feeling rules' can change more rapidly than 'emotional experience', not least by establishing ego ideals that run ahead of actual practice (Stearns and Stearns 1986: 15). But presumably the relationship can be reversed, and the dominant conventions can lag behind, for example, subtle and slow-moving changes in orientation and behaviour.

[45] For example, Stearns and Haggerty (1991) argue that child-rearing manuals in nineteenth-century America signified wider changes in public attitudes to cruelty. They advocated forms of discipline that would spare children the levels of fear that had been prevalent in the lives of earlier generations. An analysis of the history of military manuals might offer the student of international relations similar insights into changing social standards with respect to the use of force and the prohibition of 'unnecessary suffering'. With respect to emotions and world politics, Bleiker and Hutchison (2008: 131ff.) suggest that the study of aesthetic sources may prove invaluable. Spivey (2001) and Sontag (2003) are two works that bear out their conviction with respect to the specific matter of emotional attitudes to suffering (see also Bleiker 2009).

of prior, unplanned changes in collective emotions although, as earlier comments on the abolition of public execution indicated, there is always scope for disagreement about the relative influence of different causal factors and the impact of particular emotions.[46] But there is no reason to think that problems of interpretation in this domain are substantially greater than in other areas of historical investigation.

To begin to connect the discussion with the study of cosmopolitan harm conventions: it is important to note that emotionological writings have preserved the interest in attitudes to suffering that was central to early twentieth-century images of historical psychology, and they have provided support for the argument that there has been a broad civilizing movement in modern societies towards identifying with 'other people as such, regardless of social origins' (see p. 167). Rather less attention has been devoted to the matter of whether, or how far, that process has been extended beyond national borders in conjunction with increasing global interconnectedness. But interest in how far 'social origins' still matter – more specifically, how far insider–outsider dualisms continue to shape the dominant emotional responses to suffering – can be expected to grow in response to media representations of great hardship in other societies. As with the more general revival of interest in the emotions, the examination of the scope of emotional identification, and levels of sympathy for distant peoples, has returned to themes that were central to eighteenth- and nineteenth-century moral and political thinkers. Enlightenment thinkers such as Adam Smith (1982 [1759]: 9–10) and David Hume (1969 [1739–40]: 53, 474ff.) were among the first to analyse the relationship between sympathy and distance. In a classic formulation, Smith (1982 [1759]: 136) maintained that a 'man of humanity in Europe' would feel great sorrow at learning of the suffering caused by a devastating earthquake in China. His mind would gravitate to 'melancholy reflections upon the precariousness of human life'. But the ability to sympathize with others over great distances could barely compare with the way in which 'the most frivolous disaster which could befall' him 'would occasion a more real disturbance'. A person who could not sleep, knowing that he would 'lose his little finger' the following day, would 'snore with the most profound security over the ruin of a hundred millions of his brethren'.[47] The 'destruction of that

---

[46] See p. 169, n. 22 where the discussion considered the relative importance of changing attitudes to violence and middle-class disgust at the element of the 'carnivalesque' at public executions. Debates about the extent to which humanitarian sensibilities or changing economic calculations provided the impetus for the abolition of the Atlantic slave trade fall into the same category (see Crawford 2002b).

[47] Hume (quoted in Barbalet 2002: 130) made a similar point: 'Sympathy is much fainter than our concern for ourselves, and sympathy with persons remote from us much fainter than with persons near and contiguous'. As Barbalet (1998: 130) notes, Hume and Smith believed that sympathy, which had been one of the main cementing forces in society, was losing its influence because of the growing preoccupation with individual self-interest (see Mazlish 1989 for an extended discussion of the place of such themes in the origins of sociology

immense multitude' would count for little compared with his own 'paltry misfortune' (Smith 1982 [1759]: 136).[48] Exactly the same tendency to subordinate
sympathy to self-interest was evident, Smith thought, in relations between communities. Under conditions of conflict, societies displayed little or no shame in
using harmful tactics that would be regarded with 'contempt' and 'detestation'
if employed in relations between insiders (Smith 1982 [1759]: 154–5). As with
sympathy, collective shame was less likely to be aroused when suffering was distant and inflicted on those 'with whom we have no particular connexion' (Smith
1982 [1759]: 135; also Forman-Barzilai 2005).[49]

Psychological studies of the 'familiarity' or 'similarity' bias have extended such
reflections on the human tendency to confine sympathetic concern to members
of the in-group, even though the needs of outsiders may be substantially greater
(Hoffman 2000: 206ff.). In-group solidarity has often been reinforced by stigma-
tizing outsiders whose moral standing is diminished in proportion to the harms
they caused (or are believed to have caused) in the past, or because of some supposed collective defect that may be attributed to cultural, racial or related characteristics (Elias and Scotson 2008 [1994]; Goffman 1963; Hoffman 2000: 107,
206ff.). Moral favouritism has been consolidated by dependence on 'survival
units' that have acquired specific identities through decades if not centuries of
conflict. Separate cultural identities that have evolved in those ways maintain
collective support for a double-standard of morality in world politics – one for
relations between members of the same society, another for relations between
societies, and the first far more strenuous in forbidding violent and non-violent
harm (see pp. 178–9).

in the nineteenth century). It was noted in Chapter 1 that the modern emphasis on the
harm principle is best seen as part of the process in which appeals to sympathetic ties were
replaced by appeals to impersonal principles of justice.

[48] Intriguingly, Smith added the caveat that the person will only sleep soundly in the knowledge that an 'immense multitude' is suffering, 'provided he had never seen them', or had 'no
sort of connexion with that part of the world'. The implication was that those with 'humanity' cannot as easily ignore proximate suffering, or the suffering of those with whom they
are connected (see John 1999). Various works have explored the question of how far media
images of distant suffering affect the tendency for sympathy to decline over greater distances (for preliminary comments, see Linklater 2007d).

[49] Hume (1969 [1739–40]: 474) also emphasized the relationship between connectedness and
sympathy: 'There is an easy reason, why every thing contiguous to us, either in space or time,
shou'd be conceiv'd with a peculiar force and vivacity, and excel every other object, in its
influence on the imagination. Ourself is intimately present to us, and whatever is related to
self must partake of that quality'. The formulation is striking because it emphasized contigui-
ties of time as well as space, a dimension of the foreshortening of moral horizons that notions
of complex responsibility confront directly, especially with respect to the possible effects
of environmental degradation on future generations (see pp. 101–2). As discussed below,
notions of connectedness also deal with the issue of how to forge the sense of moral responsibility for harm that is caused at a distance, whether spatial or temporal (see pp. 228–30).

But the scale of the dominant survival units has changed over time. As noted earlier, the monopoly mechanism has led to larger concentrations of power that have often taken the initiative in constructing more inclusive conceptions of community and identity (see Chapter 4). In the space of a few millennia, the dominant forms of emotional identification have shifted from small, kin-based groups to highly populated modern states that can count on the loyalty of tens or even hundreds of millions of people (de Swaan 1995; Mennell 1994). The boundaries between insiders and outsiders shifted as humans were incorporated in larger political units. It may be that the contemporary era is witnessing a major step forward in the scope of emotional identification in large part because of increased sensitivities to the dangers inherent in self–other distinctions, or the 'perils of collective identities', or 'limited altruism' (see p. 83 and pp. 133ff). Because of global environmental and other challenges, pressures to develop what Lasswell called 'world identification' continue to grow (de Swaan 1995: 35–6). Proliferating international non-governmental organizations hold out the promise that stronger attachments to a universal moral community will eventually develop. The egalitarian and universalistic dimensions of 'post-traditional' moral codes provide them with critical resources for disseminating the understanding that, in some respects, all people are more or less the same (de Swaan 1995). Dimensions of the civilizing process that affirm the value of 'ordinary life' or reflect 'the secularisation of the pain' have influenced public attitudes to distant suffering – weakening the racial and cultural stereotypes that trivialized the suffering of colonized peoples in the imperial era but, as yet, inspiring only limited global measures to eliminate relievable misery (Elias 1996: 26; also pp. 183–5).

It is clearly premature to suppose that moral favouritism will retreat as new emotion codes give rise to more global forms of shame, guilt and compassion that support radical advances in cosmopolitan harm conventions. State structures, national movements, class interests and so forth retain the power to frustrate largely uncoordinated attempts to promote 'world identification'. Other organizations cannot match their influence, but many people take their political bearings from international non-governmental organizations in an era in which loyalties to nation-states are generally more conditional than they were even a few decades ago. Significant developments may be said to be immanent in the progress that has occurred at the level of the 'national *habitus*', and not least because of advances in edging 'nationalised personality structures' closer to 'post-national' or 'higher level transnational identities' that are 'unlike those … in other historical epochs' (Pickel 2004). One of the challenges for future research on the emotions is to consider whether such changes are sufficiently extensive to suggest that many societies are entering a new phase in the civilizing process – a condition in which traditional divisions between insiders and outsiders lose some of their moral importance, and in which violent and non-violent harm to other peoples, and indifference to distant suffering, lose their acceptability.[50]

Cosmopolitan emotions

The question was posed earlier of whether cosmopolitan potentialities exist in every form of life. Simone Weil provided a powerful argument for thinking that they do. She maintained that most societies would assume that one of their members who was stranded in a desert would help a stranger (by implication, someone who belonged to another society) who was facing death because of thirst – at least most would gravitate towards that view, subject to the condition that there was enough water to let both survive. Few in the in-group would think that an explanation of the decision to assist required justification; most would believe that considerations of humanity should make assistance 'automatic'. But, Weil continued, most would think that an explanation was in order, 'if having enough water in his canteen, (a potential rescuer) simply walked past, ignoring the other person's pleas' (quoted in Gaita 1994: 616; also Gaita 2002).[51] It is important to stress that Weil did not claim that rescue has always occurred in the condition described, and it is easy to think of reasons that may have been offered in different times and places for refusing assistance (and that probably commanded widespread support). They include a complete lack of sympathy for those who belong to an enemy group, to a 'corrupted and contemptible' people and so forth. But if help has been more or less automatic, or at least not unusual, in *many* such encounters over the millennia, and if failures to help *often* led to astonishment or disgust, then it would appear that common humanity may have been more influential, and may have a greater potential to shape future trajectories, than many critics of cosmopolitanism have realized.[52]

---

[50] The 'war against terror' was one such critical juncture that led to various works that are relevant to such an inquiry. An example is the discussion of 'grievability' in Butler (2004). Preliminary comments about the issues at stake are set out in Linklater (2002c, 2007e). The 'Asian Tsunami' is the other recent event that has led to reflections on emotional responses to distant suffering, Korf (2007) being one of the more challenging.

[51] There is a parallel with the claim that 'attention to the suffering of the other' is a 'supreme ethical principle', 'the only one it is impossible to question', and the argument that some moral duties should be discharged more or less automatically, 'without concern for reciprocity' (Levinas 1998: ch. 8).

[52] To be fair to the critics, most have simply rejected the idea that common humanity can rival the moral influence of ties to particular bounded communities; few have gone further by denying that acts of rescue can be motivated by anything other than a desire to end suffering. However, the claim that 'in general ... there is no such passion in human minds, as the love of mankind, merely as such' (Hume 1969 [1739–40]: 533) and the contention that the idea of world citizenship is oxymoronic and incoherent (Walzer 2002), underestimate the extent to which considerations of humanity alone can influence conduct in the circumstances described.

Interesting issues about moral agency are raised by Weil's thesis. Rescuers and beneficiaries need not belong to the same social group for that imagined ethical encounter to occur; nor do they even have to be able to communicate in the same language – or the same spoken language.[53] All that need be presumed is the existence of universally intelligible physical gestures and expressions, or a shared emotional vocabulary that allows the members of different groups to communicate distress to each other and to respond sympathetically.[54] It might be argued that low levels of assistance to the global poor point to the limitations of that argument. Solidarity of the kind that can feature in the circumstances that Weil described clearly does not exist in relations between affluent and desperate peoples at the present time; of course, many individuals do assist the most desperate, but those who do not are rarely inclined to think that inaction requires an explanation (and very few people would think it was reasonable to ask for one). That condition may be wholly indefensible from a cosmopolitan standpoint. As Singer (1972: 232) argues, 'the fact that a person is physically near to us ... may make it more likely that we *shall* assist him, but this does not show that we *ought* to help him rather than another who happens to be further away' (italics in original). The point is that ethical impartiality dictates that 'no account (is taken) of proximity or distance'. However, current practice is clearly at variance with that moral ideal. Individuals and groups do not habitually shame each other for failures to behave compassionately towards outsiders; most do not think that apathy and inaction should result in guilt or self-reproach.

The distinction between 'passive' and 'active' sympathy has particular relevance for the points raised by Weil and Singer. A person exhibits passive sympathy, it has been argued, when s/he shares in the sorrow of others, and displays active sympathy when that feeling turns into 'practical *concern*' that involves supporting 'measures or taking steps to relieve (their) suffering' (Maclagan

[53] Habermas (see McCarthy 1981: ch. 4) suggested that the first speech act already contained the promise of the unity of all humans but, as argued above, that status could just as easily be conferred on the earliest expressions of sympathy for outsiders, or on the first harm conventions that were agreed by different societies. See Barbalet (1998: 129) for the related argument that 'in sympathy ... can be located the emotional realization of the unity of humankind'. Oatley and Jenkins (1996: 310) maintain that 'if emotions are to some extent universal, then as well as separating people they can build links (and) can provide a foundation for an intercultural morality. If there were no universals of emotions, there would be no basis for concerted world action on anything, no human sympathy for the oppressed, no outrage against tyranny, no passion for justice, no concern for protecting or sharing the world's limited resources'. The Habermasian claim about the first speech act could therefore be rephrased to argue that the earliest acts of communicating sympathy for other humans qua humans contained the possibility of the moral unification of humankind.

[54] Nussbaum (2001: 169) argues that 'biology and common circumstances ... make it extremely unlikely that the emotional repertoires of two societies will be entirely opaque to one another'. Also relevant here is the earlier claim that all humans possess a similar repertoire of expressions that permits non-verbal communication and understanding between people who are, in other respects, mysterious to each other (see pp. 209–10).

1960: 211ff.; italics in original). The plain reality that passive sympathy for distant strangers may not lead to positive assistance reveals that emotions are 'inclining' rather than 'compelling' (Barbalet 1998, 2002). They define what is salient in what 'would otherwise be an unmanageable plethora of objects of attention' without necessarily triggering any course of action (Cunningham 2001: 114ff.; De Sousa 1987: xv; Nussbaum 2001: ch. 1). The proximity of another's suffering may lead to positive sympathy in the circumstances that Weil discussed; there, emotional identification with another human qua human may be strong enough to trigger assistance. But that holds little relevance for the usual state of affairs where people consider distant suffering in the light of existing emotional ties to particular groups.

The question is how sympathy can be emancipated from such constraints, if it is indeed correct to regard it as a universal (or near universal) emotion that makes advances in global solidarity possible. Some of the oldest reflections on such emotions are still hard to surpass when contemplating such matters. Aristotle's writings are salient because they stress that another's pain arouses moral concern in the following conditions: if the agony is of a kind or scale that 'one might expect oneself, or one of one's own, to suffer'; if 'destructive or painful harm' befalls someone *not deserving to encounter it*, and 'when it is near' (quoted in Konstan 2001: 34; italics in original; see also Linklater 2007d). Those observations run along parallel lines to Weil's conjecture on the generality of certain kinds of assistance: all three of Aristotle's conditions are met in that example. But, on the available evidence, the prospects for active sympathy for others, and not just for distant strangers, diminish when at least one of those conditions is absent.

Studies of the 'bystander phenomenon' have addressed many of the key issues by asking what it is about social arrangements that leads to 'a pervasive tendency to help', and what it is that promotes 'widespread non-involvement in the problems of others' (Barry 1980: 460). For present purposes, the question can be rephrased to ask what it is that converts passive sympathy into active assistance, and what leads to inaction and indifference. Analyses of the bystander phenomenon that considered the specific case of the rape of Kitty Genovese identified several reasons for failures to convert an awareness of proximate suffering into tangible assistance.[55] In subsequent interviews with witnesses, many remarked on the fear that involvement would lead to injury or reprisals; some reported the suspicion that the victim may have been responsible for her plight (thereby echoing Aristotle's point that sympathy depends on the conviction that harm is undeserved); most maintained that they ignored calls for help on

---

[55] Kitty Genovese was violently assaulted near her apartment in New York in 1964 and later died from her injuries. Thirty-eight neighbours reported hearing her screams for help, but none went to the rescue or called the police. Cohen (2001) summarizes the reasons for inaction. Bobbit (2003: ch. 15) discusses the significance for international relations.

the assumption that someone else would contact – or had already contacted – the relevant authorities. Analysts have inferred from that last point that large-scale social systems are unusually vulnerable to the crippling effects of 'diffuse responsibility', the condition in which specific duties are not clearly assigned to particular people (Latane and Darley 1970). Such dangers are at their greatest when potential rescuers and victims are strangers, for example in the anonymity of the modern city, but they are reduced to the extent that people identify with each other, thereby approximating the conditions that Aristotle regarded as necessary for the arousal of sympathy.[56]

All of the factors that have been considered thus far are relevant for understanding the bystander phenomenon in world politics although, in that domain, it is necessary to discount one element in the Genovese case – the proximity of suffering (and with failed or failing states, it is essential to remove the assumption that effective public institutions can assist the victims of suffering to some extent). The observation that it is rare for people to 'love what lies at a distance' is clearly significant for discussions of the prospects for expressing *active* sympathy in cosmopolitan harm conventions, but it is important to add the caveat that distance counts for nothing when those involved have close emotional ties (Hume 1969 [1739–40]: 533).[57] Claims about the relationship between distance and emotional responses to suffering often compress several themes that need to be disentangled. Smith's remarks about the sleeping habits of the average person captured the point that levels of moral concern for the suffering decline as one moves from the inner circles of emotional attachment to the outer reaches of social interaction – an emotional gradient that often overlaps with geographical distance to some degree. But as Aristotle recognized, it is the salience of another's suffering (whether the agony is something 'one might expect oneself, or one of one's own, to suffer'), rather than its location or intensity that matters; that decides whether sympathy is active or passive. In international relations, salience and its effects on sympathy have been governed by emotional attachments to specific 'survival units', and by divisions between insiders and outsiders. They have underpinned the belief that, in general, others in one's own society have rights to be free from 'destructive or painful harm' that outsiders do not possess, or do not have to the same degree.

The issue is how far such convictions are being eroded by evidence of harming, or of being implicated in harming, vulnerable others who are located in the distant regions of lengthening social webs (and who cannot make claims on the basis of special connections). It is undoubtedly significant that modern technologies have breached many of 'the old barriers ... which protected the

---

[56] Psychological studies of altruistic behaviour maintain that most people confine their willingness to assist to those who are like themselves (Dovidio and Penner 2004).

[57] For example, people clearly do not suffer any less because a family member has come to harm many thousands of miles away.

private individual from the outside world' with the result that large numbers of people have become 'informed and knowledgeable citizen[s] of the world' (Tester 1998: 83–4). Images of distant suffering bring the plight of distant strangers closer to the lives of the affluent; stark evidence of global inequalities makes it hard to deny that many can relieve distress with little cost to themselves; visual representations of suffering dramatize the ways in which the most powerful societies can harm the vulnerable, whether as a result of their stranglehold on global institutions that are biased towards their economic and political interests, or because of military operations in foreign places, and so forth.[58] Subtle changes in feelings of guilt and shame, and in the public willingness to shoulder cosmopolitan responsibilities, may occur in those ways. Media images may engender public support for a contemporary variant on Enlightenment notions of a world in which common sensibilities and shared sympathies underpin collective measures to reduce unnecessary suffering (Lacquer 1989: 202; also Shaw 1996).

The evidence is that any advances that have taken place towards that condition have been selective and uneven, and entangled in competing logics (Cohen 2001: 290ff.). Many journalists have defended publishing graphic images of catastrophic circumstances in the hope of promoting active sympathy, but many complications arise (McCullin 1990). The civilizing process can lead to judgments that uncompromising images of suffering breach public taste; the result may be revulsion rather than active sympathy, psychological withdrawal rather than moral and political engagement (Taylor 1998). The attendant danger is that exposing people to the horrors of the larger world may produce 'a surfeit of consciousness' of suffering (Tester 1998: 83–4). As the idea of compassion fatigue ably suggests, witnesses to suffering may respond by becoming 'anaesthetised' to transient images of painful realities (Tester 1998: 85–6; also Tester 2001). As acts of 'non-intervention' in their own right, visual representations of objectified suffering may encourage a spirit of detached observation in the very audience to which they are addressed in the hope of arousing sympathy (Sontag 1978: 11ff.).[59] Simmel's writings on the 'blasé self' who perceives suffering as an 'abstraction' that is to be 'observed from afar', and without emotion, link the discussion with the civilizing process. For Simmel, that spirit of detachment was a by-product of the 'reserve' and polite indifference that is emblematic of life in the modern city where individuated, relatively isolated people usually

---

[58] Sontag (1978) provides a valuable survey of photojournalistic images and artistic representations of suffering in war.

[59] Sontag (1978: 17ff.) argues that photojournalism cannot 'create a moral position but (it) can reinforce one – and help build a nascent one'. In that context, she remarks on the influence that the image of a naked South Vietnamese child fleeing from a napalm attack had on the emotional climate surrounding US military involvement in Vietnam. Sontag adds, however, that such images are usually interpreted in the light of, and may only reinforce, existing beliefs.

avoid more than minimum civil interaction (Tester 1998: 92–4).[60] Some observers go further by speculating that displays of suffering can satisfy cravings for 'news' entertainment, and a longing to puncture the monotonies of daily routines with an endless flow of markers of constant change that, at best, breed passive sympathy and, at worst, total indifference or even 'cruelty and callousness' (Mestrovic 1994: 84).[61] Observers are granted 'the satisfaction of being able to look … without flinching'; they are afforded 'the pleasure of flinching', should they so desire (Sontag 2003: 36).[62]

It is possible to imagine a world in which the competition for power and security is less influential than it has been in the past, in which insider–outsider dualisms have a greatly reduced significance, but where efforts to build cosmopolitan harm conventions make little if any progress. The main beneficiary of those changes could be the blasé temperament, too absorbed in personal pursuits to care about, or have time for, the distractions of suffering in far-off places. Such an orientation towards distant suffering, such levels of emotional withdrawal and disengagement, may be easier to adopt when people believe there is nothing in their relations with outsiders that they must answer for – nothing in their personal conduct, or in their complicity with private or public institutions, that raises moral questions and should arouse psychological unease. From an ethical point of view, detachment may be hard to justify in the context of rising levels of interconnectedness; but from a sociological point of view, there may be no detectable rise in the level of active sympathy. Outcomes may be different when people believe that they are directly responsible for harm, or profit from unjust enrichment simply by virtue of the existence of global political and economic structures and processes. Under those conditions, people may well be right that those who are 'closer to us' emotionally or geographically '*tend* to be more vulnerable to our actions and choices than those distant from us'; but they cannot deny that there are 'special obligations' of care to those who, despite being 'distant from us', are no less 'vulnerable to our actions and choices', and perhaps even more so because of transnational, or structural, or 'public accumulative harm' (see pp. 148–9).

---

[60] There is a parallel with Elias's notion of *homo clausus*, absorbed in privacy and isolation (see pp. 101–2).

[61] That formulation is close to Burke's observation that some pains are 'simply terrible' but at a 'certain distance and with certain modifications, they may be, and they are delightful' (Burke 1990 [1757]: 36–7). See also the discussion of the 'sublime' in Bleiker (2009: ch. 3).

[62] The civilizing process is a source of such vicarious pleasures because it largely shields modern humans from direct encounters with death and suffering. Taylor (1998: 90ff. and ch. 8) suggests that insider–outsider dualisms intensify emotional responses to portrayals of suffering that the inhabitants of pacified societies find engrossing. In Britain, the argument is, visual images of foreign cadavers are more 'acceptable' than images of dead co-nationals. The presumed 'hierarchy of death' may encourage the view that life is cheap in less 'civilized' places, and that humanitarian exercises are pointless (Taylor 1998: 90ff.).

Similar issues arise in green political theory which has been at the forefront of efforts to defend notions of personal and collective responsibility that go well beyond traditional conceptions. A recurrent claim is that justice dictates that affluent regions shoulder most of the burden for arresting and reversing harm to the commons and to other peoples (see pp. 66–7). A related argument which responds to the fact that the moral life lags behind rising levels of global inter-connectedness maintains that 'simple' responsibility – where people observe existing conventions, and do no more than they are required to – should be augmented or replaced by 'complex' responsibility – where people have a highly reflective orientation to the ways in which personal conduct and social organ-ization may harm other communities and future generations, and may change their behaviour accordingly (see pp. 101–2). The ambition is to alter conduct by defending what has been described as the 'connected self' (Staub 2003). That con-cept has been used in social psychology to show how the desire to avoid shame and guilt predisposes people to behave morally towards those with whom they are more closely associated. The idea of connectedness which, as noted earlier, is also central to the ethic of care and responsibility, has been defended as a way of confronting the moral and political challenges that have arisen because of the capacity to cause harm, intentionally or unintentionally, over much greater distances (see pp. 146–9).[63]

Support for that line of argument can be found in writings on 'transnational advocacy networks' which maintain that they are most successful when they can provide a convincing account of peoples' casual responsibility for incontrovert-ible suffering in the form of 'bodily harm to vulnerable individuals' (see p. 98). Those movements encourage practical efforts to dislodge national monopolies in the sphere of the emotions: they challenge conventional assumptions that, in general, the suffering of insiders matters more than the suffering of outsiders, that justice between co-nationals is far more significant than justice between societies, and that violating national standards is more shameful than infrin-ging global norms. They point to potentials for globalizing moral emotions that first emerge at the 'local' level, which are crucial for the survival of every way of life, but which can be extended outwards as part of the widening of the scope of emotional identification (Nussbaum 2002). They make a strong ethical case for forms of moral, legal and political accountability that are appropriately trans-national given the realities of increasing interconnectedness.[64]

---

[63] Rorty (1989: 191) has argued that 'our sense of solidarity is strongest when those with whom solidarity is expressed' are regarded as 'one of us', where 'us' means something 'smaller and more local than the human race'. As a description of how many respond to distant suffer-ing, there is undoubted merit in that claim. But the idea of the connected self points to the importance of anchoring solidarity in concerns about how actions affect other humans adversely, whether or not they are 'like us' culturally, or in some other way. See also Dobson (2005) and (2006).

[64] Accountability can take three forms: moral where it influences personal and collective con-duct; legal in that it gives the victims of harm access to judicial process; and political where

The literature on 'transnational advocacy networks' suggests that the idea of the 'connected self' provides many people with the rationale for developing cosmopolitan emotions. As specialists in global 'conscience formation', those movements have an important role to play in translating universal or near universal moral emotions into a 'world culture' that is disposed towards, and shaped by, cosmopolitan harm conventions (Boli and Thomas 1999).[65] They can rally support for global projects that validate Horkheimer's contention that compassion for the suffering is the basis of true solidarity, and they may yet enjoy greater success in converting such responsiveness to the suffering of others into active sympathy in a world in which powerful socializing agencies continue to reinforce the moral status quo (pp. 183–5).[66] Cosmopolitan potentials that exist in virtually every way of life may then find expression in specific socio- and psycho-genetic forces that finally grant the individual and humanity moral equality with sovereign states (Elias 1991: 138ff.).

From a sociological point of view, the question is whether such appeals to broaden ethical horizons will fail, or have only limited success, because of the very global asymmetries of power and wealth which they protest against. The analysis of the civilizing process stressed that functional democratization was a major driving-force behind advances in responsiveness to the interests of other people in society, irrespective of social origins (see pp. 165–7). Dependence on the lower strata compelled elite groups to share power and resources that they had previously monopolized. Ethical arguments that begin with the connected self tend to presume that no equivalent levels of functional democratization exist in international politics: they appeal to the strong to sympathize with vulnerable people who are affected by their actions or who lose as they gain from global structures and processes. Some respond to such moral appeals; others do not. For some, the injustice of interconnectedness, without functional democratization, is a reason to support projects of global reform; for others, interconnectedness without functional democratization provides no such incentive. The upshot is that notions of the connected self may inform some future transnational civilizing process – indeed its outlines already exist up to a point – but

global institutions are created so that all those who are affected by any structure, policy or action enjoy appropriate rights of representation.

[65] The evolution of international criminal law is a major example of how non-governmental organizations have contributed to progress in that area. As noted earlier, the interesting question is how far support for the humanitarian principles that are embedded in the International Criminal Court can be strengthened by cosmopolitan expressions of emotions such as compassion, indignation and shame, and how far global support for punishing human rights violators becomes 'second nature' for large numbers of people everywhere.

[66] The main analyses of socialization processes in international relations have focused on how systemic pressures compel states to compete for power and insecurity, whatever their preferences may be, and on how international society socializes new states so that they conform to practices that originated in Europe (Armstrong 1993; Waltz 1979). Pickel (2004) offers an approach to changes in 'national habitus' that is closer to the position taken here.

it is essential to look elsewhere for evidence of pressures and compulsions that will force people generally to recognize the imperative of acquiring a global conscience and the related cosmopolitan emotions, as well as the need for cosmopolitan harm conventions that may clash with immediate self-interest.[67]

Conclusion

It is not surprising that analyses of material forces – in particular, coercive power and systems of production – have dominated efforts to link historical sociology with International Relations. Studies of power and production analyse the most fundamental structural changes in the modern world such as the rise of the territorial state and its spread to all parts of the world, the establishment of capitalist social relations more or less everywhere, and the industrialization of warfare. But those perspectives do not explain how human beings have come to be bound together in modern societies. They do not account for the moral compass that guides everyday conduct and influences collective emotional responses to violence and suffering. The socio-psychological forces that are central to those domains are not 'filled in' once power and production have determined the structures of social interaction. They are as much cause as effect of the long-term developments that group people together in particular ways. Whether analysing existing social arrangements or endeavouring to identify the sources of new possibilities, they have an importance that cannot be reduced to the other phenomena mentioned above.

The bonds that unite always separate people from some others in the same group, and from other societies. Identification with the main 'survival unit' has been the norm throughout history. Sympathies have been directed towards salient others in the same society; harm to outsiders has often been regarded as essential for group security or survival, and as a source of 'group charisma' (Elias and Scotson 2008 [1994]: introduction). But there is more to the history of international relations than mastering the invention and application of the

---

[67] Reference has been made to the relationship between colonial violence and the absence of functional democratization (see p. 88, n. 24 above). That emphasis on the restraining power of reciprocity is no less important for understanding failures to rescue and the so-called bystander phenomenon – where potential rescuers do not believe that their positions with the desperate will ever be reversed. That is why ethical appeals to people to imagine future reversals of circumstances are likely to have a limited effect, in the absence of functional democratization. A related point was made by Primo Levi in his reflections on the fact that the 'Good Samaritan ethic' had no place in Auschwitz. Most people believed that there was no point extending a helping hand to those who would be dead within weeks – there was no profit in befriending those who could offer nothing in return by virtue of their 'distinguished acquaintances' or supply of 'extra rations'. In that 'Hobbesian' state, the custom was to allow 'the drowned' to 'drift by on their way to death' (Levi 2001: 39). Notwithstanding humanitarian aid and emergency assistance, something of that condition might be said to exist in the relations between the global rich and the global poor at present.

instruments of force. Various religious and secular ideologies have promoted global extensions of sympathy and solidarity. In the modern world, the unusual influence of universalistic and egalitarian norms raises the question of whether the species may yet enter a new phase of the civilizing process which is marked by stronger commitments to eliminating unnecessary harm, but only if those ideas come to have an 'elective affinity' with particular interests.

The current range of emotional responses to visual representations of distant suffering points to the openness of the future. It is impossible to discount the possibility that struggles for military power will decline in the next phase of global integration – along with pernicious representations of others – only for widespread indifference to suffering to increase.[68] The connected self captures part of what is required to avoid that blighted victory, namely the outward extension of moral emotions that most people acquire in viable communities in conjunction with a heightened sensitivity to the ways in which humans harm, and are harmed by, others – but it may be more useful in shaping ethical ideas than in trying to understand how radical change may occur at the global level. Nevertheless, success in embedding the harm principle in personality structures is essential for widening the scope of emotional identification so that cosmopolitan harm conventions can exercise greater influence on world politics. The next chapter considers the implications for the sociology of global civilizing processes.

[68] The point can be turned around in the argument that the process of individuation is one reason for the declining significance of insider–outsider distinctions, at least amongst certain social strata. That might seem to augur well as future advances in transnational solidarity are concerned. However, the weakening of feelings of connectedness with co-nationals (particularly where that is the result of growing inequalities) may have different consequences.

6

Civilizing processes and international systems

The final task is to integrate the main themes in the previous chapters by setting out the central questions for an analysis of global civilizing processes that integrates Wight's vision of the comparative investigation of states-systems with Eliasian process sociology. The questions are the prelude to an empirical inquiry into the nature and scope of cosmopolitan harm conventions in different international systems that will be the subject of future discussion. Part one considers Wight's distinctive approach to International Relations in which systems of states are the preferred level of analysis, an approach that is invaluable for efforts to build bridges with, and contribute to, process sociology. Part two turns to his conjectures about certain long-term patterns of development that may be common to all states-systems. They include, as noted earlier, the trend towards larger territorial concentrations of power, the elimination of small states, and struggles for power that result in the dominance of one power, at which point the system of states is replaced by a universal empire. Despite those realist conjectures, Wight's general thesis was that international societies have at least a temporary civilizing role. They have been domains in which many states have attempted to curb the power to inflict devastating harm; and, as the humanitarian laws of war reveal, there have been times when they have aimed not only to create order between states but to alleviate the suffering of people as moral subjects in their own right. But invariably the challenge of maintaining order between the great powers has been so great that most effort has been concentrated on protecting international harm conventions; only rarely has there been progress in weaving cosmopolitan conventions into the structure of international societies.

The clear implication of Wight's conjectures about the likely fate of states-systems is that support for all manner of harm conventions declines rapidly during final struggles for supremacy. In Elias's terms, decivilizing processes finally overpower civilizing processes. Comparing states-systems would seem to lead to pessimistic conclusions about the prospects for long-term advances in the reduction of pointless suffering. However, Wight (1977: 44–5) observed that conceptions of a universal moral community that also appear to be common to all states-systems have invariably survived the final conflicts, and that the transition from the lawlessness of a states-system in its terminal phase to a universal empire that could enforce the peace has often been greeted with relief – as

232

a blessing for human society as a whole. That comment draws attention to the need to understand the different ways in which empires and states-systems have contributed to universalizing processes that include visions of human community (Mann 1986).

Many analyses of early empires have stressed their role in creating symbols that were designed to promote at least elite identification with the new centres of political power. Sociologies of empire have referred to the rationalization of the 'symbolic sphere' – to the creation of a universalistic political imagery – as conquering elites sought to legitimate their rule and to counteract the centrifugal forces that threatened to destroy their power (Eisenstadt 1963; Mann 1986: 170ff.).[1] As already noted, whether the focus is on states-systems or empires, similar questions arise about their part in creating universal symbols or 'transcultural principles' that enable different groups to co-exist peacefully. Especially important is the question of how far that imagery was largely a front for dominant interests or at least partly an exercise in reaching an ideological compromise between the rulers and the ruled.[2] The issue of what world empires have contributed to visions of human community must consider their relations with outsiders as well as their efforts to unite conquered groups through integrative universal symbols. Empires are not, in the main, hermetically sealed systems, but enter into various trading and other relations with outsider groups, often forming larger international systems with them, as Wight emphasized in his observations about secondary and suzerain state-systems (see pp. 237–8). Wight (1991: ch. 4) highlighted the need to explore the extent to which imperial elites regarded outliers as 'savages' without rights, how far they believed that outsiders deserved some measure of respect because of their disruptive power or usefulness, and whether they believed they should be spared certain forms of violent and non-violent harm by virtue of shared humanity. Those questions are especially important for an approach to global civilizing processes that explores the extent to which images of a more inclusive community evolved as societies became more and more interconnected in different types of international system. To return to an earlier point, the issue is how far it is possible to discern in the evolution of those arrangements an overall trend in which increasing portions of the globe have been 'subjected to or incorporated within civilized social structures' (see p. 132).

As with international societies, empires are prone to collapse, but conceptions of a universal commonwealth do not necessarily lose all importance in the process. Those worldviews may survive in the shape of nostalgic longings for

[1] The earliest example, according to Mann (1986: 133ff.), was the Akkadian incorporation, circa 2310 BC, of the deities of conquered peoples in a universal pantheon. The new politico-religious order was designed to show that the empire gave expression to cosmic forces, and was not an instrument of the dominant political class.
[2] See the distinction in Mann (1986: 22ff.) between immanent and transcendent imperial ideologies.

an earlier period of unity. Imperial images of human solidarity have influenced orientations towards emerging systems of states. The impact of medieval conceptions of natural law on the quest for a new political vocabulary in early modern Europe is one example of how universal symbols that were associated with a former empire continued to have currency and influence as societies struggled to develop new principles of co-existence.[3] In the case of the modern system, it is especially significant that the idea of human dignity survived, albeit 'underground', and that political movements in later periods were able to harness it to a 'civilizing' project of protecting individual human rights from tyrannical regimes and from the horrors of warfare (Bull 1977: 83). In such ways visions of unity have been transferred from one form of world political organization to another: from international societies of states to empires and vice versa.

To develop those points it is necessary to establish new links between historical sociology and International Relations, and specifically to combine Wight's analysis of states-systems and Elias's comparative approach to civilizing processes in a higher synthesis. The task is to study international systems with a view to ascertaining what they accomplished in the way of a global process of civilization that brought advances in reducing violent and non-violent harm. It is important to add that no states-system is more important than any other for understanding the challenges that societies have confronted in trying to tame the struggle for power, to free themselves from domination, from cultural humiliation and degradation, from economic exploitation, and so forth. If the modern system has special significance, it is because the *oecumene* (or inhabited world) is no longer thought to end at the frontiers of Rome or China, but embraces humanity as a whole. It is the highest 'steering mechanism' that societies currently possess for shaping the political development of the species in the face of mounting global problems. The question that can be asked of any states-system (namely how far did the constitutive parts agree on cosmopolitan harm conventions that were designed to protect all peoples from unnecessary suffering?) has unprecedented significance in the modern system.

In the light of those comments, the third section lists central questions for the comparative sociology of global civilizing processes. That exercise draws together three dimensions of the earlier discussion – the taxonomy of forms of violent and non-violent harm that was set out in Chapter 1; the core themes advanced by leading theories of international relations which were considered in Chapter 3; and the focus on emotional identification, as initiated by process sociology and emotionology, that was introduced in Chapter 5. The synthesis incorporates the commitment to a cosmopolitan harm principle that was explained in Chapter 2 and links it with the conceptual framework that has been developed by process sociology.

---

[3] Visions of unity seem to have had a broadly similar role in the ancient Chinese system of states (see McNeill 1979b).

As argued in the introduction to this book, it is entirely legitimate to regard the detached analysis of global harm conventions as an end in itself, and to proceed without trying to decide whether any states-system is more 'ethically advanced' than the others. To return to a point that was made in Chapter 4, it is essential to guard against seeming to think that international societies in other eras faced a straight choice between 'their' values and 'ours', and made the conscious decision not to live like 'us' because of what can only be regarded as a flaw in their reasoning, or some other defect (see p. 160). Wight did not address those issues, but his sensitivity to historical context is incompatible with moral rankings of that kind. There was no intention to 'cast a slur' on other states-systems, when, for example, he observed that the modern states-system has devised complex international institutions that the Ancient Greek city-state system did not have, or when he suggested that it has a greater capacity to regulate its own course (Linklater and Suganami 2006: chs 4–6). It is certainly the case that higher levels of institutionalization represent an advance in recognizing the need for collective responses to the dangers that exist when societies are responsible for their own security and survival, and they may signify collective achievements in disrupting cycles of violence. But it is important to analyse the specific conditions, over which societies may have little control, that favour experiments of that kind, or stand formidably in the way. Such breakthroughs are virtually impossible when states are trapped in civil conflicts that have transnational dimensions, and when therefore the question of how to create international order (considered as a separate domain) simply does not arise (see pp. 11–12, n. 60).[4] It is nevertheless legitimate to refer to progress when states succeed in establishing international and cosmopolitan harm conventions, and it is meaningful to describe their accomplishments in terms of advances in greater detachment, in the ability to think from the standpoint of others, and in extending sympathy to outsiders that others can build on in later periods.[5] Through

---

[4] Examples can be drawn from both the Ancient Greek and Renaissance city-state systems.

[5] Elias paid little attention to diplomatic efforts to manage the double-bind processes which were discussed on pp. 177–8. But his study of involvement and detachment is central to understanding the processes just described (Elias 2007a [1987]). The transition from involvement in specific security dilemmas that breed competitive behaviour to a shared recognition of dangers that require collective action depends on cognitive advances, and particularly on shifts from what specific threats 'mean for me or for us' to a more detached consideration of what they are in themselves, that is 'independently' of what they mean 'for us or for me' (Elias 2007a [1987]: 122; also Kilminster 2007: ch. 5 who discusses Elias's analysis of the 'survival value' of greater detachment, but also the danger that those who support thinking from the standpoint of other people in conditions of conflict may be condemned as dangerous heretics). It is worth adding that assessments of levels of detachment in different states-systems are not necessarily *ex post facto* judgments about the rationality of actors in other periods. Volume 2 discusses that point with reference to Thucydides' comments about the increasing concentration on the ferocious pursuit of immediate self-interest as part of the decivilizing effects of the Peloponnesian War.

such developments, the species can undergo collective learning or global civil-izing processes.[6]

The concept of collective learning, which is considered in the fourth section, may arouse suspicion given its association with eighteenth- and nineteenth-century grand narratives with their belief in inevitable patterns of development that cul-minated in modern Europe. There are no grounds for trying to recover ideas that were linked with condescension towards, and contempt for, non-European societies. But the critique of such rosy self-images need not undermine efforts to understand learning processes that have influenced the development of human-ity as a whole. An example from the natural sciences is the analysis of achieve-ments in acquiring levels of detachment from the physical environment that led to significant cognitive advances and to greater power over processes that earlier societies had regarded as uncontrollable. Such movements have had ambiguous consequences, simultaneously increasing collective wealth and involving societies in more destructive forms of warfare (Elias 2007a [1987]). Similar ideas about collective learning are no less relevant for the analysis of international relations. They draw attention to developments in the capacity to cause destructive forms of harm, but they also highlight achievements in agreeing on international and cosmopolitan harm conventions – on global civilizing processes, in short.

The focus on long-term developments within different states-systems is designed to explain the relationship between diverse collective learning proc-esses in international politics – learning how to acquire and deploy destruc-tive power, how to construct principles of co-existence that win the approval of different societies, and so forth. Above all else, the challenge is to under-stand how far different systems discovered workable solutions to the problems associated with rising levels of human interconnectedness, and how far they found ways of living together with the 'minimum of domination' (Foucault, in Moss 1998: 20–1). Subject to an earlier caveat, such an approach can compare the achievements of different states-systems in making progress towards that ideal. It can extend Elias's analysis of civilizing processes which did not iden-tify states-systems as crucial objects of analysis, or focus on how the tensions between civilizing and decivilizing processes in those forms of world political organization have shaped long-term patterns of development that have affected humanity as a whole. In so doing, it draws on Wight's comparative analysis of states-systems, but takes that perspective further by creating new linkages with process sociology.

[6] It is important to explain the relationship between civilizing and collective learning proc-esses. As discussed earlier (see Chapter 4), the former refer to the social standards and pat-terns of restraint that particular peoples have developed in the course of dealing with the challenge of living together without harming each other time and time again. Collective learning processes exist in that domain, but they are also evident in advances in understand-ing how to out-manoeuvre, overwhelm and destroy adversaries. One of the purposes of civilizing processes is to reduce the dangers that result from learning in that sphere.

The final section turns to the issue of how far the modern states-system has been the site for distinctive global civilizing processes – a question that will be considered in more detail in later volumes. The contemporary order has witnessed the rise of ever-larger territorial monopolies of power and the geographical extension of social and economic relations. More controversial is what it has achieved in the way of learning how to co-exist with the minimum of violent and non-violent harm. The chapter on the process of civilization commented on the debates about whether modern societies have advanced beyond their predecessors in promoting the non-violent co-existence of people. Those disputes have mainly been centred on domestic social change, but they are also relevant to discussions of whether humanitarian principles and cosmopolitan sentiments have come to exercise unusual influence in the modern states-system, or have only limited effect when compared with human ingenuity in learning how to inflict violent harm. They invite speculations about what that system will bequeath to future generations who may confront the challenge of regulating still higher levels of global interconnectedness with all their attendant tensions and ambiguities.

The idea of a states-system

The distinguishing feature of a states-system is that the constituent parts – normally 'sovereign states' – recognize each other's right to independence (Wight 1977: ch. 1).[7] That form of world political organization can be distinguished from a suzerain state-system in which the dominant power claims a special entitlement to lay down the law to subject societies that may nevertheless retain significant internal autonomy (Wight 1977: ch. 1).[8] Building on those definitions, Wight maintained that states-systems can be 'primary' or 'secondary': primary when consisting of sovereign states or independent communities;[9] secondary when the constituent parts are empires or suzerain state-systems rather than sovereign states.[10] In both cases, recognition of the entitlement to independence (which is

---

[7] The following discussion borrows from Linklater and Suganami (2006: ch. 6).

[8] Wight's examples of a suzerain states-system include the Chinese tributary system, the Byzantine empire and the Abbasid Caliphate which came to power following the collapse of the Islamic empire.

[9] Wight's examples are the Hellenic and Hellenistic or Graeco-Roman states-systems, the world order that existed in China between 771 BC and 221 BC when the Ch'in empire was established, and the Western international order which extends from the Renaissance city-state system to the modern society of states that now encompasses the entire world.

[10] Wight's examples include the system in the Near East that embraced Egypt, the Hittites, Babylon and Crete in the second millennium BC; the relations between the Roman and Parthian empires in their 'successive manifestations'; and the closest modern analogue which was the international society that existed in the Mediterranean in the twelfth and thirteenth centuries AD, embracing Western and Eastern Christendom, and the Islamic world.

not the same as equality) tames but does not end the struggle for power. Only in modern international society have separate political communities developed the idea of 'the legal equality of states' (Wight 1977: 22ff.). That observation was qualified by the comment that the European states-system has moved through a 'succession of hegemonies' (Watson 1992: 252). Developing the point, Watson (1992: 4) maintained that 'systems of independent states certainly differ from suzerain or imperial systems', but a theory that rests on a 'simple' dichotomy between the two will fail to account for 'actual realities'. In short, the historical evidence is that 'all known ways of organising diverse but interconnected communities have operated somewhere between ... the two extremes' (Watson 1992: 4).

Various sociological works lend implicit support to the argument that the history of international systems is far more complex than the distinction between a 'system of absolutely independent states' and 'a heterogeneous empire' which is tightly administered from a central point suggests (Watson 1992: 4). One approach has observed that early agrarian empires had to rely on previously independent ruling elites to govern newly conquered territory because of the inability to rule subdued peoples directly (Mann 1986: ch. 5). Elements of 'anarchical' and 'hierarchical' orders were combined in empires such as Rome which entered into agreements with frontier societies that were, on many occasions, respected as notional equals.[11] The broader point is that the neo-realist idea of the 'international system' is insufficiently nuanced to capture the diverse qualities of different forms of world political organization; as a result further research is needed to conceptualize and classify international systems that can be placed along the spectrum from anarchy to hierarchy (Buzan 1993; Buzan and Little 2000).[12]

It is necessary to consider such conceptual issues and taxonomies before turning to the comparative sociology of global civilizing process. As a preliminary step, it is also important to ask if Wight's reflections on primary states-systems, which concentrated on the Hellenic-Hellenistic, Chinese and modern international political orders, overlooked other important examples. Watson (1992: ch. 2) included the Sumerian city-state system that survived from around 3200 BC to the unification of Sumer under King Lugalzaggisi and Sargon of

---

[11] See Waltz (1979) on the differences between anarchic and hierarchical political systems.

[12] To give one example, it is unclear whether the multi-actor systems that succeeded the Middle Kingdom around 1800 BC, and in the Muslim world from the ninth to the tenth centuries AD following the 'extinction of the Caliphate and the dismemberment of the world of Islam into a multiplicity of separate, often warring, sovereignties' (Lewis 1974: 165ff.), are primary states-systems in Wight's sense of the term. In the first example, each ruler claimed to be 'the legitimate Pharaoh of all the land' (McNeill 1979b: 32). In the second, each ruler asserted rights as the supreme caliphate. Claims to universal jurisdiction coexisted with geographically limited power. How far diplomatic relations were organized around a belief in the mutual recognition of rights to political independence is a topic for future investigation.

Akkad. He also considered the ancient Indian states-system in the Ganges region between the seventh and fourth centuries BC, at which point the separate kingdoms fell under the dominion of Magadha, soon to be conquered by Alexander's forces that entered the Indus region in 327 BC (McNeill 1979b: 166).[13] That augmented list is far from complete.[14] As Buzan and Little (2000: 172ff.) argue, an exhaustive inventory of 'multi-actor systems' should also find a place for the many systems of city-states that existed outside the European continent.[15]

In an intriguing discussion of international orders, Wilkinson (2000: 60) calculates that there have been twenty-eight systems of states in world history and twenty-three universal empires which all suffered the same fate of collapsing into multi-actor systems. Interestingly, on that argument, systems of states appear to have been 'more durable' than empires. The modern international system is not only 'the most durable of its species', but has 'outlasted any world state ever recorded'. Important definitional issues arise here. It is unclear how many of the twenty-eight states-systems were 'primary' as opposed to 'secondary', in Wight's use of those terms, or how many were 'international systems' or 'international societies' in which the constituent units recognized each other's right to political independence (Bull 1977: 9–13).[16] Beyond such conceptual matters

---

[13] Roberts (1980: 138) maintains that there were sixteen such kingdoms at the end of the seventh century.

[14] Other examples include the system of Mayan city-state polities that emerged in the latter the part of the first millennium AD (see Cioffi-Revilla and Landmann 1999; Gat 2006: 270). The constituent rulers seem to have formed a 'brotherhood of equals'. On some accounts, wars of conquest were prevalent when the Spanish arrived (Renfrew and Cherry 1986: ch. 7). Toynbee (1978: 424) refers to the post-Tiahuanacao phase of Andean history (circa AD 1000–1430) that revolved around three states in the coastal lowlands, Chimu, Cuizmanco and Chincha, that 'dwarfed' the polities of the pre-Tiahuanacao Age of 'Florescence' which ended around AD 500. It seems that there may have been a multi-state system or confederacy of societies in pre-Inca Peru, in the period after AD 250 (Scarre 2005: 655ff.).

[15] Complexities arise about distinguishing city-states from other early forms of political association such as petty kingdoms, but they must be placed to one side here (Gat 2006: ch. 10). Examples of inter-city or early states-systems were found in the Harappan culture which existed between 2500–1500 BC (in what is now Pakistan). A similar complex existed in West Africa around AD 1500 and revolved around Benin and at least ten other cities – see Watson (1992) and, in particular, Buzan and Little (2000: 174, 196) for references to those multi-actor orders. Also significant is the Phoenician system that emerged around 1150 BC but did not develop autonomously on account of being forced to pay tribute to Assyria in the ninth century BC, before losing its independence entirely in the sixth century BC, first to Nebuchadnezzar II and then to Persia (see Wesson 1978: 92–3 and Mann 1986: ch. 7). Just like the states-systems described in Wight (1977), city-state systems lasted for only a few centuries before being destroyed by internal conflict or by a predatory neighbour (Gat 2006: 310).

[16] Bull (1977: ch. 1) distinguished between an international system in which states compete for power and always face the possibility of becoming involved in generalized warfare, and an international society in which states generally observe basic principles of co-existence and support international institutions that are responsible for their creation, administration and enforcement.

lie largely unexplored questions about the role of international and cosmopolitan harm conventions in different systems of states, primary and secondary. There have been many separate discussions of early systems where considerations of order and/or justice underpinned support for the laws of war.[17] Further research is needed to clarify whether efforts to create international order always developed before attempts to observe justice in war, whether shared ideas about pointless suffering formed a common culture that facilitated the rise of a society of states, or whether international and cosmopolitan harm conventions often emerged contemporaneously. A central purpose is to understand the conditions that permitted the development of global civilizing processes in different states-systems.

The sociology of states-systems

Wight's approach to states-systems is a counterweight to Elias's tendency to deny that such global civilizing processes existed – although in part the difference was one of emphasis since Wight was clearly of the view that civilizing processes in relations between societies have always been precarious because of struggles between the great powers. Nevertheless, one of his aims was to investigate the extent to which the equivalents to modern institutions such as diplomacy, international law and the balance of power existed in earlier times. A key issue was whether societies of states had only appeared in regions where there was a common culture that was reinforced by an awareness of 'cultural differentiation' from the outside world (Wight 1977: 34–5). The impact of sensibilities that were shared by ruling elites – how far they were the basis for strong links between the members of international society, and how far they influenced conduct towards outsider groups – was a major issue for an inquiry which considered, for example, the impact of Pan-Hellenic ideas on relations between the Ancient Greek city-states, and the degree to which images of common humanity encouraged the development of a more inclusive conception of international society

---

[17] Sumerian city-states believed they were part of an international society with diplomatic conventions including the doctrine that hegemonic powers had special responsibilities for resolving disputes and for preserving the 'rules of war' (Watson 1992: 27; Mann 1986: ch. 3). The political units that formed the ancient Chinese system, and particularly those that occupied the area that had been unified culturally and politically by the Chou Empire prior to its collapse in 771 BC, recognized each other's independence for the most part, cooperated intermittently to uphold the balance of power, and observed restraints on force (Watson 1992: 86–7; Wesson 1978: 33ff.). Members of the Indian states-system, which was roughly contemporaneous with the Hellenic international order, seem to have combined the belief that it was legitimate to reduce neighbours to vassalage with the conviction that overturning the laws and customs of conquered communities was reprehensible (Watson 1992: 78; Wesson 1978: 32–3). The Institutes of Manu circa the fourth century AD provide evidence of a diplomatic code that emphasized commitments to principles of humanity in war (Wesson 1978: 32–3).

that could embrace the traditional enemy, Persia. With respect to the modern European states-system, the analysis considered the influence of 'revolutionist' sensibilities on efforts to free the underlying unity of all peoples from the grip of the ruling classes (in both revolutionary France and Bolshevik Russia); and it assessed the impact of humanitarian convictions on cosmopolitan or inter-nationalist attempts to ensure that European states behaved ethically towards 'barbarians' and 'savages' (Wight 1977: chs. 1–2; Wight 1991: ch. 4). Although not cast in these terms, Wight's reflections on such dynamics within the Hellenic and modern states-systems provided valuable insights into the nature and extent of global civilizing processes.

There are parallels between Elias's stress on the impact of the 'monopoly mechanism' on world history and Wight's reflections on long-term patterns of development in societies of states. For Wight, what there was in the way of 'soci-ety' or 'community' failed to prevent the collapse of earlier systems. In ancient China, war reduced the number of great powers from an overall average of between twenty-five to fifty states until one state, the Ch'in, transformed the sys-tem into an empire (Wight 1977: 40; also Toynbee 1978: ch. 31). Warfare had the same long-term result in Ancient Greece where the 1,500 city-states that existed in the classical era were steadily reduced in number, and where the ascendancy of two powers, Athens and Sparta, resulted in the catastrophic wars that exposed the system to Macedonian domination followed by Roman imperial rule. In the period in which Wight was developing his ideas about the sociology of states-systems, the two superpowers appeared to be on a collision course which suggested that modern international society would suffer the same fate as its predecessors.[18]

Such dynamics do not augur well as far as future levels of moral sensitiveness in world politics are concerned, although there was a degree of ambiguity in Wight's position on that subject – as in Elias's (see pp. 178–81). On the one hand, there is the legendary claim that international politics is 'the realm of recurrence and repetition', and the more specific observation that the modern states-system has lurched from one hegemon to another without making significant progress towards cosmopolitanism.[19] On the other hand, there was the comment that

[18] Toynbee (1978: 593) also subscribed to this position, as did Elias, as noted earlier (pp. 176–7).

[19] Wight's conception of cosmopolitanism was flawed. Cosmopolitanism was thought to defend 'a world society of individuals, which overrides nations or states, diminishing or dis-missing this middle link'. The objective was 'the total dissolution of international relations' in the belief that 'the only true international society is one of individuals' (Wight 1991: 45). Many forms of cosmopolitanism do not have that form, but rather defend 'friendship towards the world'; they respect local affiliations while aiming to check any tendency to exaggerate their moral significance in ways that justify violent and non-violent harm to others (Linklater 2002b). As discussed here, cosmopolitan harm conventions are not in tension with local attachments per se, but have the function of reconciling obligations to insiders with obligations to other peoples.

states-systems are not all exactly the same since there have been significant differences in the extent to which humanitarian values have influenced their development and dominant practices. In particular, Wight (1966b: 126) argued, the modern states-system may be influenced by a level of 'moral sensitiveness' that was missing from '*simpler civilizations*' such as Greece and Rome where there was little consideration of 'international ethics' (italics added).[20]

One implication of that aside is that there is merit in comparing attitudes to cruelty and suffering in particular phases in the history of any states-system, and in different states-systems. The point has been stressed that there is no reason to think that Wight was any more inclined than Elias to use pejorative language when referring to unequal levels of 'moral sensitiveness' in international societies. Wight's sympathies may have been with the relativist standpoint that has been imputed to Durkheim's approach to the sociology of morals which held that all moralities are right for the societies that created them (Durkheim 1993: 48). To think otherwise would seem to commit the hermeneutic crime of rushing to judge other cultures by contemporary 'alien' standards without pausing to consider the distinctive challenges they faced. The reference to 'simpler civilizations' raises the issue of whether Wight's remarks about differences between states-systems were influenced by implicit value-judgments. But for reasons given earlier, lower levels of 'moral sensitiveness' need not be regarded as an expression of natural wickedness, but as the product of violent conditions and their 'decivilizing' effects; and higher levels can be likened to the advances in attunement between people that Elias discussed (see pp. 159–60; also n. 7 above). The latter can be seen to be intertwined with the development of peaceful social conditions that free people from the frequently brutalizing results of being forced to compete for power and security, rather than explained in terms of 'natural' higher moral qualities.[21]

It is perfectly legitimate to argue that significant ethical advances did take place in the development of any international society, and to maintain that one society of states may have gone further than others in promoting 'moral progress', as long as those sensitivities to social context are kept in mind. Although it is pointless condemning international societies for falling short of the 'higher'

---

[20] As noted in Linklater and Suganami (2006: 213) the point was made in connection with Stalin's suggestion that the German General Staff should be liquidated at the end of the Second World War. The reference to 'simpler civilizations' points to the need for exactly the kind of comparative analysis of civilizing processes that Elias pioneered, with the emphasis on developments in relations between states and their connection with larger patterns of social and political change.

[21] Wight was clearly of the view that higher levels of moral sensitiveness often decline rapidly when power struggles intensify. Parallels between his thinking about international relations and Elias's standpoint on how civilizing and decivilizing processes always develop in tandem indicate how English School theory could profit from an engagement with process sociology.

standards of later periods, the analyst can attempt to establish how far they were cruel by the standards of their time – by what the prevailing harm conventions regarded as permissible and impermissible.[22] The evidence may be hard to uncover, but there is always scope for trying to ascertain how far particular groups resented such cruelties, and struggled for their elimination. To proceed differently is to fail to consider the extent to which the restraints on conduct that were embedded in the dominant harm conventions had no other purpose than protecting the interests and privileges of the dominant states and strata. Such an approach raises the question of whether the members of an international society made distinctions between restraints that may be necessary for the survival of such forms of world political organization, and constraints that simply work to the advantage of the great powers, and how far they developed collective projects that were designed to free all peoples from unnecessary harm (see pp. 22–3). But the central issue is not whether the majority of states in any international society had such orientations. The key point is that it is legitimate to search for and explain social learning in that domain, and not least because of its significance for global civilizing processes that promote cosmopolitan harm conventions.

To proceed in the manner described is to recognize the force of the argument that the historian's chief task is to strive to comprehend other societies 'from within'. It is to accept, with the caveat that has been noted, that shared social understandings may form 'relatively self-contained systems' with 'independent standards of intelligibility and rationality', and to acknowledge that 'criticism or assessment in the light of more recent criteria [may be] inappropriate' (Gardiner 1975: 10–11). But as that author notes, to assume that inquiry must end there is to place 'unrealistically narrow restrictions upon historical procedure'. Historians have a legitimate interest in assessing what earlier societies contributed, however unwittingly, to longer-term patterns of development; they can reasonably accord past events 'a significance not the less real for having been unenvisaged, and possibly unenvisageable' by people at the time. Although those observations were concerned with the study of earlier societies, they are also important for the sociology of states-systems. Clearly, the members of any states-system cannot foresee where innovations in military technology will lead, or predict what may come from displays of solidarity with outsiders. They may not be concerned with how their separate and collective choices will influence future generations, or pause to reflect on whether their global harm conventions are likely to improve or damage the prospects that societies can live together more amicably. Circumstances may conspire to prevent such long-term thinking. Then again, under certain conditions, they may well be conscious of how their decisions and actions will leave a legacy to future generations – for good or

---

[22] Difficulties in comparing emotional attitudes to cruelty in different eras, and in judging whether societies were cruel by their own standards, are discussed in Miller (1993).

ill – and they may alter their moral and political orientations accordingly. The study of global civilizing processes should proceed in that light.

Towards a sociology of civilizing processes in states-systems

It was noted in Chapter 4 that Elias defined the process of civilization as a dual movement in which people developed ways of satisfying basic needs without 'injuring, demeaning and in other ways harming each other time and time again', and in which they came to identify with others in their society irrespective of social origins (pp. 159–60). It follows that the sociology of global civilizing processes should focus on how far communities discovered ways in which they could promote their interests without causing violent or non-violent harm again and again; and it should investigate how far such achievements were connected with advances in thinking that insiders and outsiders are moral equals.

Chapter 1 discussed these forms of harm in world politics: deliberate killing and physical injury; actions that were designed to degrade and humiliate; unintended harm; negligence; complicit harm; exploitation; and finally omissive, structural and public harm. That taxonomy leads to various questions about civilizing processes in different states-systems that lay the foundations for future efforts to understand the extent to which conceptions of the 'problem of harm', and a collective desire to resist a 'principle of injury', influenced long-term patterns of development.[23] Amongst the more important are:

1. Did global standards and practices express the aspiration to spare enemy combatants and prisoners of war unnecessary suffering? To what extent did cosmopolitan harm conventions oppose, inter alia, the infliction of suffering on civilian populations whether by using physical force or employing military or other sanctions to starve them into submission? To what extent did a 'principle of humaneness' exercise restraint on arguments from military necessity?
2. How far did the dominant principles and practices endorse or oppose racist, xenophobic and other degrading representations of outsiders?
3. To what extent did political communities cooperate to protect all persons from deliberate harm caused by non-state actors, including the agents of 'private international violence'? Did they collaborate, by virtue of a commitment to a global civilizing process, to eradicate piracy, and to weaken or eliminate the equivalent of contemporary transnational organizations that trade persons for, amongst other things, the purpose of 'sexual slavery'?

---

[23] To repeat, the question is not whether earlier international societies created harm conventions that expressed modern ethical sensitivities about violence and cruelty. The point is to ascertain how far they believed there were problems of harm in particular areas, and acted to ameliorate the consequences. Further comments on understanding the conditions that favour global civilizing processes will be set out in volume 2. See p. 96 on 'the principle of injury'.

4. How far did the problem of exploitation emerge as a moral problem in different states-systems, and how far did it lead to revulsion towards the ruthless employment of the labour of defeated peoples, towards slavery more generally, and towards other practices that took advantage of the vulnerable, including rape in war?

5. To what degree did notions of omissive harm influence conduct in different states-systems? Were responses to famine and starvation in other societies influenced by the belief that peoples can cause harm through indifference to suffering (even when they are not causally responsible for it)? To what extent was human society as a whole troubled by inaction in the face of any evidence (and clearly information must have been extremely limited in the pre-industrial world) that governments harmed their subjects or citizens by using torture or other forms of violence to infringe what are now widely regarded as 'natural' rights?

Those questions arise as part of the comparative analysis of states-systems where the main connections between the constituent units are geopolitical rather than economic or cultural. The reference to slavery points to systems of exploitation that are anchored in economic relations – for example, where slave markets function with a degree of autonomy from state power. The following questions address the conditions in which communities are so economically interdependent that it is essential to analyse transnational in addition to international harm – and to examine transnational exploitation as well as any arguments for transnational justice (see pp. 38–9).[24] The questions are:

6. Did states believe that they had moral duties to the victims of unintended harm? The rise of global environmental harm has made this a central theme in the modern society of states, as has the ability to project military power into the heartland of other societies with the result that measures to destroy legitimate targets cause the unintended and disproportionate killing of innocent civilians. How far did moral anxieties about unintended harm appear in other states-systems?

7. Related issues arise in connection with negligent harm. Modern concerns about negligence stress the failure to exercise due care, as in criticisms of Union Carbide following the explosion at Bhopal in December 1984, but one must ask how far negligent harm was a moral problem in earlier

---

[24] Buzan and Little (2000: 80–1) maintain that 'if interaction capacity is low, then structure will have little or no effect. Higher levels of interaction capacity allow structural forces powerfully into play'. Interaction capacity refers to the extent to which people, commodities, ideas and so forth can move across space. As noted earlier, unprecedented levels of 'interaction capacity' in the modern system may be responsible for 'sectoral transformation: a shift from military-political to economic processes as the *dominant* (i.e. system defining) form of interaction' (Buzan and Little 2000: 357; italics in original). The importance of that form of sectoral change is reflected in the following questions about harm.

states-systems – for instance, with respect to a lack of care and consideration for civilians during military conflicts.

8. Complicitous harm can occur in many different areas of global social and political relations – in the economic realm where individuals belong to organizations that cause harm (as in the example of shareholder complicity in corporate harm which was discussed in Chapter 1), or where people enjoy the benefits of practices such as slave trade without any direct personal involvement. The second example reveals that the idea of 'the harm that we do in our everyday lives', which has been employed to describe various moral problems in the present phase of global interconnectedness, can be used to analyse attitudes to suffering in any states-system where there is traffic in people. The question is how far involvement in mediated harm produced widespread feelings of guilt and 'self reproach' in different states-systems.

9. Structural harm is associated with high levels of economic interconnectedness that may be capped by regulative 'global coercive regimes'. Structural harm is clearly more central in the modern states-system than in any of its predecessors, and so comparative analysis must be largely concerned with the evolution of modern international society and with degrees of 'moral sensitiveness' to the human consequences of that phenomenon.

10. Global public harm exists when states have created standards and practices that signify the sense of belonging to an international society, and when it is possible to erode trust in those arrangements or in some other way weaken their authority without necessarily intending to harm specific groups or persons. Unlike structural harm, global public harm is not a concept that applies only to the modern states-system. As noted above, in Thucydides' account of the Peloponnesian War, many violations of the laws of Hellas were regarded as offences against the gods, and as an injury to all Greeks (see p. 72). Perhaps breaches of religious principles constituted the main form of public harm in earlier states-systems. But it is important to ask how far the welfare of humanity, or the part that came within the boundaries of a system of states, was at stake in the condemnation of violations of global principles. Two issues arise: to what extent did global public harm attract criticism because it damaged international harm conventions and the institutions that were responsible for creating and administering them; and to what degree was it condemned because of setbacks to international institutions that were designed to promote and safeguard cosmopolitan harm conventions?

The last point is a reminder that one of the purposes of the sociology of states-systems is to understand long-term patterns of change and, in particular, evidence of global civilizing processes in which cosmopolitan ideas came to underpin beliefs about how peoples could co-exist with minimum violent and non-violent harm. The discussion must therefore consider specific conjectures that leading approaches to international relations raise for the inquiry (see Chapter 3). They include:

1. To what extent did great power rivalry place insuperable obstacles in the way of efforts to build cosmopolitan harm conventions? How far did arguments from military necessity, and temptations to blur the distinction between necessity and utility, repeatedly weaken any cosmopolitan harm conventions that did exist? To what extent did great power rivalries determine the long-term development of states-systems with the consequences that Wight described?

2. Some questions presume that states belong to an international system, but it is necessary to analyse patterns of development within international societies that mediate between 'systemic' constraints and visions of a universal community (see pp. 127–33, n. 16). It is important to ask how far 'pluralistic' commitments to order were complemented by 'solidarist' standards that expressed cosmopolitan aspirations to reduce suffering. English School theory raises additional questions about whether 'great responsibles' restrained the pursuit of self-interest because of commitments to cosmopolitan harm conventions. Wight's position on the collapse of earlier states-systems leads to the issue of how far any moral concerns about harm and suffering that were included within visions of world community were swept aside by the decivilizing processes that led to empire; it also invites discussion of whether such ethical sensibilities were incorporated in imperial ideologies, and survived at least in the form of anti-systemic forces that circulated in what have been called the 'interstices' of imperial orders, where they preserved the hope that people might one day enjoy freedom from unnecessary harm (Mann 1986: 15–19, ch. 10).

3. Certain traits that all past international societies seem to have in common prompt questions about the impact of insider–outsider dualisms, and specifically the role of distinctions between 'civilized' and the 'savage' or 'barbaric' peoples, on long-term developments. How far did a global 'standard of civilization' tolerate acts of violence against outsiders that were largely forbidden within international society? What part did it play in promoting the belief that 'civilized' peoples violated their own norms and ideals by treating 'savages' as if they did not possess rights? Relations with 'barbarians' test the human capacity to develop and observe moral and political principles that represent a significant degree of detachment from 'superior' worldviews – particularly in the absence of functional democratization. Questions about 'standards of civilization' belong to a larger catalogue of queries about how far pernicious distinctions between insiders and outsiders blocked advances to cultural standpoints that recognize that all people have equal rights to be free from pointless suffering. Rather different questions arise when societies

become so interconnected that peoples need to learn how to be more responsive to each other's interests. Then the issue is how far loyalties to traditional 'survival units' impede movement towards combinations of 'local' and universal affiliations that enable different peoples to cooperate to eradicate unnecessary harm.

4. Historical materialism highlights issues regarding economic exploitation that Wight's vision of a sociology of states-systems failed to address. A more synoptic perspective must analyse systems of exploitation such as slavery that have been prevalent in human history; but theoretical comprehensiveness also requires attention to moral attitudes to suffering, a dimension of social life that is usually ignored by materialist perspectives. Links between racism and the Atlantic slave trade reveal a need to discuss the ideologies that were used to justify slavery and servitude in other eras, just as the influence of religious ideas on the early nineteenth-century abolitionist movement invites comparisons with measures to alleviate or end suffering that was caused by economic domination in earlier eras. Lengthening chains of interconnectedness always raise issues about how far ethical horizons lag behind global integration, and about whether any parallel widening of the scope of emotional identification occurred. The impact of industrial capitalism on the globalization of society leads to the conjecture that the modern states-system enjoys moral potentials that did not exist in earlier forms of world political organization. Formal equality between those who own and control the forces of production, and those who must sell their labour-power to survive, are especially pertinent here. That condition of parity has to be seen in conjunction with functional democratization – with whether it is so minimal that dominant strata can withstand challenges to exploitation, or reaches a level where the former believe that concessions to subordinate groups are essential to maintain their privileges and powers. At the same time, it is important to consider whether advances in individuation look set to entrench moral indifference in affluent communities to the pernicious effects of capitalist globalization.

5. All questions about attitudes to suffering point to the issue of how far some version of an ethic of care and responsibility that is essential for the survival of every society influenced the long-term development of states-systems. To what extent did moral concerns about the effects that actions have on others check the dangers of 'limited altruism'? Did a sense of connectedness with vulnerable others generate sympathy for, and solidarity with, those who were adversely affected by new opportunities for causing distant harm that emerged with the globalization of human society? To what extent have destructive masculinities been relatively free from moral constraints in warfare with terrible consequences for adversaries and civilian populations, including women who were reduced to 'the spoils of war'? How far was uninhibited violence widely valued as an expression of the identity of the male

warrior while compassion and restraint were regarded as signs of weakness or effeminacy? To what extent were destructive masculinities regarded as praiseworthy, or as shameful and reprehensible because they violated a code of chivalry, displayed pleasure in killing and brutality, and lacked human sympathy?

Many of the issues that have been highlighted lead directly to 'emotionology' and to the analysis of the scope of emotional identification. Whether states form a society depends on how far at least the ruling strata experience a sense of 'we-feeling'. How far states relish the ruthless use of force against enemies, tolerate or sanction the rape of women in war, engage in exploiting enslaved labour, or license the humiliation of outsiders depends on levels of identification with outsiders. Whether the members of an international society are troubled by direct and indirect harm depends in part on the degree to which compassion, guilt and shame have become cosmopolitan moral emotions that have a profound impact on attitudes to harm that is suffered by distant strangers. The human capacity to emancipate such emotions from over-identification with 'survival units' points the sociology of states-systems towards the following questions:

1. What were the dominant emotional attitudes to violent and non-violent harm, how did they influence the conduct of the great powers, and were they embodied in cosmopolitan harm conventions that the strong were prepared to support?
2. To what extent did moral codes in the most influential states limit compassion, shame and guilt to relations within the in-group, or promote identification with the members of other societies? Did 'we-feeling' attach taboos to certain forms of violence, discourage degrading representations of others, constrain exploitation, and lead to opposition to other forms of harm across the states-system as a whole?
3. Great power conflict in the final phase of the Hellenic and Chinese international systems led to a coarsening of sensibilities rather than to the growth of 'world identification'. But how influential were cosmopolitan emotions in the individual phases in the life-cycle of any states-system, and how far did they survive 'elimination contests' and the transition to universal empire?

Larger questions need to be asked about the relationship between international states-systems, global civilizing processes and the moral and political development of the species. Systems of states may create a measure of order for the *ecumene* of their age but, of course, imperial expansion has frequently transformed understandings about the boundaries of the inhabited world. It is therefore important to ask what different international systems contributed to the evolution of universal political frameworks that realized immanent possibilities for freeing all people from the tyranny of unnecessary harm. The question is how far the members of states-systems made critical advances in reaching an overlapping consensus about shared vulnerabilities that underpinned contrasts between generalizable and non-generalizable interests – between purposes that every person can reasonably have, and objectives that cannot be pursued by all people if they are to succeed in living together harmoniously (see p. 96). Alternatively, the issue is to what extent did understandings of the most accessible points of solidarity between strangers emerge from beneath the shadows of pernicious systems of social exclusion and influence relations between societies?

To conclude this section it is important to repeat that no states-system is more important than any other for understanding how independent political communities have responded to the challenges of interconnectedness. If the modern society of states has special importance, it is because it is the first of its kind to face the challenge of whether it can satisfy ethical demands to take responsibility for the well-being of individuals everywhere and for the future welfare of humanity. The dominant responses to unusually high levels of interdependence that seem likely to increase in the decades and centuries ahead clearly have great significance for the human prospect for altering the balance of power between, on the one hand, the capacity to invent ever more ingenious ways of causing more destructive harm over greater distances and, on the other, the ability to promote global civilizing processes that have the purpose of controlling that distinctive feature of the evolution of the species. Further comments on that tension require some reflections on the importance of the idea of collective learning processes for the sociology of states-systems.

Collective learning in world history

The problems with nineteenth-century meta-narratives that sought to discover the meaning of history need no discussion here. More important is the impact of the critique of historical inevitability and progress for the status of efforts to understand long-term processes of change and, in particular, collective learning processes. As suggested earlier, using the notion of social learning to describe long-term changes in the moral sphere can raise concerns that the errors of the nineteenth-century philosophies of history will be repeated (see Shapcott 2001). However, the idea of 'moral-practical learning' is valuable for placing modern conceptions of harm in a world-history perspective and for understanding the prospects for a global process of civilization (Habermas 1979a).[25]

---

[25] The idea of social learning is hardly alien to International Relations scholarship. It was central to neo-functionalist approaches to inter-state cooperation and to related analyses of 'security communities' around four decades ago (Deutsch 1970; Pentland 1974). More recently, it has featured in studies of long-term change in world politics (Modelski 1990, 2000). But the concept has not been widely adopted by the International Relations community, and there has been no systematic discussion of its significance for efforts to build links with historical sociology or world history.

Habermas (1979b) provided a defence of an 'empirical philosophy of history' that analyses the different learning processes that have shaped the development of humanity (Jay 1984: ch. 15). A key objective of the approach was to understand the unique species-capacity to move from particularistic to universalistic, or 'post-conventional', ethical perspectives (Habermas 1979a: chs. 3–4). Quite how that potential had evolved was not explained, although the transition from early kinship groups to state-organized societies was cited to illustrate the part that the compulsions of interdependence had played in the shift from parochial frameworks to more 'decentred' cultural standpoints (Habermas 1979b). Kant's philosophical notion of learning how to 'think from the standpoint of others' was turned into a sociological concept that could be used to understand the development of larger, more complex social systems. Habermas's later writings concentrated on the philosophical defence of a universal ethic that links the obligation to strive to take the standpoint of other people with the responsibility to engage in open dialogue with all those who stand to be affected by one's actions (see Linklater 1998). But the overall argument is also useful for sociological purposes, and specifically for the empirical analysis of learning processes that improve the human prospect of reaching agreements about how to co-exist with minimum harm.

Habermas maintained that theory can give an account of ideal dialogic procedures, but it cannot anticipate outcomes: moral agents must themselves establish how far they can agree about universal principles or 'generalizable interests'. There is a rough parallel between the approach and the argument for a complex 'labour of translation' between ways of life which is based on the recognition that 'the universal is only partially articulated', and 'we do not yet know what forms it may take' (Butler 2002: 46, 52). Also relevant, and providing a bridge to analysing cosmopolitan harm conventions, is the Eliasian focus on greater interconnectedness between societies that has repeatedly created internal tensions between the demands to fall back and reinforce standard orientations towards outsiders, and the pressures to advance towards a position of greater detachment which involves closer attention and attunement to the concerns of others. Evidence of moral-practical learning in world politics is provided by the growing recognition that what were often dismissed as merely 'utopian' ideas (as ideas that were relevant to the internal organization of societies, but not to the harsh, unchanging realities of international politics) have become critical for meeting the challenges of global interconnectedness (McCarthy 1981: ch. 3).

The tendency for sociologists and social theorists to focus on developments within societies at the cost of analysing relations between them has meant that there has been little detailed investigation of potentials for, and constraints on, moral learning in different states-systems. Notions of the recurrent and repetitive qualities of international politics have combined with the 'methodological nationalism' of much social and political inquiry in a pincer movement that has impeded efforts to understand collective learning processes at the global level.

The study of 'the expansion of international society' is a partial exception to the general trend, although largely undertaken in isolation from broader developments in the social sciences. That process has made the question of how far societies can participate in a 'complex labour of translation' more fundamental than ever before; it continues to probe their ability to think from the standpoint of others in forms of diplomatic dialogue that explore the potential for agreements on principles and procedures that can command general if not universal consent.[26]

In the spirit of the old grand narratives, one of the purposes of the sociology of states-systems is to identify and understand moral breakthroughs in earlier periods that paved the way for cosmopolitan standpoints that are enshrined in visions of a 'universal communication community' that grant all people an equal right to protest against, and to be protected from, indefensible harm. For reasons given earlier, the approach can begin with the assumption that all societies can be thought to have 'a potential to engender universal structures and yet so far, for better or worse, few have gone very far in articulating and institutionalising universalities in the spheres of social relations and cultural designs' (Nelson in Huff 1981: 11; see also the discussion on pp. 203–4).[27] The envisaged perspective differs from other conceptions of the historical sociology of international relations by placing states-systems at the centre of an analysis of the evolution of universalistic potentialities that have provided the moral resources for struggles to eradicate the surfeit of harm that has developed with the globalization of social and economic relations – that is, as part of strategic learning in which societies have mastered more destructive technologies for the purpose of outmanoeuvring, controlling and defeating adversaries (Elias 1994: 131; and comments on Schiller in Elias 1996: 124ff.).

---

[26] As Bull and Watson (1984: conclusion) contend, it is no small achievement that the societies involved have made notable advances in agreeing on basic principles of co-existence. To translate that discussion of the expansion of international society into the language of the modes of social theory which are under consideration here, the global integration of regional international systems with long-established hierarchical conceptions of world order raised questions about the capacity for agreeing on principles that span different cultural standpoints. One of the achievements of various studies of world history is the light they cast on such universalising processes, although only rarely in connection with the analysis of international states-systems. Toynbee (1978), Roberts (1980) and Buzan and Little (2002) are important in this context. Those are matters to return to in volume 3.

[27] For the record, Habermas (1979a: 37) accused Nelson of assuming that universalistic worldviews are 'exclusively a Western phenomenon', and added that a better starting-point is that 'the universalistic potential was not … a peculiarity of occidental traditions but can be documented for all the world-views originating between 800 and 300 BC in China, India, Greece and Israel' – in what Jaspers called the 'axial age'. See Nelson's response in Huff (1981: 10–11). The argument here has been that all or most moral codes have such cosmopolitan potentials, and that Weil's writings point the way to understanding how far they reside in capacities for sympathy and solidarity that exist in all societies.

It is probably true that the great philosophers of history approached the past with the hope of identifying general trends that would 'leave us morally satisfied, or at least not morally dissatisfied' (Walsh 1967: 145). But those who believed that there had been moral progress invariably recognized that learning processes are not restricted to that sphere. Many highlighted the gulf between moral achievements and current miseries.[28] At times, the Stoic injunction to refrain from harming distant strangers was linked, implicitly or otherwise, with the recognition of how the 'other side' of learning processes created immense risks for all people.[29] It is essential to stress that forms of social learning that have led to larger territorial monopolies of power that can cause immense harm over greater distances express species-powers that are as distinctive as the ability to widen the scope of emotional identification to include all humans. For realists, strategic learning in the former domain has had the greatest impact on the course of international political history. For cosmopolitans such as Kant, the fact that revolutions in inventing new ways of causing harm have often had the upper hand should not obscure the part that moral learning plays in maintaining the hope that modern societies and their descendants are not condemned for evermore to live with the patterns of the past.

Modernity, collective learning and global civilization

At stake between realists and cosmopolitans is the issue of whether moral learning can keep pace with strategic learning. Weber argued that the dominant religious worldviews in the major civilizations had usually helped to consolidate existing centres of political power. One of the distinctive features of Occidental rationality was the division between the two worlds of ethical universals and political imperatives, and the practice of harnessing a 'higher' morality to condemn the compromises that attend the exercise of political power (see pp. 201–3). The idea of the ambiguities of interconnectedness which has been a central

[28] The classic statement can be found in Kant's *Idea for a Universal History* (see Walsh 1967: 121): 'One cannot avoid a certain feeling of disgust, when one observes the actions of man displayed on the great stage of the world. Wisdom is manifested by individuals here and there; but the web of human history as a whole appears to be woven from folly and childish vanity, often, too, from puerile wickedness and love of destruction: with the result that at the end one is puzzled to know what idea to form of our species which prides itself so much on its advantages'. Kant proceeds to discuss the emerging universal political association that might free humanity from such forces.

[29] Mazzini's moral advocacy is worth noting in this context. 'Ask yourselves', he argued, 'as to every act you commit within the circle of family or country: If what I now do were done by and for all men, would it be beneficial or injurious to Humanity? And if your conscience tells you it would be injurious, desist: desist even though it seems that an immediate advantage to your country or family would be the result' (quoted in Wight 2004: 112). As with many recent approaches to environmental ethics, that particular defence of a cosmopolitan harm principle was linked with the notion that more and more people share a similar fate.

feature of Western political thought since the Enlightenment points to the tensions between those spheres; on the one hand, as Kant (1965 [1797]: 126, 1970b [1795]) argued, there is progress in the sphere of human rights but, on the other, there is the increased possibility of causing 'evil' in more distant places. Heirs to that perspective deny that social and political life can be reduced entirely to advances in strategic learning, and they support every effort to end senseless harm, but most acknowledge that the struggle to alter the balance of power between moral and strategic learning is not one the species is certain to win.

Those who have some confidence that the balance can shift decisively in favour of moral learning can point to several advances in contemporary international society – the humanitarian laws of war, the human rights culture, and advances in international criminal law that all defend equal rights to be free from 'serious bodily and mental harm'. For many liberals, the potentials for a radical break with the past depend on the globalization of liberal states, given the evidence that they have an unusual commitment to the non-violent resolution of political differences, at least in their relations with each other (Gat 2006; MacMillan 1998). Such standpoints preserve the separation between ethics and politics by denying that humanitarian sensibilities are simply ways of reconstituting domination and power (see pp. 187–90). As previously noted, many have argued that the realities either are, or could turn out to be, rather different.[30] This is not the occasion to speculate about how the tensions between ethics and politics will develop in the modern states-system. Suffice it to note that geopolitical struggles and 'elimination contests' have not yet come to an end; however, because of rising levels of interconnectedness, societies face intense pressures to exercise foresight and restraint in order not to harm the social and political structures (and the biosphere) on which all depend. Those comments point towards an examination of a collective learning processes system that is centred on the following questions:

1. To what extent is modern international society witnessing a sharp trend towards the 'obsolescence of war' between great powers, a reduced tolerance of force more generally, and a broad movement towards enforcing the

---

[30] The reference is to the earlier comment that liberal revulsion for violence contains the danger of violence against regimes that are deemed to be unacceptably cruel, as well as indifference to the suffering that the 'uncivilized' inflict on each other because of their unrestrained, 'atavistic' appetite for violent conflict (see pp. 108–10). It is also worth recalling the study of ancient empires which shows how universal ideologies that had flown along channels that no single power could control were finally hijacked by the dominant state in the region (see Mann 1986: 22ff.) for a discussion of how 'transcendent' ideas (that had escaped incorporation in systems of domination) became 'immanent' (intermeshed with, and legitimizing, particular structures of power). The opening years of the current millennium may have provided a foretaste of how some future hegemon will harness a 'transcendent ideology' to its particularistic cause, convincing itself in the process that it is acting as a guardian of universal human interests.

humanitarian laws of war that represents a civilizing advance in which the collective interest in 'taming the sovereigns' now rivals the earlier task of 'taming the warriors' within European states? To what extent has 'the civilizing process' found expression in an inter-liberal peace which reveals that Enlightenment ideals might yet provide the basis for further steps towards global pacification which can be consolidated by support for a cosmopolitan harm principle that is anchored in 'the affirmation of everyday life'? (see pp. 4–5.

2. How far does the legal prohibition of sovereign acts that involve the 'cruel and degrading' treatment of citizens distinguish the modern states-system from its predecessors? Do restrictions on national sovereignty embody unique cosmopolitan understandings about the ideal relationship between obligations to co-nationals and responsibilities to other peoples?

Those questions are designed to highlight advances in expanding the geographical 'scope of moral concern' (see O'Neill 2000b: 188) – without losing sight of progressions in the sphere of strategic learning. The aim is to assess the significance of progress in recognizing equal rights to be free from the cruelties inflicted in civil conflicts and inter-state war, in placing moral restraints on what is claimed on the basis of military necessity, in opposing harmful collective identities with pernicious distinctions between insiders and outsiders, and in promoting a global care ethic that attempts, amongst other things, to reduce the power and appeal of destructive masculinities. But as critics of the Western practice of privileging legal and political rights over social and economic entitlements have argued, it is imperative to consider the depth as well as the scope of such rights in the light of threats to economic and environmental security that are posed by states, transnational business enterprises, market forces and global regimes. On that argument, the 'liberalism of privilege' should broaden its conception of individual rights with a view to creating a 'humane and equitable' international order that addresses the problem of harm to the world's poorest communities (Richardson 1997, 2000). Such concerns about the social consequences of 'free market liberalism' raise questions about forms of non-violent harm that were discussed in Chapter 1. They include:

3. Where do the main potentials lie for dealing with forms of structural harm that can be easily overlooked by liberal ideas that 'cruelty is the worst thing we do'? What are the most promising responses to the problem of exploitation in the sense of taking advantage of the vulnerable, and to the challenge of reducing negligent or inadvertent harm particularly when it adds to the problem of global environmental degradation (which may yet prove to be the main test of how far the modern states-system can protect the interests of humanity)? How far do legal efforts to create new conceptions of national sovereignty that recognize the duty to avoid transnational harm represent unusual progress in meeting the challenges associated with rising levels

of global interconnectedness?[31] To what extent can visions of 'ecologically responsible statehood', and related ideas of moral, legal and political account-ability, embed cosmopolitan emotions in new global sociogenetic and psy-chogenetic combinations? (Eckersley 2004: 236–8).

Those questions are a reminder that the modern states-system is unique in having to confront an extraordinary variety of harms whether caused by state-building, geopolitics and war, or notions of cultural, racial or religious suprem-acy, or industrial systems of production and capitalist social relations that have no equivalent in other eras. Modern international society does not lack the moral resources with which to deepen and enlarge the scope of moral concern – they reside in the universalistic and egalitarian ideas that are part of its Enlightenment legacy. Whether those beliefs will ever be the main 'pacemaker of social evolu-tion', or are destined to be so marginal as to justify the bleak observation that there has been no real 'progress outside the technological sphere', is impossible to predict (Toynbee 1978: 590). But there is evidence that modern international society is turning one corner as far as a global civilizing process is concerned – in making a cosmopolitan harm principle more central to its organizing prin-ciples. Some confidence about the future can be derived from evidence that environmental harm may produce a sharp increase in support for the cosmo-politan principle that all people have an equal right to be consulted about prac-tices and decisions that affect them. The belief that distinctions between citizens and non-citizens are morally irrelevant when harm ignores national frontiers may win new advocates as a result. Concerns about complicit harm through involvement in unfair trading practices or unethical investment is pronounced in some circles, along with a measure of guilt or unease with respect to omissive harm when serious human rights violations meet with inaction. Perhaps the central issue is whether progressive forces in global civil society can persuade national and international institutions to convert universalistic and egalitarian values into stronger cosmopolitan harm conventions, and to turn current levels of passive sympathy into active sympathy (see pp. 223–4).[32] Advances in that area and, where appropriate, the enforcement of relevant obligations through further innovations in international criminal law ultimately depend on new, 'post-national' personality structures that give cosmopolitan expression to uni-versal – or almost universal – moral emotions such as compassion, shame, guilt, indignation and disgust. The following questions arise in that context.

---

[31] The reference is to the *International Law Commission Articles on Responsibility of States for Internationally Wrongful Acts* and *Draft Articles on Prevention of Transboundary Harm from Hazardous Activities* (Crawford 2002a).

[32] For an illustrative discussion, see the account of the development of the 1998 Rome Statute for an International Criminal Court in Thakur and Malley (1999). See also the discussion in Clark (2007).

4. What evidence is there to suppose that higher levels of interconnectedness are promoting a widening of the scope of emotional identification, generating more compassionate responses to violence and cruelty, and producing a greater sense of 'complex responsibility' for the victims of harm? (see pp. 101–2). Is there reason to think that an increasing sense of the inadequacies of nation-centred standpoints is leading to rising levels of support for ideas of world citizenship? It is essential to add that one of the preconditions of cosmopolitan political progress, namely the weakening of the ties between the individual and the state, may create new dangers. The question therefore arises of whether future generations may look back on the modern era as a turning-point in which advancing individuation weakened the insider–outsider dualisms that have blocked cosmopolitan moral advances for millennia only to allow widespread indifference to distant suffering to prevail. The central question is where do the countervailing forces of functional democratization lie?

This chapter has shown how elements from Wight's sociology of states-systems and Elias's perspective on civilizing processes can be combined to form a new empirical research agenda. Themes drawn from critical theory have informed the outline of a comparative sociological inquiry that investigates what different international systems have contributed to a global civilizing process. The critical-theoretical interest in understanding the potentials for global solidarity, and in supporting a mode of scholarship that lends 'a voice to suffering', will shape future inquiry into how far potentials for creating cosmopolitan harm conventions can be realized in what many regard as the hostile condition of international anarchy, or the unpromising environment of capitalist globalization, and so forth. Large issues arise. All that need be added is that attempting to deal with all of them with sufficient depth could occupy a lifetime. Selectivity must win out. For that reason, the following volume will focus on the analysis of civilizing and decivilizing processes in successive states-systems in the West, the aim being to understand how far 'things that were once permitted are now forbidden'.

~

Conclusion

The case has been made for a sociology of global civilizing processes that analyses how far a cosmopolitan harm principle was embedded in the normative structure of different states-systems. Societies of states have central importance because they are the highest 'steering mechanisms' available to independent political communities grappling with the challenges of interconnectedness. They are arenas in which the capacity to solve the problems associated with the ambiguities of interconnectedness has been put to the test; domains where societies have faced pressures to become attuned to each other (unless one is so dominant that it can effectively ignore the rest), and where they have discovered the extent of their capacity to become detached from parochial codes and to think from the other's standpoint; spheres in which, assuming a rough equilibrium of power, communities reveal how far they can observe self-restraint given the fear of disturbing the order on which all depend and, finally, in which they have demonstrated the extent to which they can widen the scope of emotional identification and support cosmopolitan principles that protect all people from the harms to which they are vulnerable. The modern states-system merits particular attention because it is the first form of world political organization that encompasses humanity as a whole. Whether it is, or can become, the site for unique civilizing processes that rein in the power to harm therefore has immense significance for the coming phase of global integration.

As realists stress, major obstacles stand in the way of global civilizing processes. For their critics, the challenge is to identify prospects for transnational solidarities that are not utopian or fanciful, but which have the potential to keep pace with the development of the power to hurt in world politics. Several conceptions of the moral good have been canvassed in connection with that ideal, only to flounder because they are perceived to reflect parochial standpoints that cannot command general support, and because they cannot be universalized without domination. Common vulnerabilities to mental and physical suffering that have provided the foundation for the laws of war in different forms of world political organization do not have that handicap. Tensions between realists and their opponents largely revolve around the issue of whether diplomatic agreements to protect persons and communities from unnecessary violence can only moderate the violence that is inherent in the 'logic of anarchy' (and which is frequently released because of 'military necessity') or may yet provide the basis for radical changes in the ways in which people are bound together at the global level.

Attitudes to suffering in communities that are so tied together – and particularly in those that have the greatest ability to shape global standards and institutions – are clearly central to conjectures about how far future advances in interconnectedness are likely to be accompanied by cosmopolitan imaginaries. It would be unwise to expect a radical break with the norms that have governed relations between societies for millennia. Loyalties to specific survival units continue to mean that people identify more closely with the suffering of others in their community than with vulnerable outsiders. Dominant narratives that recount collective ordeals in warfare strengthen such social bonds while driving wedges between societies. On the other hand, awareness of distant suffering has never been as great as it is today. People have never been as conscious of their power to alleviate suffering, or as cognizant of how they can harm, and be harmed by, distant strangers whether as a result of power struggles between states, or transnational corporate behaviour, or the silent operation of transnational processes. Many will argue that those sensibilities have done little to weaken the prevalent moral and political orientations towards the outside world. From that standpoint, any widening of moral horizons that has taken place in particular societies has made little impression on how the dominant moral codes direct sympathy and compassion towards co-nationals or fellow citizens. Others are perhaps more optimistic, or less pessimistic, about what those cultural changes may mean for efforts to govern interconnectedness in the eras that lie ahead.

Nation-states possess grand narratives that, inter alia, remind citizens of earlier threats to their existence, and commemorate collective ordeals in war. If it is to be a site for major global civilizing processes, an emergent world society will need equivalent accounts of its origins and development, of transformative moments that should be celebrated, of common dangers, as well as inspiring visions of collective hopes and unfulfilled ambitions. There is no immediate prospect of an agreed account of how the species came to form a community of shared desires and aspirations, of how it responded to common threats in ways that reveal how the pursuit of self-interest can be transcended in joint endeavours. We are perhaps only at the beginning of a phase when closer interconnectedness encourages the development of narratives of universal significance that document the struggles of the species, celebrate its achievements, and explain threats to its survival and to its ability to live decently – narratives that may encourage cosmopolitan identification by showing how, over the millennia, humans used their inventiveness with regard to the capacity to harm to eliminate rival species, to colonize and populate almost every region of the world, to develop longer social webs that now entangle all societies, and to unleash a series of military and technological revolutions that have led to the real possibility of the elimination of all life on earth. Such narratives do not rely on assumptions about a common fate – as if people everywhere face the same dangers and have identical interests – but they do point to certain trajectories of development that have affected the species as a whole. The part that many transnational movements play in building universal webs of significance and global attachments around such long-term directions should not be underestimated. Their role in publicizing the need for greater foresight about the possible consequences of allowing current trajectories to continue unchecked, in encouraging the difficult movement from myopic attachments to new transnational solidarities that bridge divisions between peoples, and in encouraging support for cosmopolitan harm conventions provides a reminder of the moral potentials that are inherent in the present phase of global interconnectedness. Those movements provide an alternative source of identification to the nation-state, a common point of reference for emergent transnational publics, and an obvious means of converting any sense of the limitations of particular ways of life into universal structures of consciousness that bring 'higher' and 'lower' loyalties together in new forms of political community.

It is useful to consider the potential significance of those phenomena for the future development of the global economic and political system. As noted earlier, some observers have argued that transnational advocacy networks enjoy most success when there is clear evidence of distant suffering, and a widely shared account of the forces that caused it. That observation about transnational movements draws attention to the role that specific harm narratives can play in encouraging the members of different societies to support humanitarian endeavours. It suggests how at least partial inroads into the dominant social moralities have been made, and how the idea of world citizenship and the elements of a global conscience can be combined – however slowly – with existing loyalties to particular national groups.

Universal social movements promote specific narratives that connect explanations of the causes of relievable suffering in particular places with concrete programmes of action. They are not in the business of supplying grand narratives that have the different purpose of understanding how the species evolved over very long-term intervals. Some movements may distrust such sweeping historical accounts, fearing the consequences of replacing 'totalizing' national narratives with accounts that purportedly address the whole of humanity but remain trapped within particular cultural horizons and reflect quite specific moral standpoints and political interests. On that argument, efforts to promote a transition from the narrative forms that have contributed to the success of nation-states to 'universal' representations of the past that identify common ground between all members of the species should probably be resisted.

Different strands of critical theory have explained what is at stake in debates about collective narrations that aim to support community and solidarity. Moving to ground that has not been central to those discussions, it is important to ask whether transnational movements owe any of their success to grand narratives that have analysed the evolution of humanity over thousands of years, and particularly to celebrated works that have brought long-term changes in the relations between human societies and nature during the current inter-glacial period to the attention of mass publics, encouraging in the process greater detachment from national horizons and greater identification with humanity as a whole, but also promoting reflections on long-term political projects that may be critical for future well-being and survival (Diamond 1997, 2005). It is possible that some parallels between the outlooks of many international non-governmental organizations (that address specific social and political problems) and proliferating grand narratives (that deal with thousands of years of social and political evolution) are now sufficiently extensive to suggest that subtle cultural shifts with significant cosmopolitan potential are taking place at least around the edges of the *habitus* of large numbers of people in many regions. Current interest in ideas of world or cosmopolitan citizenship, good international citizenship and global environmental citizenship might be regarded as evidence of an emerging recognition of the need for new moral and political concepts, new combinations of local and global loyalties, and new orientations to other people and towards nature, in the context of ever-advancing global interconnectedness. Such sensibilities (which are part of the everyday experience of many people in different cultures) may signify the emergence of a world society where common reference-points are found in an awareness of the urgent need for exercising more than limited control over processes that now affect the whole of humanity.

At the core of those beliefs is an awareness of the need to rein in the power to harm, an orientation towards the world that is tied up with a deeper understanding of the evolution of that human capacity over many thousands of years of social and political change, and with a greater appreciation of the inter-related problems it creates for societies today. Different forms of harm have encouraged the development of universal structures of consciousness with significant cosmopolitan potential. They include shock and revulsion at the useless violence of the First World War, fear of the possible consequences of using the most destructive instruments of violence not only for the adversaries involved but for the species and the fragile biosphere on which it depends, a precariousness that has become all the more apparent to people everywhere with evidence of increasing, and possibly irreversible, global warming. Indeed global environmental challenges may prove to have a greater impact than has the nuclear revolution on the dominant moral codes and their distinctions between insiders and outsiders. That is not because those challenges will necessarily turn out to be a greater threat to human society and survival, but because the effects may be more tangible for hundreds of millions of people, or they may seem more directly connected than was the nuclear threat with the realities of everyday life, and more easily linked with beliefs about how alterations to daily routines might yet alter the course of events if they are repeated globally and sustained for long periods, and if they are accompanied by major changes in social organization and public policy. Also important for repairing damaged human self-images is the late realization that societies must take vigorous action to protect non-human species from astonishing success in accumulating sufficient destructive power to cause permanent change to the environment.

No one can be certain that those developments will generate a substantial rise in 'world identification'. Explanations of how preoccupations with short-term interests may undermine collective responses to global challenges with potentially disastrous results are not hard to come by. But the immanent possibilities for individual and collective identities that grant a more central role to ideas of world citizenship, and which recognize that there is more to politics than protecting the interests of co-nationals, are to be found in the widespread realization that the species has entered, or may be rapidly approaching, a critical stage in its development, if not the 'point of no return'.

Studies of long-term processes of social development can complement the efforts by transnational advocacy networks to promote appropriate conceptions of global moral and political responsibility. Complementarity hinges on their respective harm narratives, with 'world history' focusing on the collective learning that has shaped the evolution of the power to harm over the millennia (and on the largely responsive civilizing processes), while analyses of suffering in specific locations identify constellations of power that prevent people from enjoying the freedom from threats and insecurities that is now widely regarded as their natural right. Complementarity refers to their reciprocal relationship. Large-scale harm narratives can shed light on the patterns of social and political development that have led to the problems that advocacy networks wrestle with in particular places. The latter's preoccupations are unlikely to be intelligible unless they are placed within those longer-term developmental processes. But to turn the point around, specific harm narratives that aim to understand specific locales can point to the difficulties in conceptualizing broader transformations; they can connect warnings about the inherent dangers of totalizing narratives with an emphasis on how the success of practical measures to reduce harm depends on a particular sensitivity to distinctive relationships in different locales, and to diverse ties between local arrangements and global power structures and processes.

Investigations of long-term change encourage a degree of detachment from immediate preoccupations so that societies can confront the scale of the cultural change that is needed to promote the humane governance of lengthening webs of interconnectedness – and to improve the prospects that progress in implementing a cosmopolitan harm principle can keep pace with further advances in strategic learning. Such narratives draw attention to the ingenuity with respect to the power to hurt that was crucial for the early success of the species – when even its survival was far from guaranteed – and which allowed it to triumph over other species (that may have included other hominid groups) at that evolutionary point when its dominance over rivals was far from assured. Such representations of the human past explain inventiveness in refining the capacity to harm in ways that ensured the 'survival of the fittest' in struggles between communities. They cast light on the extraordinary dimensions of social evolution that have been analysed by process sociologists – the overall trend towards ever larger monopolies of power, the formation of longer social webs within and between highly pacified territories, and significant shifts in emotional identification and in reworking insider–outsider dualisms.

Reconstructed grand narratives have therefore promoted public recognition of the long development of the destructive power that gave humans their preeminent position on the planet, continuing the process of eliminating other species that appeared alongside the first experiments in complex forms of social and political organization, and now bending back on the species itself as more communities are exposed to the danger of climate change. Such analyses of global interconnectedness have extended earlier studies of how lengthening chains have brought prosperity to some social strata, and poverty, vulnerability and dependence to others. In dismantling what proved to be short-lived beliefs that science and technology can guarantee security and happiness, they have stressed the increased capacity for destructive violence following the diffusion of state-organized societies to all areas of the world, and they have highlighted the 'democratization' of the ability to inflict harm over greater distances (as a result of the proliferation of destructive weaponry, and the emergence of subnational and transnational political forces that can harness new technologies to organize acts of terror in different societies). Spanning those inquiries is a growing realization in some quarters of how continuing loyalties to traditional survival units have lagged behind the forces that have led to the current phase of global integration. Shortfalls in learning how to become better attuned to the interests of people over greater distances continue to delay the regulation of uncontrolled processes, an ideal that remains one of the most important legacies of the Enlightenment.

Narratives that have focused on the history of ingenious ways of exercising power and inflicting harm, and a corresponding decline in confidence in the 'project of Enlightenment', may generate fatalism and feelings of hopelessness. They have certainly undermined false optimism about human possibilities, and created enduring suspicions that emancipatory visions contained potentials for repression that their exponents failed to grasp or did not take seriously. The thesis that societies simply lurch from one form of domination to another, and the belief that there is little evidence of progress outside the technological sphere, hardly encourage optimism about the future – although, in Toynbee's case, such images of the past were combined with the advocacy of fundamental global change and, in Foucault's writings, with support for particular struggles and modes of resistance. But complex questions remain about the relationship between cosmopolitan aspirations and the dominant forms of social learning and patterns of change – about whether the former are utopian ideals that jar with the main historical trends, whether they will continue to orbit above them until the sense of an impending crisis forces political actors to incorporate them in their strategies for survival, and about whether they are immanent in actual social relations – that is, part of the identity of an increasing number of people who are willing to support responses to global problems that do not compromise cosmopolitan ethical ideals.

The 'harm narrative' that may come to command greater support in different parts of the world tends towards a negative utopianism – to the aspiration to see an end to particular systems of domination, oppression and exploitation rather than to try to breathe new life into one of the discredited visions of human reconciliation that depended on a naïve faith in perfectibility. Certainly, those who support a utopia of shared aversions need not flinch from defending a narrative of partial progressions over the last two centuries that focuses on, amongst other things, the abolition of the Atlantic slave trade and colonial slavery, struggles to end other imperial cruelties and imperial domination itself, the expansion of international society to include all peoples who have organized themselves as states, measures to combat racism, genocide and torture, and related steps to embed egalitarian and universalistic commitments in cosmopolitan harm conventions that are designed to protect important, if still limited, human rights.

Those developments may not be permanent; they face reversal when fears for security and survival intensify. They may not suspend the usual practices of international politics, or dramatically alter what some regard as their 'propelling principles' over many millennia. They may struggle, or fail, to keep pace with changes in other sectors of social and political life. Moreover, practical success in many of those areas (such as ending the overseas European empires) may have owed less to humanitarian motives than to the pragmatic recognition that political concessions and compromises were necessary to appease disruptive groups; such advances may have occurred because dominant social groups cared as much, if not more, for upholding their civilized self-image and belief in their basic decency as for the plight of people elsewhere. Nevertheless, universal and egalitarian legal and moral norms provide national and transnational actors with crucial resources that can be harnessed in struggles to reduce or eradicate pointless and relievable harm. They make it possible for such groups to combine visions of the moral obligations and responsibilities of world citizens with a realistic assessment of potentials for inventing new ways of inflicting harm.

It may be that such collective reflections on the power to harm are essential for global political progress, precisely because societies are not poised to agree on positive images of the good life. The achievement of higher levels of moral and political universality has been slow to occur, and remains brittle. Securing them and promoting further advances may depend on growing support for the forms of grand narrative that were outlined earlier. Far from being incompatible with the 'project of the Enlightenment', that conjecture draws on an approach to the human past that can be traced back to late eighteenth-century European political thought, and is perhaps nowhere more evident than in Kant's 'Copernican revolution' that considered the problem of harm in world politics from the vantage-point of universal history (Kant 1970a [1784], 1970b [1795]).

How much of Kant's grand narrative remains relevant for the contemporary project of cosmopolitanism is too complex a matter to discuss here. It is more important to stress that Kant recognized the transformative effect of rising levels of human interconnectedness, that he was prescient in recognizing the need to shift the focus of political analysis from the state to humanity, and that he devised a universal ethical framework that addressed the problem of how people could become more accountable to one another over greater distances. It is important to recall that such cosmopolitan aspirations were not anchored in rose-tinted images of society and politics. As noted earlier, Kant observed melancholically that history is as much a monument to folly and puerile destructiveness as to noble and civilized qualities. Feelings of disgust and revulsion could be reduced through progress in granting all people the right to be free from unnecessary harm – although such emotions would have been avoided had humans incorporated that principle in their social and political relations from the earliest times. The compulsions of interdependence forced the realization – at least amongst the more enlightened – that respect for what had long been regarded as an optional ethical principle, at least as far as relations with outsiders were concerned, had become essential for future success in learning how to co-exist with the minimum of violent and non-violent harm.

That is not to suggest that Kant believed that the species should limit its ambitions to curbing harm, or that he assumed that there was little point trying to encourage benevolence in human affairs. There is, in any case, more to the harm principle than 'negative' duties to refrain from causing mental suffering, physical injury and other 'setbacks' to core interests. 'Positive' obligations are also involved, including dismantling unjust global institutions and establishing systems of accountability that give vulnerable groups voice and representation wherever decisions are taken that may harm them. Related sentiments are evident in Kant's claim that heads of state are obliged to publicize the maxims on which they plan to act in universal political arrangements that work to ensure that societies do not harm each other unnecessarily. That cosmopolitan ideal reflects Kant's overall approach to the ambiguities of interconnectedness – to the reality that the material and cultural benefits of global commerce, and the ability to assist distant strangers by bringing human rights abuses to the attention of the whole world, have been accompanied by unprecedented opportunities for causing evil in remote areas. In short, dismay at the genius of the species in inventing new ways of causing harm was combined with some confidence in its capacity to undergo a long civilizing process that would enable political communities to live together with no more harm than is necessary for the survival of decent social and political relationships. That confidence was linked with the idea that growing interconnectedness raises the cost of thinking and acting differently.

Kant's focus on universal history had the explicit aim of promoting identification with the entire species. Analysing long-term developments was designed to support cosmopolitan structures of consciousness. In more recent times, some world historians have echoed those sentiments by stating that an appreciation of the labours of humanity can help foster the moral aspiration to end the lethality of inter-group encounters. They point the way to combining accounts of the history of the power to harm, and analyses of efforts to curb the aptitude and appetite for causing harm, with ethical reflections on the global civilizing process that humans must undergo if they are to live without war, domination, exploitation, humiliation and so forth. Whether the contemporary society of states has an unusual capacity to promote such advances is a contested issue. Promising signs have been noted, including international legal developments that make universal vulnerabilities the basis of support for a cosmopolitan harm principle, and transnational movements that make resistance to pointless harm a central aspiration. Those cosmopolitan breakthroughs suggest that a principal feature of world society is the growing number of people in different locales with a recognizably similar 'harm narrative'. One can only speculate about how far such narratives will give rise to universal orientations that can alter the course of history over approximately the last 6,000 years. Placing such contemporary developments in long-term perspective clarifies the ethical issues that are at stake, ensuring that the more optimistic interpretations of future possibilities are not detached from realistic assessments of the likely tensions and clashes between civilizing and decivilizing processes in the period that lies ahead.

BIBLIOGRAPHY

Adcock, M., White, R. and Hollows, A. (1989) *Significant Harm: Its Management and Outcome*. Croydon: Significant Publications.

Adler, E. and Barnett, M. (eds.) (1998) *Security Communities*. Cambridge: Cambridge University Press.

Adorno, T. (1973) *Negative Dialectics*. London: Routledge.

(2000) *Problems of Moral Philosophy*. Cambridge: Polity Press.

Agamben, G. (1998) *Homo Sacer: Sovereign Power and Bare Life*. Stanford: Stanford University Press.

Ahmed, F. E., Harris, N., Braithwaite, J. and Braithwaite, V. (eds.) (2001) *Shame Management Through Integration*. Cambridge: Cambridge University Press.

Aho, J. (1981) *Religious Mythology and the Art of War: Comparative Religious Symbolisms of Military Violence*. London: Aldwych Press.

Aiken, W. and La Follette, H. (eds.) (1977) *World Hunger and Moral Obligation*. Englewood Cliffs, NJ: Prentice Hall.

Alderson, K. and Hurrell, A. (eds.) (2000) *Hedley Bull on International Society*. London: Macmillan.

Amore, R. C. (1996) 'Peace and Non-Violence in Buddhism'. In Dyck 1996.

Anderson, P. (1974) *Lineages of the Absolutist State*. London: New Left Books.

Apfel, R. J. and Simon, B. (eds.) (1996) *Minefields in their Hearts: The Mental Health of Children in War and Communal Violence*. New Haven: Yale University Press.

Arendt, H. (1994) *Eichmann in Jerusalem*. Harmondsworth: Penguin.

Aries, P. (1974) *Western Attitudes Toward Death in Western Thought: From the Middle Ages to the Present*. London: Johns Hopkins University Press.

Aristotle (1955) *Ethics*. Harmondsworth: Penguin.

Armstrong, D. (1993) *Revolution and World Order: The Revolutionary State in International Society*. Oxford: Clarendon Press.

Armstrong, K. (2004) 'Through the Tears', *The Guardian*, 9 October.

Arneson, R. (1998) 'The Priority of the Right over the Good Rides Again'. In Kelly 1998.

Aronfreed, J. (1968) *Conduct and Conscience: The Socialization of Internalised Control Over Behavior*. London: Academic Press.

Asad, T. (1997) 'On Torture, or Cruel, Inhuman and Degrading Treatment'. In Kleinman *et al.* 1997.

Ashworth, J. (1987) 'The Relationship Between Capitalism and Humanitarianism', *American Historical Review*, 92 (2), 813–28.

Augustine (1972) *Concerning the City of God against the Pagans*. Harmondsworth: Penguin.

Baard, E. (2003) 'The No Mourning After Pill', *The Times*, 10 July.

Baldry, H. C. (1965) *The Unity of Mankind in Greek Thought*. Cambridge: Cambridge University Press.

Banner, S. (2002) *The Death Penalty: An American History*. Harvard: Harvard University Press.

Barbalet, J. (1998) *Emotion, Social Theory and Social Structure: A Macrosociological Approach*. Cambridge: Cambridge University Press.

Barbalet, J. (ed.) (2002) *Emotions and Sociology*. Oxford: Blackwell.

Barbu, Z. (1960) *Problems of Historical Psychology*. London: Routledge and Kegan Paul.

Barkan, E. (2000) *The Guilt of Nations: Restitution and Negotiating Historical Injustices*. London: Johns Hopkins University Press.

Barker-Benfield, G. J. (1992) *The Culture of Sensibility: Sex and Society in Eighteenth-Century Europe*. Chicago: University of Chicago Press.

Barry, B. (1980) 'Review of L. S. Scheleff, The Bystander: Behavior, Law, Ethics', *Ethics*, 90 (4), 457–62.

(1995) *Justice as Impartiality*. Oxford: Oxford University Press.

Bauman, Z. (1989) *Modernity and the Holocaust*. Cambridge: Polity Press.

(1993) *PostModern Ethics*. Oxford: Blackwell

Baumeister, L. (1997) *Evil: Inside Human Violence and Cruelty*. New York: W. W. Freeman.

Baylis, J. and Smith, S. (eds.) (2001) *The Globalization of World Politics*. Oxford: Oxford University Press.

Beck L. W. (1963) *Kant on History*. Indiana: Bobbs–Merrill.

Beck, U. (1992) *Risk Society: Towards a New Modernity*. London: Sage.

(2002) 'The Cosmopolitan Society and its Enemies', *Theory, Culture and Society*, 19 (1–2), 17–44.

Bendelow, G. and Williams, S. (eds.) (1998) *Emotions in Social Life: Critical Themes and Contemporary Issues*. London: Routledge.

Bending, L. (2000) *The Representation of Bodily Pain in Late Nineteenth Century English Culture*. Oxford: Oxford University Press.

Benhabib, S. (1993) *Situating the Self: Gender, Community and Postmodernism in Contemporary Ethics*. Cambridge: Polity Press.

Benhabib, S., BonB, Wolfgang and McCole, John (eds) (1993) *On Max Horkheimer: New Perspectives*. Cambridge: MIT Press.

Bentham, J. (1970) [1789] *The Principles of Morals and Legislation*. Darien, CT: Hafner.

Bergh, G. van Benthem van den (1992) *The Nuclear Revolution and the End of the Cold War: Forced Restraint*. Basingstoke: Macmillan.

Bernstein, J. M. (2002) *Adorno: Disenchantment and Ethics*. Cambridge: Cambridge University Press.

Bernstein, M. H. (1998) *On Moral Considerability: An Essay on Who Matters Morally*. Oxford: Oxford University Press.

Bleiker, R. (2009) *Aesthetics and World Politics*. Basingstoke: Palgrave Macmillan.

Bleiker, R. and Hutchison, E. (2008) 'Fear no More: Emotions and World Politics', *Review of International Studies*, 34 (special issue), 115–35.

Blomert, R. (2002) 'Re-Civilizing Processes as a Mission of the International Community', *Figurations: Newsletter of the Norbert Elias Foundation, 17* (available at: http://elias-i.nsfhost.com/elias/figs.htm).

Blowfield, M. and Frynas, J. G. (eds.) (2005) 'Critical Perspectives on Corporate Social Responsibility', *International Affairs*, 81 (3).

Blum, L. (1980) 'Compassion'. In Rorty 1980.

Bobbit, P. (2003) *The Shield of Achilles: War, Peace and the Course of History*. London: Penguin.

Boeckmann, R. J. and Turpin-Petrosino, C. (eds.) (2002) 'Understanding the Harm of Hate Crime', *Journal of Social Issues*, 58 (2).

Bogner, A. (1987) 'Elias and the Frankfurt School', *Theory, Culture and Society*, 4 (2–3), 249–85.

Bohman, J. (1999) 'Critical Theory and Democracy'. In Rasmussen 1999.

Boli, J. and Thomas, G. (eds.) (1999) *Constructing World Culture: International Non-Governmental Organisations since 1875*. Stanford: Stanford University Press.

Booth, K. (2001a) 'Ten Flaws of Just Wars'. In Booth (2001b).

Booth, K. (ed.) (2001b) *The Kosovo Tragedy: The Human Rights Dimensions*. London: Frank Cass.

Booth, K. (ed.) (2005) *Critical Security Studies and World Politics*. Boulder, CO: Lynne Rienner.

Booth, K. (2008) *Theory of World Security*. Cambridge: Cambridge University Press.

Booth, K. and Dunne, T. (eds.) (2002) *Worlds in Collision*. Basingstoke: Palgrave Macmillan.

Booth, K. and Wheeler, N. J. (2008) *The Security Dilemma: Fear, Cooperation and Trust*. Basingstoke: Palgrave Macmillan.

Bourke, J. (1999) *An Intimate History of Killing: Face-to-Face Killing in Twentieth-Century Violence*. London: Granta Books.

Bourne, J. (2001) 'The Life and Times of Institutional Racism', *Race and Class*, 43 (2), 7–22.

Bowden, B. and Seabrooke, L. (eds.) (2006) *Global Standards of Market Civilization*. London: Routledge.

Bowker, J. (1975) *Problems of Suffering in the Religions of the World*. Cambridge: Cambridge University Press.

(1997) 'Religions, Suffering and Society'. In Kleinman *et al.* 1997.

Box, S. (1983) *Power, Crime and Mystification*. London: Tavistock.

Bradley, F. H. (1962) *Ethical Studies*. Oxford: Oxford University Press.

Bratspies, R. M. and Miller, R. A. (eds.) (2006) *Transboundary Harm in International Law: Lessons from the Trail Smelter Arbitration*. Cambridge: Cambridge University Press.

Braudel, F. (1982) *Civilization and Capitalism, 15th-18th Century (volume 2), The Wheels of Commerce*. London: William Collins.

Bremmer, J. and Roodenburg, H. (eds.) (1991) *A Cultural History of Gestures*. Cambridge: Polity Press.

Breuer, S. (1993) 'The Long Friendship: On Theoretical Differences between Adorno and Horkheimer'. In Benhabib *et al.* 1993.

Brewer, M. B. and Hewstone, M. (eds.) (2004) *Emotion and Motivation*. Oxford: Blackwell.

Briant, P. (1999) 'The Achaemenid Empire'. In Raaflaub and Rosenstein 1999.

Brissenden, R. F. (1974) *Virtue in Distress*. London: Macmillan.

Brown, C. (1988) 'The Modern Requirement? Reflections on Normative International Theory in a Post Western World', *Millennium*, 17 (2), 339–48.

Brown, D. E. (1991) *Human Universals*. New York: McGraw-Hill.

Brown, R. M. (1990) 'The Holocaust as a Problem in Moral Choice'. In Wiesel *et al.* 1990.

Brown, P. G. and Shue, H. (eds.) (1981) *Boundaries: National Autonomy and its Limits*. Totowa, NJ: Rowman and Littlefield.

Bull, H. (1977) *The Anarchical Society: A Study of Order in World Politics*. London: Macmillan.

(1979a) 'Human Rights and World Politics'. In Pettman 1979.

(1979b) 'The State's Positive Role in World Affairs'. In Alderson and Hurrell 2000.

Bull, H. (ed.) (1984a) *Intervention in World Politics*. Oxford: Clarendon Press.

Bull, H. (1984b) 'European States and African Political Communities'. In Bull and Watson 1984.

(2000) 'Justice in International Relations'. In Alderson and Hurrell 2000. Originally published in 1984 as *The Hagey Lectures*, University of Waterloo, Ontario.

Bull, H. and Watson, A. (eds.) (1984) *The Expansion of International Society*. Oxford: Clarendon Press.

Burguiere, A. (1982) 'The Fate of the History of *Mentalities* in the *Annales*', *Comparative Studies in Society and History*, 24 (4), 424–37.

Burke, E. (1960) *The Philosophy of Edmund Burke: A Selection from his Speeches and Writings*. Ann Arbor: University of Michigan Press.

(1990) [1757] *A Philosophical Enquiry into the Origin of our Ideas of the Sublime and the Beautiful*. Oxford: Oxford University Press.

Burke, P. (ed.) (1973) *A New Kind of History from the Writings of Lucien Febvre*. London: Routledge and Kegan Paul.

Burke, P. (1993) *The Art of Conversation*. Cambridge: Polity Press.

(2003) 'The Annales, Braudel and Historical Sociology'. In Delanty and Isin 2003.

Burke, P., Harrison, B. and Slack, P. (eds.) (2000) *Civil Histories: Essays Presented to Sir Keith Thomas*. Cambridge: Cambridge University Press.

Butler, J. (2002) 'Universality in Culture'. In Nussbaum 2002.

(2004) *Precarious Lives: The Powers of Mourning and Violence*. London: Verso.

Butterfield, H. (1953) *Christianity, Diplomacy and War*. London: Epworth Press.

Butterfield, H. and Wight, M. (eds.) (1966) *Diplomatic Investigations: Essays in the Theory of International Politics*. London: Allen and Unwin.

Buzan, B. (1993) 'From International System to International Society: Structural Realism and Regime Theory meet the English School', *International Organization*, 47 (3), 327–52.

(2004) *From International to World Society? English School Theory and the Social Structure of Globalisation*. Cambridge: Cambridge University Press.

(2010) 'Culture and International Society', *International Affairs*, 86 (1), 1–25.

Buzan, B. and Little, R. (2000) *International Systems in World History: Remaking the Study of International Relations*. Oxford: Oxford University Press.

(2001) 'Why International Relations has Failed as an Intellectual Project and What to Do About It', *Millennium*, 30 (1), 19–39.

(2002) 'International Systems in World History: Remaking the Study of International Relations'. In Hobden and Hobson 2002.

Calhoun, C. (ed.) (1994) *Social Theory and the Politics of Identity*. Oxford: Blackwell.

Carman, J. (ed.) (1997) *Material Harm: Archaeological Studies of War and Violence*. Glasgow: Cruithne Press.

Carman, J. and Harding, A. (eds.) (1999) *Ancient Warfare: Archaeological Perspectives*. Stroud: Sutton.

Carneiro, R. L. (1970) 'A Theory of the Origin of the State', *Science*, 169, 733–8.

(1986) 'Political Expansion as an Expression of the Principle of Competitive Exclusion'. In Cohen and Service 1986.

Carr, E. H. (1945) *Nationalism and After*. London: Macmillan.

(2001) *The Twenty Years' Crisis 1919–1939*. Basingstoke: Palgrave.

Carrasco, D. (1999) *City of Sacrifice: The Aztec Empire and the Role of Violence in Civilization*. Boston: Beacon Press.

Chang, I. (1997) *The Rape of Nanking*. London Penguin.

Chapman, J. (1999) 'The Origins of War in Central and Eastern Europe'. In Carman and Harding 1999.

Childress, J. F. (1974) 'Reinhold Niehbur's Critique of Pacifism', *Review of Politics*, 36 (4), 467–91.

Cicero (1967) *On Obligation*. London: Faber and Faber.

Cioffi-Revilla, C. and Landmann, T. (1999) 'Evolution of Maya Polities in the Ancient Mesoamerican System', *International Studies Quarterly*, 43 (4), 559–98.

Clark, I. (2005) *Legitimacy and International Society*. Oxford: Oxford University Press.

(2007) *International Legitimacy and World Society*. Oxford: Oxford University Press.

Claude, I. (1969) *National Minorities: An International Problem*. London: Greenwood Press.

Clausewitz, C. von (1989) [1832] *On War*. Princeton: Princeton University Press.

Clement, G. (1996) *Care, Autonomy and Justice: Feminism and the Ethic of Care*. London: Westview Press.

Cohen, E. (1996) 'The Hundred Years' War and Crime in Paris: 1332–1488'. In Johnson and Monkkonen 1996.

Cohen, S. (2001) *States of Denial: Knowing about Atrocities and Suffering*. Cambridge: Polity Press.

Cohen, R. and Service, E. (eds.) (1986) *Origins of the State*. Philadelphia: Institute for the Study of Human Institutions.

Collins, R. (1974) 'Three Faces of Cruelty: Towards a Comparative Sociology of Violence', *Theory and Society*, 1 (4), 415–40.

Connell, R. W. (1995) *Masculinities*. Berkeley: University of California Press.

Cook, M. (2000) *Commanding Right and Forbidding Wrong in Islam*. Cambridge: Cambridge University Press.

Cooley, C. (1998) *On Self and Social Organization*. Chicago: University of Chicago Press.

Corbin, A. (1996) *The Foul and the Flagrant: Odour and the Social Imagination*. London: Macmillan.

Crawford, J. (2002a) *The International Law Commission's Articles on State Responsibility*. Cambridge: Cambridge University Press.

Crawford, N. C. (2001) 'The Passions of World Politics: Propositions on Emotions and Emotional Relationships', *International Security*, 24 (4), 116–56.

(2002b) *Argument and Change in World Politics: Ethics, Decolonization and Humanitarian Intervention*. Cambridge: Cambridge University Press.

Crosby, A. (1986) *Ecological Imperialism: The Biological Expansion of Europe, 900–1900*. Cambridge: Cambridge University Press.

Crossley, N. (1998) 'Emotion and Communicative Action: Habermas, Linguistic Philosophy and Existentialism'. In Bendelow and Williams 1998.

Csordas, T. J. (ed.) (1994) *Embodiment and Experience: The Existential Ground of Culture and the Self*. Cambridge: Cambridge University Press.

Cunningham, A. (2001) *The Heart of What Matters: The Role for Literature in Moral Philosophy*. Berkeley: University of California Press.

Curtin, P. D. (1984) *Cross-Cultural Trade in World History*. Cambridge: Cambridge University Press.

Dallmayr, F. (2001) 'Conversation Across Boundaries: Political Theory and Global Diversity', *Millennium*, 30 (2), 331–47.

Dan-Cohen, M. (2002) *Harmful Thoughts: Essays on Law, Self, and Thoughts*. Princeton: Princeton University Press.

Darnton, R. (2001) *The Great Cat Massacre and Other Episodes in French Cultural History*. London: Penguin.

Davis, B. D. (1970) *The Problem of Slavery in Western Culture*. Harmondsworth: Pelican.

Davis, W. (ed.) (2001) *Taking Responsibility: Comparative Perspectives*. London: University Press of Virginia.

Dawson, D. (1996) *The Origins of Western Warfare: Militarism and Morality in the Ancient World*. Boulder, CO: Westview Press.

De Maistre, J. (1965) *The Works of Joseph de Maistre*. London: George Allen and Unwin.

De-Shalit, A. (1998) 'Transnational and International Exploitation', *Political Studies*, 46 (4), 693–708.

De Sousa, R. (1987) *Rationality of the Emotions*. Cambridge, MA: MIT Press.

Deigh, J. (1983) 'Shame and Self-Esteem: A Critique', *Ethics*, 93, 225–45.

Delanty, G. and Isin, E. (eds.) (2003) *Handbook of Historical Sociology*. Oxford: Sage.

Denemark, R. A., Friedman, J., Gills, B. K. and Modelski, G. (eds.) (2000) *World System History: The Social Science of Long-Term Change*. London: Routledge.

Deutsch, K. (1970) *Political Community in the North Atlantic Area*. London: Archon Books.

Diamond, J. (1997) *Guns, Germs and Steel: A Short History of Everybody for the Last 13,000 Years*. London: Jonathan Cape.

(2005) *Collapse: How Societies Choose to Fail or Survive*. London: Viking Penguin.

Dibblin, J. (1988) *Day of Two Suns: US Nuclear Testing and the Pacific Islanders*. London: Virago.

Dillon, R. (1992) 'Respect and Care: Toward Moral Integration', *Canadian Journal of Philosophy*, 22 (1), 105–32.

Divale, W. T. and Harris, M. (1976) 'Population, Warfare and the Male Supremacist Complex', *American Anthropologist*, 78 (3), 521–38.

Dobson, A. (2003) 'States, Citizens and the Environment'. In Skinner and Strath 2003.

(2005) 'Globalisation, Cosmopolitanism and the Environment', *International Relations*, 19 (3), 259–73.

(2006) 'Thick Cosmopolitanism', *Political Studies*, 54 (1), 165–84.

Dobson, A. and Eckersley, R. (eds.) (2006) *Political Theory and the Ecological Challenge*. Cambridge: Cambridge University Press.

Donelan, M. D. (1990) *Elements of International Political Theory*. Oxford: Clarendon Press.

Dovidio, J. F. and Penner, L. A. (2004) 'Helping and Altruism'. In Brewer and Hewstone 2004.

Duchesne, R. (2005) 'Centres and Margins: The Fall of Universal History and the Rise of Multicultural World History'. In Hughes-Warrington 2005.

Dunne, T. (2003) 'Society and Hierarchy in International Relations', *International Relations*, 17 (3), 303–20.

Dunne, T. and Wheeler, N. J. (eds.) (1999) *Human Rights in Global Politics*. Cambridge: Cambridge University Press.

Dunning, E. (1986) 'Preface'. In Elias and Dunning 2008b.

   (2008) 'Social Bonding and Violence in Sport'. In Elias and Dunning 2008b.

Dunning, E. and Mennell, S. (1998) 'Elias on Germany, Nazism and the Holocaust: On the Balance between "Civilizing and Decivilizing Trends"', *British Journal of Sociology*, 49 (3), 339–57.

Dunning, E. and Mennell, S. (eds.) (2003) *Norbert Elias*, vol. I, London: Sage.

Durkheim, E. (1993) *Ethics and the Sociology of Morals*. New York: Prometheus Books.

Dyck, H. L. (ed.) (1996) *The Pacifist Impulse in Historical Perspective*. London: University of Toronto Press.

Eaton, L. D. and Guddat, K. H. (eds.) (1967) *Writings of the Young Marx on Philosophy and Society*. New York: Anchor Books.

Eckersley, R. (2004) *The Green State: Rethinking Democracy and Sovereignty*. Cambridge, MA: MIT Press.

   (2006) 'Communitarianism'. In Dobson and Eckersley 2006.

Edelman, N. (1990) 'Global Prohibition Regimes: The Evolution of Norms in International Society', *International Organization*, 44 (4), 479–526.

Edkins, J. (2003) *Trauma and the Memory of Politics*. Cambridge: Cambridge University Press.

Eisenstadt, S. (1963) *The Political System of Empires*. New York: Free Press.

Ekman, P. and Friesen, W. V. (1998) 'Constants across Culture in the Face and Emotion'. In Jenkins *et al.* 1998.

Elias, N. (1978) *What is Sociology?* New York: Columbia University Press.

   (1990) 'Further Aspects of Established-Outsider Relations: The Maycomb Model'. In Elias and Scotson 2008.

   (1991) *The Symbol Theory*. London: Sage.

   (1994) *Reflections on a Life*. Cambridge: Polity Press.

   (1996) *The Germans: Power Struggles and the Development of Habitus in the Nineteenth and Twentieth Centuries*. Cambridge: Polity Press.

   (1998) 'An Interview in Amsterdam'. In Goudsblom and Mennell 1998.

   (2000) *The Civilizing Process: Sociogenetic and Psychogenetic Investigations*. Oxford: Blackwell.

   (2001a) *The Loneliness of the Dying*. London: Continuum.

   (2001b) *The Society of Individuals*. London: Continuum.

   (2006a) 'The Expulsion of the Huguenots from France'. In Elias 2006c.

   (2006b) 'On Seeing in Nature'. In Elias 2006c.

   (2006c) *Early Writings*. Dublin: University College Dublin Press. [Collected Works, vol. I].

(2006d) *The Court Society*. Dublin: University College Dublin Press. [Collected Works, vol. II].

(2007a) [1987] *Involvement and Detachment*. Dublin: University College Dublin Press. [Collected Works, vol. VIII].

(2007b) [1992] *An Essay on Time*. Dublin: University College Dublin Press. [Collected Works, vol. IX].

(2008a) 'The Genesis of Sport as a Social Problem: Part One'. In Elias and Dunning 2008b.

(2008b) 'The Civilising of Parents'. In N. Elias (2008) *Essays II: On Civilising Processes, State Formation and National Identity*. Dublin: University College Dublin Press. [Collected Works, vol. XV]. First published in Goudsblom and Mennell 1998.

(2008c) 'Technisation and Civilisation'. In N. Elias (2008) *Essays II: On Civilising Processes, State Formation and National Identity*. Dublin: University College Dublin Press. [Collected Works, vol. XV]. First published in *Theory, Culture and Society*, 1995, 12 (3), 18–41.

(2009a) 'Towards A Theory of Social Processes'. In N. Elias (2009) *Essays III: On Sociology and the Humanities*. Dublin: University College Dublin Press. [Collected Works, vol. XVI]. First published in *British Journal of Sociology*, 1997, 48 (3), 355–83.

(2009b) [1986] 'The Retreat of Sociologists into the Present'. In N. Elias, *Essays III: On Sociology and the Humanities*. Dublin: University College Dublin Press. [Collected Works, vol. XVI]. First published in *Theory, Culture and Society*, 1987, 4 (2–3), 223–34.

(2009c) 'On Human Beings and their Emotions: A Process-Sociological Essay'. In N. Elias (2009) *Essays III: On Sociology and the Humanities*. Dublin: University College Dublin Press. [Collected Works, vol. XV]. First published in *Theory, Culture and Society*, 1987, 4 (2–3), 339–61.

(2010) *Humana Conditio*. Dublin: University College Dublin Press. [Collected Works, vol. VI].

Elias, N. and Dunning, E. (2008a) 'Leisure in the Spare-Time Spectrum'. In Elias and Dunning 2008b. [Collected Works, vol. VII].

(2008b) [1986] *The Quest for Excitement: Sport and Leisure in the Civilizing Process*. Dublin: University College Dublin Press. [Collected Works, vol. VII].

Elias, N. and Scotson, J. L. (2008) [1994] *The Established and Outsiders: A Sociological Inquiry into Community Problems*. Dublin: University College Dublin Press. [Collected Works, vol. IV].

Elliott, L. (2006) 'Cosmopolitan Environmental Harm Conventions', *Global Society*, 20 (3), 345–63.

Elshtain, J. B. (1987) *Women and War*. Brighton: Harvester Press.

Elshtain, J. B. (ed.) (1992) *Just War Theory*. Oxford: Basil Blackwell.

Elshtain, J. B. (1999) 'Really Existing Communities', *Review of International Studies*, 25 (1), 141–6.

Elster, J. (1999) *Alchemies of the Mind: Rationality and the Emotions.* Cambridge: Cambridge University Press.

Ember, C. R. and Ember, M. (1997) 'Violence in the Ethnographic Record: Results of Cross-Cultural Research on War and Aggression'. In Martin and Frayer 1997.

Emmanuel, A. (1972) *Unequal Exchange: A Study of the Imperialism of Trade.* London: Monthly Review Press.

Engels, F. (1969a) 'Principles of Communism'. In Engels 1969b.

(1969b) *Selected Works.* Moscow: Progress Publishers.

Erskine, T. (ed.) (2003) *Institutions and Responsibility.* Basingstoke: Palgrave Macmillan.

Erskine, T. (2008) *Embedded Cosmopolitanism: Duties to Strangers and Enemies in a World of 'Dislocated Communities'* Oxford: Oxford University Press.

Evans, D. (2001) *Emotion: The Science of Sentiment.* Oxford: Oxford University Press.

Evans, M. (ed.) (1994) *International Law Documents.* London: Blackstone Press.

Evans, R. (1997) *Rituals of Retribution: Capital Punishment in Germany, 1600–1987.* Harmondsworth: Penguin.

Ewing, A. C. (1959) *Second Thoughts on Moral Philosophy.* London: Routledge and Kegan Paul.

Featherstone, M., Hepworth, M. and Turner, B. S. (eds.) (1991) *The Body: Social Process and Cultural Theory.* London: Sage.

Feinberg, J. (1973) *Social Philosophy.* Englewood Cliffs, NJ: Prentice Hall.

(1984) *Harm to Others: The Moral Limits of the Criminal Law.* Oxford: Oxford University Press.

(1985) *Offence to Others: The Moral Limits of the Criminal Law.* Oxford: Oxford University Press.

(1986) *Harm to Self: The Moral Limits of the Criminal Law.* Oxford: Oxford University Press.

(1990) *Harmless Wrongdoing: The Moral Limits of the Criminal Law.* Oxford: Oxford University Press.

(1992) *Freedom and Fulfilment: Philosophical Essays.* Princeton: Princeton University Press.

Ferguson, R. B. (1997) 'Violence and War in Prehistory'. In Martin and Frayer 1997.

(1999) 'A Paradigm for the Study of War and Society'. In Raaflaub and Rosenstein 1999.

(2000) 'The Causes and Origins of "Primitive Warfare": On Evolved Motivations for Warfare', *Anthropological Quarterly*, 73 (3), 159–64.

Finer, S. (1997) *A History of Government.* Oxford: Oxford University Press.

Finzsch, N. and Jutte, R. (1996) *Institutions of Confinement: Hospitals, Asylums and Prisons in Western Europe and North America 1500–1950.* Cambridge: Cambridge University Press.

Firestone, R. (1999) *Jihad: The Origin of Holy War in Islam*. Oxford: Oxford University Press.

Fischer, A. H. (ed.) (2000) *Gender and Emotion: Social Psychological Perspectives*. Cambridge: Cambridge University Press.

Fischer, M. (1992) 'Feudal Europe, 800–1300: Communal Discourse and Conflictual Practices', *International Organization*, 46 (2), 427–66.

Fletcher, A. (1995) *Gender, Sex and Subordination in England 1500–1800*. New Haven: Yale University Press.

Fletcher, J. (1997) *Violence and Civilisation: An Introduction to the Work of Norbert Elias*. Cambridge: Polity Press.

Foot, R. (2006) 'Torture: The Struggle over a Peremptory Norm in a Counter-Terrorist Era', *International Relations*, 20 (2), 131–51.

Forbes, I. and Hoffman, M. (eds.) (1993) *Political Theory, International Relations and the Ethics of Intervention*. London: Macmillan.

Forman-Barzilai, F. (2005) 'Sympathy in Space(s): Smith on Proximity', *Political Theory*, 33 (2), 189–217.

Forsyth, M., Keens-Soper, M. and Savigear, P. (eds.) (1970) *The Theory of International Relations: Selected Tests from Gentile to Treitschke*. London: Allen and Unwin.

Foucault, M. (1973) *Madness and Civilization: A History of Insanity in the Age of Reason*. New York: Vintage Books.

(1979) *Discipline and Punish: The Birth of the Prison*. Harmondsworth: Penguin.

(1984) 'What is Enlightenment?' In Rabinow 1984.

Frankena, W. (1963) *Ethics*. Englewood Cliffs, NJ: Prentice Hall.

Fraser, N. (2000) 'Rethinking Recognition', *New Left Review*, 3 (May–June), 107–20.

(2007) 'Transnationalizing the Public Sphere: On the Legitimacy and Efficacy of Public Opinion in a Post-Westphalian World', *Theory, Culture and Society*, 24 (4), 7–30.

Freeman, M. (2003) 'Is Limited Altruism Morally Wrong?' In Garrard and Scarre 2003.

Freud, S. (1939) *Civilisation and its Discontents*. London: Hogarth Press.

(1998) [1932] 'Why War?' In Rundell and Mennell 1998.

Gaita, R. (1994) 'Critical Notice', *Philosophical Investigations*, 17 (4), 613–28.

(2002) *A Common Humanity: Thinking about Love and Truth and Justice*. London: Routledge.

Gardiner, P. (ed.) (1975) *The Philosophy of History*. Oxford: Oxford University Press.

Garland, D. (1990) *Punishment and Modern Society: A Study in Social Theory*. Oxford: Oxford University Press.

(2000) *The Culture of Control: Crime and Social Order in Contemporary Society*. Oxford: Oxford University Press.

Garrard, E. and Scarre, G. (eds.) (2003) *Moral Philosophy and the Holocaust*. London: Ashgrave.

Gat, A. (2000) 'Reply to Ferguson', *Anthropological Quarterly*, 73 (3), 164–8.

(2006) *War in Human Civilization*. Oxford: Oxford University Press.

Gatrell, V. A. C. (1994) *The Hanging Tree: Execution and the English People, 1770–1968*. Oxford: Oxford University Press.

Gay, P. (1994) *The Cultivation of Hatred: The Bourgeois Experience*. London: Harper Collins.

(1998) *My German Question: Growing Up in Nazi Germany*. London: Yale University Press.

Geras, N. (1995) *Solidarity in the Conversation of Humankind: The Ungroundable Liberalism of Richard Rorty*. London: Verso.

(1998) *The Contract of Mutual Indifference: Political Philosophy after the Holocaust*, London: Verso.

(1999) 'The View from Everywhere', *Review of International Studies*, 25 (1), 157–63.

Gerth, H. H. and Mills, C. W. (eds.) (1948a) 'Introduction: The Man and his Work'. In Gerth and Mills 1948b.

Gerth, H. H. and Mills, C. W. (eds) (1948b) *From Max Weber: Essays in Historical Sociology*. London: Routledge and Kegan Paul.

Geuss, R. (2005) 'Suffering and Knowledge in Adorno', *Constellations*, 12 (1), 3–20.

Gibney, M. (2004) *The Ethics and Politics of Asylum: Liberal Democracy and the Response to Refugees*. Cambridge: Cambridge University Press.

Giddens, A. (1985) *The Nation-State and Violence*. Cambridge: Polity Press.

Gilbert, P. and Andrews, B. (eds.) (1998) *Shame: Interpersonal Behavior, Psychopathology and Culture*. Oxford: Oxford University Press.

Gill, S. (1995) 'Globalisation, Market Civilisation, and Disciplinary NeoLiberalism', *Millennium*, 24 (3), 399–423.

Gilligan, C. (1982) *In a Different Voice: Psychological Theory and Women's Development*. Cambridge, MA: Harvard University Press.

Glover, J. (1990) *Causing Death and Saving Lives*. Harmondsworth: Penguin.

Glucklich, A. (2001) *Sacred Pain: Hurting the Body for the Sake of the Soul*. Oxford: Oxford University Press.

Gnirs, A. M. (1999) 'Ancient Egypt'. In Raaflaub and Rosenstein 1999.

Goffman, E. (1963) *Stigma: Notes on the Management of Spoiled Identity*. London: Penguin.

Goldhagen, D. J. (1996) *Hitler's Willing Executioners: Ordinary Germans and the Holocaust*. London: Little Brown.

Goldstein, J. S. (2001) *War and Gender: How Gender Shapes the War System and Vice Versa*. Cambridge: Cambridge University Press.

Gong, G. (1984) *The Standard of Civilization in International Society*. Oxford: Clarendon Press.

Goodin, R. E. (1987) 'Exploiting a Situation and Exploiting a Person'. In Reeve 1987.

Goodin, R. E., Pateman, C. and Pateman, R. (1997) 'Simian Sovereignty', *Political Theory*, 25 (6), 821–49.

Gordon, R. S. C. (2001) *Primo Levi's Ordinary Virtues: From Testimony to Ethics.* Oxford: Oxford University Press.

Goudsblom, J. (1992) *Fire and Civilization.* London: Penguin.

(1996) 'Human History and Long-Term Social Processes: Toward a Synthesis of *Chronology* and *Phaseology*'. In Goudsblom *et al.* 1996.

(2004) 'Christian Religion and the European Civilizing Process: the Views of Norbert Elias and Max Weber Compared in the Context of the Augustinian and Lucretian Traditions'. In Loyal and Quilley 2004.

(2006) 'Pacification and the Monopolization of Organized Violence' (unpublished paper).

Goudsblom, J. and Mennell, S. (eds.) (1998) *The Norbert Elias Reader.* Oxford: Basil Blackwell.

Goudsblom, J., Jones, E. and Mennell, S. (1996) *The Course of Human History: Economic Growth, Social Process and Civilization.* London: M. E. Sharpe.

Goveia, E. V. (2000) 'The West Indian Slave Laws of the Eighteenth Century'. In Sherene and Beckles 2000.

Gray, J. (1996) *Mill on Liberty: A Defence.* London: Routledge.

Grayling, A. (2006) *Among the Dead Cities: Was the Allied Bombing of Civilians in WWII A Necessity or a Crime?* London: Bloomsbury.

Green, T. H. (1906) *Prolegomena to Ethics.* Oxford: Clarendon Press.

Greenberg, K. J. and Dratel, J. L. (eds.) (2005) *The Torture Papers.* Cambridge: Cambridge University Press.

Greenspan, P. S. (1995) *Practical Guilt: Moral Dilemmas, Emotions and Social Norms.* Oxford: Oxford University Press.

Greenwald, D. F. and Harder, D. W. (1998) 'Domains of Shame: Evolutionary, Cultural and Psychotherapeutic Aspects'. In Gilbert and Andrews 1998.

Gregor, T. (1990) 'Uneasy Peace: Intertribal Relations in Brazil's Upper Xingu'. In Haas 1990.

Grieco, J. (1988) 'Anarchy and the Limits of Cooperation: A Realist Critique of the Newest Liberal Institutionalism', *International Organization*, 42 (3), 485–507.

Grossman, D. (1996) *On Killing: The Psychological Cost of Learning to Kill in War and Society.* New York: Little Brown.

Gunder Frank, A. (1978) *Dependent Accumulation and Underdevelopment.* London: Macmillan.

Haas, J. (1990) *The Anthropology of War.* Cambridge: Cambridge University Press.

(1999) 'The Origins of War and Ethnic Violence'. In Carman and Harding 1999.

Habermas, J. (1975) *Legitimation Crisis.* Boston: Beacon Press.

(1979a) *Communication and the Evolution of Society.* London: Heinemann.

(1979b) 'History and Evolution', *Telos*, (39), 5–44.

(1987) *The Philosophical Discourse of Modernity: Twelve Lectures.* Cambridge, MA: MIT Press.

(1989) *The Theory of Communicative Action, volume two: The Critique of Functionalist Reason*. London: Heinemann.

(1990) *Moral Consciousness and Communicative Action*. Cambridge: Polity Press.

(1998a) 'Paradigms of Law'. In Rosenfeld and Arato 1998.

(1998b) 'Reply to Symposium Participants'. In Rosenfeld and Arato 1998.

Haldon, J. (1999) 'The Byzantine World'. In Raaflaub and Rosenstein 1999.

Hallpike, C. R. (1988) *The Principles of Social Evolution*. Oxford: Clarendon Press.

Halttunen, K. (1995) 'Humanitarianism and the Pornography of Pain', *American Historical Review*, 100 (2), 303–34.

Hamblin, W. J. (2006) *Warfare in the Ancient Near East to 1600BC: Holy Warriors at the Dawn of History*. Abingdon: Routledge.

Hamilton, J. B. (1963) *Political Thought in Sixteenth-Century Spain*: Oxford: Oxford University Press.

Hampson, N. (1968) *The Enlightenment: The Pelican History of European Thought 4*. Harmondsworth: Penguin.

Handl, G. (2006) '*Trail Smelter* in Contemporary International Environmental Law: Its Relevance in the Nuclear Energy Complex'. In Bratspies and Miller 2006.

Hanson, V. D. (1989) *The Western Way of War: Infantry Battle in Classical Greece*. New York: Alfred Knopf.

(2002) *Why the West has Won: Carnage and Culture from Salamis to Vietnam*. London: Faber.

Harcourt, B. E. (1999) 'The Collapse of the Harm Principle', *Journal of Criminal Law and Criminology*, 90 (1), 109–94.

Hardcastle, V. G. (1999) *The Myth of Pain*. Cambridge, MA: MIT Press.

Hare, R. M. (1963) *Freedom and Reason*. Oxford: Oxford University Press.

Harré, R. and Parrott, W. G. (eds.) (1996) *Emotions: Social, Cultural and Biological Dimensions*. London: Sage.

Harris, M (1977) *Cannibals and Kings: The Origins of Cultures*. New York: Random House.

Harris, P. (1974) 'The Marxist Conception of Violence', *Philosophy and Public Affairs*, 3 (2), 192–220.

(1989) *Children and Emotions: The Development of Psychological Understanding*. Oxford: Blackwell.

Harris, W. V. (2001) *Restraining Rage: The Ideology of Anger Control in Classical Antiquity*. Harvard: Harvard University Press.

Hart, H. L. A. (1961) *The Concept of Law*. Oxford: Oxford University Press.

(1968) *Law, Liberty and Morality*. Oxford: Oxford University Press.

Hart, H. L. A. and Honore, T. (1985) *Causation in the Law*. Oxford: Clarendon Press.

Harvey, P. (2000) *An Introduction to Buddhist Ethics*. Cambridge: Cambridge University Press.

Hashmi, S. H. (1996) 'Interpreting the Islamic Ethics of War and Peace'. In Nardin 1996.

Haskell, T. H. (1985) 'Capitalism and the Origins of the Humanitarian Sensibility', *American Historical Review*, 90 (2), 339–61 and 547–66.

Hassig, R. (1999) 'The Aztec World'. In Raaflaub and Rosenstein 1999.

Hay, D. (1992) 'War, Death and Theft in the Eighteenth Century: The Record of the English Courts', *Past and Present*, 95, 117–60.

Hegel, G. W. F. (1952) [1821] *The Philosophy of Right*. Oxford: Clarendon Press.

Held, D. (ed.) (1991) *Political Theory Today*. Cambridge: Polity Press.

Held, D. (1995) *Democracy and World Order: From the Modern State to Cosmopolitan Governance*. Cambridge: Polity Press.

Herodotus (2004) *The Persian Wars*. Cambridge, MA: Harvard University Press.

Herz, J. (1959) *International Politics in the Atomic Age*. New York: Columbia University Press.

Hill, C. J. and Smith, M. (eds.) (2010) *The International Relations of the European Union*. Oxford: Oxford University Press.

Hillyard, P., Pantazis, C., Tombs, S. and Gordon, D. (eds.) (2004) *Beyond Criminology: Taking Harm Seriously*. London: Pluto Press.

Hinnells, J. R. and Porter, R. (eds.) (1999) *Religion, Health and Suffering*. London: Kegan Paul International.

Hobbes, T. (1949) [1651] *De Cive or the Citizen*. New York: Appleton-Century-Crofts.

Hobden, S. and Hobson, J. (eds.) (2002) *Historical Sociology of International Relations*. Cambridge: Cambridge University Press.

Hobson, J. (2004) *The Eastern Origins of Western Civilization*. Cambridge: Cambridge University Press.

Hoffman, M. L. (2000) *Empathy and Moral Development: Implications for Caring and Justice*. Cambridge: Cambridge University Press.

Honderich, T. (1980) *Violence against Equality: Inquiries in Political Philosophy*. Harmondsworth: Pelican.

Honneth, A. (1995) *The Struggle for Recognition: The Moral Grammar of Social Conflicts*. Cambridge: Polity Press.

Horkheimer, M. (1974a) 'Schopenhauer Today'. In Horkheimer 1974b.

(1974b) *Critique of Instrumental Reason*. New York: Seabury.

(1993) *Between Philosophy and Social Science: Selected Early Writings*. Cambridge, MA: MIT Press.

Horwitz, G. J. (1991) *In the Shadow of Death: Living Outside the Gates of Mauthausen*. London: I. B. Tauris.

Huff, T. E. (1981) *On the Roads to Modernity: Conscience, Science and Civilizations*. Totowa, NJ: Rowman and Littlefield.

Hufton, O. (1995) *The Prospect Before Her: A History of Women in Western Europe, volume one 1550–1800*. London: HarperCollins.

Hughes-Warrington, M. (ed.) (2005) *World Histories*. Basingstoke: Palgrave Macmillan.

Huizinga, J. (1970) *Homo Ludens: A Study of the Play Element in Culture*. London: Temple Smith.

Hume, D. (1962) [1777] *An Inquiry Concerning Human Understanding*. New York: Collier Books.

   (1969) [1739–40] *A Treatise of Human Nature*. Harmondsworth: Penguin.

Hunt, L. (ed.) (1989) *The New Cultural History*. Berkeley: University of California Press.

Hurrell, A. (2007) *On Global Order: Power, Values and the Constitution of International Society*. Oxford: Oxford University Press.

Iganski, P. (ed.) (2002) *The Hate Debate: Should Hate be Punished as a Crime?* London: Profile Books.

Jackson, R. H. (2000) *The Global Covenant: Human Conduct in a World of States*. Oxford: Oxford University Press.

Jackson Preece, J. (1998) 'Ethnic Cleansing as an Instrument of Nation-State Creation: Changing State Practices and Evolving Legal Norms', *Human Rights Quarterly*, 20 (4), 817–42.

Jaspers, K. (1947) *The Question of German Guilt*. New York: Dial Press.

Jay, M. (1984) *Marxism and Totality: The Adventures of a Concept from Lukacs to Habermas*. Berkeley: University of California Press.

Jenkins, J. M., Oatley, K. and Stein, N. L. (eds.) (1998) *Human Emotions: A Reader*. Oxford: Blackwell.

John, A. (ed.) (1999) *Dreadful Visitations: Confronting Natural Catastrophe in the Age of Enlightenment*. London: Routledge.

Johnson, E. A. and Monkkonen E. H. (eds.) (1996) *The Civilization of Crime: Violence in Town and Country since the Middle Ages*. Chicago: University of Illinois Press.

Johnson, J. T. (1992) 'Threats, Values and Defense: Does the Defense of Values by Force Remain A Moral Possibility?'. In Elshtain 1992.

Jouanna, J. (1999) *Hippocrates*. Baltimore: Johns Hopkins University Press.

Kalberg, S. (1980) 'Max Weber's Types of Rationality: Cornerstones for the Analysis of Rationalisation Processes in History', *American Journal of Sociology*, 85 (5), 1145–79.

Kaldor, M. (1999) *New and Old Wars: Organized Violence in a Global Era*. Cambridge: Polity Press.

Kant, I. (1965) [1797] *The Metaphysical Principles of Virtue*. New York: Bobbs-Merrill.

   (1963) [1786] *Conjectural Beginning of Human History*. In Beck 1963.

   (1970a) [1784] 'Idea for a Universal History from a Cosmo-political Point of View'. In Forsyth *et al*. 1970.

   (1970b) [1795]'Perpetual Peace'. In Forsyth *et al*. 1970.

   (1978) [1798] *Anthropology from a Pragmatic Point of View*. London: Southern Illinois London Press.

Kapteyn, P. J. G. (1996) *The Stateless Market: The European Dilemma of Integration and Civilization*. London: Routledge.

Kapteyn, P. (2004) 'Armed Peace: On the Pacifying Condition for the "Cooperative of States"'. In Loyal and Quilley 2004.

Kaspersen, L. B. and Gabriel, N. (2008) 'The Importance of Survival Units for Norbert Elias's Figurational Perspective', *Sociological Review*, 56 (3), 370–87.

Katz, L. (1999) 'Responsibility and Consent: The Libertarian's Problems with Freedom of Contract'. In Paul *et al.* 1999.

Kaufman-Osborn, T. K. (2001) 'What the Law Must Not Hear: On Capital Punishment and the Voice of Pain'. In Sarat 2001.

Keal, P. (1983) *Unspoken Rules and Superpower Dominance*. London: Macmillan.

  (2003) *European Conquest and the Rights of Indigenous Peoples: The Moral Backwardness of International Society*. Cambridge: Cambridge University Press.

Keck, M. and Sikkink, K. (1998) *Activists Beyond Borders: Advocacy Networks in International Politics*. Cornell: Cornell University Press.

Keegan, J. (1994) *A History of Warfare*. London: Pimlico.

Keeley, L. H. (1996) *War Before Civilization: The Myth of the Peaceful Savage*. Oxford: Oxford University Press.

Keenan, T. (1987) 'The Paradox of Knowledge and Power: Reading Foucault on a Bias', *Political Theory*, 15 (1), 5–37.

Kekes, J. (1996) 'Cruelty and Liberalism', *Ethics*, 106 (4), 834–44.

Kelly, P. (ed.) (1998) *Impartiality, Neutrality and Justice: Re-Reading Brian Barry's Justice as Impartiality*. Edinburgh: Edinburgh University Press.

Keohane, R. O. (1986) 'Reciprocity in International Relations', *International Organization*, 40 (1), 1–27.

  (1989) *International Institutions and State Power: Essays in International Relations Theory*. Boulder, CO: Westview Press.

Kern, P. B. (1999) *Ancient Siege Warfare*. London: Souvenir Press.

Khulumani et al. v. *Barclays National Bank* (www.khulumani.net/press-releases).

Kiernan, V. (1998) *Colonial Empires and Armies, 1815–1960*. Stroud: Sutton Publishing.

Kilminster, R. (2007) *Norbert Elias: Post-Philosophical Sociology*. Abingdon: Routledge.

Kilminster, R. and Mennell, S. (2003) 'Norbert Elias's. In Ritzer 2003.

Kleinig, J. I. (1978) 'Crime and the Concept of Harm', *American Philosophical Quarterly*, 15 (1), 27–36.

Kleinman, A., Veena, D. and Lock, M. (eds.) (1997) *Social Suffering*. Berkeley: University of California Press.

Klostermaier, K. K. (1996) 'Himsa and Ahimsa Traditions in Hinduism'. In Dyck 1996.

Konstan, D. (2001) *Pity Transformed*. London: Duckworth.

Korf, B. (2007) 'Antinomies of Generosity: Moral Geographies and post-Tsunami Aid in South- East Asia', *Geoforum*, 38 (2), 366–78.

Kramer, H. and Sprenger, J. (1971) *The Malleus Maleficarum*. New York: Montague Summers.

Kratochwil, F. (2008) 'Sociological Approaches'. In Reus-Smit and Snidal 2008.

Krieken, R. van (1998) *Norbert Elias*. London: Routledge.

Kurki, M. and Sinclair, A. (2010) 'Hidden in Plain Sight: Constructivist Treatment of Social Context and its Limitations', *International Politics*, 47 (1), 1–27.

Kutz, C. (2000) *Complicity: Ethics and Law for a Collective Age*. Cambridge: Cambridge University Press.

Kyle, D. G. (1998) *Spectacles of Death in Ancient Rome*. London: Routledge.

Lacquer, T. W. (1989) 'Bodies, Details and the Humanitarian Narrative'. In Hunt 1989.

Ladd, J. (ed.) (1973) *Ethical Relativism*. Belmont: Wadsworth.

Lara, M. P. (ed.) (2001) *Rethinking Evil*. Berkeley: University of California Press.

Larrabee, M. J. (ed.) (1993) *An Ethic of Care: Feminist and Interdisciplinary Perspectives*. London: Routledge.

Latane, B. and Darley, J. M. (1970) *The Unresponsive Bystander: Why Doesn't He Help?* Englewood Cliffs, NJ: Prentice Hall.

Lawler, P. (1994) *A Question of Values: Johan Galtung's Peace Research*. Boulder, CO: Lyne Rienner.

Lebow, N. (2003) *The Tragic Vision of Politics: Ethics, Interests and Orders*. Cambridge: Cambridge University Press.

LeDoux, J. (1998) *The Emotional Brain: The Mysterious Underpinnings of Emotional Life*. London: Weidenfeld and Nicolson.

Levi, P. (1988) *The Drowned and the Saved*. London: Michael Joseph.

(2000) *If This is a Man; The Truce*. London: Everyman.

(2001) *The Voice of Memory*. Cambridge: Polity Press.

Levinas, E. (1998) *Entre Nous: On Thinking-of-the-Other*. New York: Columbia University Press.

Levinson, S. (ed.) (2004) *Torture: A Collection*. Oxford: Oxford University Press.

Lewis, B. (1974) 'Politics and War'. In Schacht and Bosworth 1974.

Lichtenberg, J. (1981) 'National Boundaries and Moral Boundaries: A Cosmopolitan View'. In Brown and Shue 1981.

Liddell, H. G. and Scott, R. (1980) *An Intermediate Greek-English Lexicon*. Oxford: Clarendon Press.

Lifton, R. J. (1974) *Home from the War: Vietnam Veterans, Neither Victims nor Executioners*. London: Wildwood House.

Linklater, A. (1982/1990) *Men and Citizens in the Theory of International Relations*. London: Macmillan.

(1990) *Beyond Realism and Marxism: Critical Theory and International Relations*. London: Macmillan.

(1998) *The Transformation of Political Community: Ethical Foundations of the Post-Westphalian Era*. Cambridge: Polity Press.

(2001) 'Citizenship, Humanity and Cosmopolitan Harm Conventions', *International Political Science Review*, 22 (3), 261–77.

(2002a) 'Towards a Critical Historical Sociology of Transnational Harm'. In Hobden and Hobson 2002.

(2002b) 'The Problem of Harm in World Politics: Implications for the Sociology of States-Systems', *International Affairs*, 78 (2), 319–38.

(2002c) 'Unnecessary Suffering'. In Booth and Dunne 2002.

(2004) 'Norbert Elias, "The Civilizing Process" and International Relations', *International Politics*, 41 (1), 3–35.

(2005) 'Discourse Ethics and the Civilising Process', *Review of International Studies*, 31 (1), 141–54.

(2006a) 'Cosmopolitanism'. In Dobson and Eckersley 2006.

(2006b) 'The Harm Principle and Global Ethics', *Global Society*, 20 (3), 429–43.

(2007a) *Critical Theory and World Politics: Sovereignty, Citizenship and Humanity*. Abingdon: Routledge.

(2007b) 'Towards a Sociology of Global Morals with an Emancipatory Intent', *Review of International Studies*, 21 (1), 135–50.

(2007c) 'Transnational Public Spheres and Global Civilizing Processes', *Theory, Culture and Society*, 14 (4), 31–7.

(2007d) 'Distant Suffering and Cosmopolitan Obligation', *International Politics*, 44 (1), 3–35.

(2007e) 'Torture and Civilisation', *International Relations*, 21 (1), 119–30.

(2009) 'Human Interconnectedness', *International Relations*, 23 (3), 481–97.

(2010) 'A European Civilising Process?' In Hill and Smith 2010.

Linklater, A. and Suganami, H. (2006) *The English School of International Relations: A Contemporary Reassessment*. Cambridge: Cambridge University Press.

Liston, K. (2007) 'Revisiting the Feminist-Figurational Sociology Exchange', *Sport in Society*, 10 (4), 623–46.

Liston, K. and Mennell, S. (2009) 'Ill-Met in Ghana: Jack Goody and Norbert Elias on Process and Progress in Africa', *Theory, Culture and Society*, 29 (7–8), 52–70.

Little, R. (2000) 'The English School's Contribution to the Study of International Relations', *European Journal of International Relations*, 6 (3), 395–422.

Liverani, M. (2001) *International Relations in the Ancient Near East: 1600–1100 B.C.* Basingstoke: Palgrave.

Locke, J. (1960) [1689] *Two Treaties of Government*. Cambridge: Cambridge University Press.

Löwenheim, O. (2007) *Predators and Parasites: Persistent Agents of Transnational Harm and Great Power Authority*. Michigan: University of Michigan Press.

Loyal, S. (2004) 'Elias on Class and Stratification'. In Loyal and Quilley 2004.

Loyal, S. and Quilley, S. (eds.) (2004) *The Sociology of Norbert Elias*. Cambridge: Cambridge University Press.

Lu, C. (2000) 'The One and Many Faces of Cosmopolitanism', *Journal of Political Philosophy*, 8 (2), 244–67.

(2007) 'Shame, Guilt and Reconciliation after War', *European Journal of Social Theory*, 11 (3), 367–83.

Lucas, J. R. (1966) *The Principles of Politics*. Oxford: Clarendon Press.

Lupton, D. (1998) *The Emotional Self*. London: Sage.

Lyon, M. L. and Barbalet, J. M. (1994) 'Society's Body: Emotion and the "Somatization" of Social Theory'. In Csordas 1994.

McAleer, K. (1994) *Dueling: The Cult of Honor in Fin-de-Siecle Germany*. Princeton: Princeton University Press.

Macaulay, Lord (1880a) 'Notes on the Indian Penal Code'. In Macaulay 1880b.

(1880b) *Miscellaneous Works of Lord Macaulay*. New York: Harper.

McCarthy, Thomas (1981) *The Critical Theory of Jurgen Habermas*. London: MIT Press.

McCarthy, T. (1998) 'Legitimacy and Diversity: Dialectical Reflections on Analytic Distinctions'. In Rosenfeld and Arato 1998.

McCullin, D. (1990) *Unreasonable Behaviour: An Autobiography*. London: Jonathan Cape.

Machiavelli, N. (1950) [1532] *The Prince and the Discourses*. New York: Modern Library.

(1994) 'Guilty Bystanders? On the Legitimacy of Duty to Rescue Statutes', *Philosophy and Public Affairs*, 23 (2), 157–91.

Mackie, J. (1977) *Ethics: Inventing Right and Wrong*. Harmondsworth: Penguin.

Mackinnon, C. and Dworkin, A. (eds.) (1997) *In Harm's Way: The Pornography Civil Rights Hearings*. Cambridge, MA: Harvard University Press.

Macklin, R. (1977) 'Moral Progress', *Ethics*, 87 (4), 370–82.

Maclagan, W. G. (1960) 'Respect for Persons as a Moral Principle: I', *Philosophy*, 35 (134), 193–217.

MacMillan, J. (1998) *On Liberal Peace: Democracy, War and the International Order*. London: I. B. Tauris.

McIntyre, A. (1967) *A Short History of Ethics*. London: Routledge and Kegan Paul.

McNeill, W. H. (1979a) *Plagues and Peoples*. Harmondsworth: Penguin.

(1979b) *A World History*. Oxford: Oxford University Press.

(1983) *The Great Frontier: Freedom and Hierarchy in Modern Times*. Princeton: Princeton University Press.

(1986) *Mythistory and other Essays*. Chicago: University of Chicago Press.

(1989) *Arnold Toynbee: A Life*. Oxford: Oxford University Press.

(1990) 'The Rise of the West after Twenty Five Years', *Journal of World History*, 1 (1), 1–26.

Malcolmson, R. (1973) *Popular Recreations in English Society: 1700–1850*. Cambridge: Cambridge University Press.

Mann, M. (1986) *The Sources of Social Power, vol. one, A History of Power from the Beginning to 1760*. Cambridge: Cambridge University Press.

Mansbach, R. and Ferguson, Y. (1996) *Polities: Authorities, Identities and Change*. Columbia, SC: University of South Carolina Press.

Mapel, D. R. (1996) 'Realism and the Ethics of War and Peace'. In Nardin 1996.

Margolis, J. (1971) *Values and Conduct*. Oxford: Oxford University Press.

Marlatt, G. A. (ed.) (1998) *Harm Reduction: Pragmatic Strategies for Managing High-Risk Behaviors*. London: Guilford Press.

Martin, D. L. and Frayer, D. W. (eds.) (1997) *Troubled Times: Violence and Warfare in the Past*. Amsterdam: Gordon and Breach.

Marx, K. (1967) [1844] 'Economic and Philosophical Manuscripts'. In Eaton and Guddat 1967.

(1970) [1887] *Capital, volume one*. London: Lawrence and Wishart.

(1973) [1857–58] *Grundrisse*. Harmondsworth: Penguin.

Mason, M. (1999) *Environmental Democracy: A Contextual Approach*. London: Earthscan.

(2001) 'Transnational Environmental Obligations: Locating New Spaces of Accountability in a post-Westphalian Order', *Transactions of the Institute of British Geographers*, 26 (4), 407–29.

(2005) *The New Accountability: Environmental Responsibility Across Borders*. London: Earthscan.

(2006) 'Citizenship Entitlements Beyond Borders? Identifying Mechanisms of Access and Redress for Affected Publics in International Environmental Law', *Global Governance*, 12 (3), 283–303.

Mayall, J. (1999) *World Politics: Progress and its Limits*. Cambridge: Polity Press.

Mayerfeld, J. (1999) *Suffering and Moral Responsibility*. Oxford: Oxford University Press.

Mazlish, B. (1989) *A New Science: The Breakdown of Connections and the Birth of Sociology*. Oxford: Oxford University Press.

(2006) *The New Global History*. Abingdon: Routledge.

Mearsheimer, J. (2001) *The Tragedy of Great Power Politics*. New York: Norton.

Melden, A. I. (ed.) (1958) *Essays in Moral Philosophy*. Seattle: University of Washington Press.

Melzack, R. and Wall, P. (1982) *The Challenge of Pain*. Harmondsworth: Penguin.

Mennell, S. (1990a) 'The Globalization of Human Society as a Very Long-Term Social Process: Elias's Theory', *Theory, Culture and Society*, 7 (2), 359–71.

(1990b) 'Decivilizing Processes: Theoretical Significance and Some Lines of Research', *International Sociology*, 5 (2), 205–23.

(1994) 'The Formation of We-Images: A Process Theory'. In Calhoun 1994. Reprinted in Dunning and Mennell 2003, vol. II.

(1998) *Norbert Elias: An Introduction*. Dublin: University College Dublin Press.

(2007) *The American Civilizing Process*. Cambridge: Polity Press.

Mestrovic, S. (1994) *The Barbarian Temperament: Toward a Postmodern Critical Theory*. London: Routledge.

Midgley, M. (1992) *Wickedness: A Philosophical Essay*. London: Routledge.

Mill, J. S. (1972) *Utilitarianism, On Liberty and Considerations on Representative Government*. London: Everyman.

Miller, W. I. (1993) *Humiliation and Other Essays on Honor, Social Discomfort and Violence*. London: Cornell University Press.

Minois, G. (1995) *History of Suicide: Voluntary Death in Western Culture*. Baltimore: Johns Hopkins University Press.

Modelski, G. (1990) 'Is World Politics Evolutionary Learning?', *International Organization*, 44 (1), 1–24.

(2000) 'World System Evolution'. In Denemark *et al.* 2000.

Montaigne, M. (1965) [1580] 'On Cruelty', in *Montaigne's Essays, volume 2*. London: Everyman.

Moore, B. (1972) *Reflections on the Causes of Human Misery and upon Certain Proposals to Eliminate Them*. London: Allen Lane.

Moore, G. E. (1959) *Principia Ethica*. Cambridge: Cambridge University Press.

Moore, M. S. (1999) 'Causation and Responsibility'. In Paul *et al.* 1999.

Moorehead, C. (1998) *Dunant's Dream: War, Switzerland and the History of the Red Cross*. New York: Carroll and Graff.

Morgenthau, H. (1971) *Politics in the Twentieth Century*. Chicago: University of Chicago Press.

(1973) *Politics Among Nations: The Struggle for Power and Peace*. New York: Alfred A. Knopf.

Morris, D. B. (1997) 'About Suffering: Voice, Genre, and Moral Community'. In Kleinman *et al.* 1997.

Moss, J. (ed.) (1998) *The Later Foucault: Politics and Philosophy*. London: Sage.

Murphy, J. G. (1990) 'The Retributive Emotions'. In Murphy and Hampton 1990.

Murphy, J. G. and Hampton, J. (eds.) (1990) *Forgiveness and Mercy*. Cambridge: Cambridge University Press.

Murray, A. (1997) *Reconstructing Realism: Between Power Politics and Cosmopolitan Ethics*. Edinburgh: Keele University Press.

Nardin, T. (ed.) (1996) *The Ethics of War and Peace: Religious and Secular Perspectives*. Princeton: Princeton University Press.

Neiberg, M. S. (2001) *Warfare in World History*. London: Routledge.

Nelson, B. (1971a) 'Note on the Notion of Civilization by Emile Durkheim and Marcel Mauss', *Social Research*, 38 (4), 808–13.

(1971b) 'Discussion on Industrialization and Capitalism'. In Stammler 1971.

(1973) 'Civilizational Complexes and Inter-Civilizational Relations', *Sociological Analysis*, 34 (2), 79–105.

(1976) 'On Occident and Orient in Max Weber', *Social Research*, 43 (1), 114–29.

Nettleton, S. and Watson, J. (eds.) (1998) *The Body in Everyday Life*. London: Routledge.

Nichols, T. (1997) *The Sociology of Industrial Injury*. London: Mansell.

Nielsen, K. and Ware, R. (eds.) (1997) *Exploitation*. New Jersey: Humanities Press.

Nieman, S. (2002) *Evil in Modern Thought: An Alternative History of Philosophy*. Princeton: Princeton University Press.

Nietzsche, F. (1956) [1867/1872] *The Birth of Tragedy and the Genealogy of Morals*. New York: Doubleday Anchor Books.

Norman, R. (1995) *Ethics, Killing and War*. Cambridge: Cambridge University Press.

Northrup, D. (2005) 'Globalization and the Great Convergence: Rethinking World History in the Long-Term', *Journal of World History*, 16 (3), 249–68.

Nussbaum, M. C. (2001) *Upheavals of Thought: The Intelligence of Emotions*. Cambridge: Cambridge University Press.

(2002) 'Duties of Justice, Duties of Material Aid: Cicero's Problematic Legacy', *Journal of Political Philosophy*, 8 (2), 176–206.

et al. (2002) *For Love of Country* (edited by J. Cohen). Boston: Beacon Press.

Oakley, R. (1992) *Morality and the Emotions*. London: Routledge.

Oatley, K. and Jenkins, J. M. (1996) *Understanding Emotions*. Oxford: Blackwell.

Okowa, P. N. (2000) *State Responsibility for Transboundary Air Pollution in International Law*. Oxford: Oxford University Press.

O'Neill, O. (1989) 'Justice, Gender and International Boundaries', *British Journal of Political Science*, 20 (4), 439–59.

(1991) 'Transnational Justice'. In Held 1991.

(1996) *Towards Justice and Virtue: A Constructive Account of Practical Reason*. Cambridge: Cambridge University Press.

(2000a) 'Distant Strangers, Moral Standards and Porous Boundaries'. In O'Neill 2000b.

(2000b) *Bounds of Justice*. Cambridge: Cambridge University Press.

Orwell, G. (1970) 'England, Your England', *Collected Essays, Journalism and Letters*. Harmondsworth: Penguin.

Parekh, B. (1972) 'Liberalism and Morality'. In Parekh and Berki 1972.

Parekh, B. and Berki, R. N. (eds.) (1972) *The Morality of Politics*. London: Allen and Unwin.

Parker, G. (2002) 'The Etiquette of Atrocity: The Laws of War in Early Modern Europe'. In Parker 2002a.

(2002a) *Empire, War and Faith in Early Modern Europe*. London: Allen Lane.

Parrott, W. G. and Harré, R. (1996) 'Embarrassment and the Threat to Character'. In Harré and Parrott 1996.

Passmore, J. (1975) 'The Treatment of Animals', *Journal of the History of Ideas*, 46 (2), 195–218.

Patterson, O. (1982) *Slavery and Social Death: A Comparative Study*. Cambridge, MA: Harvard University Press.

Paul, E. F., Miller, F. D. and Paul, J. (eds.) (1999) *Responsibility*. Cambridge: Cambridge University Press.

Pentland, C. (1974) *International Theory and European Integration*. London: Faber and Faber.

Perrott, M. (ed.) (1990) *A History of the Private Life, volume 4: From the Fires of Revolution to the Great War*. Cambridge, MA: Harvard University Press.

Pettman, R. (ed.) (1979) *Moral Claims in World Affairs*. London: Croom Helm.

Pickel, A. (2004) 'Homo Nationis: The Psycho-Social Structure of the Nation-State', *Global Society*, 18 (4), 325–46.

Pijl, K. van der (1998) *Transnational Classes and International Relations*. London: Routledge.

  (2007) *Nomads, Empires, States: Modes of Foreign Relations and Political Economy, volume 1*. London: Pluto Press.

Pinker, S. (2003) *The Blank State: The Modern Denial of Human Nature*. London: Penguin.

Pogge, T. (2002) *World Poverty and Human Rights*. Cambridge: Polity Press.

Popper, K. (1966) *The Open Society and its Enemies, Volume One*. London: Routledge and Kegan Paul.

Portmann, C. (2000) *When Bad Things Happen to Other People*. London: Routledge.

Pouncey, P. R. (1980) *The Necessities of War: A Study of Thucydides' Pessimism*. New York: Columbia University Press.

Price, J. (2001) *Thucydides and Internal War*. Cambridge: Cambridge University Press.

Price, R. M. (1997) *The Chemical Weapons Taboo*. Cornell: Cornell University Press.

Pugash, J. Z. (1977) 'The Dilemmas of the Sea Refugee: Rescue without Refuge', *Harvard International Law Journal*, 18 (3), 577–604.

Quint, D. (1998) *Montaigne and the Quality of Mercy: Ethical and Political Themes in the Essais*. Princeton: Princeton University Press.

Quinton, A. (1973) *Utilitarian Ethics*. London: Macmillan.

Raaflaub, K. and Rosenstein, N. (eds.) (1999) *War and Society in the Ancient and Medieval Worlds: Asia, the Mediterranean, Europe and Mesoamerica*. London: Harvard University Press.

Rabinow, P. (ed.) (1984) *The Foucault Reader*. New York: Pantheon Books.

Rae, H. (2002) *State Identities and the Homogenisation of Peoples*. Cambridge: Cambridge University Press.

Rahman, A. and Toubia, N. (2000) *Female Genital Mutilation*. London: Zed Books.

Rasmussen, D. (ed.) (1999) *The Handbook of Critical Theory*. Oxford: Blackwell.

Rawcliffe, C. (1998) 'Medicine for the Soul: The Medieval English Hospital and the Quest for Spiritual Health'. In Hinnells and Porter 1999.

Rawls, J. (1971) *A Theory of Justice*. Cambridge, MA: Harvard University Press.
  (1993) *Political Liberalism*. New York: Columbia University Press.

Raymond, G. A. (1997) 'Problems and Prospects in the Study of International Norms', *Mershon International Studies Review*, 41 (2), 205–45.

Raz, J. (1986) *The Morality of Freedom*. Oxford: Oxford University Press.

Redfield, R. (1973) 'The Universally Human and the Culturally Variable'. In Ladd 1973.

Reeve, A. (ed.) (1987) *Modern Theories of Exploitation*. London: Sage.

Renfrew, C. and Cherry, J. (eds.) (1986) *Peer Polity Interaction and Socio-Political Change*. Cambridge: Cambridge University Press.

Reus-Smit, C. (1999) *The Moral Purpose of the State: Culture, Social Identity, and Institutional Rationality in International Relations*. Princeton: Princeton University Press.

(2002) 'The Idea of History and History with Ideas'. In Hobden and Hobson 2002.

(2009) 'Constructivism'. In S. Burchill and A. Linklater (eds.) *Theories of International Relations*. Basingstoke: Palgrave Macmillan.

Reus-Smit, C. and Snidal, D. (eds.) (2008) *The Oxford Handbook to International Relations*. Oxford: Oxford University Press.

Rey, R. (1998) *The History of Pain*. Harvard: Harvard University Press.

Richardson, J. (1997) 'Contending Liberalisms', *European Journal of International Relations*, 3 (1), 5–33.

(2000) *Contending Liberalisms in World Politics: Ideology and Power*. Boulder, CO: Lynne Reinner.

Richter, J. (2001) *Holding Corporations Accountable: Corporate Conduct, International Codes and Citizen Action*. London: Zed Books.

Richter, M. (1964) *The Social Philosophy of T.H. Green*. London: Weidenfeld and Nicolson.

Ritzer, G. (ed.) (2003) *The Blackwell Companion to Major Contemporary Social Theories*. Oxford: Blackwell.

Roberts, A. and Guelff, R. (eds.) (2000) *Documents on the Law of War*. Oxford: Oxford University Press.

Roberts, J. (1980) *The Pelican History of the World*. Harmondsworth: Penguin.

Robinson, F. (1999) *Globalizing Care: Ethics, Feminist Theory and International Relations*. Boulder, CO: Westview Press.

Robinson, W. I. and Harris, J. (2000) 'Towards a Global Ruling Class? Globalization and the Transnational Capitalist Class', *Science and Society*, 64 (1), 11–54.

Rorty A. O. (ed.) (1980) *Explaining Emotions*. Berkeley: University of California Press.

Rorty, R. (1989) *Contingency, Irony and Solidarity*. Cambridge: Cambridge University Press.

Rosecrance, R. (1986) *The Rise of the Trading State: Commerce and Conquest in the Modern World*. New York: Basic Books.

Rosenberg, J. (1994) *The Empire of Civil Society: A Critique of the Realist Theory of International Relations*. London: Verso.

Rosenfeld, M. and Arato, A. (eds.) (1998) *Habermas on Law and Democracy: Critical Exchanges*. Berkeley: University of California Press.

Ross, W. D. (1930) *The Right and the Good*. London: Clarendon Press.
  (1939) *Foundations of Ethics*. London: Clarendon Press.
Rousseau, J.-J. (1968) [1765] *A Discourse on the Origin of Inequality*. London: Dent.
Rowse, T. (1998) *White Flour, White Power. From Rations to Citizenship in Central Australia*. Cambridge: Cambridge University Press.
Ruggie, J. (1983) 'Continuity and Transformation in the World Polity: Towards a Neo-Realist Synthesis', *World Politics*, 35 (1), 261–85.
Rundell, J. and Mennell, S. (eds.) (1998) *Classical Readings in Culture and Civilization*. London: Routledge.
Sadowski, Y. (1998) *The Myth of Global Chaos*. Washington, DC: Brookings Institution Press.
Sanderson, S. K. (1988) *Macrosociology: An Introduction to Human Societies*. New York: Harper and Row.
Sarat, A. (ed.) (2001) *Pain, Death and the Law*. Ann Arbor: University of Michigan Press.
Scarre, C. (ed.) (2005) *The Human Past: World PreHistory and the Development of Human Societies*. London: Thames and Hudson.
Scarry, E. (1985) *The Body in Pain: The Making and Unmaking of the World*. Oxford: Oxford University Press.
Schacht, J. and Bosworth, C. E. (eds.) (1974) *The Legacy of Islam*. Oxford: Clarendon Press.
Scheff, T. (1988) 'Shame and Conformity: The Deference-Emotion System', *American Sociological Review*, 53 (3), 395–406.
  (1994) *Bloody Revenge: Emotions, Nationalism and War*. Boulder, CO: Westview Press.
Schelling, T. C. (1966) *Arms and Influence*. London: Yale University Press.
Schopenhauer, A. (1995) [1840] *On the Basis of Morality*. Oxford: Berghahn.
Schore, A. (1998) 'Early Shame Experiences and Infant Brain Development'. In Gilbert and Andrews 1998.
Schwarzenberger, G. (1941) *Power Politics*. London: Jonathan Cape.
Sebald, W. G. (2003) *On the Natural History of Destruction*. London: Hamish Hamilton.
Sennett, R. (2002) *Flesh and Stone: The Body and the City in Western Civilization*. London: Faber and Faber.
Sennett, R. and Cobb, J. (1972) *The Hidden Injuries of Class*. New York: Vintage.
Sereny, G. (1995) *Into that Darkness: From Mercy Killing to Mass Murder*. London: Pimlico.
Shapcott, R. (2001) *Justice, Community and Dialogue in International Relations*. Cambridge: Cambridge University Press.
Sharpe, J. A. (1990) *Judicial Punishment in England*. London: Faber.
Shaw, M. (1996) *Civil Society and Media in Global Crises: Representing Distant Violence*. London: Pinter.

Sherene, V. and Beckles H. McD. (eds.) (2000) *Caribbean Slavery in the Atlantic World*. Oxford: Ian Randle Publishers.

Sherratt, A. (1995) 'Reviving the Grand Narrative: Archaeology and Long-Term Change', *European Journal of European Archaeology*, 3 (1), 1–32.

Shiva, V. (2000) 'Ecological Balance in an Era of Globalization'. In Wapner and Ruiz 2000.

Shklar, J. (1984) *Ordinary Vices*. Cambridge, MA: Harvard University Press.

Shrivastava, P. (1992) *Bhopal: Anatomy of a Crisis*. London: Paul Chapman Publishing.

Shue, H. (1981) 'Exporting Hazards'. In Brown and Shue 1981.

Shun, K.-L. (1997) *Mencius and Early Chinese Thought*. Stanford: Stanford University Press.

Silverman, L. (2001) *Tortured Subjects: Pain, Truth, and the Body in Early Modern France*. Chicago: Chicago University Press.

Simons, K. W. (1999) 'Negligence'. In Paul *et al*. 1999.

Singer, M. G. (1963) *Generalization in Ethics*. London: Eyre and Spottiswoode.

Singer, P. (1972) 'Famine, Affluence and Morality', *Philosophy and Public Affairs*, 1 (3), 229–43.

(1977) *Animal Liberation: Towards an End to Man's Inhumanity to Animals*. London: Paladin.

(1981) *The Expanding Circle: Ethics and Sociobiology*. Oxford: Oxford University Press.

(2002) *One World: Ethics and Globalization*. New Haven: Yale University Press.

Skinner, Q. and Strath, B. (eds.) (2003) *States and Citizens*. Cambridge: Cambridge University Press.

Skocpol, T. (1979) *States and Social Revolutions*. Cambridge: Cambridge University Press.

Smart, J. J. C. (1973) 'An Outline of a System of Utilitarian Ethics'. In Smart and Williams 1973.

Smart, J. J. C. and Williams, B. (1973) *Utilitarianism: For and Against*. Cambridge: Cambridge University Press.

Smith, A. (1982) [1759] *The Theory of Moral Sentiments*. Indianopolis: Liberty Fund.

Smith, D. M. (1998) 'How Far Should We Care: On the Spatial Scope of Beneficence', *Progress in Human Geography*, 22 (1), 15–38.

(2000) *Moral Geographies: Ethics in a World of Difference*. Edinburgh: Edinburgh University Press.

Smith, D. (2001) *Norbert Elias and Modern Social Theory*. London: Sage.

Snow, N. E. (1991) 'Compassion', *American Philosophical Quarterly*, 28 (3), 195–205.

Solomon, R. C. (1993) *The Passions: Emotions and the Meaning of Life*. Indianapolis: Hackett.

Sontag, S. (1978) *On Photography*. London: Allen Lane.

  (2003) *Regarding the Pain of Others*. London: Hamish Hamilton.

Spierenburg, P. C. (1991) *The Broken Spell: A Cultural and Anthropological History of Preindustrial Europe*. Brunswick: Rutgers University Press.

  (2004) 'Punishment, Power and History: Foucault and Elias's, *Social Science History*, 28 (4), 607–36.

Spivey, N. (2001) *Enduring Creation: Art, Pain and Fortitude*. Berkeley: University of California Press.

Stammler, O. (ed.) (1971) *Max Weber and Sociology Today*. Oxford: Basil Blackwell.

Staub, E. (2003) *The Psychology of Good and Evil: Why Children, Adults and Groups Help and Harm Others*. Cambridge: Cambridge University Press.

Stavrianos, L. (1990) *Lifelines from Our Past: A New World History*. London: I. B. Tauris.

Stearns, P. N. and Haggerty, T. (1991) 'The Role of Fear: Transition in Emotional Standards for Children, 1850–1950', *American Historical Review*, 96 (1), 63–94.

Stearns, P. N. and Stearns, C. Z. (1985) 'Emotionology: Clarifying the History of Emotions and Emotional Standards', *American Historical Review*, 90 (4), 813–36.

Stearns, P. N. and Stearns, C. (1986) *Anger: The Control of an Emotion in the United States*. Chicago: University of Chicago Press.

Steintrager, J. A. (2004) *Cruel Delight: Enlightenment, Culture and the InHuman*. Bloomington: Indiana University Press.

Stevens, C. (1994) *White Man's Dreaming: Killipaninna Mission 1866–1915*. Melbourne: Oxford University Press.

Stirk, P. M. (1992) *Max Horkheimer: A New Interpretation*. Hemel Hempstead: Harvester Wheatsheaf.

Stone, L. (1979) *The Family, Sex and Marriage in England: 1500–1800*. London: Weidenfeld and Nicolson.

  (1983) 'Interpersonal Violence in English Society: 1300–1980', *Past and Present*, (101), 22–33.

  (1985) 'The History of Violence in England: Some Observations. A Rejoinder', *Past and Present*, (108), 216–24.

Sunstein, C. R. (2005) *Laws of Fear: Beyond the Precautionary Principle*. Cambridge: Cambridge University Press.

Swaan, A. de (1995) 'Widening Circles of Identification: Emotional Concerns in Sociogenetic Perspective', *Theory, Culture and Society*, 12 (2), 25–39.

  (1997) 'Widening Circles of Disidentification: On the Psycho- and Socio-genesis of the Hatred of Distant Strangers: Reflections on Rwanda', *Theory, Culture and Society*, 14 (2), 105–22.

Sznaider, N. (2001) *The Compassionate Society: Care and Cruelty in Modern Society*. Oxford: Rowman and Littlefield.

Tanaka, Y. (2002) *Japan's Comfort Women: Sexual Slavery and Prostitution During World War II and the US Occupation*. London: Routledge.

Tangney, J. P. and Dearing, R. L. (2002) *Shame and Guilt*. London: Guilford Press.

Taylor, C. (1989) *Sources of the Self: The Making of Modern Identity*. Cambridge: Harvard University Press.

Taylor, J. (1998) *Body Horror: Photojournalism, Catastrophe and War*. Manchester: Manchester University Press.

Teitel, R. G. (2000) *Transitional Justice*. Oxford: Oxford University Press.

Ten, C. L. (1980) *Mill on Liberty*. Oxford: Clarendon Press.

Teschke, B. (2003) *The Myth of 1648: Class, Geopolitics and the Making of Modern International Relations*. London: Verso.

Tester, K. (1998) 'Bored and Blasé: Television, the Emotions and Georg Simmel'. In Bendelow and Williams 1998.

(2001) *Compassion, Morality and the Media*. Buckingham: Open University Press.

Thakur, R. and Malley, W. (1999) 'The Ottowa Convention on Landmines: A Landmark Humanitarian Treaty in Arms Control?', *Global Governance*, 5 (3), 273–301.

Thomas, H. (1979) *An Unfinished History of the World*. London: Hamish Hamilton.

Thomas, K. (1984) *Man and the Natural World: Changing Attitudes in England, 1500–1800*. Harmondsworth: Penguin.

(2009) *The Ends of Life: Roads to Fulfilment in Early Modern England*. Oxford: Oxford University Press.

Thomas, W. (2001) *The Ethics of Destruction: Norms and Violence in International Relations*. Cornell: Cornell University Press.

Thompson, J. (2002) *Taking Responsibility for the Past: Reparation and Historical Injustice*. Cambridge: Polity Press.

Thomson, G. (1987) *Needs*. London: Routledge.

Thornberry, P. (2002) *Indigenous Peoples and Human Rights*. Manchester: Manchester University Press.

Thucydides (1928) *History of the Peloponnesian War*. Cambridge, MA: Harvard University Press.

Tibi, B. (1996) 'War and Peace in Islam'. In Nardin 1996.

Tilly, C. (1993) *Coercion, Capital and the European States: AD 900–1992*. Oxford: Blackwell.

Todorov, T. (1999) *Facing the Extremes: Moral Life in the Concentration Camps*. London: Weidenfeld and Nicolson.

Tombs, S. and Hillyard, P. (2004) 'Towards A Political Economy of Harm: States, Corporations and the Production of Inequality'. In Hillyard *et al.* 2004.

Tooke, J. (1965) *The Just War in Aquinas and Grotius Middle Ages*. London: SPCK.

Toynbee, A. (1978) *Mankind and Mother Earth*. London: Paladin.

Tritle, L. A. (2000) *From Melos to My Lai: War and Survival*. London: Routledge.

Tronto, J. (1994) *Moral Boundaries: A Political Argument for an Ethic of Care.* London: Routledge.

Tunick, M. (2005) 'John Stuart Mill and Unassimilated Subjects', *Political Studies,* 53 (4), 833–48.

Turner, B. S. (1987) *Medical Power and Social Knowledge.* London: Sage.

(1991) 'Recent Developments in the Theory of the Body'. In Featherstone *et al.* 1991.

(1992) *Regulating Bodies: Essays in Medical Sociology.* London: Routledge.

(1993a) 'Outline of a Theory of Human Rights', *Sociology,* 27 (3), 489–512.

(1993b) *Max Weber: From History to Modernity.* London: Routledge.

(1996) *The Body and Society.* London: Sage.

(2006) *Vulnerability and Human Rights.* London: Sage.

Turney-High, H. H. (1991) *Primitive War: Its Practices and Concepts.* Columbia: University of South Carolina Press.

Urmson, J. O. (1958) 'Saints and Heroes'. In Melden 1958.

Vencl, S. (1999) 'Stone Age Warfare'. In Carman and Harding 1999.

Verkamp, B. J. (1993) *The Moral Treatment of Returning Warriors in Early Medieval and Modern Times.* Scranton: University of Scranton Press.

Vincent, L. (2006) 'French Accused of Pacific Nuclear Cover-Up', *Observer,* 1 January.

Vincent, R. J. (1986) *Human Rights and International Relations.* Cambridge: Cambridge University Press.

Vincent, R. J. and Wilson, P. (1993) 'Beyond Non-Intervention'. In Forbes and Hoffman 1993.

Wallerstein, I. (1979) *The Capitalist World-Economy.* Cambridge: Cambridge University Press.

(1991) *Geopolitics and Geoculture: Essays on the Changing World-System.* Cambridge: Cambridge University Press.

Walsh, W. H. (1967) *An Introduction to the Philosophy of History.* London: Hutchinson.

Waltz, K. N. (1979) *Theory of International Politics.* Reading, MA: Addison-Wesley.

Walzer, M. (1980) *Just and Unjust Wars: A Moral Argument with Historical Illustrations.* Harmondsworth: Penguin.

(1996) 'War and Peace in the Jewish Tradition'. In Nardin 1996.

(2002) 'Spheres of Affection'. In Nussbaum 2002.

Wapner, P. and Ruiz, E. L. J. (eds.) (2000) *Principled World Politics: The Challenge of Normative International Relations.* Boulder, CO: Rowman and Littlefield.

Ware, V. (1992) *Beyond the Pale: White Women, Racism and History.* London: Verso.

Warnock, G. (1971) *The Object of Morality.* London: Methuen.

Warren, B. (1980) *Imperialism: Pioneer of Capitalism.* London: Verso.

Watson, A. (1982) *Diplomacy: The Dialogue between States.* London: Methuen.

(1987) 'Hedley Bull, States Systems and International Societies', *Review of International Studies*, 13 (2), 147–53.

(1992) *The Evolution of International Society: a Comparative Historical Analysis*. London: Routledge.

Weber, M. (1948a) 'Social Psychology of the World Religions'. In Gerth and Mills 1948.

(1948b) 'Religious Rejections of the World and their Directions'. In Gerth and Mills 1948.

(1948c) 'India: The Brahmans and the Caste'. In Gerth and Mills 1948.

Wendt, A. (2003) 'Why a World State is Inevitable', *European Journal of International Relations*, 9 (4), 491–542.

Wertheimer, A. (1996) *Exploitation*. Princeton: Princeton University Press.

Wesson, R. G. (1978) *State Systems: International Pluralism, Politics and Culture*. London: The Free Press.

Wheeler, N. J. (2000) *Saving Strangers: Humanitarian Intervention in International Society*. Oxford: Oxford University Press.

(2002) 'Dying for Enduring Freedom: Accepting Responsibility for Civilian Casualties in the War Against Terrorism', *International Relations*, 16 (2), 205–25.

Wheeler, N. and Bellamy, A. (2001) 'Humanitarian Intervention in World Politics'. In Baylis and Smith 2001.

Wheeler, N. J. and Dunne, T. (1998) 'Good International Citizenship: A Third Way for British Foreign Policy', *International Affairs*, 74 (4), 847–70.

Wierzbicka, A. (1999) *Emotions Across Languages and Cultures: Diversity and Universals*. Cambridge: Cambridge University Press.

Wiesel, E., Dawidowicz, L., Rabinowitz, D. and Brown, R. M. (eds.) (1990) *Dimensions of the Holocaust*. Evanston, IL: Northwestern University Press.

Wight, M. (1966a) 'Why Is There No International Theory?' In Butterfield and Wight 1966.

(1966b) 'Western Values in International Relations'. In Butterfield and Wight 1966.

(1977) *Systems of States*. Leicester: Leicester University Press.

(1978) *Power Politics*. Leicester: Leicester University Press.

(1991) *International Theory: The Three Traditions*. Leicester: Leicester University Press.

(2004) *Four Seminal Thinkers in International Relations: Machiavelli, Grotius, Kant and Mazzini*. Oxford: Oxford University Press.

Wilkinson, D. (2000) 'Civilisations, World Systems and Hegemonies'. In Denemark *et al.* 2000.

Williams, B. (1973) *Morality: An Introduction to Ethics*. Harmondsworth: Penguin.

Williams, M. C. (2005) *The Realist Tradition and the Limits of International Relations*. Cambridge: Cambridge University Press.

Williams, S. J. and Bendelow, G. (eds.) (1998) *The Lived Body: Sociological Themes. Embodied Issues*. London: Routledge.

Wittgenstein, L. (1974) *Philosophical Investigations*. Oxford: Basil Blackwell.

Wolin, S. S. (1960) *Politics and Vision: Continuity and Vision in Western Political Thought*. Boston: Little Brown.

Wollstonecraft, M. (1992) [1792] *A Vindication of The Rights of Woman*. London: Everyman.

Wood, A. W. (1997) 'Exploitation'. In Nielsen and Ware 1997.

Wouters, C. (1998) 'How Strange to Ourselves are Our Feelings of Superiority and Inferiority', *Theory, Culture and Society*, 15 (1), 131–50.

    (2004) 'Changing Regimes of Manners and Emotions: From Disciplining to Informalizing'. In Loyal and Quilley 2004.

Wright, Q. (1964) *A Study of War*. Chicago: University of Chicago Press.

Yao, X. (2000) *An Introduction to Confucianism*. Cambridge: Cambridge University Press.

Young, A. (1997) *The Harmony of Illusions: Inventing Post-Traumatic Stress Disorder*. Princeton: Princeton University Press.

Young, I. M. (1990) *Throwing Like A Girl and Other Essays in Feminist Philosophy and Social Theory*. Bloomington: Indiana University Press.

    (2006) 'Responsibility and Global Justice: A Social Connection Model', *Social Philosophy and Policy*, 23 (1), 102–30.

INDEX

Adorno, T., 3, 23, 106, 121, 191
affectedness, principle of, 91, 92, 96,
    100, *see also* Habermas, Quinton
affirmation of ordinary life, 4, 255
ahimsa, 1, 84, 87, *see* Buddhism, world
    religions
animal suffering, 17, 31, 92, 96,
    142, 170, 186, 188, 189, 218,
    see also Schopenhauer, Singer,
    speciesism
apartheid, 21, 69, 108, 136
Aristotle, 69, 210, 224, 225
Arneson, J., 89
Augustine, St, 150

balance of power, 10, 20, 181, 240
balance of terror, 178
Barkan, E., 69
Barry, B., 42, 48, 83
Beck, U., 53, 74
Benhabib, S., 147, 148
Bentham, J., 92, 94
Bhopal Incident, 68, 245
body, the 33, 35, 51, 91, 93, 105, 106,
    159, 185, 186, 187, *see also* pain,
    vulnerability
Box, S., 109
Buddhism, 92, *see ahimsa*, Jainism,
    world religions
Bull, H., 36, 86, 87, *see also* societies of
    states
Bull, H. and Watson, A., 8
Butler, J., 251
Buzan, B. and Little, R., 26, 199, 238,
    245, *see also* neo-realism
bystander phenomenon, 59, 64, 224, 225,
    see also moral indifference, Wiesel

campaigns of compassion, 189
capital punishment, 91, 171, 188,
    see also systems of punishment
Carneiro, R., 119, 121
Carr, E. H. 38
Cicero, 78, *see* Stoicism
citizenship vs humanity, 24, 76, 180,
    255, *see also* world citizenship
civilization, the idea of, 129, 134,
    see also Elias, insider–outsider
    distinctions, Nelson, standard of
    civilization, Weber, Wight
Clausewitz, von C., 120
Clement, G., 149
collective learning, 66, 236, 250–3,
    254, 262, *see also* ambiguities of
    interconnectedness, cosmopolitan
    harm conventions, global
    civilizing process, Kant
Collins, R., 173
comfort women, 69
compassion, 20, 59, 67, 71, 80, 95,
    96, 98, 99, 102, 171, 174, 180,
    214, 216, 223, 229, 249, 257,
    259, *see also* cruelty, emotions,
    Foucault, Horkheimer, pity,
    solidarity, sympathy
complicity, 55–7, 58, 70, 71, 101, 143,
    227, 246
connected self, 82, 228, 229,
    see also ethic of care and
    responsibility
constructivism, 21, 195, 200
corporate social responsibility, 68
cosmopolitan democracy, 100
cosmopolitan environmental harm
    conventions, 39

299

crimes against humanity, 62, 69, 73, 108

critical theory, 5, 23, 144, 187, 257, 260, *see also* emancipation, Foucault, Marx, process sociology

cruel and unusual punishment, 91, 107, 171

cruelty, 4, 5, 15, 17, 21, 22, 30, 33, 37, 39, 48, 53, 89, 107, 109, 126, 150, 173, 174, 188, 227, 242, 255, 257, *see also* animal suffering, Febvre, Montaigne, Nietzsche, Schopenhauer, Shklar

De Maistre, J., 112

De Sousa, J., 211

decivilizing processes, 18, 19, 20, 21, 128, 130, 162, 247, *see also* Elias on the civilizing process

Declaration of the Rights of Man and the Citizen, 31

De-Shalit, A., 38

detachment, 26, 27, 35, 133, 138, 163, 177, 247, 251, 262, *see also* Elias on the civilizing process, foresight, grand narratives, Kant, Nelson, self-restraint, world history

disgust, 72, 89, 159, 169, 171, *see also* Elias on the civilizing process

distant suffering, 20, 221, 224, 227, 259, *see also* mass media, moral indifference, Smith, transnational advocacy networks

Dobson, A., 67, 98

Duchesne, R., 25, 26

Dunning, E., 165

duties,
    negative and positive, 71, *see also* citizenship vs humanity, harm principle, Pogge, Ross

duties to the environment, 40, 262

Eckersley, R., 98

Elias, N., x, xi, 22, 32, 34, 211, *see also* decivilizing processes, emotions, Foucault, global civilizing process, historical social psychology, process sociology, Weber, Wight

Elias, approach to civilizing processes, 157–63

Elias, on civilizing process, 16–18, 163–72

Elias on emotions, 205–6

Elias on functional democratisation, 161, 167, 174, 183, 188, 189, 192

Elias, on global integration and disintegration, 175–85

Elias on interconnectedness, 20, 102, 182

Elias, N. and Dunning, E., 170

Elshtain, J.-B, 3, 150

emancipation, 24, 140

emotional identification, 118, 137, 146, 183, 217–22, 249, 257, *see also* Elias on the civilizing process, insider-outsider distinctions, emotionology

emotionology, 218, 219, 249, *see also* harm conventions, historical social psychology, process sociology

emotions, 21, 32, 95
    cosmopolitan, 198, 208, 229, 249, 256, *see also* compassion, Elias on the civilizing process, emotional identification, guilt, harm conventions, historical social psychology, shame

empathy, 97, 126, 147, 149, 213, *see also* compassion, pity

empire, 8, 26, 33, 65, 69, 119, 120, 121, 142, 144, 203, 233, 249, *see also* Mann, societies of states, Wight, Wilkinson

Engels, F., 65

Enlightenment, 4, 5, 16, 22, 41, 93, 131, 172, 186, 219, 226, 254, 255, 256, 263, 265, *see also* Foucault

environmental apartheid, 68

environmental degradation, 2, 26, 29, 37, 39, 40, 67, 72, 137, 255

ethic of care and responsibility, 94, 145–51, 248, *see also* connected self

evil, 3, 42, 44, 150
exploitation, 53–5, 69–70, 139, 245,
    248, 249, 255

Febvre, L., 21, 208
Feinberg, J., 46
    on exploitation, 54
    on harm, 14, 45, 47
    on rescue, 58, 59
    on the moral minimum, 48
    on types of harm, 50
    on welfare interests, 46–7,
    see also harm principle, liberalism,
    Mill
female genital mutilation, 15, 63
foresight, 53, 101, 183, 254, 260,
    see also Elias on the civilizing
    process, responsibility simple vs
    complex, precautionary principle,
    self-restraint
Foucault, M., 5, 15, 186, 187, 188, 189,
    190, 263
Frankfurt School, 23, 106,
    see also Adorno, Habermas,
    Horkheimer
Freud, S., 2, 3, 6, 17, 117, 158, 179,
    205
functional democratisation, 203, 229,
    247, 248, see also Elias

Galtung, J., 60
Gardiner, P, 243
Garland, D., 174
Gay, P., 59
generalizability in ethics, 94, 96
generalizable interests, 12, 13, 91, 96,
    99, 102, 103, 250, 251
genocide, 17, 21, 37, 108, 134, 136, 180,
    264, see also Elias
Geras, N., 88, 102
Giddens, A., 195
Gilligan, C., 81, 146, 147, see also ethic
    of care and responsibility
global civilizing process, 17, 19, 20,
    21, 38, 41, 50, 67, 76, 94, 102,
    109, 123, 221, 244, 250, 259,
    see also Elias on the civilizing
    process, collective learning,

constructivism, cosmopolitan
    harm principle, critical theory,
    harm principle, Nelson, societies
    of states, systems of states, Wight,
    world history
global or world risk society, 39, 65, 66,
    67, 68, see also Beck
Glover, J., 79
Goudsblom, J., 2, 132
grand narratives, 163, 252, 259, 260,
    261, 263, 264, see also ambiguities
    of interconnectedness, Kant,
    world history
Green, T. H., 101
group rights, 135, 136,
    see also indigenous peoples,
    minority nations, post-national
    identities
guilt, 34, 180, 214, 216, 223, 246, 249,
    see also connected self, emotions,
    infant moral development, shame,
    Tangney and Dearing

Habermas, J., 12, 13, 91, 100, 107, 110,
    148, 204, 251
Hague Conventions, 62, 108
Hare, R. M., 96
harm, 2
harm, concept of, 6, 12, 14, 15, 41–3
harm, concrete vs abstract, 38
harm, cultural justifications for, 32
harm, examples in world politics,
    62–73
harm, hierarchy of, 105–11
harm, international vs transnational, 38
harm, problem of, ix, 6, 7, 8, 14,
    see also Elias on the civilizing
    process, complicity, cruelty,
    exploitation, Feinberg, harm
    principle, humiliation, liberalism,
    Mill, negligence, public harm,
    rescue, structural harm
harm, types of, 51–61
harm conventions, 33
    cosmopolitan, 8, 10–11, 16, 36, 37,
    40, 62, 90, 206, 234, 244, 246, 247,
    249
    primary vs secondary, 59, 72, 103

harm conventions (*cont.*)
  sociology of, 6, 7–8, 15, *see also*
    civilizing process, emotions,
    global civilizing process, societies
    of states, systems of states
harm conventions, universality of, 6–7,
    29–30
harm narratives, 260–6
harm principle, 23, 76, 88, 89, 100, 102,
    104
  cosmopolitan, 23, 111, 133, 149,
    191, 255, 256, 258, 262, 266,
    see also duties (negative and
    positive), Feinberg, Geras, Mill,
    Ross
harm principle and international
    politics, 86–8
harm principle, critique of, 88–90
harm principle, defence of, 79–84
Harmon Doctrine, 66
Hart, H. L. A., 44, 47, 59, 82
hate crimes, 52
hazardous waste, 39, 68, *see also* Shue
Hegel, G. W. F., 96, 123, 210
Herodotus, 89
Herz, J., 39
Hierocles, 110
Hippocratic Oath, 30
Hippocratic School, 94
historical social psychology, 21, 207,
    217, 219
historical sociology, 204, 213
  and International Relations,
    199–207, 234, *see also*
    emotionology, historical social
    psychology
Hobbes, T., 3
Holocaust, 17, 69, 88, 173
Honderich, T., 56
Horkheimer, M., 23, 106, 191, 229
human rights culture, 10, 13, 14,
    21, 37, 63, 64, 73, 105, 107,
    109, 129, 133, 135, 234, 254,
    256, 264, *see also* group rights,
    humanitarian intervention,
    Kant, state sovereignty, *Universal
    Declaration of Human Rights*,
    Vincent

humanitarian intervention, 10, 63,
    64, *see also* The English School,
    human rights culture
humanitarianism, 5, 189,
    see also Foucault
Hume, D., 210, 219, 220, 225
humiliation, 42, 97, 133, *see also* cruelty,
    Levi, Rorty, Wouters

indigenous peoples, 52, 69, 70, 108,
    134, *see also* group rights
infant moral development, 7, 29, 80,
    212–213, *see also* guilt, shame
insider-outsider distinctions, 10, 13, 24,
    40, 83, 92, 122, 133, 137, 141, 206,
    207, 213, 221, 225, 227, 228, 247,
    255, 261, 263
  Elias on, 178, 183, *see also* emotional
    identification, global civilizing
    process, harm conventions, mass
    media, moral indifference, Nelson,
    Rorty, solidarity, war, Weber
institutional racism, 61
interconnectedness
  ambiguities of, 10, 16, 26, 112, 151,
    253, *see also* Elias, Kant, societies
    of states
International Labour Organisation, 108,
    135
international law, 61, 68, 76,
    see also human rights culture,
    Nuremberg Principles, realism
International Red Cross, 62
international society
  contemporary, 10, 15, 108, 254, 256
  expansion of, 26, 132, 134, 138, 252,
    see also Bull, The English School,
    societies of states, Wight
international vs transnational harm, 37,
    38, 39, 40, 66, 109, 141, 255

Jainism, 1, 84, 92
just war, 37, 67, 87, 150, *see also* harm
    principle, military necessity
justice, 57, 85, 98, 134, 138, 228
  international vs transnational,
    38, *see also* Aristotle, Bull,
    compassion, ethic of care and

responsibility, generalisable interests, Pogge, Smith, unjust enrichment

Kant, I., 16, 27, 28, 94, 251, 253, 265, *see also* ambiguities of interconnectedness, generalisability in ethics, Rorty, Schopenhauer, world history
Keck, M and Sikkink, K., 98
Keohane, R. O. 103
Kutz, C., 56, *see also* complicity, solidarity

Lasswell, H., 221
laws of war, 48, 62, 83, 87, 123, 129, 130, 150, 232, 255, 258, *see also* just war, moral learning, systems of states
legitimacy, 131, 135, *see also* Wight
Levi, P., 59, 97, 230
Levinas, E., 37, 59, 222
liberalism, 5, 22, 46, 55, 86, 144, 255, *see also* Feinberg, Geras, Marx, Mill, Parekh, social harm perspective
Lieber Code, 62
Lucas, J., 89, 90, 99

Macklin, R., 108
malleus malifecarum, 31
Mann, M., 195
Margolis, J., 110
Marx, K., 4, 16, 28, 38, 54, 60, 61, 92, 139, 140, 141, 142, 210, *see also* exploitation, structural harm
Marx, K. and Engels, F., 65
Marxism, 103, 113
masculinity, 118, 150, 165, 189, 214, 249, *see also* ethic of care and responsibility
mass media, 34, 64, 219, 226, *see also* Singer, Smith, Sontag, Tester
Mayerfeld, J., 110
McNeill, W., 26, 27, 132
Mennell, S., 20, 67, 173, 178
military necessity, 122–7, 150, 244, 247, 259, *see also* realism

military threshold, 119, 121
Mill, J. S, 14, 84
Mill, on harm, 43–4
minority nations, 135, *see also* group rights
Montaigne, M., 105, 106
Moore, M. S., 58
moral indifference, 38, 39, 43, 59, 68, 73, 83, 88, 102, 109, 142, 175, 216, 222, 227, 245, 248, 257, *see also* bystander phenomenon, Smith
moral learning, 13, 251, 254, *see also* collective learning, Kant, strategic learning
moral progress, 108, 112, 134, 242, 253, *see also* Macklin
multiple identities, 137, 138, *see also* emotional identification, post-national identities

negative utilitarianism, 84, 86
negative vs positive duties, 77, 78, 79, 86, 89, 265
negligence, 52–3, 67–8, 245–6, 255
Nelson, B., 203, 204, 252
neo-realism, 113, 194, 199, 238
Nielsen, K. and Ware, R., 53
Nietzsche, F., 174
nuclear colonialism, 68
Nuremberg Code (1947), 107
Nuremberg Principles, 37, 62, 70, *see also* international law

omissive harm, 102–3, 245, 256, *see also* rescue
O'Neill, O., 13, 38–9, 96, 99, 102, *see also* generalisable interests, principle of injury

pain, 7, 8, 13, 82, 90–4, 224, *see also* affirmation of ordinary life, the body, Elias on the civilizing process, harm conventions, humanitarianism, moral progress, principle of injury, Rorty, solidarity
Parekh, B., 88

Pickel, A., 221
pity, 21, 215, *see also* Aristotle,
    compassion, emotions, Rousseau,
    Smith
Pogge, T., 70, 72, 73
post-national identities, 137, 138,
    221, 256, *see also* emotional
    identification, multiple identities
post-traumatic stress disorder, 34, 35
precautionary principle, 44, 66
principle of injury, 13, 96, 97, 107, 130,
    150, 244, *see also* O'Neill
process sociology, xi, 185–91, 194,
    197, 232, *see also* critical theory,
    Frankfurt School, Horkheimer
progress, 5, 15, 16, 18, 22, 26, 144, 148,
    160, 178, 264
public harm, 59–60, 72–3, 246

Quinton, A., 84, 91

racism, 108, 248, 264
Rape of Nanking, 69
Rawls, J., 23, 78, 82
realism, 1, 22, 105, 139, 141, 147, 176,
    178, 199, 253, *see also* military
    necessity, neo-realism, security
    dilemma, strategic learning
rescue, 41, 57, 64, *see also* Feinberg,
    Geras, omissive harm, Weil
responsibility, 56, 101, 104, 148, 184,
    225
  simple vs complex, 101, 257,
    see also connected self, corporate
    social responsibility, ethic of
    care and responsibility, harm
    conventions, solidarity
Rey, R., 93, 105
Rorty, R., 40, 51, 95, 216, 228,
    see also cruelty, Shklar
Ross, W. D., 79–80, 82
Rousseau, J.-J., 85, 210, 215, 216

Scarry, E., 43
Scheff, T., 212
Schopenhauer, A., 92, 95, 96, 106, 216
secularisation of pain, 93
security dilemma, 81, 126, 177

self-restraint, 18, 21, 66, 87, 118,
    120, 126, 127, 131, 149, 258,
    see also Elias on the civilizing
    process
sentience, 92, *see also* Bentham,
    Schopenhauer
sex slaves, 53, 69, 244
sex tourism, 69
shame, 159, 180, 211, 214, 228, 249,
    see also Elias on the civilizing
    process, guilt, infant moral
    development, Scheff, Tangney and
    Dearing
Sherratt, A., 8
Shklar, J., 40, 105
Shue, H., 45, 99
Singer, P., 25, 71, 96–7, 102, 223
slave labour, 69
slavery, 21, 36, 38, 130, 142, 186, 189,
    245, 264, *see also* sex slaves
Smart, J. J. C., 91
Smith, A., 99, 210, 219, 225
social harm perspective, 43, 109, 142
societies of states, 11, 12, 36, 129, 258,
    see also Bull, systems of states,
    Wight
solidarity, 3, 4, 13, 24, 35, 40, 57,
    82, 90, 102, 103, 133, 204, 207,
    214, 220, 224, 248, 250, 257,
    see also compassion, Horkheimer,
    Levi, pain, Rorty, sympathy, Weil,
    world religions
Sontag, S., 226, 227
speciesism, 92
standard of civilization, xi, 203, 247
Stangl, F., 56
state sovereignty, 10, 37, 63, 64, 136,
    138, 255, *see also* global civilizing
    process, Harmon Doctrine, Trail
    Smelter Arbitration
state-formation, 120, 199, *see also* Elias
    on the civilizing process, insider–
    outsider distinctions, solidarity
Stearns, C. and Stearns, P., 218
Stoicism, 76, 87, 110, 210, 253
strategic learning, 252, 253, 254, 255,
    262, *see also* collective learning
structural harm, 73, 246, 255

structural violence, 60–1, *see also* Galtung, structural harm

superfluous injury, 37, 62, 108, 138, *see also* unnecessary suffering

sympathy, 13, 97, 226
  passive vs active, 223, 224, 225, 256, *see also* Aristotle, bystander phenomenon, compassion, emotional identification, emotions, insider–outsider distinctions, Smith A.

systems of punishment, 17, 32, 48, 83, 169, 186, *see also* Elias on the civilizing process

systems of states, xi, 9, 20, 28, 127, 232, 234, 237–44, 246, 249, *see also* global civilizing process, harm conventions, Wight, Wilkinson

Sznaider, N., 53, *see also* campaigns of compassion

Tangney, J. P. and Dearing, R. L., 212

Taylor, C., 4, 51

Ten, C., 89

Tester, K., 226

The English School of International Relations, 18, 26, 181, *see also* Bull, harm principle, societies of states, Wight

Thompson, J., 69, 70

Thucydides, 15, 16, 19, 21, 72, 124

Tombs, S. and. Hillyard, P., 60, *see also* social harm perspective

torture, 37, 43, 107, 108, 109, 126, 175, 189, 245, 264

Toynbee, A., 5, 25, 256, 263

Trail Smelter Arbitration, 66

transnational advocacy networks, 98, 228, 229, 260, 262, *see also* connected self

transnational public spheres, 100

UN General Assembly *Declaration on the Elimination of Violence against Women*, 63

unequal exchange, 73, 143, *see also* exploitation, unjust enrichment

unintended harm, 52, 65, 245, 255

Universal Declaration of Human Rights, 63, 107

unjust enrichment, 53, 69, 70, 100, 143, 227, *see also* exploitation, harm principle, unequal exchange, Vincent

unnecessary suffering, 37, 62, 67, 108, 138, 244, *see also* Hague Conventions, superfluous injury

Vincent, R. J., 70–1, 131

violence, 51, 62, 64, 69, 164, 247, 249, *see also* Elias on the civilizing process, cruelty, harm, harm conventions, structural violence, war

vulnerability, ix, 9, 30, 31, 51, 263, *see also* the body, exploitation, generalizable interests, harm conventions, harm principle, hate crimes, pain, solidarity, unjust enrichment

vulnerability principle, 106

Wallerstein, I., 73

Walzer, M., 125, 149

war, 2, 249, *see also* Elias on civilizing process, global civilizing process, harm conventions, historical sociology, just war, laws of war, masculinity, military necessity, world history

war and injury, 116–22

Ware, V., 78

Warnock, G., 83

Watson, A., 8, 200

Weber, M., 195, 201, 202, 205, 253

Weil, S., 222

Wertheimer, A., 53, 54

Wheeler, N. J., 67, 131

Wiesel, E., 59

Wight, M., ix, 15, 20, 128, 232, 233, *see also* the English School, societies of states, systems of states

Wilkinson, D., 239

Wollstonecraft, M., 1, 98

Wood, A., 53–4, 55

world citizenship, 257, 260, 261,
     262, *see also* ambiguities of
     interconnectedness, citizenship vs.
     humanity
world history, 2, 25, 27, 120, 143,
     184, 266, *see also* Buzan and
     Little, collective learning, grand

narratives, Habermas, harm
     narratives, Kant, McNeill
world religions, 8, 13, 84, 85, 197,
     213, *see also ahimsa*, Buddhism,
     Jainism, Weber
Wouters, C., 218
Wright, Q., 123, 127